C0-AWH-534

Library of
Davidson College

Enacting the Reformation
in Germany

Professor Gerald Strauss

Gerald Strauss

Enacting the Reformation in Germany

Essays on institution and reception

VARIORUM

943.03
S912e
c.1

This edition copyright © 1993 Gerald Strauss.

Published by VARIORUM
      Ashgate Publishing Limited
      Gower House, Croft Road,
      Aldershot, Hampshire GU11 3HR
      Great Britain

      Ashgate Publishing Company
      Old Post Road,
      Brookfield, Vermont 05036
      USA

ISBN 0-86078-351-0

British Library CIP data
      Strauss, Gerald
      Enacting the Reformation in Germany: Essays on Institution and
      Reception. – (Variorum Collected Studies Series; CS 418)
      I. Title II. Series
      943

Library of Congress CIP data
      Strauss, Gerald, 1922–
      Enacting the Reformation in Germany: Essays on Institution and
      Reception/Gerald Strauss. p. cm. (Collected Studies Series; CS418)
      ISBN 0-86078-351-0: (alk. paper): £42.50 (est.) ($81.95 est.)
      Essays originally published 1958–1991.
      Includes bibliographical references and index.
      1. Reformation-Germany. 2. Germany-History-1517–1648.
      I. Title II. Series: Collected studies; CS418.
      BR305.2.S84 1993   93-4444
      274.3'06-dc20   CIP

The paper used in this publication meets the minimum requirements of
American National Standard for Information Sciences – Permanence of
Paper for Printed Library Materials, ANSI Z39.48-1984.   TM

Printed by Galliard (Printers) Ltd
      Great Yarmouth, Norfolk, Great Britain

      COLLECTED STUDIES SERIES CS418

A DB-4148

CONTENTS

This book contains xiv + 298 pages

PUBLISHER'S NOTE

The articles in this volume, as in all others in the Collected Studies Series, have not been given a new, continuous pagination. In order to avoid confusion, and to facilitate their use where these same studies have been referred to elsewhere, the original pagination has been maintained wherever possible.

Each article has been given a Roman number in order of appearance, as listed in the Contents. This number is repeated on each page and quoted in the index entries.

PREFACE

The title I have chosen for this collection, "Enacting the Reformation", expresses my working assumption that historical events do not just happen; they are made, enacted, by individuals both prominent and obscure, responding to possibilities and struggling against constraints in unique circumstances that facilitate action and in turn channel it, pursuing objectives not always clearly grasped and constantly shifting as they encounter unanticipated consequences in the world. The process that makes events happen in this way is never completely recoverable. But much can be found out and said about it, at least where information is plentiful, and this is what I have tried to do for the German Reformation, the sources for which are gratifyingly abundant and expressive.

The thirty-five years spanned by the original publication dates of these articles (1958–1993) are a very long time, not only in the career of their author, but also, and more interestingly, in the development of Reformation scholarship. Something of the character of this development may be gleaned from these papers. If taken in chronological order, they exhibit a slow passage from a rather trustingly positivistic and normative outlook on the explanation of historical phenomena to a much more critical descriptive posture and a self-conscious awareness of the essential ambiguity of the past, and from a conventional preoccupation with the products of high culture and the affairs of high office to a more experimental concern with the reception of these products and the social impact of these affairs. They also reflect my discipline's growing eagerness to move beyond its traditional choice of materials to explore little-tried and therefore more problematic sources. New kinds of questions about meaning and significance abound in recent historical literature on the Reformation, and these, too, begin to surface in the articles I wrote from about 1967 on. Scholarship being a collaborative enterprise, it will be obvious to specialists, and evident also to non-specialist readers who take the trouble to look through my notes, that I have profited much over the years from the work of colleagues in the field. On the other hand I hope not to be mistaken when I think that some of my own efforts have been of use to them as well.

Inevitably, but no less regrettably for that, a gathering of pieces written over a long period by a single scholar with a rather narrowly focused interest will accommodate some overlapping and duplication. I have tried to compensate for this nuisance by clustering articles around a few salient topics or themes that have occupied me in my attempts to gain some understanding of the Reformation in Germany. Some of these themes have been there from the beginning; others appeared as my conceptual and methodological horizons widened. In a general way they are indicated by the titles of the five parts in which this book has been arranged. But the themes are both broader and more pervasive than these headings suggest, and it may therefore be useful to enumerate them here so that the individual articles can be seen in relation to a common core of interpretive interests.

One theme, running through the three chapters forming Part One, concerns an early and tentative phase of what today we would call Germany's long search for an acceptable identity. Some striking parallels to more recent episodes in the history of German identity construction are likely to occur to readers of these chapters; however, in writing them it was my aim only to draw a portrait of the national mood among the literate and the concerned in the early decades of the sixteenth century as their country faced the momentous consequences of Luther's revolt against Rome. Keenly sensitive to the cultural and political disadvantages of a nation separated by geography and history from the classical springs of civilization, these men sought to find the determining characteristics of their land and people in the physical and cultural features of a landscape never before adequately explored and described, and in the – sometimes triumphant, but more often lamentable – experiences of a collective historical past. Much of what they surveyed and chronicled could be pointed to with pride. But much, too, had to be related in righteous anger as German history turned out to be a story of recurrent victimization by foes of greatly superior craft and cunning. In their adversarial telling of it, history became a sounding board for voicing a sense of aggrieved national outrage and, as such, a precondition of the massive response to Luther's appeal for support. But it also furnished the country with an inspiring image of its ancestors whose upright and rugged lives in the ancient Germanic forests, and whose heroic building of cities and empire in more recent times, could serve their descendants as a source of moral strength and civic resolve.

A second theme is the centralized state that in the course of the sixteenth century began to dominate the political scene in the German principalities and free cities: its claims and demands, its effort to act on these pretensions, and the modus vivendi it worked out with the Lutheran Reformation, specifically its seizure, from the late 1520s on, of the many opportunities created by the Reformation for a significant enlargement of the state's responsibilities. A summary statement of my thoughts on this subject appears in an essay written in 1989 but not published before now, "The Idea of Order in the German Reformation" (Chapter XIV), which attempts to grasp the corporeal reality behind the abstractions "state" and "Reformation" by focusing on the human agents of this enlargement of the scope of governmental influence and power. Linking many of the issues raised in earlier articles, this essay also tries to define in its broadest sense the idea of "reform" that underlies all programs and policies of the German Reformation.

The protean concept of "reform" explains the prominence in this volume of a third theme: the place of education in the enactment of the Reformation. In exploring this subject, I emphasize the astonishing wealth of pedagogical ideas, methods, and materials available to Lutheran reformers. I also examine the implications of their consequent dependence on the classical and medieval traditions of learning and teaching, and point to the resulting creative tension in the Reformation's pedagogical and social thought between a practical optimism concerning the possibilities of schooling and the anthropological pessimism mandated by their theology. Education, in the extended sense of the word, served the overall objectives of reform by locating the site of desirable change in the individual person, whose mental and moral shaping (in the case of the select few) and behavioral conditioning (for the majority) were taken as the requisites for a renewal, or at least an improvement ("reform" meant both of these) of religion and society. Putting this belief into practice, reformers relied on the classical curriculum for the task of molding future leaders in church and state while devising for the masses a simple program of religious and civic indoctrination intended to bring them to approved standards of thinking and acting. Needless to say, results were always less than what was hoped. Several of my articles, particularly those in Part Four, attempt to explain why this was so.

A fourth theme expresses my growing conviction – it turns up first in a 1967 article on the Reformation in Nuremberg – that ideas become historically operative only to the extent that they are incorporated in concrete historical situations. To be embraced, to be acted on, ideas must make sense within frames of reference defined by these situations. Such an assertion sounds banal when disembodied as a general proposition. But once it is aimed at specific problems it raises useful questions. Why would an urban oligarchy of hard-headed merchants, such as the councillors of Nuremberg, agree to adopt officially a religious posture of such uncompromising unworldly tenets as Lutheranism? I tried to find an answer in the political and social predispositions of the city's ruling elite, and while there are some things about the article I wrote on this subject in 1967 that seem dated today – an enormous amount of first-rate research on Nuremberg in the Reformation period has come out in the twenty-five years between then and now – the central thesis I proposed at that time still strikes me as sound. What explains the powerful hold exerted by the texts of the classical curriculum on the cultural policy makers of the Reformation period (and, of course, of the centuries after that time)? Might some fresh insight into the Faust book of 1587 be gained by an examination of the social and confessional setting in which it was produced? Where should we look to find our standards for judging the results of the Reformation? Most of the chapters in Parts Two, Three, and Four of this volume advance arguments for evaluating ideas in relation to their reception and utilization by identifiable human groups and their situation among the landmarks of concrete circumstances.

An interest in historical judgments, and in the personal and situational perspectives that prompt us to make them in certain ways, has suggested the fifth theme, which I address in the last two chapters of this volume. Chapter XV examines the grounds on which we must come to terms with Luther's notoriously harsh reaction to the peasant rebellion of 1525; Chapter XVI attempts an analysis of the sympathies and antipathies we bring to our responses to what is now usually called "history from below". Perhaps not inappropriately in the concluding part of a retrospective collection, I intrude into these two essays with some personal thoughts about what I have long felt to be the risky steps historians must take in balancing their two lives, in the past and in the present. The contrasting scenes on which we must act offer very different incentives for choosing and deciding, and they distribute very dissimilar kinds of rewards for making these choices. This disjunction touches our work intensely, and in the final chapter I have tried to think about the consequences of this for our discipline.

Re-reading older pieces produced at successive life stages and in various states of mind and preparation is bound to occasion some uncomfortable reflections. Most awkward among them is the question of accuracy. How sure can one be that one has got it right? Having had the benefit of second and third thoughts about my past efforts, I can say that the arguments I have made in these articles seem to hold up, and that the picture I have drawn of Germany in the century of the Reformation appears to possess the quality of verisimilitude. Whether this quality is tantamount to truth, I cannot say. Writing in the preface to his *German History in the Age of the Reformation*, the great Leopold von Ranke, recalling the countless hours he spent in more than a dozen archives and libraries while preparing his major work, acknowledges that some future historians might well find additional documents that would allow them to correct this or that detail in his account. But his basic perceptions, he was certain, must be confirmed by the new discoveries, "for", he concluded, "*Die Wahrheit kann nur Eine sein* – there can be but one truth."[1] We have moved a vast distance from such declarations, for the reassuring, if demanding, belief in which we have substituted an agnostic, though devout and pious, respect for the stupendous richness and variety of historical actuality. To work through a fraction of this wealth in our research, and to give a faithful representation of it in our writing, is not a mean undertaking. I have aimed at no more exalted accomplishment than this.

GERALD STRAUSS

Amherst,
Massachusetts, 1993

---

[1] Leopold von Ranke, *Deutsche Geschichte im Zeitalter der Reformation* (6th ed., Leipzig, 1881), I, x.

ACKNOWLEDGEMENTS

Grateful acknowledgement is made to the following publishers, journals and editors, for kindly permitting the reproduction in this volume of articles published by them: Northern Illinois University Press, Dekalb, Il. and G.C. Sansoni S.P.A., Italy (I); Heldref Publications, Washington, D.C. (II); the editor of *Medievalia et Humanistica*, Denton, Tx (III); the Past and Present Society, Oxford (IV, XI, XVI); the American Society of Church History, Chicago (V); Clarendon Press, Oxford (VI); Johns Hopkins University Press, Baltimore (VII); the editor of *History of Education Quarterly*, Bloomington, IN (VIII); the editor of *Journal of Social History*, Pittsburgh (IX); George Allen & Unwin, London (X); Cornell University Press, Ithaca, N.Y. (XII); Max Niemeyer Verlag, Tübingen (XIII); and Wayne State University Press, Detroit (XV).

I

THE COURSE OF GERMAN HISTORY:
THE LUTHERAN INTERPRETATION

Cicero's remark that « to be ignorant of what happened before you were born is to remain forever a child »[1] was not merely a ubiquitous commonplace in the sixteenth century. It summarized the reflections of many thoughtful men on their past, notably in a country as preoccupied with its destiny and its problems as Germany. Political and moral maturity could scarcely be attained without an awareness of one's history. But what *was* that history? Did the numberless events of the distant and recent past coalesce into a meaningful pattern? Was there, in the grand unfolding of the divine will which was history, room for the distinct development of a particular nation? That development having been grasped and related, what bearing did it have on the present? These questions, though remaining largely implicit, impelled much of the historical writing done in Germany in the sixteenth century.

While a coherent pattern of national history emerged only in the second half of that century, German historical scholarship was vigorous from its beginnings. Partly in the interest of self-discovery, partly to dispel the general ignorance concerning Germany which, it was thought, prevailed in the world, German literary men devoted much of their time to the elucidation of their nation's past. The story of this endeavor has been often told. Professional scholars and amateurs, national enthusiasts and local patriots, produced a mass of source publications, critical studies, historical investigations and descriptions on the full range of subjects relating to ancient and medieval Germany. The result was a spate of works of considerable merit and great utility, extending from the local chronicles of Sigismund Meisterlin written in the 1450's to Beatus Rhenanus' *Three Books on Germany* of 1531 — a high point in German antiquarian scholarship — to large-scale descriptions of country and people such as Sebastian Münster's *Cosmography* of 1544, in whose crowded

---

[1] Cicero, *Orator, ad M. Brutum*, 34, 120.

pages the ambition to discover and set down what could be learned about ancient and modern Germany seemed to have reached fulfillment [2].

Special problems received the largest share of attention: the question of boundaries, particularly the western borders of the Empire in medieval and recent times; ancient survivals into the present — place names, foundations, regional customs; tribal names, languages, the modern consequences of the migrations; the whole question of the relationship of the German heartland to the Holy Roman Empire. Ancient Germanic society, especially in its military and religious aspects, remained an endlessly fascinating subject. Biographies had to be written, inscriptions and coins collected. Description and chronicling — a kind of stock-taking of the country's natural and spiritual stores — engaged the fervor of scholars and writers caught up in the zeal of their nascent national consciousness. A thousand years of neglect had to be made good, whole chapters of obloquy expunged from the pages of printed history. Complaints, denials, accusations concerning shabby historical treatment at the hands of jealous foreigners were incessantly reiterated. Laments and accusations persisted as a stereotype in German historical writing throughout the century and lent it an air of tension and a polemical, often aggressive tone. But there must also have been felt the satisfaction of a job well done. By and large, the ambition of German intellectuals to describe their country and bring its history « from the shadows into the light of day » (as they said) [3] had, by the second half of the century, been accomplished.

Satisfactory in scholarship, often excellent in description and characterization, these works represent a substantial scholarly and publicistic achievement. It cannot be said, however, that they express or reflect a coherent view of German history. As interpretive history they offer little food for thought. No attempt

---

[2] See Gerald Strauss, *Sixteenth-Century Germany, its Topography and Topographers* (Madison, Wisc., 1959) for a discussion of this topic and references to the literature.

[3] For example, Reuchlin, writing in the preface to Johann Nauclerus' *Memorabilium omnis aetatis et omnium gentium chronici commentarii ...* (Tübingen, 1516), III recto: Nauclerus has brought to light again « et gesta et literas Germanorum, quae multos iam annos in tenebris et situ deliturant ».

was made to find in German history a recognizable process of development or a meaningful historical pattern. Apart from inscrutable divine purpose, only the caprice of human volition was recognized, producing isolated actions and reactions in discrete situations.

The evidence suggests that at least some contemporaries hoped for something better. German history, it was said, equal to, and even surpassing, that of Greece and Rome, called for a major historical talent to tell it justly. If only a new Thucydides were to arise to record the wars against Rome or the exploits of the Hohenstaufen! Many an industrious compiler prefaced his own modest effort with apologies for its lack of breadth, and expressed the heartfelt wish for the appearance on the scene of a historian of vision and power [4]. He may have thought of style, proportion, form when calling upon such a man. But some writers, at least, seem to have been aware that compendia and chronicles were no longer enough, that the historian preparing to take on a great subject should draw meaning from, and give shape to, the recital of events. The discipline of history was no longer the preserve of the learned. It was a favored interest of the laity as well as of the scholarly community. Most works first written in Latin were translated into German, and from the 1530's on an increasing number of writers composed their histories in German or produced them in two languages, vernacular versions usually being longer and richer in color and personality [5]. Historical evidence was also seen to have practical value. Political and constitutional crises often revealed historical documentation as an invaluable ally to negotiation [6],

---

[4] E. g. Huldreich Mutius, *De Germanorum prima origine* ... (Basel, 1539), preface. The more elegant the work's style, the easier to fulfill its purpose of enlightening men of learning in Italy and elsewhere. Mutius himself was retained by the Basel professor Eustathius Quercetanus to turn his large collection of German chronicles and documents into a Latin history to be addressed « ad Graecos et Latinos » (A recto).

[5] See Melanchthon's preface to Kaspar Hedio's translation of Johann Cuspinian's *de Caesaribus ... opus: Ein ausserlessne Chronica von Julio Caesare ... bis auf Carolum Quintum* (Strassburg, 1541).

[6] E. g. the guilds of Cologne, following their successful rebellion against the city government in 1513, demanded that an archive be established. Jacob Wimpheling, *Germania* (Strassburg, 1501, dedication) argues that the ge-

and authorities were being urged to ensure the survival of essential records and preserve the memory of important events [7]. This apparent growth in historical consciousness, coinciding as it did with persistent uneasiness over the political problems facing the country, suggests that a comprehensive interpretive synopsis of the course of German history would have been warmly received.

In the event, German historiographers were slow and tentative in their response. Unable or unwilling to stray from the well-paced tradition of adapting and extending older chronicles, they made it clear that the desired synthesis would not be drawn from the sources themselves. Until well past the middle of the sixteenth century, historiography in Germany remained chronicling. The inherited form was flexible enough to accommodate a few idiosyncratic departures. But a commitment to a responsibility other than that of enumerating events in the order in which they happened was required before a chronicle of facts, with or without comment, could turn into history.

A few among the chronicles attained the rank of paradigms, their authority being preserved by new editions and imitations. For much of the sixteenth century the model par excellence was the chronicle of Johann Nauclerus (or Verge, his family name), a teacher of law at the University of Tübingen in the 1470's. From about 1480 until his death in 1510 Nauclerus labored on the book that made his reputation, a world chronicle extending from the Creation to the year 1500 [8]. Though apparently encouraged by the Emperor Maximilian [9], Nauclerus made few concessions to either national or dynastic history. His book records

---

neral historical ignorance prevailing in Germany enabled Louis XI to press his claims to the German lands west of the Rhine.

[7] E. g. beginning in 1482 the election capitulations of the Archbishops of Mainz obliged incumbents to establish archives for all important political documents (Bayerisches Staatsarchiv Würzburg, *Mainzer Domkapitel Urkunden*, Libell 5, 6, etc.). Wimpheling, *Germania*, Book II, urges the Strassburg Council to cause records to be kept of every memorable event in the affairs of city, territory, and Empire, « so that future generations may be mindful of these things ». *Tutschland Jacob Wympfflingers ...* (Strassburg, 1648) Cii recto.

[8] *Memorabilium omnis aetatis et omnium gentium chronici commentarii a Ioanne Nauclero ... digesti in annum salutis MD* (Tübingen, 1516).

[9] Ernst Joachim, *Johannes Nauclerus und seine Chronik* (Göttingen, 1874).

the deeds of the peoples of Europe, or rather of their sovereigns, with nearly equal weight given to all the nations. More important than any single group is the papacy, a continuing institution and the connective thread leading the chronicler through the centuries [10]. Apart from the Church, Nauclerus' theme is the instability of temporal things. Perhaps it was in response to an increased concern with German history that he devotes a little more than their share of space to the affairs of the Empire [11], but his manner of reporting them permits no distinction between his own country and others. Germans deserve detailed attention as the bearers of the imperium. But their history is no less transitory, nor is it more immediate to the chronicler, than the fate of ancient Rome.

Nauclerus' chronicle was acclaimed from the moment of its appearance in 1516 [12]. Erasmus praised the author as a meticulous and honest collector of facts [13], still the best criterion for success as a historian. More important: Nauclerus continued to exert an influence through those who imitated or, in at least one case, copied him. He was an important source for Johann Carion's chronicle in the 1530's. Huldreich Mutius' German history of 1539 is, despite its claim to have been drawn from all the old chronicles and other sources its author could put his hands on [14], for the most part lifted from the pages of Nauclerus and his follower Nicolaus Baselius [15]. Mutius' book is an efficiently written chronicle of political events, but it advances no argument and urges no interpretation, unless it be the by now obligatory patriotic sentiments that invade the narrative

---

[10] Or rather of the history of the sixth age. Nauclerus' historical scheme is that of the six World Ages, each divided into generations. The sixth age begins with the birth of Christ.

[11] German history proper is contained on pp. 105-304 out of 495 pages. Roman history, for example, takes up 123 pages.

[12] It seems to have circulated in manuscript before publication. Cf. Ernst Joachim, *Johannes Nauclerus*.

[13] In his prefatory epistle to the 1516 edition of the Chronicle. See above, note 8.

[14] *De Germanorum prima origine, moribus, institutis, legibus et memorabilibus ....ex probatioribus Germanicis scriptoribus in Latinam linguam translati* ... (Basel, 1539).

[15] For an examination of Mutius' sources, see K. E. H. Müller, *Die Chronik des ... Huldreich Mutius* (Prenzlau, 1882).

whenever the subject permits them [16]. As long as the historian's job was served by a bare recital of events, Nauclerus, and others like him, continued to be appreciated. In 1568 he was still the model for Laurentius Surius, a Carthusian monk in Cologne who sought to oppose the « poison of wicked, perverted teachings introduced by historians in order to mislead the common man » [17], by setting plain facts against the lies of Lutheran historians and by chronicling the events of his own time in the pedestrian manner of Nauclerus [18]. Actually, Surius argues a good deal, but in conception and arrangement his book is entirely derivative. Events — important or trivial as the case may be — are placed side by side in unbending succession, suggesting nothing other than the passage of time and the good or evil intentions of their instigators.

There are other examples of such survivals into the later sixteenth century. The so-called Ursberg Chronicle, compiled by the prior of the Premonstratensian monastery of Ursberg during the reign of Frederick II, was first printed in 1515 [19] and again in 1537, at which time Melanchthon added a short preface, praising the author's skill in portraying the whole sweep of human history, and stressing the importance of gaining an understanding of the great changes in history [20]. The Ursberg Chronicle probably attracted attention as an early example of partisan anti-papal historiography [21]. It was reprinted several times in the sixteenth century [22] and was one of the chief sources

---

[16] E. g., pp. 160-1.

[17] Laurentius Surius, *Commentarius brevis rerum in orbe gestarum ... ex optimis quibusque scriptoribus congestus* (Cologne, 1568). A German translation, by Heinrich Fabricius, appeared in the same year: *Kurtze Chronik oder Beschreibung der vornembsten händeln und Geschichten ...* (Cologne, 1568). The words quoted are from the translator's preface, A II verso.

[18] See Surius' own statement, *Commentarius ...*, A IIII recto.

[19] In Augsburg, from the one surviving manuscript of the entire work in the possession of Konrad Peutinger. An earlier edition of part of the work had been printed at Augsburg, c. 1474.

[20] Cf. Melanchthon's preface to the Strassburg edition of 1537, II verso.

[21] Melanchthon's preface to the Ursberg Chronicle in Kaspar Hedio, *Ein ausserlessne Chronik ...* (Strassburg, 1543) CCIII recto.

[22] Strassburg, 1540; Basel, 1569; Strassburg, 1609. There is a critical edition: Oswald Holder-Egger and Bernhard von Simson (eds.), *Die Chronik des Propstes Burchard von Ursberg* (*Scriptores rerum Germanicarum in usum scholarum*) (Hanover and Leipzig, 1916).

of medieval history for the Magdeburg Centuries. To David Chytraeus it was, as late as 1564, the most useful and penetrating of the old chronicles [23]. In 1539 the Strassburg preacher Kaspar Hedio turned out a German translation, and in 1543 he added to it other chronicle material in order to bring it up to date [24]. Interestingly enough, there is less spirit in Hedio's contribution than in his thirteenth-century source. Apart from an occasional bit of sniping in the direction of Rome, Hedio recites events one after the other without transitions or interpretation.

How hard it was to breathe new life into a dated form is shown by chronicles of institutions and places where new and exciting things were happening. Neither the monastic reform movement, nor the surge of urban culture in the fifteenth and sixteenth centuries found adequate historiographical expression in the work of local historians, and this despite the influence of humanist ideas and techniques on historical thought [25]. German humanist historians were probably too deeply immersed in disputes over special problems to gain the distance required for the synoptic view. The problem of the Empire loomed too large for German writers to make their way around the subject without expending a great deal of time and energy on such politically acute, but historiographically subsidiary, debating points as the *translatio imperii*, the election rights of pope and emperor with respect to each other, the devolution of the sovereign's authority to lesser rulers, imperial and curial reform, and the many other politically sensitive issues that were inseparable from the Empire as an institution, especially as a legal institution [26]. Few writers, indeed, seem to have been inclined to heed the summons for a German Thucydides to seize the facts of

---

[23] *De lectione historiarum recte instituenda* (Wittenberg, 1564), 1 recto.

[24] Kaspar Hedio, *Ein ausserlessne Chronik von Anfang der Welt bis auff das iar ... 1543 ...* (Strassburg, 1543). Hedio had been responsible for the 1537 Latin edition, to which he also added new material.

[25] Paul Joachimsohn, *Zur städtischen und klösterlichen Geschichtsschreibung Augsburgs im 15. Jahrhundert* (Bonn, 1895), pp. 33-49. Id., *Die humanistische Geschichtsschreibung in Deutschland I: Die Anfänge. Sigismund Meisterlin* (Bonn, 1895).

[26] For a good summary of this « problem of the Empire » and a sketch of its background, see Morimichi Watanabe, *The Political Ideas of Nicholas of Cusa ...* (Geneva, 1963).

national history and place them in context. So experienced a historical scholar as David Chytraeus, who had been a student of Melanchthon's and lectured on history at the University of Rostock in the third quarter of the sixteenth century, where he wrote numerous works on chronology and methodology as well as chronicles of Prussia and Saxony and a documentary history of the Augsburg Confession, evinced no interest in the interpretation of German history [27]. Even opinionated and committed men like Sebastian Franck and Johannes Aventinus failed to venture into general interpretations. Aventinus, like most world chroniclers before him, was mainly intent on showing that the Holy Roman Empire was not likely to escape the fate which had overtaken Persia and Macedon. His interest is no more confined to German history than it is — despite the title of his major work, the *Bavarian Chronicle* — to his home province. His concern is for humanity, human society, the human condition. Unhistorical in his mental habits, he used history as a vehicle for advancing his passionately held and forcefully argued opinions [28]. No more do we find a consistent interpretation in Sebastian Franck's *German Chronicle* of 1538, a work whose title [29] leads one to expect a national history and whose expressed intention of «pointing out the true kernel and main themes of our history» [30] raises hopes of an attempt at interpretation. In fact, Franck is content on most points to quote Nauclerus and Hartmann Schedel. He, too, wants to see German history take its rightful place [31]. But he has no use for the patriotic trumpeting of one's own national virtues [32] and thinks it foolish

---

[27] Of Chytraeus' many works, see especially *Chronicon Saxoniae ... ab anno 1500 usque ad MDXCIII* (Leipzig, 1593) and its German translation (Leipzig, 1597); *Historia der Augsburgischen Confession ...* (Rostock, 1576), and *De lectione historiarum recte instituenda* (Wittenberg, 1564). On Chytraeus' historical lectures and his immense correspondence on historical matters, see Detloff Klatt, « Chyträus als Geschichtslehrer und Geschichtschreiber », *Beiträge zur Geschichte der Stadt Rostock*, V (1909), 4-202.

[28] On Aventinus' mind and methods, see Gerald Strauss, *Historian in an Age of Crisis: The Life and Work of Johannes Aventinus* (Cambridge, Mass., 1963).

[29] *Germaniae chronicon: Von des gantzen Teutschlands, aller Teutschen Völcker herkommen ... von Noe bis auf Carolum V* (Frankfurt am Main [?], 1538).

[30] *Ibid.*, AA iii verso.

[31] See the conventional statement, *ibid.*, AA ii recto.

[32] *Ibid.*, LXXXI recto; CCXXIV verso; etc.

to concentrate on the deeds of a single segment of humanity. In writing a German history he merely wished to redress the balance overthrown by chauvinistic historians of other countries.

Aventinus and Franck are immensely attractive writers. Their compelling personalities emerge strongly from their books, making them a joy to read. But as historians they represent no gain on so jejune an exercise in chronicling as Schedel's *liber chronicarum* of 1493, a work which, because of its usefulness as a compendium and attractiveness as a piece of book making, cast a prolonged spell on sixteenth-century historical writing. A thoughtful thumbing through of Schedel's *Nuremberg Chronicle* (as it is usually called) [33] reveals some interesting clues to the reasons for the current indifference to interpretive history. Content to think within a historical framework which could not help but drain historical actuality of life and pertinency, Schedel added neither point nor direction to the chronological, biographical, and descriptive fragments of which his chronicle is composed. Human history is biography. Even the city descriptions for which Schedel's chronicle is famous are biographies. A picture attracts the eye; essential facts are registered. Events are more interesting as vignettes, illustrated by woodcuts, than as pieces in a consecutive narrative. There is no development. Sacred and secular history occur apart from each other, their segregation made visually evident on facing pages. To be sure, Schedel's *Chronicle* reflects the smug self-assurance of Nuremberg's well-to-do bourgeoisie, as it does the cautious commercial policies of its publisher, Koberger. The great problems of world and national history remained largely beyond its narrow horizon, and in this respect the work is akin to most municipal chronicling, which tended to concern itself only with those events of external history that pertained directly to the main preoccupations of the city [34]. In the case of Schedel's chronicle, its very popularity as a work of historical reference and edification suggests that its author's conventional habits by no means misrepresented the general trend of historical thought in the early decades of the sixteenth century. Even where stronger

---

[33] Hartmann Schedel, ... *Buch der Croniken* (Nuremberg, 1493).

[34] Cf. Heinrich Schmidt, *Die deutschen Städtechroniken als Spiegel des bürgerlichen Selbstverständnisses im Spätmittelalter* (Göttingen, 1958).

674

convictions and a keener grasp of political problems showed up the inadequacy of conventional procedures, the inherited pattern remained largely intact.

Of this tenacity of received ideas and methods Jacob Wimpheling's treatise on German history is a particularly interesting example. Often spoken of as the first work on German history written from the national point of view [35], the *Epitoma Germanicarum rerum* of 1505 was, indeed, published to provide Germans with a first introduction to their national history [36] and to demonstrate the continuity of that history from antiquity through the medieval centuries, the age of Carolingians, Hohenstaufen, and other imperial dynasties being revealed as a time of high deeds, and a fitting succession to the heroic migration period. In relating the deeds of medieval emperors, Wimpheling conveys the excitement of discovery. His is the first German history, the only serious attempt so far to put to rest the lingering notion that Germany has no history, indeed, that Germans are unworthy of having a history at all. Identifying himself on the first page of his work as an Alsatian [37], and thereby adding urgency to the discussion of problems of territorial and political sovereignty [38], he passes quickly over the ancient tribes to the crucial questions of the origins of Charlemagne [39] and the transfer of authority from the Carolingian to the Saxon dynasties [40]. On this important point, the transmission of the imperial title, Wimpheling was well briefed with arguments, being about to prepare Lupold von Bebenburg's *Tractatus de*

---

[35] Paul Joachimsen, *Geschichtsauffassung und Geschichtschreibung in Deutschland unter dem Einfluss des Humanismus* (Leipzig and Berlin, 1910), p. 66.

[36] I use the Basel edition of 1532, p. 315.

[37] *Ibid.*, p. 315.

[38] On these points see, in addition, Wimpheling's *Germania* (Strassburg, 1501), Book I, written against Louis XI's (then the dauphin) contention that ancient Gaul, and therefore modern France, extended to the shores of the Rhine. For counter arguments, see Thomas Murner's *Germania nova* of 1502.

[39] *Epitoma*, chapter 9 « De Carolo magno primo Germanorum imperatore ... et de inhumano facinore Gallorum modernorum ». Also chapter 22 with its massing of evidence to show that Charlemagne and his father were ethnically German.

[40] *Ibid.*, chapter 22 « De defectione stirpis Caroli magni in Gallis; deque indignatione Gallorum in electorum institutionem ». Especially p. 330.

iuribus regni et imperii for the press [41]. But these tasks of demonstration having been accomplished, the remainder of his narrative relapses into chronicle, a mere recital of deeds and wars succeeding the arguments so vigorously pressed before. Having indicated the point of departure of German national history and identified the direction in which events and agents were moving, he was content, for the rest, to report salient events, only occasionally lacing the recital with references to national accomplishments and appeals to his countrymen to crown their history by seizing the leadership of the Christian crusade against the Turks.

Wimpheling's limitation to an epitome suggests that he intended nothing more at the time than a first try at national history. As such the book was a success and, more important, a signpost. For although lacking erudition and patience for the sustained practice of the historian's craft, Wimpheling was driven by a powerful motive for writing and propagating history: his enlistment in the Alsatian resistance to French political and cultural encroachment. History as a weapon for contending a vital interest, history as a means of gaining support for a noble cause — here was a task for the practicing historian which, though hardly new, was bound to make him cast a critical look at historiographical ideas and procedures no longer adequate to the imperatives of the day.

When a coherent interpretation of the course of German history did emerge after the middle of the sixteenth century, it came not as a result of redoubled efforts by the chronicler, nor in consequence of the transplantation to Germany of humanist ideas. Chroniclers, while accustomed to taking the long view, were too deeply enmeshed in their infinite world of petty details, while humanist scholars, though their source criticism and their pursuit of questions of origin and derivation were vital and fruitful, were not by their outlook impelled toward a reassessment of the whole course of German history [42]. Nor

---

[41] Originally written in 1340, the *Tractatus* was published in Strassburg, 1508.

[42] For a somewhat different view, see Paul Joachimsen, *Geschichtsauffassung* ..., in which it is argued that humanism precipitated the decisive break with medieval traditions of historiography in German historical scholarship. See especially pp. 74-77, 104-5.

did the great undertaking of the *Germania illustrata*, whose objective it was to portray Germany in her present condition, ever turn to the task of giving shape to, and making sense of, the historical events of the preceding ages. The many territorial and local descriptions which were the fruit of the impetus given the *Germania illustrata* idea by Celtis and his colleagues in the first decade of the sixteenth century, are essentially eulogies of the splendor of Germany and of the good life being lived there. They tended to avoid risky questions of interpretation. Sebastian Münster, one of the ablest among the descriptive guides to the German scene [43], stoutly proclaimed his desire to remain above political and other controversies in order to perform his task without injuring person or party [44].

Münster was, in any case, and along with most of his fellow writers on human affairs, much too conscious of the inadequacy of his knowledge and the fallibility of his judgment [45] to display the kind of self-confidence needed for the job of interpreting history. No such lack of self-assurance troubled those who were eventually to accomplish this task. Historical reassessments have always coincided with turning points in history, and have been closely associated with the movements responsible for them. In their sweep and scope these historical interpretations reflect the movement's uncompromising confidence and self-absorption. It would be astonishing if the Lutheran Reformation had not brought about a searching review of German history, or if it had failed to produce a consistent interpretation of the course of that history. Although not important to the movement as a source of self-knowledge, history was of evident value as a weapon in the struggle against religious and political oppo-

---

[43] Münster's *Cosmographia* (published Basel, 1544; I use German version of 1545 and Latin version of 1550) covers, of course, the entire world. But the bulk of the book, pp. 189-591 out of 818 pp. in the 1545 edition, is taken up by the third book on Germany. Münster states it as his principal objective to « emphasize the German nation as much as possible ... ». *Cosmographia* (Basel, 1545), a vi recto.

[44] *Ibid.*, preface, a vi recto.

[45] Karl Heinz Burmeister (ed.) *Briefe Sebastian Münsters* (Ingelheim, 1964), *passim*. Nearly every one of Münster's surviving letters shows the man's respect for facts, his passion for bringing as many facts as possible into his possession, his desire to avoid controversy at all costs, and the sense of his own fallibility.

nents. With Melanchthon showing the way, and his son-in-law Caspar Peucer to execute the design, the themes and arguments advanced by earlier writers were joined into a coherent body of historical opinion. The resulting historical portrait of Germany — a country besieged, despoiled, violated, her guileless, trusting people defrauded by sly foreigners — is not a pretty one, but as a tool of propaganda it had great power, negatively as a means of identifying the enemy, positively as an instrument for rallying popular support.

The ability of history to sway opinions had, of course, long been recognized. Wimpheling and Aventinus had utilized it for this purpose, the latter with considerable skill. Of the careworn portrait of Germany arising from Peucer's *Chronicle* in the 1570's, every line and wrinkle had been drawn before. The power of history to personalize and dramatize the great issues and controversies was evident to all. No one having read Johann Stumpf's tragic chronicle of the reign of Henry IV was likely to remain unaffected by its scenes of perfidy, filial treachery, and popular inconstancy [46], nor fail to agree with Stumpf that the struggle between the unfortunate emperor and the overweening pope was the beginning of the Empire's time of troubles, the end of which was not yet in sight [47]. The facts of history had often before been seized as weapons of attack and defense. But never had the entire course of German history come under such pointed review. Now, however, writers and publishers in the service of the Lutheran Reformation applied to the entire course of German history the lessons drawn from earlier fragmentary examinations of events and personalities, creating for the first time an interpretation of German history which made it possible to grasp both its scope and its essence.

A fundamental lack of interest in the intrinsic processes of history prevented the first generation of Lutheran historians from abandoning the traditional scheme of world monarchies, or from consigning to the rubbish heap such transparent and already exposed, but nonetheless useful, forgeries as the false

---

[46] Johann Stumpf, *Keyser Heinrychs des vierdten ... fünftzigjärige Historia ...* (Zurich, 1556).

[47] A point also made in Stumpf's main work, *Gemeiner loblicher Eydgnoschaft ... Beschreybung* (Zurich, 1548) ff. 49 v-50 r.

678

« Berosus » of Annius of Viterbo. Frequent protestations not-withstanding, it was not so much historical truth that counted; what mattered was the utility of historical exemplification, and the impact of historical argument. In its general outline the course of German history as seen in Wittenberg was accurate enough, based as it was, for the most part, on well established facts and much-debated points of view. But the Wittenberg authors did not primarily seek the critical approval of the scholarly community. Their appeal was to a wider public and their purpose to teach or, more properly, indoctrinate.

Melanchthon's role in the production of Johann Carion's world chronicle of 1532 has by now been clearly established [48]. Carion, a professional astrologer and mathematician, had drawn up some notes and reflections on world events and taken them to Melanchthon, whose respect for the science of astrology and its practitioners seems to have prompted him to revise a manuscript singularly conventional and lacking in form. Carion's brief chronicle and its various translations and continuations [49] therefore reflected from its first edition Melanchthon's historical ideas, as these are known to us also from his various prefaces and univerity lectures [50]. Though too brief to press any of its arguments conclusively, the little chronicle mirrors not only Melanchthon's views on history, but also the spirit in which history, and particularly German history, had been written since the beginning of the sixteenth century. Every incident is introduced as an *exemplum*. Emperors represent virtue, France

---

[48] See Robert Stupperich, « Geschichtliche Arbeit und Geschichtsbetrachtung », in *Der unbekannte Melanchthon ...* (Stuttgart, 1961), pp. 72-84, for a discussion of the literature on this point. Most informative: Gotthard Münch, « Das Chronikon Carionis Philippicum », *Sachsen und Anhalt* I (1925), 199-283.

[49] *Chronica, durch Magistrum Johan Carion vleissig zusamen gezogen ...* (Wittenberg, 1532). New editions Wittenberg, 1533, 1538, 1549; Augsburg, 1533, 1540; Magdeburg, 1534; Frankfurt, 1546; continued by Johann Funck, Frankfurt, 1555. All these in German. Latin translations 1537, 1539, 1550, 1555. Other editions and translations are listed by Georg Theodor Strobel, *Miscellaneen ...* VI (Nuremberg, 1782), 159-206. I cite according to Wittenberg, 1532.

[50] On Melanchthon's historical ideas see Robert Stupperich, *loc. cit.* and Attilio Agnoletto, « Storia e non storia in Filippo Melantone », *Nuova rivista storica* 48 (1964), 491-528, with bibliography.

and the papacy the powers of greed and envy whose machinations (« *Praktiken* ») have plunged Germany into ruination [51]. Hope is confined to the expectation of the world's end, which cannot now be more than a few generations away [52].

That a much more comprehensive, detailed, and polemical survey of German history than this should have transformed the later versions of the *Chronica Carionis*, despite the Lutheran belief in the imminence of Doomsday and the consequent irrelevance of temporal history, cannot be due to anything other than the nature of the Lutheran movement as a struggle. Melanchthon had strong convictions about the power of history to teach by example, not only how to act in given situations, but also how to relate one's own strivings to the great currents of world history. This explains the great importance he attached to general history — « whole chronicles » (as he put it) « from beginning to end » [53]. History was an invaluable aid to his theological pedagogy. As revised by Melanchthon in 1558 and 1560 (as far as Charlemagne) [54] and continued by Caspar Peucer through the reign of Maximilian [55], the so-called Chronicle of Carion in its long Latin and German versions of 1572 and 1573,

---

[51] 129 verso; 149 recto; 151 recto; 163 recto and verso, and *passim*.

[52] 169 recto and verso.

[53] See Melanchthon's preface to Kaspar Hedio's translation of Cuspinian's *de Caesaribus atque Imperatoribus Romanis opus* ... of Strassburg, 1541, reprinted in Robert Stupperich, « Geschichtliche Arbeit », pp. 183-91. For an ill-tempered and anti-Protestant, but not inaccurate, review of Melanchthon's attitude to history, see Richard Fester, « Sleidan, Sabinus, Melanchthon », *Historische Zeitschrift*, 89 (1902), 11-12.

[54] Printed in *Corpus Reformatorum* XII. For a discussion of Melanchthon's version of the *Chronica*, see Gotthard Münch in « Das Chronikon », pp. 258-75.

[55] Peucer completed the Latin version of the *Chronica Carionis* with the publication of part V (Wittenberg, 1565, to the death of Maximilian). All parts together appeared in 1572. This last edition was translated into German: *Chronica Carionis ... vermehret und gebessert durch Herrn Philippum Melanchthonem und Doctorem Casparum Peucerum* (Wittenberg, 1573). Peucer's difficulties in Wittenberg did not begin until 1574, when he was tried and imprisoned. The Elector August of Saxony sought, despite his theological antipathy to Peucer, to persuade him to complete the *Chronica* with a final part on contemporary affairs. But Peucer resolutely refused to comply while in prison and under suspicion, and the last section of the chronicle was never written. See Caspar Peucer, *Historia carcerum* ... (Zurich, 1605), pp. 302-3.

though preachy and obtrusively pedantic in its parade of book learning, advances an absorbing and, in its total impact, stirring interpretation of the course of German history. Nothing in Melanchthon's various pronouncements on history suggests that he himself had taken a special interest in German history. But Peucer, who was invited by the academic senate of the University to carry on Melanchthon's lectures and continue the chronicle [56], turned the narrative decisively in that direction. So completely did German history come to dominate the final versions of what had started out as an epitome of a world chronicle that, from the fourth book (the beginning of Peucer's authorship) onward, the discussion of other countries and peoples is confined to occasional notes on « conditions in England » and « conditions in Poland » [57].

German history proper begins at a point when a great change in the structure of the Roman Empire divided the western from the eastern regions. First among the new western rulers were the German Franks who « conquered the occidental empire and, through their wisdom and manly deeds, maintained and continued it in Germany » [58]. The appearance and character of German lands and peoples, as portrayed in Peucer's description of the country at the time of Charlemagne (pp. 411-44), reveal the might now in the hands of Germans, though the discussion of the extent and privileges of their conquest is set against a backward glance to the fate of ancient empires. The ups and downs of history, the reader is reminded, should admonish him, even as pride in his own country swells his breast, that life is but exile and the future can bring only calamities. The claims of conscience thus satisfied, Peucer proceeds to the question of Charlemagne and of the imperial title (pp. 451 ff.). Of the legitimacy of this title there are many proofs. Charles won it by conquest and the right of war, and it was bestowed on him by the Roman nobility with the approval of the eastern emperor. Charles was not created emperor by the pope, who has neither

---

[56] See the documents printed in Georg Theodor Strobel, *Miscellaneen*, VI (Nuremberg, 1782), 190-91.

[57] A great deal of space is, of course, given to the Church. But secular history in Peucer's version of Carion's *Chronica* is the history of the Holy Roman Empire.

[58] I cite according to *Chronica Carionis ...* (Wittenberg, 1573), p. 409.

the right nor the power to dispose over the kingdoms of the world. A long look at Charles' public and private life suggests a man of exemplary virtues, in sum « one of the truly good and wholesome monarchs through whom God chooses to reign » (p. 470). But the ensuing swift breakdown of the Carolingian empire illustrates the nature of human history and furnishes scores of « examples, which rulers would be wise to take as a warning to themselves » (p. 490).

Meantime the papacy had usurped the rule of the Church and subverted the traditional supremacy of the emperor over the pope into a papal hegemony [59]. Glancing back over the fifteen hundred years since the coming of Christ, Peucer finds an uninterrupted growth in papal power and a corresponding decay of everything else (p. 511). During the first five hundred years of this long span of time truth remained ascendant, but the succeeding half millennium saw the battles of truth against lies, heresy, and superstition become ever more violent as vice gained on virtue, the wicked felt their strength, and the good grew feeble. « In the last five hundred years », he concludes, « idolatry, superstition, and ambition have grown ripe in the Church. Of its erstwhile discipline nothing is left but a shadow ». The papacy is not seen here as a historical phenomenon, as it is in the work of another Protestant historian, Johann Sleidan [60], who shows how the steady growth and success of papal power must be explained as the result of stealth and the ruthless, single-minded pursuit of the politics of domination. Melanchthon and Peucer saw Rome as a supernatural force. It simply exists; no one is to blame for having allowed it to arise, but everyone must see it as an admonition to heed the judgment of God on men's sins (p. 537).

Wicked power requires a victim for the perpetration of its mischief, and this is the role in which the German nation sees itself cast. Papal designs and Italian intrigue cause « *Empörung*

---

[59] The reversal of the traditional relationship of emperor and pope was generally accepted as the source of all German troubles with the Church. Cf. Sebastian Münster, *Cosmographia* (Basel, 1545), ff. 49 v-50 r; 62 r; 69 r and v.

[60] Especially in *Oration an alle Stende des Reichs. Vom römischen Neben-haupt, im Keisertum erwachsen* (1542), printed in *Bibliothek des litterarischen Vereins in Stuttgart* CXLV (Tübingen, 1879).

und Aufrur » to break out again and again (p. 571). This is the background of German history during the middle ages. Heroic efforts were required to withstand assaults unleashed from Rome, but even though Germany could boast her share of determined rulers, her history records more defeats than victories. The reign of Henry IV is a climactic moment in this struggle, as well as one possessing the peculiar character of one of history's *fatales periodi* in which great mutations occur in human affairs (pp. 634 ff.). The Church's transformation of itself into a secular monarchy having been consummated [61], fundamental alterations were bound to throw the Empire into turmoil, as « the sovereignty and majesty of imperial dignity were undermined by papal cunning and, ultimately, destroyed and brought into the utmost contempt » (p. 641). Stopping at nothing, the popes did not rest until they had crushed the German emperors into docile subjects, « torturing them cruelly and steeping them in disgrace ». A mere shadow now of her former autonomy, Germany had been irretrievably altered into « an alien shape and condition » (« *ein gar frembde gestalt und form* » p. 641). With no object other than the extension of their hegemony over Germany by means of fomenting dissension and civil war, the popes and other « arrogant Italians » succeeded in ruining the country through « the shedding of noble German blood », « the extirpation of the most distinguished of her princely houses », and « the subversion of her ancient laws and customs » (p. 642). Now and then a handful of stalwart men struggled to their feet, but it was no use. The pope's power was too vast now, and the common rabble too blinded by superstition (p. 643) to reverse the Roman triumph.

Why did emperors and princes acquiesce in this destruction of the nation's manhood? Peucer raises the question in anticipation of protests from even the most resigned believers in God's inscrutable direction of events. True to the by now customary stereotype of the naive and artless German whose simple piety left him naked to Latin cunning, the very virtues of the

---

[61] Approximately 1000 years having passed since the apostles first began to preach, the Church was about to enter its « third period of 500 years during which its doctrines, discipline, and organization were to take on a new shape ». *Chronica Carionis* ..., p. 634.

German character are shown to have brought on his undoing. « Not because of terror or timidity », did the emperors succumb, « nor through any flinching in the face of danger, painful though it must have been to gaze upon the pitiful ruination of their fatherland, the gruesome massacre of their subjects, and the terrible destruction of so many of their truest and dearest friends. The main cause of our sovereigns' reticence in the face of provocation was their unswerving love of the Christian faith, which made them unwilling to offer resistance to the popes. This is the principal, indeed almost the only, reason why pious German emperors submitted to the popes » (pp. 721-22).

Under the sign of papal tyranny nothing went right. At best the country could patch its divisions and muddle through its difficulties (p. 775). After the death of Frederick II, the last monarch to rise to self-defense against the pope, « everything went to rack and ruin » (p. 811). What follows — not only in national, but also in regional and local history — is unrest, invasions, civil strife, a story of general disintegration. Instances of public and individual corruption proliferate. The revival of studies and letters, brought west by refugee scholars from Constantinople (p. 1044) is a bright note, as is the introduction of printing into Germany, for to these is due the cleansing of Christian doctrine and the renewal of religion (p. 1046). But the human story continues in gloom. We are assured that the Roman Empire will last to the end of time (and « prophecy and soothsaying » confirm the belief [p. 776]). But might not the imperium be once again transferred to another people? Peucer thinks not. Only the Turks stand as a possible successor, and they do not constitute, he thinks, a civilization (p. 776), But the nagging doubt, by no means mere rhetoric in the historical thought of the time, made the backward glance over the course of German history a peculiarly poignant experience.

This picture of German history was the generally accepted one in the Protestant historical literature of the later sixteenth century. It is implicit, where not explicitly affirmed, in regional descriptions and local chronicles [62]. Older works brought up

---

[62] For a comprehensive, though superficial, survey of the literature of regional and local historiography in Germany, see Franz X. von Wegele, *Geschichte der deutschen Historiographie* (Munich and Leipzig, 1885), pp. 143-78; 372-464.

to date or translated carried insertions or addenda to make them fit the pattern [63]. There is, to be sure, a counterpoint, namely the hope, or expectation, of a brighter destiny for the pitiful figure of wasted and impotent Germany. Without in any way altering the impression conveyed by the historical retrospect, this interpretation sees Luther's Germany as a risen and steeled nation which, having regained the light of true religion, and shed the blindfolds of her Roman slavery along with the ignorance of her own history, now serves God's purpose in the world. Sleidan puts this point of view forcefully, not in his best known work, the *Commentaries* of 1555, in which it is implicit, but in his *Address to the Estates of the Empire* of 1542, a no-holds-barred polemic, republished several times in the later sixteenth century. Look at our history, he says, learn from it and be proud of it. Barbarians at first, we have grown polished and refined. Victimized throughout the centuries by ruthless pontiffs and foreigners we were conditioned by adversity. « And as if to offer proof that God has chosen us to accomplish a special mission, there was invented in our land a marvelous, new, and subtle art, the art of printing » [64]. This opened German eyes, even as it is now bringing enlightenment to other countries. « Each man became eager for knowledge, not without feeling a sense of amazement at his former blindness » [65]. The cultural and religious renewal now in evidence in Germany is sure indication of other blessings to come.

Germany as a nation with a divine mission was another stereotype in historical literature. Matthias Flacius, chief historian and administrator of the Magdeburg Centuries, points to the presence of a small band of German warriors in the army with which Caesar defeated Pompey as a sign that God had, from the beginning, destined the Germans as possessors of the Empire [66]. Some writers saw a German mission of suffering,

---

[63] E. g. Basilius Faber who, in 1582, translated into German Albert Krantz's *Saxonia* of 1520, apologized for his author's deficient understanding of papal and imperial affairs. Albert Krantz, *Saxonia*... (Leipzig, 1582), f. IIII r.

[64] Johann Sleidan, *Oration an alle Stende*... (see note 60, above), p. 79.

[65] *Ibid.*, p. 80.

[66] *De translatione imperii Romani ad Germanos* (Basel, 1566); *Von Ankunfft des römischen Keysertums an die Deutschen* (Ursel, 1567), d 3 recto. In the

like that of ancient Israel. Indeed, much that was written in Germany at the time carries overtones suggesting an image of Germany as sacrificial victim [67]. Others could not believe that the Empire of Charles V was all shadow and no substance. « I conclude », writes Sleidan, « that never in her history has our German nation stood as high. Who knows, she may be the greatest in the world » [68].

Sleidan's confidence — or near-confidence, for he catches himself up short with a reminder that nearest the top one is also closest to one's downfall — arose from the conviction, gained in a half century's successful endeavor to portray Germany's riches and splendors, that the country's position in the world was solidly based on natural and man-made wealth. Matthias Quad summarized this belief at the beginning of the next century in a book appropriately titled *Teutscher Nation Herrligkeit* [69]. The optimistic, not to say boastful, view of German society given by Quad had been present throughout the second half of the sixteenth century. It gave voice to what was, no doubt, a genuine and widely-held sense of pride and gratitude. But it is an unreflective strain, not only because materialistic and quantitative, but because it is unhistorical. It never posed the real question: why had the Empire's splendid physical and human resources not been translated into strength, unity, and order? Why were calls for an end to strife and a healing of divisions fated to remain plaintive rhetoric? No informed and candid reply was given to the question until Pufendorf supplied it in 1667. Meanwhile the historical retrospect provided in Peucer's chronicle fashioned an integrated view of history which not only explained much that had been confusing in the distant and recent past, but also generated that sense of aggrieved self-righteousness which is so useful to an embattled movement.

The circulation of the *Chronica Carionis* in Peucer's final

Centuries themselves, the arrangement of material is too schematic to permit proper presentation of the course of German history. Affairs in the Empire come up at the beginning of Chapter 16 of each century.

[67] See my forthcoming collection *Manifestations of Discontent in Germany on the Eve of the Protestant Reformation*.

[68] Johann Sleidan, *Oration an alle Stende ...*, p. 81.

[69] Cologne, 1609.

redaction has never been precisely investigated [70], but all indications suggest that it was widely used in the Protestant world as a text for university lectures and as a teaching book in schools and for the instruction of young princes [71]. It was frequently republished, not only in Wittenberg, but also in Geneva, Lyons, Frankfurt, Rostock, and Dordrecht [72]. Its view of the course of German history must have been passed on to at least a generation of people called upon to understand the place of their country in the political and religious world of their time. No doubt, brooding speculations on disintegration and demise were, in any case, more congenial to the religious mood of the sixteenth century German than visions of eminence. The persistent image of Germany as long-suffering victim may therefore be yet another piece of evidence of that country's intense and honest religiosity.

---

[70] For some evidence, see Gotthard Münch, « Das Chronikon », pp. 276-83.

[71] See also Franz Schnabel, *Deutschlands geschichtliche Quellen und Darstellungen* (Leipzig and Berlin, 1931), pp. 45-6.

[72] For editions and translations see Georg Theodor Strobel, *Miscellaneen*, VI, 159-206. The *Chronica Carionis* is still given as a source for general world history in Johann Christoph Gatterer's *Handbuch der Universalgeschichte* I (Göttingen, 1763).

II

THE IMAGE OF GERMANY IN THE SIXTEENTH CENTURY

IT WAS IN THE sixteenth century that German men of letters first undertook a systematic description of their country. Not only the many profound transformations of the time—Turks, plagues, religious strife, trans-oceanic voyages, and insistent demands for political reform—rallied them to a fresh attempt at orientation. It was an implicit objective of their profession as humanists to know themselves and their environment. What was "Germany"? A territory? A sum of historical experiences? An ethnic community? Is Germany today coterminous with the Empire, or are her true boundaries those of ancient Germania? Is there a common national denominator under the profusion of regional cultures? These were questions of serious import at a time when every thoughtful person could see a new age rising above the historical horizon.

The efforts of the humanist community were such that before the middle of the century the answers to these questions had been given, and much more besides. The German humanists knew that no thorough examination of German geography and history had ever been made. They therefore harnessed their special skills to a great collaborative enterprise. Germany was to be described, or "illustrated," as they said. Highly competent techniques of historical research and criticism, professional training in geography, a narrative style no longer hampered by the chronicler's slow pace enabled them to present their contemporaries with a vivid image of the German scene. If we today found ourselves suddenly set down in the Germany of 1600, we would have no difficulty in shifting for ourselves with the aid of these volumes. The many territorial descriptions, and especially the massive "cosmographies" of Sebastian Münster and Johann Rauw, in which the whole country is described, furnish scenic descriptions to help us choose our route, maps to point our way, illustrations of cities and landmarks to facilitate recognition, historical comments to deepen our appreciation of the current scene. Passing through a town, we would be prepared to admire its points of interest, we would know commodities profitably to be purchased and what local specialties to order at the *table d'hôte*. We could tell the social standing of a passer-by from his apparel, and if he engaged us in conversation we could chat without reluctance, for we would know not only his language, the local idiom, but would be acquainted with the town's history, its institutions, its past and present notables. All of

Reprinted from Gerald Strauss, "The Reformation and its Public in an Age of Orthodoxy", in *The Germanic People and the Reformation*, edited by R. Po-Chia Hsia. Copright © 1988 by Cornell University Press. Used by permission of the publisher, Cornell University Press.

the German lands were thus described. Everywhere scholars were at work ("geographistorians," Jean Bodin aptly called them in his *Methodus*) in pursuit of the common goal. The composite image which results is one of a fine, prosperous land with a proud heritage and an assertive spirit. The wholesomeness of this national culture, as they themselves had discovered it in their travels and in their search of the archives, was one of the major sources of humanist patriotism. No opportunities were lost to point with pride.

Particular satisfaction came from the opportunity to set the record of antiquity straight. It never ceased to gall the German humanists that their revered authorities had paid such scant attention to Germany and its people in ancient times, and that what they did say was scarcely complimentary. The "bristling forests" and "reeking swamps" which Tacitus names as typical of German geography, and the crude and irascible nature he ascribes to the tribal warriors offended their pride of ancestry. Tacitus was the fullest source, but who would say that ancient Germany had received her due from him? The rest of the classical writers, the few, that is, who deigned to consider Germany at all, had been far less generous. Strabo's dryasdust topographical survey no more suggested the true grandeur of the German landscape than his niggardly acknowledgment of Roman respect for the Germans' bellicosity could appraise their valor.[1] Pliny seemed to give nothing more than a list of tribes.[2] But worse even than their neglect was disparagement by others, Seneca, for example:

> Consider the peoples beyond the limits of the Roman Empire [he writes]. I speak of the Germans and of all those vagrant tribes which one meets around the Danube. Living on a sterile soil, they must bear a perpetual winter and a gloomy sky. A mere thatched roof protects them from rain. They walk about on swampy ground hardened to ice by the cold. They nourish themselves on the wild beasts which they hunt in the forests. . . . They have no shelter and no home other than the place where fatigue forces them down each night. Their most common food must first be procured by the labor of their hands. They are exposed to the intemperance of a frightful climate and have no clothing to protect their bodies.[3]

Pomponius Mela, a widely read epitomizer of Strabo, similarly speaks of

[1] *Geography* VII. 1. ii-v; 2, i-iv.
[2] *Natural History* IV. 13–15.
[3] *De Providentia* 4 (Dialogues, Book I). This treatise circulated in the fifteenth and sixteenth centuries under the title *De gubernatione mundi* (Cf. Seneca, *Opera moralia et epistolae* (Naples, 1475; Hain-Copinger No. 14590). The essay opens with the question: Is the world governed by a Providence, and, if so, why do the good suffer so many afflictions? Seneca here justifies the existence of evil by pointing to the salutory effects hardship has on those who learn to inure themselves to it. The Germans are introduced as an example of a whole tribe to which insecurity and privation are normal existence.

a country made impassable by forests and swamps and almost uninhabitable by a miserable climate[4] and describes the Germans as follows:

> They are a hardy and robust people who find in war an outlet for their natural ferocity and in strenuous exercise an employment for the vigor of their bodies. They take pleasure in braving the cold and go about naked until the age of puberty (which comes late to them). . . . They make war against all their neighbors, for no reason other than caprice. . . . They know no law but force, and no scruples prevent them from engaging in brigandage. . . . Their manner of living is crude and barbarous; they even eat raw the flesh of their cattle and of wild beasts, being content, when the meat is no longer fresh, to beat it with hands and feet without even removing the skin.

Obviously, the Germany found in the books of the ancients was not the country the humanists knew. There was much debate, and some heated controversy, over whether modern men and women were, in fact, superior to the tribes-people to whose pristine purity of character Tacitus testified. But about the country itself there could be no argument. Either enormous transformations had taken place, or the ancients were guilty of misrepresenting the facts. Injured pride wanted to believe the latter. "Dies hand di Römer geschriben von unserm edlen und fruchtbarsten landt," writes Sebastian Münster, "nachdem si do so lange zeit und mit solchen grossen kosten gefochten hand. Ist aber kein wunder, dann ir keiner hat es recht gesehen."[5]

Clearly, the first question was: Did Greek and Roman writers really know Germany? It hardly seemed possible, considering the state of their misinformation. Taking their cue from Enea Silvio de' Piccolomini, who had declared in his *Europa* that the ancient literature on German affairs would lead one to suspect that the country were located somewhere outside the inhabited world,[6] the German humanists began to adduce reasons for ancient ignorance. It was suggested, for example, that the common superstition of Germany as a country of raging rivers and impenetrable forests must have discouraged the most intrepid historian from making his way into her interior.[7] Others believed that since the tribes never had fixed habitations and were constantly on the move, the old writers could hardly have gathered much information about them.[8] Hence we may assume, writes Peter Albinus, "das die alten nach Ge-

---

[4] *De situ orbis*, written about the middle of the first century A.D. The section on Germany occurs in Book III, chapter iii.
[5] *Cosmographia: Beschreibung aller lender* . . . (Basel, 1544), p. 160.
[6] *Cosmographia Pii Papae in Asiae et Europae eleganti descriptione* . . . (I use ed. Paris, 1509) "Europa," chapter xxiii. Repeated verbatim by Hartmann Schedel, *Liber cronicarum* . . . (Nuremberg, 1493), 267 recto.
[7] Schedel, op cit., 299 recto. This point, too, was first made by Enea Silvio.
[8] Franciscus Irenicus, *Germaniae exegeseos volumina duodecim* . . . (Hagenau, 1518), 6 verso. Repeated verbatim by Willibald Pirckheimer, *Germaniae ex variis scriptoribus perbrevis explicatio* (Nuremberg, 1530), A 3 recto.

dunken und Wahn von Teutschlandt geschriben, denn es ir keiner recht besehen; und derhalt zu glauben, das es auch in der erste so gar ungeschlacht nicht gewesen, als dafür mans ausgeschrien."[9] To make up for the evidence they lacked, Greek and Roman authors drew on their imagination or, worse, their prejudices. Everyone knows their habit of suppressing such facts as were not conducive to their own greater glory.[10] Given the almost total absence of chroniclers among the Germans themselves, they were free to spread lies and slanders:[11] "Ire feinde habens tun [record their deeds] müssen und dieselben haben, wi man achten kann, das beste unterdrückt und sovil si haben gekonnt, den preis und glimpf auf sich selbs gezogen."[12]

The ignorance and/or malice of Caesar, Livy, Seneca, Strabo, Tacitus, Pliny, and others became the spur with which the more vociferously patriotic of German humanists goaded their contemporaries. Bebel, Wimpheling, Irenicus were only too willing to see treachery in every *Wälsche*, ancient or contemporary. Others, however, accepted the classical picture of tribal Germany as substantially correct and discovered in the middle ages the heroic period of their race. Indeed, the more primitive the conditions in ancient days, the greater, obviously, the achievement of those who cleared the forests, drained swamps and tamed rivers, built cities, laid roads, ploughed up the soil and made the land productive.

Again, it was Enea Silvio who showed how the crudeness of their forbears might be made the major premise from which to argue the German genius. In 1458 Enea, then a Cardinal in the service of Pope Calixtus III, and himself about to ascend the throne of St. Peter, had written a long open letter to Martin Mayr, chancellor of the Archbishop of Mainz, to oppose Mayr's public allegations of curial arrogance in Germany. Mayr's complaint was one of a long series of expressions of Germany's gravamina against Rome. The rapacity of popes has impoverished Germany, he declared. "Our nation, once of such great fame, which acquired with her courage and blood the Roman Empire and was Mistress and Queen of the world, has become poor and a tribute-paying maid!" Enea's answer was a lengthy treatise on the present state of Germany.[13] To refute Mayr's charge, Enea culls from the ancient authors

9 Peter Albinus, *Commentarius novus de Mysnia, oder Newe Meysnische Chronica* . . . (Wittenberg, 1580), p. 616.
10 Heinrich Bebel, *Epitoma laudum Suevorum.* I use ed. in Melchior Goldast, *Rerum Suevicarum scriptores* (Ulm, 1727), pp. 6–7. Also Braun and Hogenberg, *Civitates orbis terrarum*, German ed. (Cologne, 1574 ff.), Vol. I, fol. 1 B recto.
11 Heinrich Bebel, *De laude, antiquitate, imperio, victoriis rebusque gestis veterum Germanorum.* I use ed. in *Schardius redivivus* (Giessen, 1673), I, 126.
12 Thomas Kantzow, *Ursprunck und geschicht der Pomern und Rhügianer* . . . ed. Georg Gaebel (Stettin, 1897 and 1898), II, 7.
13 Usually entitled *De ritu, situ, moribus et conditione Germaniae descriptio.* Most conveniently found in Enea's *Opera* (Basel, 1571), pp. 1034–1086.

a crass account of primitive Germany, then abruptly shifts to his own day and to a glowing portrayal of German civilization in the fifteenth century, the result of the culture mission of the Roman Church. It is a pretty picture he now draws. With that plasticity of style uniquely his own, Enea sets down quick impressions of intensively cultivated fields and hills in the countryside. He enumerates produce and fruits, grains and wines, domestic animals and game. But his most flattering words are reserved for the brightest jewels of modern Germany, her cities. He pays high respect to the great commercial families of Leipzig, Nuremberg, and Frankfurt; he describes German trade; he counts up armies and arsenals; he even has some kind words for the universities.

Well before Enea's treatise was printed in Leipzig in 1496, it circulated in manuscript among the members of the humanist community. "Let us see," writes Enea at the beginning of his discourse, "what Germany was like in the old days, and how she looks today." No investigation could have been more appropriate for the humanists to undertake. Enea's vivid juxtaposition of the two Germanies, the ancient and the new, became their *Leitmotiv*, and his use of Tacitus and others for contrast became their method of exploitation of the sources. Enea's chief contention, that it was the civilizing power of the Church which had emancipated Germany from barbarism, was generally ignored. But his technique became a commonplace in humanist historiography and geography in the century which followed.

The ancestral characteristics of moral uprightness and rugged simplicity which had been recorded by Tacitus and Seneca continue to elicit proud comments, but the reader's attention is now directed to the startling progress made since antiquity. If only the ancient writers could see Germany now, how their eyes would pop! "Today, O Pomponius," we hear, or "Today, O Cornelius,"[14] Germany is no longer the bleak and barren place you knew! There was pleasure in the mere recitation of attractions now to be found in Germany:

Sehen wir doch jetz zu unser zeyt das wider spil, das wir gemeinlichen einen günstigen himel hand, und ein geschlachten boden. Die bühel bringen uns was uns lieb ist, wir hand hübsch und lustige weld, überfluss der frücht, weinträgige berge, gross und klein fliessende wasser die das ertrich begiessen, lustige wolschmeckende und gesunde brunen, vil quellen heisses wassers, vil salz gruben und brunen, mere erz gruben dann kein land um uns gelegen, ich geschweig hie wie zierlich das teutsch land mit grossen und kleinen stetten, märkten, castellen, dörfern und schlössern erbauen ist."

Thus Sebastian Münster in his *Cosmographia* of 1544,[15] a big book which describes and illustrates the enumerated features in loving detail.

---

14 Bebel, *Quod Germani sunt indigenae, Schardius Redivivus*, I, 105.
15 Pp. 161–162.

Authors competed with one another for the opulence of their summaries
of Germany's newly developed treasures. The theme is retained even in
Matthew Merian's topographies of the following century. Once upon a
time Germany was "rau" and "wüst," writes the editor, a "traurige Woh·
nung, ungeschlachtes und merentheils unerbautes ertrich." But rare in·
deed is the charm which is not now to be found in Germany. We have
splendid and mighty cities, fortresses, castles, monasteries, hamlets and
villages, and standing in them lavishly appointed churches, magnificent
townhalls, spacious schools, libraries, cemeteries, hospitals, orphanages
and homes for the aged and indigent, warehouses, arsenals, granaries,
public stables, mills, bath houses, mechanical clocks, public theatres,
water works, harbors, fountains, bridges, shooting galleries, dance halls
and inns, museums and exhibition halls, monuments, numismatic and
other collections, luxurious private dwellings, pretty and useful gardens,
and so on and on. And these are only the man-made marvels. Natural
bounties comprise an inventory twice as long.[16] Such catalogues never
seemed to tire the German reader, and every descriptive work featured
them. What better way was there to count his blessings?

While the geographistorians described the current scene, learned phi·
lologists undertook to clear up misunderstandings by launching lengthy
commentaries upon ancient views of Germany. Franz Irenicus, a Swab·
ian humanist, attempted nothing less than a complete catalogue of refer·
ences, with explanations and running glosses. His vast compilation, the
Germaniae exegeseos volumina duodecim or, as it was more often called,
Exegesis Germaniae,[17] is the most singular work of humanist scholarship
of the entire century. Confronting his material with the confident en·
thusiasm of his own twenty-three years and of the youthful humanist
movement itself, Irenicus compounded a curious blend of exegetical,
narrative, and hortatory writing. He explicates all texts which make
mention of Germany, from the Jewish authors to the Byzantine histor·
ians. He appraises the writings of his colleagues. He upbraids and, in
turn, encourages his contemporaries. And all the while he describes and
relates. The entire second half of his work is devoted to the physical
geography of the German lands as seen by the ancient authors. To de·
scribe the great Hercynian forest he excerpts Herodian of Syria on the
density of the vegetation, Strabo on the trees, Pliny on the hills and
mountains, and Tacitus on forest products. For the Rhine we get a com·
pendium of passages from Herodian, Claudian, Caesar, Plutarch, Pom·
ponius Mela, Tacitus, Strabo, Ammianus Marcellinus, Dracontius, Pliny,
Dionysius Periegetes, Appian, Virgil, and Hegesippus. They make up a
more generous account than many of his colleagues suspected, but Ireni·
cus was able to point out inadequacies and complement it with obser-

16 Preface to the first volume of the editions of 1652 and 1677, fol. 2 recto and verso.
17 See note. 8.

II

vations taken from Otto of Freysing, Nauclerus, Boccaccio, Leonardo Bruni, Enea Silvio, and Konrad Celtis. His erudition was enormous and even if his contemporaries scorned his wooly style and his frequently obnoxious tirades, they were glad to go to the book for reference.

Naturally enough, the most intensive exegesis was concentrated upon Tacitus' *Germania*. The little work was of paramount importance in fixing an authoritative image of Germany and the Germans in the first century of the Christian era, and, when held up against the cultural conditions of the sixteenth century, it became an irresistible theme for comment and comparison. The manuscript of the *Germania*, brought to Italy in 1455, was first printed at Venice in 1470 and three years later again at Nuremberg. At first it seemed to attract little notice in Germany, but after its exploitation by Enea Silvio in his treatise against Martin Mayr, the German humanists suddenly awoke to the possibilities of the work. In the early years of the sixteenth century, moreover, Tacitus' *Annales* were published in Rome, and Book I of this work, printed here for the first time, deals with the great hero of Germanic antiquity, Arminius. The time was auspicious for analysis and emendation.

The first German editions of the *Germania*, both by Konrad Celtis, appeared in 1500 and 1505. Neither of them is a substantial work of scholarship, but they further apprised the German humanists of the value of Tacitus' description. Celtis also lectured on Tacitus, again the first to do in Germany. Numerous commentaries on the *Germania* soon made their appearance, but only one of them turned out to be of lasting significance, Andreas Althamer's *Comments Upon Tacitus' Germania*, published in 1536.[18] Althamer's work is a model of humanist scholarship, dedicated in its treatment of the source and the interpretive problems. Every sentence, almost every word of Tacitus becomes the starting point of a discourse on etymological, geographical, historical, and occasionally philosophical matters. The many publications, by German humanists, of sources illustrating the German Middle Ages made it possible for Althamer to add significantly to Tacitus' outline of tribal culture. We hear more about "their ancient songs, their only way of remembering and recording the past," about their tactics in the Roman wars, their religious usages and family associations. Far from being doggedly antiquarian, Althamer never fails to point out that much of Tacitus' description is, of course, no longer valid. His treatise, and other similar ones by Jodocus Willich, Melanchthon, and Beatus Rhenanus, thus make a natural transition to the later descriptive works. The German past, now definitely established, is seen as a foil against which the present stands out in all its brilliant hues.

18 *Commentaria Germaniae in P. Cornelii Taciti Equitis Rom. libellum de situ, moribus, et populis Germanorum* (Nuremberg, 1536). An earlier version had been published in 1529.

The Swiss scholar Joachim Vadian accomplished the same purpose with a book of glosses on Pomponius Mela. Like Althamer, he is intent on suggesting the dramatic contrast between the then and the now. Eager to correct all the faulty impressions conveyed by Pomponius, Vadian compiles an impressive list of German intellectual achievements to take the place of Pomponius' examples of crudeness. A piqued summary of modern law codes answers Pomponius' assertion that "Germans know no law but force." And he even declares earnestly that "what Pomponius reports concerning our eating raw meat is no longer true today."[19]

The point would not have been made so insistently if it had not been felt that the ancient stereotype still persisted in all its rank malice. A German who, around 1500, happened to take up Zacharias Lilius' *Orbis breviarium*, an otherwise useful geographical encyclopedia, learned to his surprise that his country is bounded by Rhine and Danube, that the land, where not swampy, is overgrown with immense forests and overrun by wild oxen the size of elephants, and that he himself is of a warlike disposition and especially noted for his ability to go about naked in freezing weather.[20] Was this refusal to recognize that things had changed in Germany motivated by ignorance or malice? The latter, it would seem, for foreigners in Germany had a habit of making no secret of their utter disdain for the country, even while they enjoyed its hospitality. Giovanni Antonio Campano, for example, an intimate of Enea Silvio, when he attended the Diet of Regensburg in 1471, released the full stream of his scorn to his correspondents in Italy to whom he wrote enough letters from Germany to fill the entire sixth book of his epistolary.[21] He detests the climate (p. 352). The coarse food revolts his urbane palate and upsets his delicate stomach (pp. 356–357). Everything one touches is dank, everything smells; the German themselves exude an odor of decaying bodies (pp. 346, 396). "O! What a chasm separates the Danube from the Tiber!" he calls out (p. 356). As his stay in Germany is prolonged the letters, at first unhappy, grow peevish, ultimately vituperative. The very name of the country now sickens him: "non ad mores modo, sed ad nomen quoque Germaniae subnauseo" (p. 334). Meanwhile, his yearning for the day of his reunion with the land of sunshine and laughter has become well-nigh unbearable: "Quando erit illa dies? quando erit illa dies?" (p. 402).

We know that the letters were read in Germany from an invective against them by one Conrad von Leonberg, or Leontorius.[22] The reaction of the humanists may easily be imagined. Their suspicions of the

19 *Pomponii Melae Hispani Libri de situ orbis tres, adiectis Ioachimi Vadiani Helvetii in eosdem scholiis. . . .* (Vienna, 1518), fol. 96 verso.
20 *Orbis breviarium* (Florence, 1493), f i recto–f ii verso.
21 *Joh. Antonii Campani Epistolae*, ed. J. B. Mencken (Leipzig, 1707). My citations are to this edition.
22 Printed by Joseph Schlecht in *Hist. Jahrb. d. Görresges.*, XIX (1898), 351 ff.

good faith and honesty of Italians were all too readily aroused. The Italians, more than any other people, were now held responsible for the ignorance of German deeds which prevailed in the world. A common charge was that they suppressed those records of antiquity which were thought to draw a favorable picture of Germany. "Let them restore to us the entire history of Tacitus which they have hidden away," challenges Albert Krantz, a Saxon chronicler,[23] "let them give back Pliny's twenty books on Germany." These latter, we learn from another writer, "werden von den Italis, so den Teutschen keinen rum gönnen, neidischer weis unterdrückt."[24] Konrad Celtis accused contemporary Italian historians of intentional slander and deceit. In general, Italians, as opposed to the Germans who recognized their distinction in their moral traits, were considered shrewd, crafty, cunning, and ruthless,[25] hardly attributes of dispassionate historians.

The list of grievances and accusations might easily be expanded. Even when allowance is made for rhetorical hyperbole, enough remains to reveal genuine resentment and hurt feelings. An early expression of these feelings, and a determining one for the subsequent course of the humanist movement, was Konrad Celtis' address in 1492 at the University of Ingolstadt, where he had been appointed to a chair in rhetoric. The customary oration on the dignity of his subject was, on this occasion, charged with all his resentment of Italian superciliousness.[26] As he exhorts his listeners to strain every nerve to contribute to the intellectual glory of their country, to shun no effort to discover and present to the world the true image of Germany, he raises the specter of a Germany defenseless against the deprecations of her ruthless neighbors. Our object, he says, must be to "do away with that old disrepute of the Germans in Greek, Latin, and Hebrew writers who ascribe to us drunkenness, cruelty, savagery, and every other vice bordering on bestiality." Now that we have drained the marshes and cut down the forests and built splendid cities, it is time to lay that ghost to rest. "Let us be ashamed that certain modern historians should speak of our most famous leaders merely as 'the barbarians' in order to disparage the reputation of all Germans."[27] But why is it, he continues, that we do nothing to defend our-

---

23 *Saxonia* (Cologne, 1520), a ii verso. Again, I, 16. Repeated by Pirckheimer, op. cit., dedication.

24 Peter Albinus, op. cit., p. 70.

25 These adjectives are used by Felix Fabri, *Descriptio Sueviae*, ed. Herman Escher, *Quellen zur schweizer Geschichte*, VI (1884), 134.

26 *Oratio in Gymnasio in Ingolstadio publice recitata.* There is an English translation by Leonard Forster, *Selections from Conrad Celtis* (Cambridge, 1948) pp. 36–65, from which I quote.

27 The reference is specifically to Flavio Biondo whose *Historiarum ab inclinatione Romanorum Decades* were published around 1483, and to Marcus Antonius Sabellicus, *Historiae rerum Venetarum ab urbe condita libri XXIII*, printed in 1487. I am dealing here only with questions of physical geography and the appearance of the

selves against these accusations? "Let us be ashamed, I pray, that not one of you should be found today to hand down to posterity the deeds performed by German courage, while many foreigners will be found who, in their historical works, but contrary to all historical truth, will hiss like vipers against our courage, . . . and seek with falsifications and lying inventions . . . to belittle our glorious achievements."

This was a call to action. Still the jealous chorus against Germany by convincing it of the fraudulence of its allegations. Draw up a true portrait of the land, and the detractors will be silenced. "Then we shall see," writes Sebastian Münster, "what kind of land our ancestors conquered for their home: not a wild, uncivilized country, but a paradise and pleasure garden in which everything necessary to man's happiness is found."[28]

Thus came to life the idea of Celtis' master project, the *Germania illustrata*, a parallel description of ancient and modern Germany. It was to be a great collaborative effort, involving every public-spirited man of letters in Germany, and as Celtis presently devoted himself to its direction, his basic plan emerged with some clarity. First the correct nomenclature of the physical features would have to be worked out. Boccaccio's complaint that "names of mountains are nowadays mistaken for those of rivers, and lakes are confused with forests or cities or provinces,"[29] was most apposite in Germany where a traveler who tried to orient himself on a map based on Ptolemy would soon have got lost. Shifting populations and boundaries had left hardly a Latin or Greek name standing. "Under 20 bergen, stetten oder regionen [hat] nit eine iren alten namen mer," complains Sebastian Franck.[30] Celtis therefore set in motion a determined effort to trace the survivals of the old names and to discover the meanings of the new ones. Meanwhile scholars in all of the German lands would survey their native regions and describe them in a manner which Celtis himself proceeded to demonstrate with his little book on Nuremberg, an ingenious and high-spirited description of the

[28] *Erklerung des Newen Instruments der Sunnen, . . . Item ein vermanung Sebastiani Münster an alle liebhaber der künstenn, im hilff zu thun zu warer und rechter beschreybung Teutscher Nation* (Oppenheim, 1528).

[29] *De montibus, sylvis, fontibus, lacubus, fluminibus . . .* (Venice, 1473), unnumbered first page.

[30] *Weltbuch: spiegel und bildtniss des gantzen erdtbodens . . .* (Tübingen, 1534), fol. 3 verso.

land, not with the honor accorded to classical letters in Germany. The latter question was, of course, one of major concern at the time. The popular literature, especially, abounds with assurances that modern Germany provided a more fitting home for the eternal fame of the ancient authors. The humanists were not so sure. They did not think that Apollo had so far been lured to Germany. On the humanist drama see the recent *Forschungsbericht* by Wolfgang F. Michael, "Das deutsche Drama und Theater vor der Reformation," *Vierteljahresschrift für Literaturwissenschaft,* XXXI (1957), 106–153.

city's appearance and community life.[31] Combined into great compilations, or published separately and to be read in sequence, these volumes would "illustrate" Germany's landscape, her history, institutions, the diversity of her regional cultures and the constant Germanic character binding them. It was to be the most revealing investigation ever undertaken. It would catch the image of Germany's past and reflect the achievements which had attended her political and cultural growth.

The *Germania illustrata* remained a fragment. Celtis' death in 1508 deprived the project of its central impetus. But its essential purpose, the illustration of Germany's physical geography and history to establish an authoritative image of the country, was realized in scores of individual treatises and books. Pirckheimer's work on nomenclature settled that problem for the whole century. Beatus Rhenanus' solid, objective analytical study, the *Rerum Germanicarum Libri Tres* of 1531, was not surpassed as an exposition of ancient Germany until the appearance of Philip Clüver's magisterial *Germania antiqua* of 1616.

But it was in the great number of regional descriptions which soon came from every corner of the Empire that Germany really became aware of her own likeness. At a time at which a feeble national consciousness was badly in need of encouragement, the panoramic view which German readers found in these brimming books was heartening indeed. Attractive, prosperous, endowed with natural riches and a sturdy, industrious people, Germany must have seemed to them on the threshold of a brilliant future. Let the foreigner now intone the churlish phrases of Seneca and Pomponius Mela. A reference or two to Münster's *Cosmographia*, to Johann Stumpf's *Description of the Swiss Confederation*, to Peter Albinus' book on Meissen or Sebastian Brant's on the Rhine valley or Philip Apian's on Bavaria will set him straight.

> O Teutschland wie war dein Gestalt
> Vor Zeiten so gering und alt.
> So fern der klare Sonnenglanz,
> Dein Boden überleuchted ganz;
> War alles an dir rau und wild,
> Ganz unerbaut und nichts gezielt;
> Unfruchtbar, und von wilden Leuten
> Bewohnet zu denselben zeiten.
> Wie bist du aber jetz zumal
> So schön und herrlich überall,
> Glückselig reich und wolgeziert,
> Ganz fruchtbar und aufs schönst formirt.
> Vil hochgelerter weiser Leut
> Die sind in dir zu finden heut;

31 *Norimberga*, ed. Albert Werminghoff (Freiburg i. B., 1921).

234

Vil grosse stett und schöne Bäu
In dir erwachsen sind aufs neu.
Wie bist du doch so ganz und gar
Verändert in so manchem jar.[32]

The sentiment of the jingle echoes in Latin hexameters, in prose narrative, in the stately rhetoric of public addresses and private letters. All resound with the joy of a new-found pride. Undisputed now was the splendor of the German lands. Dispelled for all time the ancient notion that Germany is a wasteland peopled by oafs and ruffians!

---

[32] Translation of a Latin poem recited by Salomon Frenzel, a crowned poet, in 1585. The translation forms the preface to the German edition of Marx Welser's *Chronica der . . . Stadt Augsburg* (Frankfurt, 1595), unnumbered fol. 4 recto. The entire poem covers eight folio pages.

III

THE PRODUCTION OF JOHANN STUMPF'S DESCRIPTION OF THE SWISS CONFEDERATION

AMONG the most substantial achievements of humanist scholarship in sixteenth-century Germany, and probably the most enduring against the winds of time and taste, are the topographical descriptions produced by widely scattered groups of writers in the various German lands. A concerted effort to "illustrate" Germany's history and scenery occupied the humanist community throughout the century, and created many handsome books to whose brimming pages we still turn for our most intimate portrait of Reformation Germany. In their own age these books were read with intense pleasure, as masterpieces of the printer's art and as mirrors held up to the land and the people. But a graver accomplishment, too, compelled acclaim. For the first time the German lands were here made systematically aware of their political and cultural identity.

We do not know as much about the production of these chorographies, as they were called, as we would wish; but the main outlines, at least, of the typical process are clear. All such books were collaborative projects, many of them compilations, in which case the author was really collector and editor. He made the contacts and sent out the initial requests which would eventually place on his desk the raw material of his book, descriptions of towns and landscapes, documentary material to illustrate their history, biographies of men of local renown, genealogies, antiquities, inscriptions, and so on. While his correspondents were gathering information, the author himself went through the standard classical and medieval sources, as well as such modern chronicles as were available to him, copying out passages or whole pages which might find their way, often all but unchanged, into his manuscript. As contributions arrived they were inserted into the narrative outline, combined with his own notes. Finally illustrations and maps, some procured in the field, others from the printer's files, were selected. Care had only to be taken that the resulting compilation did not altogether lack balance and proportion.

One of the most successful of the great sixteenth-century chorographies, Johann Stumpf's *Description of the Swiss Confederation*,[1] has left a record of its production which enables us to trace in some detail the stages in which the idea of a description of the Swiss cantons became a massive topographical-historical volume.[2] Because of Stumpf's conscientiousness in saving every pertinent scrap

---

[1] *Gemeiner loblicher Eydgnoschaft, Stetten, Landen, und Völckeren chronikwirdiger Thaaten, Beschreybung* . . . , first ed. (Zurich, 1548).

[2] On Stumpf see Attilio Bonomo, *Johannes Stumpf, der Reformator und Geschichtschreiber* (Genoa, 1923) and Hans Müller, "Der Geschichtschreiber Johann Stumpf," *Schweizer Studien zur Geschichtswissenschaft*, N.F., VIII (1945).

Stumpf was born in Bruchsal in the Bishopric Speyer in 1500, left home after an altercation with his father over the choice of a profession, entered the priesthood and joined the Johannite Order. Only twenty-two years old, he attained the priorship of the Order's house at Bubikon. There he fell in with the Zurich reformers and went over to the new religion. In 1543 he took charge of the congregation at Stammheim, northeast of Zurich, near the German border. There he remained until his retirement from the ministry. He died in Zurich in 1578.

of paper, and thanks to the filial piety of his son and literary executor, Johann Rudolph, and the lasting concern of those who were Stumpf's associates in authorship, much of the relevant correspondence has survived.[3] The letters and documents are eloquent evidence of the learning, dedication, and hard work that went into the production of such books as Stumpf's. They also tell us something about the many large and petty difficulties which occasionally obstructed the way of their makers.

The point of departure for the author of a chorography was usually an existing published or manuscript chronicle which could be expanded with new descriptive and illustrative material. In Stumpf's case this was the *Swiss Chronicle* of the Zurich churchman Heinrich Brennwald,[4] Stumpf's father-in-law. Brennwald had written this long work to replace the older and slighter chronicle of Petermann Etterlin. He completed it in 1522, a most detailed history but no departure from the time-honored annalistic inventory. His order of narration is unswervingly chronological, proceeding from year to year, month to month, often from day to day where his sources were full enough. The author's personality is not to be found in this mass of material, but there is a great deal of valuable information in it. It was not mere family loyalty which led Stumpf to undertake the revision and augmentation of the Brennwald manuscript. He credited the older man with arousing his own interest in the art of history. Once stimulated, however, these interests struck out in a direction which was to take Stumpf far beyond the older man's conventional annals. By 1540 the principles of chorography had been clearly formulated, and an active group of writers were turning out topographical-historical treatises in accordance with them. Stumpf brought their ideas and equipment to his labors on the *Chronicle.* He soon found that the old scheme would not hold the new techniques, and resolved to make a fresh start. "People in other countries," he notes in the *Description*[5] "assume that the Alpine regions are nothing more than rocky wastes. . . . If they will but read this book they shall see that even the highest Alps have their fertile valleys and smiling pastures." To show honorable antiquity and historical importance was not enough. A country's attractiveness had to be demonstrated, and only the topographical method could do that.

*   *   *

It would be an oversimplification to represent Stumpf's *Description* as the product of one man's desire to display the physical wonders and human achievements of the country in which he made his home. There were almost as many

---

In addition to the *Eydgnoschaft* he wrote an account of the Luther-Zwingli controversy, a treatise on the Council of Constance, and a history of the reign of Henry IV of Germany.

[3]The letters and documents pertaining to Stumpf's biography have been collected by Attilio Bonomo in two typescript volumes at the Zentralbibliothek in Zurich, *Mss. Z I 103 and 103a.* I shall cite them as *Bonomo,* followed by the page number. The pagination of the two volumes is consecutive. Much, though not all, of the correspondence may also be found in Ernst Götzinger's edition of Vadian's *Deutsche historische Schriften,* II (1877). Vadian's letters may be consulted in the edition of his correspondence by Emil Arbenz, "Die Vadianische Briefsammlung der Stadtbibliothek St. Gallen," *Mitt. z. vaterl. Gesch. herausgg. v. hist. Ver. in St. Gallen, XXIV-XXV;* XXVII-XXX.

[4]Published only in the modern edition of Rudolf Luginbühl, *Heinrich Brennwalds Schweizerchronik* in *Quellen zur schweizer Geschichte,* N.F., I (1908) and I$_2$ (1910).

[5]*Eydgnoschaft,* Book IX, 293 verso.

ambitions for the large work as there were collaborators. Only an examination of the steps which led to its publication will reveal its many-sided nature.

The dominating figure in the circle about Stumpf was Heinrich Bullinger, the successor of Zwingli in Zurich. Bullinger was not only his superior—Stumpf was, until 1543, minister of the congregation of Bubikon, a little town southeast of Zurich—but he was also very much his spiritual mentor. Quite naturally, therefore, Stumpf turned to Bullinger for help with some historical problems which delayed the completion of his Brennwald revision. Early in 1536 he had continued the Chronicle to the year 1534,[6] but the seventh and eighth of the nine books were still incomplete[7] and the first three, because they had been put together hastily,[8] did not satisfy Stumpf. Before these sections could be readied for the printer, Bullinger had to procure source material to close the gaps and to subject the whole manuscript to his careful review; but work continued to lag, and Stumpf was never happy with the result. In September 1536 a rumor that Gilg Tschudi was about to publish a Swiss chronicle prompted him to ask the Zurich authorities to support the printing of his own work, "however inferior and full of faults it may be," in order to set the Protestant point of view against that of the Catholic Tschudi.[9] But the pieces came together slowly, certainly not until late in 1539,[10] and in the meantime the notion of a new and different kind of description must have occurred to either Stumpf or Bullinger. The publication, in 1538, of Tschudi's *Alpisch Rhetia* in a Latin translation by Sebastian Münster,[11] brought an early example of the topographical-historical genre before their eyes. Not long afterwards Stumpf must have begun the preliminary investigations for the new work, the *Description of the Swiss Confederation*. The first indication of the new plan is Stumpf's request of an "illustrated Ptolemy" from Bullinger in March 1541,[12] probably Münster's edition of the *Geography* with forty-eight new maps in xylograph, which had appeared in Basel in 1540.[13] It seems that Bullinger was successful in locating a copy,[14] and no doubt the study of Ptolemy's text and of the fine maps, which had also speeded Münster's work on his *Cosmographia*, intensified Stumpf's and Bullinger's topographical interests. Chorography was, in any case, very much a part of the German intellectual atmosphere in the mid-sixteenth century. Stumpf could not fail to be aware of its possiblities.

Work seems to have moved ahead swiftly now. Late in 1542 Bullinger approved the division of the volume into thirteen books and expressed pleasure at the imminent completion of the second book on Germany.[15] At the same time some important collaborators are heard from. One was Nicolaus Briefer, Dean

---

[6]Stumpf to Bullinger, 2 December, 1535; *Bonomo,* 122.

[7]Stumpf to Bullinger, 3 January, 1536; *Bonomo,* 124.

[8]Stumpf to Bullinger, 18 May, 1536; *Bonomo,* 128.

[9]Stumpf to Bullinger, 17 September, 1536; *Bonomo,* 130.

[10]*Cf.* the letter of Petrus Fabricius, a proofreader for Stumpf's printer Froschauer, to Stumpf, 28 January, 1540; *Bonomo,* 154.

[11]Most easily found in *Schardius redivivus* (Giessen, 1673) I, 269-303. The work was written in 1528.

[12]Bullinger to Stumpf, 15 March, 1541; *Bonomo,* 165.

[13]*Cf.* Justin Winsor, "A Bibliography of Ptolemy's Geography," *Library of Harvard University: Bibliographical Contributions* No. 18 (1884), 18-23.

[14]Hans Müller, *op. cit.,* 28.

[15]Bullinger to Stumpf, 24 November, 1542; *Bonomo,* 168.

of St. Peter's in Basel, a man learned in Swiss antiquities. He has learned from the printer Christof Froschauer that Stumpf is engaged on a description of Switzerland and surroundings, and he offers his assistance, urging Stumpf strongly not to omit a consideration of the origins of the Swiss localities. Some material for the political history of several cities and regions was included in the letter. He offers this information, Briefer declares, because he knows that Stumpf has a special talent for combining many sources "into an orderly and elegant exposition, just as you have done, not long ago, in your treatise on the Council of Constance."[16] Bullinger, too, sent a sheaf of extracts made at various libraries,[17] and in the summer of 1544 Sebastian Münster inquired about Stumpf's plans and suggested the mutual exchange of notes.[18] Less than a year later, when the scope and format of the *Description* had become known to him, Münster's friendship for the man and his cause cooled. In the meantime Stumpf helped himself liberally to portions of the *Cosmographia* when it appeared that year.

At the end of 1543 Stumpf was transferred from Bubikon to Stammheim, near the German border.[19] His new position seems to have afforded him greater leisure; consequently the year 1544 opens a period of intensive occupation with the *Description* which was to last until July 1546.[20] During the summer of 1544 Stumpf was able to undertake a fact-finding journey to the south, especially the Valais and Lausanne.[21] He observed eagerly and kept a note book in which he recorded his findings with meticulous care.[22] He examined documentary material:

> As soon as we arrived we called on the Abbot and inquired about the monastery's charter. The Abbot then brought out a magnificently illuminated volume in which the foundation charter had been recorded.[23]

He wrote out copies and German translations of records bearing on monastic and municipal histories.[24] He made mention of details of architecture and decoration:

> *Nota bene*: the fine floor mosaic behind the altar.[25]

Above all, he notes topographical detail:

> The Roth See, a half hour's walk from Luzern, extends north-east to within a half hour's walk from the village Ebikon. . . .[26]

Or

> Distance in miles from Zurich to Grimsel: From Zurich to Zug 2 miles, from Engelberg to Grund on the Aare 2 miles, from Grund to Guttannen 1 mile, from Guttannen to Spittal a little more than 1 mile, from Spittal to Grimsel 1 mile. Total: 12 miles, or more nearly 13 miles.[27]

Much of the eleventh book on the Valais region was assembled from these notes.

---

[16]Nicolaus Briefer to Stumpf, 17 December, 1542; *Bonomo*, 169-173. The reference is to Stumpf's *Des grossen Conciliums zuo Constentz . . . Beschreybung . . .* (Zurich, 1541).

[17]*Bonomo*, 177.

[18]Münster to Stumpf, 16 July, 1544; *Bonomo*, 222.

[19]*Bonomo*, 181, 192.

[20]Stumpf to Vadian, 4 January, 1547; *Bonomo*, 291.

[21]Bullinger to Vadian, 28 August, 1544; *Bonomo*, 223.

[22]"Reisebericht aus dem Jahre 1544," Hermann Escher, ed., *Quellen zur schweizer Geschichte*, VI (1884). Stumpf travelled with a group, but does not identify the other members.

[23]*Ibid.*, 233.

[24]*Ibid.*, 289-298.

[25]*Ibid.*, 274.

[26]*Ibid.*, 233.

[27]*Ibid.*, 240. On the Swiss *Wegstunde* and mile, see Richard Klimpert, *Lexikon der Münzen, Masse, Gewichte, Zählarten und Zeitgrössen* (Berlin, 1896), 221f.

The summer of 1544 also saw the opening of a new phase in the fortunes of the *Description*, the entrance of Joachim Vadianus into the ranks of its authors.[28] It was Bullinger who brought the project to Vadian's attention. In August 1544 he acquainted him with Stumpf's itinerary for that summer and asked him to undertake the revisions of the book on the Turgau, that is, the entire northeast of Switzerland. "You owe this to our country," Bullinger wrote him,[29] but the patriotic appeal was not necessary. Soon Vadian had staked out a major portion of the Turgau book for himself and, through frequent correspondence with Stumpf, Bullinger, and Froschauer, made himself the center of the little group.

That Bullinger and Stumpf should turn to Vadian is hardly surprising. The record of his voluminous correspondence shows clearly enough how much this universal humanist was at the hub of all political, religious, and intellectual concerns in the Switzerland of his time, and in matters of geography Vadian had special competence. No one engaged in the production of a large-scale chorography could fail to know that it was Vadian who had given exact statement to the principles and limits of this genre. In the methodological preface to his major geographical work, the commentary on Pomponius Mela, he had adapted the classical definitions of cosmography, geography, and chorography to the purposes of those of his colleagues who were then groping for a form into which to cast their projected descriptions of the German lands.[30] This preface has with good reason been called "the manifesto of the political geographers."[31] There is no topographical-historical work of the century which does not know it, and since many of his subsequent publications exemplified the method outlined in it, Vadian soon enjoyed the special authority of a pioneer in the genre. Moreover, Vadian was intimately familiar with the Turgau generally and the town and monastery of St. Gall in particular. The participation of such a man would let the whole book speak with a stronger, more confident voice. In the late summer of 1544, therefore, Stumpf submitted the draft for the Turgau book—Book Five of the finished *Description*—to Vadian for criticism and emendation.

Vadian expressed polite satisfaction with the effort, but found it insubstantial.[32] What Stumpf offered was only a bare list of places and a skeleton history. Plans for elaboration were made, but his manifold responsibilities allowed him little leisure for scholarly labors just then. Vadian in 1544 was no longer the free intellectual he had been in his Vienna days before 1517. Political and confessional problems were paramount now, and there could be no thought of scholarly activity without reference to them.[33] The pressure of official duties left few moments for quiet reflection. "I should like to see myself alone in a forest for a month or two," he wrote to Bullinger the following spring.[34] He refused to hurry

---

[28]For a review of the literature on Vadian see Werner Näf, *Vadian und seine Stadt St.Gallen*, I (St.Gall, 1944), 3-12. The second volume of Näf's biography (1957) had not appeared when this paper was written.

[29]Bullinger to Vadian, 28 August, 1544; *Bonomo*, 223.

[30]"Rudimentaria in Geographiam catechesis," *Pomponii Melae Hispani, Libri de situ orbis tres, adiectis Ioachimi Vadiani Helvetii in eosdem scholiis* . . . (Vienna, 1518), a 3 verso ff.

[31]Lucien Gallois, *Les géographes allemands de la renaissance* (Paris, 1890), 160.

[32]Bullinger to Stumpf, 26 September, 1544; *Bonomo*, 224.

[33]For the political situation which motivated Vadian's interest in the history of St.Gall, *cf.* Werner Näf, *op. cit.*, I, 19-108.

[34]Vadian to Bullinger, 14 May, 1545; *Bonomo*, 240-243.

the writing[35] though Stumpf urged haste,[36] and not until early 1546 did he deliver the last pages of his manuscript to Stumpf.

In the meantime Sebastian Münster had completed his *Cosmographia*. Because of the keen competition among authors and printers of such large illustrated volumes as Münster's and Stumpf's, the Zurich circle had awaited the publication of Münster's masterpiece with some trepidation. In September 1544 Froschauer went to Basel to procure a copy and Bullinger promised Stumpf an objective appraisal as soon as Froschauer returned.[37] Bullinger had learned that Münster was already at work on a new edition which would probably be issued in time to rival their work. The quality and appearance of the *Cosmographia* was therefore a matter of considerable concern to them.

A week later Bullinger was able to set these anxieties at rest. "My predictions have come true," he writes.[38] "Münster's book does not fulfill what it promised. The style is atrocious. He carries together a great deal but furnishes little evidence. Much he relates imperfectly, even wrongly." Bullinger therefore urges Stumpf to make every effort to excel where Münster falls short. Not only this present work must be surpassed, but the new version anticipated. A number of sections are quite well done, the description of the Valais and of the city of Augst, for example. But in general, "as black is different from white, so is this book different from yours." Secure in this knowledge Stumpf may now proceed with confidence and with all due speed.

Stumpf must have been cheered by this adverse judgment on his competitor's big effort, but in Basel there was much nervousness now. News of the elaborate preparations had come to Münster's ears, of the massive material being gathered by Stumpf and the sumptuous decorations which a whole team of artists was engraving in Froschauer's shop. He now regretted his earlier offer of cooperation, and worried especially that the Zurich people might abandon their original design and turn out a general cosmography rather than a mere description of Switzerland. In February 1545 Münster wrote an agitated note to a friend in the other camp, Conrad Pellikan, a professor of Hebrew at Zurich.[39] How near completion is this chronicle in the vulgar tongue, he wanted to know, and what form is it taking? "I have heard talk that it is to be more magnificent than mine. . . . We know that their original plan was for a history of Switzerland, but my new book may have persuaded them to turn it into a cosmography." He was aware, of course, that whole sections of his work would now be incorporated into the Zurich manuscript. What would they have done "if I had not preceded them as a pioneer?" A comparison of the two works later will easily establish their debt to him.

Münster himself realized that his printer, Heinrich Petri, could not afford to bring out an enlarged edition of the 1544 *Cosmographia* if a similar work was to appear in Zurich,[40] and his misgivings were only too justified. To the opulent volume which left Froschauer's press in 1547, with its maps, its ornate borders

[35]*Ibid.*
[36]Froschauer to Vadian, 10 May, 1545; *Bonomo*, 239.
[37]Bullinger to Stumpf, 26 September, 1544; *Bonomo*, 224.
[38]Bullinger to Stumpf, 3 October, 1544; *Bonomo*, 225.
[39]Münster to Pellikan, 9 February, 1545; *Bonomo*, 237.
[40]*Ibid.*

and devices, and its nearly two thousand illustrations including many large representations of Swiss cities, the first edition of the *Cosmographia* was a poor country cousin. Münster could only be impressed. His adoption of many of Froschauer's features for his 1550 edition reversed his earlier claim to originality in the field.

As work on the *Description* progressed, offers of collaboration came from a widening circle of scholars. Nicolaus Briefer reiterated his active interest in the work in hand,[41] and Tschudi wrote most cordially, sending along a digest of the annals of Glarus suitable for inclusion in the manuscript and inviting Stumpf to come to see him for consultation.[42] Stumpf made wide use of Tschudi's manuscript writings,[43] and had there been more frequent personal contact between the two men, much of the partisan bickering which disfigured the reception of the completed work might have been averted. Beatus Rhenanus was another who freely offered his aid. He called Stumpf's attention to the works of the Vienna physician Wolfgang Lazius, "who is to Austria what Tschudi is to Switzerland,"[44] and sent some documents pertaining to the History of Schlettstadt.[45] His correspondents were well aware of the difficulty of Stumpf's task and they praised not only his patience, but his good judgment. "I can tell you that it is easier to become a Doctor of Medicine or of Law or of Theology than to put together such a volume as yours," Briefer assured him in 1546, at the height of Stumpf's activity.[46]

All this time Vadian was engaged on his portion of the fifth book. In January 1545 he returned Stumpf's draft for the Turgau section which had been submitted to him the previous summer, and began to develop it with a major treatise on the monastery and town of St. Gall.[47] This treatise, he wrote to Bullinger, was to include a chronicle of the abbots, based on a series of critical biographies which he had written in the late 1520's and revised in 1530[48] after exploring the monastic archives during the exile of the abbot.[49] Vadian expected much from this work. "It will reveal the history of our native country from the year 900, and in such a manner that nothing will be left in doubt, not even to the monks."[50] Vadian, it will be seen, approached his share of the work in a very different spirit from Stumpf. The latter aimed to inform the reader, Vadian to persuade. As his narrative gathered momentum it expanded in all directions. In May Bullinger grew impatient for a sign of completion, and Vadian had to put him off. The trouble is, he writes him,[51] that the scale of the work continues to increase under his pen. "But it is all for the sake of History. Few people today

[41]Christophorus Piperinus to Stumpf, 26 January, 1545; *Bonomo*, 231.

[42]Tschudi to Stumpf, 22 February, 1545; *Bonomo*, 238.

[43]Gustav Müller, *Die Quellen zur Beschreibung des Zürich- und Aargaus in Johannes Stumpfs Schweizerchronik* (Zurich, 1916), 85-119.

[44]Rhenanus to Pellikan, 13 June, 1546; *Bonomo*, 279.

[45]Briefer to Stumpf, 11 July, 1546; *Bonomo*, 283.

[46]Ibid.

[47]Vadian to Bullinger, 15 January, 1545; *Bonomo*, 230.

[48]On the chronology of Vadian's older chronicle of abbots, cf. Werner Näf, *op. cit.*, II (1957), 379-383. Näf's discussion supplants Götzinger's.

[49]*Cf.* the comprehensive list of sources used by Vadian in Götzinger, II (1877), VI-XVII.

[50]Vadian to Bullinger, 30 December, 1544; *Bonomo*, 229.

[51]Vadian to Bullinger, 14 May, 1545; *Bonomo*, 240-243.

realize what the actual state of our faith and of the monasteries and religious houses was in early times, that is, in the age of the ancient Frankish kings who ruled our country and Bavaria and Swabia too, and who established the monasteries which became so corrupt during the later middle ages." He has therefore found it necessary, Vadian continues, to include an epitome of the reigns of these monarchs from the time of Clovis in order "to tell the general reader something of the customs of olden times, and what new practices have become the fashion since then, especially among the clergy." The whole of it has been drawn "from old chronicles, not only printed ones, but manuscripts, and documented with ancient letters and charters."

Stumpf was able to make only occasional use of this broad background treatise,[52] but some of it fitted into his third book on France. The rest of Vadian's scheme must have seemed even more digressive to him. There was to be a treatise on the origin of monasticism, Vadian informs Bullinger, then an account of the German monasteries under the Franks. "These chapters," Vadian predicts, "will cause our present pack of priests and monks not a little discomfort, but they will have to admit the truth." A fourth section will deal with the origins of St. Gall itself, again based on unimpeachable sources, and then will come the major piece, the lives of the abbots.[53] This part may require some additional documentary study and Vadian anticipates difficulties, but he hopes to have it all assembled by late August.

Stumpf, to whom this letter was forwarded by Bullinger, could not have been happy with the polemical nature of Vadian's projected treatise. It was very well for Vadian to invite "the Pope to leave it or lump it,"[54] speaking of his intended comments on monastic conduct, but Stumpf had to think of the sale of the volume in the Catholic cantons. In his editorial work on Vadian's material he consistently softened the line, not so much as to mask its Protestant tone, but enough to dull the edge. Vadian, of course, expected cutting. He knew his contributions were too bulky, and he trusted Stumpf to use his blue pencil well. "Stumpf is not only richly endowed with integrity and wisdom in the arts," he told Bullinger, "but he has an innate understanding of matters of historical research."[55]

In June Stumpf completed the fourth book, the general history of Switzerland in antiquity and the early middle ages. It contained many glowing tributes to the Swiss, their courageous stand against the Romans and the military and political genius displayed in their early struggles for independence. Since Stumpf was a German by birth, these words of praise would sound even sweeter to Swiss ears, a fact which did not escape Vadian's notice as a major asset of Stumpf's authorship.[56] Bullinger was greatly pleased with the book[57] and did not think it could be improved. It was now time to complete work on the Turgau section, and in late June or early July Stumpf appeared in St. Gall to show Vadian the early parts of his *Description* and to consult with him on the organization of

---

[52]It is included in *Götzinger*, III, 49-164.
[53]Vadian later reversed the order of sections four and five.
[54]*Bonomo*, 240.
[55]Vadian to Bullinger, 28 May, 1545; *Bonomo*, 244.
[56]Vadian to Bullinger, 8 July, 1545; *Bonomo*, 249.
[57]Bullinger to Stumpf, 3 June, 1545; *Bonomo*, 245.

Book Five.[58] On July 8 Vadian informed Bullinger of the results of this visit.[59] The two men compared their versions, Stumpf's very much the shorter, and made arrangements for a final draft, agreeing on the places to be described and the sources for the historical portion. Stumpf was to take from the *History of the Frankish Kings* whatever suited his purpose, and Vadian was to proceed with his history of St. Gall. To avoid duplication, Stumpf left him his completed sections and the outline of the whole work. He, in turn, lent Stumpf a satchel full of books and documents to help him with other parts of the book.

Vadian gained a favorable impression of Stumpf during this meeting. "He is truly an untiring compiler," he wrote, "and has a talent for clear and plain statement. He seems to me to be born for this work."[60] Nice compliment though this is, Vadian did not fully appreciate Stumpf's stature as an independent writer. He regarded him primarily as a skillful editor who could bring order and unity of purpose to an often haphazard collection of historical and geographical data. But Stumpf was far more than a writing tool. It was he who gave the *Description* a voice and a soul. From raw material sent in by dozens of contributors[61] he fashioned an organic structure, giving it direction and infusing it with a point of view. Far more than most other such compilations, the *Description* bears the mark of a single mind.

Vadian must have spent the summer and autumn hard at work, for at the end of September he sent Bullinger the chapters on monasticism, and in January of the following year the *History of the Abbots*. Each manuscript was accompanied by a lengthy covering letter containing Vadian's thoughts on the repercussions to be expected. It was necessary, he writes,[62] to go into detail, because so many foolish monkish notions had to be disproven. Reforms had to be urged, at least by implication. But he maligned no one and has referred to the Catholic cantons only in terms of the highest respect. What unpleasant things needed to be said were said in quotations from Augustine, Jerome, and St. Bernard, and let whoever will draw the inferences. After all, the truth never hurt anyone. In many of the biographies he might have been more outspoken, but he did not want to lay himself open to charges of immoderation and has refrained from criticizing their lives unless they deviated flagrantly from the principles of pristine monasticism.[63] Much is allowed to remain in doubt. Still, Stumpf would do well, he continues, to write a prefatory note anticipating some of the objections that are bound to come, and declaring that he has not aimed to affront anyone but has set it all down for the sake of truth alone. He should assert further "that no claim is made that this book is concerned with theology, though occasionally it has been found necessary to point out why this or that creed is the right one, and how, in every historical period, certain religious institutions have become

---

[58]Bullinger to Vadian, 3 June and 14 June; Vadian to Bullinger, 8 June, 1545; *Bonomo*, 246, 247; *Götzinger* II, LIX.

[59]Vadian to Bullinger, 8 July, 1545; *Bonomo*, 248-249.

[60]*Ibid.*

[61]A full alphabetical list of authors, ancient and modern, who have been consulted or who participated stands at the beginning of the book. The prefaces to Books XI and XII express the author's gratitude to those who have personally assisted him. *Cf.* also Hans Müller, *op. cit.*, 35-49, where the collaborators are named and their contributions listed.

[62]Vadian to Bullinger, 30 September, 1545; *Bonomo*, 252-255.

[63]Vadian to Bullinger, January, 1546; *Bonomo*, 259-264.

corrupt." He might also say a few words "about the motives of those who, during such periods of corruption, have attempted to reclaim the Christian life and faith. The reader may take from this what his religion permits him to. Each man is free to do so."[64] (Stumpf never wrote this preface.) In any case, Vadian concludes, Stumpf and Bullinger may decide how to make use of the *History of the Abbots*. They may include all of it or only portions, just as they wish.[65]

*   *   *

Again and again in these letters Vadian affirms his ideal of historical truth, but a careful reader of them cannot quite escape the suspicion that he protests too much. Objectivity was implicit in the purpose of the *Description* as seen by Stumpf. The world was to be shown the splendors of the Swiss lands, and the Helvetians themselves were to be reminded of their ancient glories so that the sterling characters and sturdy habits of their forefathers might become the inspiration of the present.[66] History, Stumpf knows, is a stage on which "good and bad men, praise- and blameworthy deeds, . . . noble virtues and base vices" display themselves for us to draw our object lessons.[67] Stumpf had no ulterior motives for his work, not even the patriotic fervor which impelled so many German humanists of the period.

Vadian, on the other hand, had a lance to break and he regarded Stumpf's pages as his lists. Were his treatise on monasticism and monastic reformers to appear by itself and under his name, he admits to Bullinger, only partisans would read it. But as part of a popular work of history and geography its effect will be widespread.[68] His own identity, he thinks, should be concealed, his name mentioned only in a general catalogue of contributors.[69] Stumpf must appear to be the author of the entire work. Since he is not a native Swiss, his readers will readily accept his strictures because they will think him objective.[70] This is an ideal method of influencing the opinions of general readers, and Vadian advises Bullinger to see to it that his observations on the lives of monks be somehow attached to the account of the wars for independence. Everyone will eagerly turn to these heroic events and will have to take Vadian's views along with them.[71] Not that Vadian condones hate-mongering. "I do not approve, nor would I allow, scurrilous abuse. But I am in favor of a more subtle kind of attack, one laced with sly overtones and sarcasm which appears to bestow praise while, in reality, it imparts a more painful sting."[72] There are numerous examples of such twists in Vadian's narrative, and the sting was felt where intended. Of detachment and objectivity there can be no question in these sections, nor in those passages where he was intent on proving the independence of the town of St. Gall from monastic control.[73] Neither can it be said that he was carried away

---

[64]*Ibid.*, 263.

[65]Reserving the right to publish the work independently, Vadian asked Bullinger to see to it that the manuscript is left intact and is returned to him. *Ibid.*

[66]Book IV, 264 verso-265 recto.

[67]Preface, ii recto.

[68]Vadian to Bullinger, 30 September, 1545; *Bonomo*, 252.

[69]Vadian to Stumpf, 29 August, 1545; *Bonomo*, 250f.

[70]Vadian to Bullinger, 8 July, 1545; *Bonomo*, 249.

[71]Vadian to Bullinger, 30 September, 1545; *Bonomo*, 252-255.

[72]Vadian to Bullinger, 12 February, 1546; *Bonomo*, 274.

[73]This is one of his expressed purposes in writing the original version of the *History of the Abbots*. *Cf.* letters of 14 May, 1545; *Bonomo*, 242, and January, 1546; *Bonomo*, 259ff.

while writing. His letters to Bullinger during the early months of collaboration plotted the line of attack with calm deliberation. Later, during a bitter altercation with Tschudi, Vadian's reaction again disclosed his true motives. In matters of religion he could not be objective. Everything points to the conclusion that he regarded his work with Stumpf as an opportunity to disseminate his passionately held and zealously defended convictions. And Stumpf was just the sort of person to stand as the author of these sentiments, a plain-spoken, decent man, not known to be either a scholar or a controversialist, not especially eloquent, a simple minister in a country town.

Stumpf knew Vadian's motives, and in his cutting of the manuscripts submitted to him he did his best to preserve the character of his own work. Stumpf enjoyed the most cordial of personal relations with his Catholic colleagues who were as eager as he to place the natural attractions and political accomplishments of the Confederation before the world's eyes. Tschudi, a Catholic and the leading Swiss historiographer of his time, was a sympathetic and self-effacing supporter who never turned against him, even when controversy erupted later. Men of good will on both sides were saddened by the religious schism. They knew it could not be closed, but their pride in their common land and its tradition was a bridge on which they met. Stumpf's abilities were recognized, and his collaborators were not restrained by confessional lines. That is why Stumpf trimmed Vadian's treatises, and not just because they were too long. Partisanship, he knew, might scuttle the whole enterprise. He had little liking for Vadian's disputations; his letters do not show this, but his cuts do. But because of his deep respect for Vadian's scholarship, and, perhaps, because of his own strong though less bellicose opinions, enough bite remained to cause resentment. This was inevitable, given the retention of Vadian's views on monks and certain of the abbots. Stumpf invited charges of bad faith by retaining these passages which were, as Tschudi later pointed out, after all digressions from the book's main business.

The initial chapter of Book Five, entitled "The Turgau, Its Situation and the Character and Customs of Its Inhabitants," is identical in Stumpf's original draft, in Vadian's manuscript, and in the version printed in the finished volume.[74] Chapter Two, however, on the origin and history of monasticism, shows considerable independence in Stumpf's handling. To take the place of his meager original draft, Vadian had presented him with an extensive treatise which covers 100 pages of print in its modern edition. By liberal excision and compression, Stumpf reduced this bulk to an account of no more than 13 folio pages, which does not arrest the chorographic description and, at the same time, preserves the tone of high scholarship of the original.[75] For a transition from the first chapter he retained the initial paragraph of his draft in which he justified the lengthy historical recital "because the town stems from the monastery, and the monastery owes its origin to the institution of monasticism."

---

[74] I cite material from the *Eydgnoschaft* according to the 1548 edition, by Book and folio signature, and Vadian's contributions and Stumpf's original draft according to the edition of Götzinger. *Eydgnoschaft*, V, 2 verso-3 verso; Vadian in *Götzinger* I, 1-3; Stumpf's draft, *Ibid.*, II, XXXVI.

[75] *Eydgnoschaft*, V, 3 verso-7 recto; Vadian in *Götzinger* I, 3ff.; Stumpf's draft, *Ibid.*, II, XXXVI-XXXIX.

The draft then continued with some rather naïve paragraphs on the first anchorites in Egypt and Syria, but after reading Vadian Stumpf produced a tighter, more professionally styled version. References to Jerome's *Life of St. Paul the First Hermit* give the account greater weight. Dates are made precise. Authorities are fully cited; however, Stumpf is loath to discard some favorite etymological experiments. Where Vadian correctly traces the derivations of "Bischof" and "Pfarrer,"[76] Stumpf arrives at the former from "bi den schafen," and at the latter by way of "pfärch," stable.[77] In general he followed Vadian's outline, sometimes producing a verbatim sentence, an entire paragraph, more often eliminating a whole section. Vadian's excursus on the explicit recognition by the early Church of the separation of ecclesiastical and secular authority is left out entirely.[78] Many other passages that would have offended in one way or another were also discarded, the extravagant praise of Erasmus, for example,[79] whom Vadian sees as the modern type of a true man of God, and the frequent cracks at contemporary monasticism. Vadian describes how monks fast. They say to the cook, 'Cook, prepare a good meal, for tomorrow we fast.' The following day: 'Cook, let us have some nourishing food, for we intend to fast today.' The next day: 'Cook, a fine meal today; we fasted yesterday.'[80] Stumpf decided that the chuckle was not worth the recriminations that must follow. He was careful, too, to keep the tone of his text informative. Vadian's is too often didactic. And of Vadian's conclusion to this second part, a savage attack on simony and lechery,[81] there is not a word in the *Description*. On the contrary, Stumpf closes the chapter with assurances of good will to everyone. "I have tried, in this chapter, to be as plain and concise as possible. What I have written is intended for no one's benefit and to no one's harm."[82]

Now Vadian opens a new section, entitled "The Pious Hermit St. Gall and the Origin, Development, and Character of his Monastery."[83] In Stumpf's draft the account of St. Gall's coming to Switzerland occupied less than a page and was part of the preceding section on monasticism, but in the *Description* it becomes a full chapter, opening with a paragraph on Irish houses and the activities of the Irish monks in France. But the succeeding description of the site of the newly founded cell, with an enumeration of the Frankish nobility residing nearby, is passed up for the moment. Such material came more naturally in a later topographical section.[84] But he takes over Vadian's next two chapters on the growth of the woodland cells into a set of buildings which soon included a church, a hospital, and a lodging place for pilgrims. Vadian intersperses generous excerpts from the documents which were at his disposal, but Stumpf's purpose was different. He wrote for the interested layman, not the historian. He made

[76]*Götzinger*, I, 39.
[77]V, 6 recto.
[78]*Götzinger*, I, 47-50.
[79]*Ibid.*, I, 6f.
[80]*Ibid.*, I, 10.
[81]*Ibid.*, I, 97-103.
[82]V, 9 verso.
[83]*Eydgnoschaft*, V, chapter 4; Vadian in *Götzinger*, I, 104-143; Stumpf's draft *Ibid.*, II, XXXVIII-XXXIX.
[84]E.g.: Rosenberg, V, 87 verso; Ramschwag, 92 verso.

good use of Vadian's research, however, and writes an informative and readable survey of the monastery's infancy.

At this point begins the major section of Vadian's part of the fifth book, "The Abbots of the Monastery of St. Gall" a historical account covering 826 years. A line from Juvenal sets the mood for what follows:

De moribus ultima fuit quaestio.[85]

Stumpf omits this, but the substance of what ensues, a chronicle of the administrations of fifty-seven abbots,[86] is derived entirely from Vadian. His draft had contained little more than a list of names[87] and an incomplete one at that. Vadian's manuscript enabled Stumpf to round out his catalogue and to correct his chronology. But because the proportions of the entire work had to be maintained he could give only an occasional taste of the rich fare offered by Vadian. The administration of Conrad von Busnang from 1226 to 1238, for example, was to Vadian a historical turning point of paramount significance, beginning a new chapter in the monastery's history. Vadian thought that it was during the stewardship of this abbot that the traditional pursuit of the arts and the classical languages was abandoned in favor of Conrad's avid search after worldly riches and honors. He therefore wrote a carefully considered account of the state of the monastery under Conrad.[88] There are many digressions. The mention of Conrad's ancient lineage leads to some paragraphs on the Swiss aristocracy in the thirteenth century and its prerogatives. The subject of the abbot's friendship with King Henry, the son of the Emperor Frederick II, gives him occasion to write at length about these men, about Gregory IX, about Guelphs and Ghibellines, crusades, and the Turks. Conrad's involvement with these men and events made for an exciting career which Vadian relates with gusto, though with disapproval. But Stumpf had no space for any of this. In his handling[89] the historical importance of the twelve-year period dominated by Conrad is not apparent. What he tries to convey instead is the impact of the man's personality, "a handsome, cunning, experienced, well-spoken man, . . . a haughty and disdainful prince." But though he could only skim the surface of what Vadian furnished, he was able to produce a balanced portrait, far more realistic than the sketch in the Draft where Conrad was passed off as "a terrible tyrant and oppressor of the poor."[90]

When Vadian reached the year 1190 in his work he was able to draw on his earlier *Chronicle of the Abbots*, composed in the 1520's, which commences with the election of Ulrich V that year. Because of the exceedingly generous scale on which this chronicle had been drawn Vadian had to condense it as he went along, using only a fraction of his original material. Stumpf, of course, found the new version still too bulky and abridged it further. The older chronicle ended with the year 1491, but Vadian continues to 1530, though because of the mass of material on recent events and the haste with which he had to master it, he could do no more than follow his sources from year to year. 1530 was a hopeful time for

---

[85]*Götzinger*, I, 144.
[86]*Eydgnoschaft*, V, 12 recto-42 verso.
[87]*Götzinger*, II, XXXIX-XLIX.
[88]*Ibid.*, I, 272-296
[89]*Eydgnoschaft*, V, 24 verso-25 recto.
[90]*Götzinger*, II, XLIII.

Vadian and the Protestants of St. Gall, and a good date to leave off. Two years before, the town, whose fight for independence provided so much of the content for the late medieval part of the chronicle, had adopted the new religion and in 1530 the monastery was closed. Vadian barely mentions the election of Diethelm as abbot that year, while the unhappy consequences of the second battle of Kappel and the return of the abbot later in 1531 are evident only in the bitter mood of the closing pages. He cannot find a gracious word to conclude his history, but Stumpf, ever the peace maker, sounds the right note. "Thus the citizens were able to preserve the churches of St. Lorenz and St. Mangen for their faith, ... and each party leaves the other to pursue its religion unmolested. May the all-merciful God unite us all in His word and in His true faith and in the knowledge of eternal truth, and may He remove all misunderstanding and dissension from us. Amen."

Vadian furnished two more portions of the Turgau book, a description of the situation and the institutions of the town of St. Gall with a year by year chronicle of important events,[91] and a detailed topographical survey of Lake Constance.[92] Stumpf follows his model closely in these chapters. Those on St. Gall are used almost as Vadian wrote them, and to Stumpf's outline description of the lake Vadian was able to add considerable material from local sources and personal knowledge. In the process many descriptions became proper chorographic vignettes. The scheme of the municipal descriptions was Stumpf's; the text Vadian's. Their aims were fully in consonance here, for by the middle of the sixteenth century a procedure for depicting a town and its life had been worked out with which both men were familiar. This description of Lake Constance begins Stumpf's topographical survey of the entire region, and other sources besides Vadian are now drawn upon, as Constance, the Zeller See and its islands and adjacent towns, Stammheim, Schaffhausen, the Thur valley, the Appenzell area are brought into focus.[93] The descriptive method varies little here. The amount of municipal history offered depends on the size of the place, but every village is at least mentioned by name. The narrative follows the natural lines of drift, along the lake first, then down the river valleys, beginning with the Thur, and the Sitter and Töss next. At every town, monastery, and castle, Stumpf pauses to set down what information he had gathered from local chronicles. When the northeastern border of the canton Zurich, his next division, is reached, Book Five is concluded.

*   *   *

Vadian's two covering letters of September and January had left Bullinger apprehensive about the polemical nature of what Vadian was writing. When he saw the manuscripts they did nothing to allay his fears. Bullinger's aims for the *Description* were identical with Stumpf's and he did not like to see the originality and usefulness of the work obscured by the nasty recriminations that must inevitably come. Vadian attempted to reassure him, asserting, as always, his conviction that the truth hurts no one. "Not only our faith, but the integrity of the

---

[91]*Eydgnoschaft*, V, 42 verso-49 recto; Vadian in *Götzinger*, II, 418-430; Stumpf's draft, *Ibid.*, II, XLIX-LII.

[92]*Eydgnoschaft*, V, 49 verso-56 recto. Vadian in *Götzinger*, II, 431-448; Stumpf's draft, *Ibid.*, II, LII-LVI.

[93]*Eydgnoschaft*, V, 56 recto ff.

historian demands that we publish nothing that strays from the truth,"[94] and his presentation, he insists, is scrupulously objective and moderate.[95] Bullinger let it go at that, trusting Stumpf's good sense in editing the material, and hoping for the best.

Stumpf spent the spring and summer of 1546 on the remaining sections. Vadian, though his formal collaboration ended with the Turgau book,[96] sent him a general maxim for the selection of material. "The more you tell your readers about little known places the more pleased they will be. What is familiar arouses little interest, but what is strange and unknown will be received with gratitude and pleasure by all."[97] Stumpf followed this advice without being led to the sensationalism which is a feature of so many topographical- historical books. There was no need to seek out the outlandish and the fantastic, for he remembered that to most of his countrymen the regions beyond their native horizons were as strange and unknown as the eastern Indies.

Brennwald's chronicle remained his running source, enriched wherever possible with information culled from other chroniclers, such as Petermann Etterlin. Bullinger furnished him with important documentary material, as did Tschudi, who had access to some monastic libraries which were closed to Protestants. Both men made collections of archival material for Stumpf's use, and Tschudi copied inscriptions. According to his own account, Stumpf brought a substantial mass of documents and records into his possession.[98] Tschudi's *Alpisch Rhetia* was helpful both as a source and as a model of a regional description. Acknowledgments were due, of course, to a far longer roster of names than these, and Stumpf lists most, though not all, of his authors at the beginning of his volume.[99] Book Twelve, on the Valais region, was largely his own creation. "I have myself," he writes[100] "walked the length and breadth of this magnificent land. I have surveyed it and have, as well as I could, recorded the location and appearance of all noteworthy towns and villages, rivers, and valleys. As for the excerpts from ancient chronicles which you will find here included, I have gathered them partly there, partly in other regions." As the manuscript grew, it came to look like a scrap book, with insertions on sheets of paper, slips stuck in here and there, marginal additions and elisions.[101]

In October Stumpf was nearly finished, for he got ready to return all borrowed books and documents to Vadian.[102] Some months before, Froschauer had begun to set the completed portions in type. In August he ran off the first two books on Europe and Germany and sent a copy of each to Vadian.[103] In Decem-

---

[94]Vadian to Bullinger, 12 February, 1546; *Bonomo*, 274.

[95]Vadian to Bullinger, 18 February, 1546; *Bonomo*, 275f.

[96]For incidental use of some of Vadian's material here and there in the *Eydgnoschaft*, cf. the tabulation in *Götzinger*, II, LXXXI

[97]Vadian to Stumpf, 1 April, 1546; *Bonomo*, 277.

[98]*Eydgnoschaft*, ii verso.

[99]For a careful investigation of Stumpf's sources, cf. Gustav Müller, *op. cit.*, and August Bernoulli, "Die Basler Quellen zu Stumpfs Beschreibung der Eidgenossenschaft," *Basler Ztschrft. f. Gesch. u. Altertumskunde* XI (1912), 244-252 and XII (1914), 191ff.

[100]*Eydgnoschaft* XI, 338 verso.

[101]Gustav Müller, *op. cit.*, 17f.

[102]Stumpf to Bullinger, 10 October, 1546; *Bonomo*, 284. They were actually returned in January, 1547. *Ibid.*, 291f.

[103]Froschauer to Vadian, 20 August, 1546; *Götzinger* II, LXXIV.

ber Vadian examined Book Three, the history of ancient Gaul and modern France with parallel accounts of the Roman and Byzantine empires. He liked it all immensely. "How tastefully and richly it is done! What a wealth of material it contains!"[104] By late February of the following year he had seen and approved Books Four and Five,[105] the latter, of course, his own Turgau section. The other eight books seem not to have gone to St. Gall for criticism, but Stumpf had occasion to turn to his mentor in other matters. There was the problem of the financial arrangements with the printer. Stumpf had no experience in such affairs and hesitated to name a sum lest it be considered excessive. Vadian, he hoped, would advise him.[106] Since Vadian's suggestions were made orally in Zurich we do not know what his proposal was, but the matter was settled to everyone's satisfaction, with Bullinger acting as mediator between Stumpf and Froschauer.[107]

Late in October the great volume was ready to be bound. Froschauer had taken great pains to make its appearance as appealing to the eye as its content was to be to the mind. He closely supervised all phases of the publication. He saw to it that local artists were engaged to provide accurate drawings of Swiss towns,[108] and insisted that his engravers read the manuscript to be able to illustrate it more fittingly. He encouraged Stumpf to come to Zurich himself to give a personal view of the work to all those engaged in its production.[109] But before the volume could be issued, the Zurich authorities decided that a book so closely linked to leading officials of Swiss Protestantism should first be inspected for theological orthodoxy. For this purpose the Council of the city appointed Bullinger, the man next to Stumpf most familiar with the work, and the municipal secretary Johann Escher to be the censors.[110] This was the final delay. In November Bullinger wrote out the entire title page and the text of the introduction,[111] the latter based on a preface which Stumpf had written some ten years earlier for the Brennwald chronicle.[112] The publication date given as part of the title is November, 1547,[113] and late that month Stumpf's seventeen-year-old son Johann Rudolph travelled to the Five Forest Cantons to offer presentation copies to the town officials. He was cordially received by the Catholic authorities there:

> On the 27th of November, 1547 [he reported home] I was on my way to Zug. . . . There I called on the Chief Magistrate, the brother of Peter Collinus. On the 28th I handed him a copy of the Chronicle and the covering letter. On the 29th I journeyed to Luzern and spent the night at the Crown Inn near the Reuss bridge. . . . On the 30th I presented Chronicle and letter to the Council and received, on the 1st of December, 10 crowns from the hands of the bailiff. On the following day I continued my journey to Winkel, a village not far from

---

[104]Vadian to Bullinger, 11 December, 1546; *Bonomo*, 285.

[105]Vadian to Stumpf, 23 February, 1547; *Bonomo*, 293.

[106]Stumpf to Vadian, 4 January, 1547; *Bonomo*, 291f.

[107]*Ibid.*

[108]Froschauer to Vadian, 10 May, 1545; *Bonomo*, 239

[109]Froschauer to Stumpf, 20 November, 1544; *Bonomo*, 227.

[110]*Cf.* Stumpf's Dedication of his later digest of the *Eydgnoschaft* to this Johann Escher. *Schwytzer Chronica, Auss der grossen in ein handbuechle zusamen gezogen* (Zurich, 1554), a ii verso.

[111]*Bonomo*. 296.

[112]Hans Müller, *op. cit.*, 49, note 82.

[113]This is the date of the thirteen presentation copies. The general trade edition is dated 1548.

Luzern, where I boarded a vessel which took me on a stormy trip to Altnach, where I spent the night. On the 3rd, bright and early, I travelled to Sarnen, the chief town of Unterwalden, and that very afternoon presented Chronicle and letter to the Council there. Both were received with expressions of high gratitude.[114]

From Schwyz came 10 crowns, from Uri 12, and from Zug and Unterwalden like amounts were expected.[115] Stumpf's cautious treatment of the religious division thus appeared to have succeeded in making the volume acceptable to the other party, while the flattering words in which he recounted the remote past of the several cantons and cities naturally pleased everyone. Zurich was particularly delighted. Early in 1548 both Stumpfs, father and son, were made honorary citizens, "he, Hans," read the citation, "having accurately and diligently set forth the memorable deeds and actions of the Confederation, to the honor and praise of Switzerland, and having made a present of a printed and bound copy of his chronicle to the undersigned."[116]

Careful reading, however, could not fail to turn up partisan treatment of sensitive issues, and it did not take long for objections to Vadian's prejudicial comments in the fifth book be voiced. The first of these was also the most disturbing, because it came from a warm friend of the authors and their enterprise, Gilg Tschudi. On December 15th, 1547, the Zurich professor Johann Friess forwarded to Stumpf a letter from Tschudi received four days earlier.[117] It is a disturbed and unhappy communication from which speaks the historian's infinite sadness over the religious dissensions which rend his country and which must be perpetuated by thoughtless and senseless acts such as Stumpf's. Tschudi does not, of course, know that most of the offending passages come from Vadian's pen. ("What would he say," Vadian wrote to Stumpf a little later, and with just a touch of glee, "if he had read my treatise in its original form!"[118]) If only, Tschudi exclaims to Friess, recalling his earlier invitation to Stumpf, he had let me see his manuscript before sending it to the printer. All this unpleasantness could easily have been avoided. "Why was it necessary to deliver a long harangue on monks and how they have invented good works for their profit? Why must he make remarks about images that are bound to embitter the Catholic party?"[119] It is quite proper to describe factually the reprehensible deeds of some monks, as he himself has done, but theological questions should be discussed only by theologians in books of a more restricted circulation, not by chroniclers. A historian's first duty is to be unbiased and to give no one cause to suspect his motives. The good people of the Seven Catholic Cantons will hardly think Stumpf objective. How sad that this otherwise splendid work has been spoiled by a few passages that should have been left unwritten. "I grieve for all his industry and care, for the book will serve only to cause bad feeling."

The Zurich group took the protest seriously, mostly out of personal regard for Tschudi. His pathos surprised them,[120] and it was agreed to submit a formal

---

[114]*Bonomo*, 651f.

[115]Bullinger to Vadian, 21 or 31 December, 1547; *Vadianische Briefsammlung*, VI, 688.

[116]Decree of the Mayor and Council of the City of Zurich, 15 February, 1548; *Bonomo*, 321.

[117]Friess to Stumpf, *Bonomo*, 299. Tschudi's letter, *Ibid.*, 297-298.

[118]Vadian to Stumpf, 30 December, 1547; *Bonomo*, 302f.

[119]This discussion of images occurs in the Byzantine section of Stumpf's third book. Tschudi holds that Stumpf's words come dangerously close to the Greek position and might encourage iconoclasm.

reply, though Bullinger thought the matter hopeless. "We can, no doubt, appease him, since he is human," he wrote,[121] "but we shall convince him of nothing." Vadian wished to keep his own name out of the altercation and thought that in any case an answer should come from the author of the whole work. But as he did not trust Stumpf to compose a persuasive enough brief[122] he decided to draw up a letter to be signed by Stumpf. On the 30th of December the draft reply to Tschudi was in Stumpf's hands.[123] There is no need to trace in detail the argument of this long document. Essentially, it is a defense not of the inclusion of inflammatory passages in the *Description* (to which Tschudi had objected), but of the partisan position taken in them. In fact, the letter goes a long way toward proving Tschudi's side of the controversy. There are many passages in which Vadian's petulance is only too clearly evident. I have not let my pen be rancorous, he writes, but others in my party have; and, pretending to contrast the moderation of his own words with the violence of others, he attaches a detailed indictment of the secular and regular priesthood drawn from the writings of various controversialists. Had I been intent on a dispute, he continues, I should have inserted long quotations from Jerome, Augustine, Gregory, and Bernard to prove my points (these are now given). Since Catholics address us almost daily with tracts and other writings, he goes on, shifting his ground, I thought it right that the beliefs of our party be set forth soberly and plainly, drawn from both Catholic and Protestant sources. That is what Sebastian Franck has done not long ago, he writes, but the reference is disingenuous, because Franck was a genuine non-partisan, denied by Protestants and Catholics alike, a true religious independent.

The letter begins and concludes with assurances of sincerity, but it could not possibly have cleared the air. Tschudi never denied the essential truth of Vadian's contentions on monastic mores; he had accused Stumpf only of an ill-considered action in warming up the controversy. Stumpf saw this clearly, and in rewriting the draft reply over his own signature he showed the same quiet sagacity he had displayed in his earlier editorial work.[124] Realizing how Vadian's disputatious citations of the Bible and the Fathers would irritate the exceedingly well read Tschudi, he omitted them all. "I shall not let this letter argue with you," he writes instead, "but shall try to convince you of my good faith." His whole letter is conciliatory in mood and modest in language, as well as much briefer.

But Tschudi was right. The few controversial pages clouded the general excellence of the work. The following March, Johann Rudolph reports to his father that the *Description* had been banned in the Empire. Any printer and bookseller who attempts to sell it will be arrested, said the Imperial decree.[125] Soon after that, the Seven Catholic Cantons appointed a commission to examine the book closely, identify passages "wherein several of our Lords and Authorities

[120]Vadian to Stumpf, 30 December,1547; *Bonomo*, 302f.

[121]Bullinger to Vadian, 3 January, 1548; *Bonomo*, 319.

[122]Vadian to Bullinger, 30 December, 1547; *Bonomo*, 286.

[123]The draft reply accompanied Vadian's letter of 30 December to Stumpf. *Bonomo*, 304-315.

[124]*Cf. Bonomo*, 316f. for Stumpf's letter to Tschudi.

[125]Johann Rudolph Stumpf to Stumpf, 30 March, 1548; *Bonomo*, 324f.

have been maligned or belittled," and answer them in a counter tract.[126] A year later the Abbot of St. Gall, to whom a copy of the work had been presented immediately after its publication, [127] was heard to utter threats against Stumpf.[128] As late as 1554 the Zurich authorities were obliged to draw up a list of objections being voiced against portions of the *Description* and called on Stumpf to furnish answers to them.[129]

After that the controversy seems to have run down. Catholic resentment over the Zurich views was, after all, a very minor incident in the course of Swiss religious struggles, and Stumpf's *Description of the Confederation* a very major accomplishment. It was soon recognized as that. The work's merits had been obvious to Tschudi even while he objected to its *obiter dicta*.[130] In 1574 Josias Simler, a good critic, called Stumpf "the finest writer on Swiss affairs,"[131] and in Jean Bodin's catalogue of historians Stumpf stands as the only representative of Swiss historiography.[132] He was, in fact, one of the most effective of the sixteenth-century chorographers, informative, plain spoken, a source of enlightenment and entertainment to his readers and a mine of facts for subsequent writers. Popular response was lasting,[133] as the editions of 1586 and 1606 show, and modern critics have sustained his reputation. The grand ambition of the "geographistorians," as Bodin called them, to write a comprehensive description of the German lands and peoples produced few better works.

---

[126]Resolution of the Seven Catholic Cantons, 12 June, 1548; *Bonomo*, 329b.

[127]Froschauer to Vadian, 24 December, 1547; *Bonomo*, 301.

[128]Stumpf to Vadian, September, 1549; *Bonomo*, 358f.

[129]Mayor and Council of the City of Zurich to Stumpf, 24 May, 1554; *Bonomo*, 492.

[130]Tschudi to Friess, 11 December, 1547; *Bonomo*, 298.

[131]Preface to the *Vallesiae descriptio* in W.A.B. Coolidge, *Josias Simler et les origines de l'alpinisme* (Grenoble, 1904), 8.

[132]*Methodus ad facilem historiarum cognitionem*, (Paris, 1572), 606.

[133]See the Preface of the Reader by Johann Wolff, printer of the third edition of 1606, un-numbered leaf 6 recto and verso.

IV

PROTESTANT DOGMA AND CITY GOVERNMENT:
THE CASE OF NUREMBERG

IN THE LATE MIDDLE AGES, NUREMBERG WAS GOVERNED BY A BENEVOLENT oligarchy.[1] For more than two centuries before 1500, the affairs of the imperial city had been directed by a small band of distinguished mercantile families who were also the chief beneficiaries of Nuremberg's growing influence and wealth. The fourteenth-century revolution which replaced patrician rule in many other German cities, or tempered it with artisan participation, failed disastrously in Nuremberg; in fact, so complete was the victory of the old ruling circles after only the briefest interlude of political turmoil, that after the middle of the fourteenth century there was no longer any question of division or distribution of power. Forty-three patrician families — the number was limited by law — ruled a city of 20,000 and a territory of some twenty-five square miles inhabited by another 20,000. Only members of the forty-three could hold places on the Inner Council, the body in which all power was concentrated. Nor were all patricians equal. Within the Inner Council itself real power lay with a committee of Seven Elders open to a mere handful among the patricians. This élite came from the so-called First Old Families whose roots in the city went back to the early thirteenth century. From the middle of the fourteenth century a remarkable uniformity settled on Nuremberg's political affairs. The same names appear year after year on the rolls of Governing Mayors, Treasurers, Elders, Members of Council, Commanders of Militia. No explanations were advanced to justify the exclusion of everyone else, only the assertion that this was the way it had always been done. In any case, the system worked. Wealth and esteem increased. Manufactures reached a recognized standard of excellence. A net of trade spanned western and eastern Europe. Envious territorial barons met defeat in their attempts to cut themselves in on the bounty. There were no class antagonisms to split society into hostile camps. Nearly everyone lived with more than adequate creature comforts. Peasant rebellions, religious

---

[1] For a detailed account of politics and society in late medieval Nuremberg, see my *Nuremberg in the Sixteenth Century* (New York, 1966), where a selective bibliography may also be found. A shorter version of this paper was read to a joint meeting of the American Historical Association and the American Society for Reformation Research in New York in December 1966.

* This article first appeared in *Past and Present: A Journal of Historical Studies*, no. 36 (April 1967), pp. 38-58 (World Copyright: The Past and Present Society, 175 Banbury Road, Oxford, England).

disputes, even the German Civil War failed to upset the placid and profitable life of this burgher community. No wonder Nurembergers congratulated themselves on their deserved good fortune, and foreign observers agreed that Nuremberg was indeed a splendidly governed place.

Technically the system depended on the total concentration of power and responsibility in the hands of the Inner Council. This Council of forty-two, or rather its nucleus of seven Elders, was the whole government, at once legislative, executive, judicial. It was not merely the supreme authority; it was the only authority. Its membership was self-perpetuating. It made all appointments but never shared authority. It took advice but delegated no decisions. It bore all responsibility but was itself accountable to no one. There was nothing, literally nothing, in the life of the city that it did not consider its business. Councillors spent long sessions deliberating on weighty matters of state, then conferred as long and as gravely on the length of skirts, the script of a salacious carnival play, the week's menu in the municipal hospitals, the number of pounder blows required to settle a paving stone in its bed. Big things and little things were indistinguishable in practical government.[2] Everything that was made, that moved, could be weighed, measured, tested, appraised passed through the hands of the Council's agents. Guild organizations having been outlawed in the aftermath of the abortive rebellion of 1349, it was the Council that set prices and working hours, made apprenticeship rules, drew up production specifications and rules for procurement and for quality of workmanship. Social activities, pastimes, religious duties, family life from birth to burial were regulated by the most meticulous prescriptions and proscriptions. Such proceedings naturally spawned a mountain of documents, and from these the story of Nuremberg's government may be reconstructed in its profuse detail. The records have been studied by generations of local historians, and there is today little argument over what the sources say.

[2] The best evidence for this is provided by records of the Committee of Elders (*Verlässe der Herren Älteren*) and by the *Ratschlagbücher*, collections of legal and practical advice given by the Council's legal experts sitting as a committee. Both are in the Staatsarchiv, Nuremberg. While the *Verlässe* record mainly summary instructions and a few brief points raised in the discussions among the Elders, the *Ratschlagbücher* give a most interesting inside view into governmental business as it arose. As the councillors themselves had little formal knowledge of the law, the advice given them by their half-dozen legal experts was based on common sense and practical experience rather than on academic jurisprudence. And as these opinions were not intended for outside eyes, the lawyers spared rhetoric and fine phrases and spoke their minds in plain language.

What do they say about the circumstances of the coming of the Reformation? Needless to state, Nuremberg's ecclesiastical establishment had long before the Reformation been brought within the reach of civic authority. Nuremberg's church overlord, the bishop of Bamberg, had never been able to offer more than feeble resistance to the Council's growing hegemony. Members of the Council assumed the titles of *Kirchenpfleger* or *Gotteshauspfleger* and supervised affairs in every church, convent, and monastery. Each one of these was tied to the government by means of regulations that limited members not only by number but also by personal acceptability to the Council, controlled expenditures and revenues, supervised construction, and so on. The Council itself chose preachers for the important pulpits; at first this could be done only if the vacancy occurred in a so-called papal month, but in 1513 the last of a long series of agreements extended the Council's appointive powers to episcopal months as well. Where reform was advisable — and reform was an elastic word — the Council did not hesitate to intervene even more directly.

No doubt, all this sounds more authoritarian than it really was. Complaints about what remained of clerical independence continued to point out malfeasance and corruption, and demand more sweeping controls. In the very years when Martin Luther's name began to give the old call for reform a new urgency, Council books record appeals from many quarters for decisive action. No lack, therefore, of good reasons to push on with "reform". The years immediately following 1517 saw the formation of a pressure group to provide theological signposts for the movement of events. Johann Staupitz, a frequent visitor to Nuremberg, had preached the Advent sermons there in 1516 on predestination and the impotence of the human will. Staupitz was a powerful orator and a moving personality. A circle of friends gathered round him and continued to meet after his departure. It was a distinguished group, including the city's two treasurers and several other members of first patrician families. In the spring of 1517 they were joined by a man who was to form a direct connection between Nuremberg and Luther, Wenzeslas Linck, formerly prior of the Augustinians and professor of theology at Wittenberg. In 1518 he preached thirty Advent sermons on the Beatitudes, breathing the spirit of Luther's faith. A year later Lazarus Spengler, secretary to the Council and a prominent man who was to marry into one of the senior patrician families, wrote his apologia of the Lutheran creed as he understood it, entitled *Defense and Christian Reply of a Lover of Divine Truth as Contained in Holy Scripture* (Nuremberg, 1519). All this bore fruit in Council decisions on practical matters. When new priors had to be chosen for the city's two parish churches, Wittenberg men were named in both cases. Hector Bömer, who went to St. Lorenz, was at the time of his election still a student at Wittenberg; Georg Pessler, named to St. Sebald, had also studied there. When a preacher's post opened at St. Sebald's church late in 1521, the Council asked Luther to suggest a candidate and appointed the man recommended, Dominicus Schleupner. At about the same time Andreas Osiander was named preacher at St. Lorenz's. He began at once to preach in an unmistakably Lutheran manner and to speak aggressively against the Pope and Roman doctrines.

These developments placed the Council in an awkward situation. The Diet of Worms had revitalized the Empire's languishing Governing Council and Chamber Court. Both were located in Nuremberg. So were the Imperial Diets of 1522 and 1524. Thus the authority of the imperial government was placed in direct conflict with affairs in the very city where the national government was meeting. The Council reacted to this dilemma by temporizing. The Worms Edict was posted but not enforced. Preachers were instructed to avoid polemics, but pleas and threats by the Archduke Ferdinand and the papal nuncio to clear the pulpits of Lutherans went unheeded. Booksellers were enjoined from selling Lutheran books, but Chieregati, the nuncio, saw them offered openly for sale. Nuremberg's emissaries to the Archduke protested their government's goodwill in upholding imperial decrees, but pleaded its impotence against public clamour for change. It is true that there was some clamour, but it was no more than the Council could easily handle. In fact, the Council instructed its ambassador to the Court of Charles V to deny and refute the allegation that it was giving in to mob pressure.[3] No doubt the Lutheran preachers had won a great following for their creed, but mass sentiment had little — if any — influence on policy in Nuremberg. The Council was not about to lose control over events.

Early in 1525 an incident in one of the monasteries gave occasion to bring matters to a head. All preachers, Lutheran and Roman, were summoned to the Town Hall and directed to furnish lists of essential articles of belief. From these the Council abstracted twelve basic points and ordered a public disputation to discuss them. The Lutherans were eager for battle, but the orthodox objected, knowing the affair to be rigged from the start. Four men of well-known Lutheran sympathies were to preside over the debate, speeches were

[3] Council to Dr. Rotenhan, 15 Jan. 1522, Briefbuch 95 (Staatsarchiv, Nuremberg).

to be in German, and before as many citizens as could be squeezed into the Great Hall of the *Rathaus*. A large and predictably anti-Roman crowd was expected in the square outside. The outcome was assured before the event.[4] But protests notwithstanding, the Council had its way, as usual. From the 3rd to the 14th of March the preachers exhorted each other and the audience on such fundamental questions as "What is Justification"? "What is Original Sin"? "How is the Old Adam to be Killed"?[5] There was never any doubt about which side would win. Three days after Osiander's peroration to the debate, the Council began its systematic programme for ending all vestiges of clerical autonomy, beginning with the expulsion of the noisiest opponents and concluding with the promulgation of the joint Brandenburg-Nuremberg *Kirchenordnung* eight years later. Though the fluctuations of politics and diplomacy in the 1530s and 40s occasionally forced the Council to moderate its Protestant bent, the Reformation itself was irreversible in Nuremberg after 1525.

This, in rough outline, is the familiar story. It has been frequently told[6] and a re-examination of the sources fails to turn up anything startlingly new. However, no historian would nowadays suggest that the documents themselves reveal all there is to know. They may, if read critically, tell us nothing but the truth, but they do not tell us the whole truth. The kind of truth we get depends on how we use them. Records of governmental bodies tend to institutionalize decisions and turn procedures into abstractions. They create an impression of logic and of inevitability inconsistent with the doubt, hesitancy, timidity, haphazardness of human action. The Council was not a disembodied institution. It was a close-knit group of individuals, each of whom possessed a variable quantity of wisdom, knowledge, good sense, confidence. As laymen and merchants and city fathers long accustomed to looking at the practical side of things, the councillors inhabited an intellectual world altogether different from that of the preachers who had succeeded in persuading them that

---

[4] The record of discussions among the *Ratskonsulenten*, the Council's legal advisers, leave no doubt that by March 1525 everyone who counted in the city had made up his mind.

[5] The record of the Disputation was published by the Council: *Handlung eines ersamen weysen Rats zu Nürnberg mit iren Prädikanten* (Nuremberg, 1525).

[6] Adolf Engelhardt, "Die Reformation in Nürnberg", *Mitteilungen des Vereins für Geschichte der Stadt Nürnberg*, xxxiii-iv (1936-7), xxxvi (1939); Hans von Schubert, *Lazarus Spengler und die Reformation in Nürnberg* (Leipzig, 1934); Georg Ludewig, *Die Politik Nürnbergs im Zeitalter der Reformation* (Göttingen, 1893); Gerhard Pfeiffer, "Die Einführung der Reformation in Nürnberg als kirchenrechtliches und bekenntniskundliches Problem", *Blätter für deutsche Landesgeschichte*, lxxxix (1952), pp. 112-33.

Martin Luther's doctrine was the true doctrine. How did it happen that the councillors became convinced of this truth ? Why did they wish to become convinced ? We cannot think about what these men did without asking why they did it.

What was there about the Lutheran creed, as announced by Luther and echoed by the Council-appointed preachers in the city, that appealed to the councillors ? Obvious political advantages were to be gained from it, and the administrative changes following at once upon the Disputation of 1525 show that the councillors were bent on seizing every new opportunity for completing the bourgeois society towards which their city had long been advancing. New and stricter marriage laws were enacted, for example, disallowing ecclesiastical provisions permitting children to marry without parental consent. Christoph Scheurl, one of the Council's legal advisers, made it clear that the real issue was property: "If children marry without the knowledge and approval of their parents", he wrote in his opinion on the matter, "they deprive and defraud them of their flesh and blood, their goods and chattels, which is a deed comparable to theft".[7] But such practical advantages meant little more than extensions of long-established procedures. They could have been had without taking on the Lutheran creed itself. And yet this creed was embraced and its implications accepted, not as useful merely, but as true. Which refines our question somewhat: How, exactly, did the councillors interpret the Lutheran creed to themselves ? What was there about it, as it was presented to them, that distinguished it from Roman doctrines ? What made it seem true and pristine where the teachings of the Church seemed to have gone astray ? Which of the elements of this integrated theology appeared so suitable as a creed for the community at large, as well as a belief for each individual soul ?

That the Lutheran creed was widely accepted in the city is a matter of certainty. Not only was it publicly preached from all the most important pulpits, it also found its way into popular literature. In the summer of 1523 Hans Sachs published his Wittenberg Nightingale, a long paean to the Reformer setting out in narrative form the whole history of Luther's struggle and explaining his theology. It is interesting to note where Sachs places the emphasis:

> First Luther tells us that we all
> Inherit sin from Adam's fall,
> In evil lust and foul intent
> And avid pride our lives are spent;
> Our hearts are black and unrefined,
> Our wills to horrid sins inclined,

[7] *Nürnberger Ratschlagbuch*, no. 26, 1v.

44

> And God, who judges soul and mind
> Has damned and cursed all human kind.
> In our hearts we know this state,
> Feel burdened with a dreadful weight
> Of anguish, fear, bewilderment
> That we should be so impotent.
> Sure of man's inability
> We change pride to humility
> And then, and only then, we see
> The Gospel, sent to make us free,
> For in it we find Christ, God's son
> Who for us men so much has done,
> Fulfilled the law, wiped clean the stain
> And won God's grace for us again.[8]

Recognition of human depravity and impotence, and unquestioning submission to God as a consequence of this recognition: that is the essence of Luther's faith as Sachs conveys it. The theme of human baseness runs through much of Sachs' work from 1523 on. The world is *grund-böse*. Man is like a beast, sunk in vile depravities, by instinct refractory and rebellious:

> Of woman born, he bears the wrath
> Of God upon his carnal self;
> He cannot walk God's chosen path.[9]

Sachs treats his readers to long catalogues of the low thoughts and deeds of men, of iniquities which they cannot understand, much less restrain. The Lutheran creed recognizes the enormity of this degradation and makes it the foundation of its preaching. This is its virtue. While Catholicism, in Sachs' caricature of it, speaks soothingly of wax candles and pilgrimages,

> Feasts by day and fasts by night,
> Confessions to your heart's delight,[10]

the Lutheran convinces man that there is nothing good in him:

> His heart corrupt with lust and greed,
> He carries poison in his seed.[11]

All this is taken from the sermons Sachs heard and from his own reading of Luther's works, of which he possessed a large number. It might be asked, why did Sachs succumb to so dismal a view of man

---

[8] *Die wittenbergisch nachtigall, die man ietzt höret überall* (1523). Printed in the edition of Sachs' works, *Bibliothek des litterarischen Vereins in Stuttgart*, ed. A. von Keller and E. Goetze (Tübingen, 1870 etc.) vol. cx, pp. 368-86. The quoted lines are on p. 377.
[9] *Inhalt zweyerlei Predig, iede inn einer kurtzen sum begriffen* (1525) in *Bibliothek des litterarischen Vereins . . .*, vol. cii, p. 397.
[10] *Ibid.*, p. 399.
[11] *Was das nützest und schädlichest tier auf erden sei* (1541) in *Bibliothek des litterarischen Vereins . . .*, vol. civ, p. 452.

and of human life? He should have been a contented man. He made a good living; he had a comfortable house; he had made two happy marriages; he was popular among his own kind for his plays and verses. Life was generous to him. Why go on so about human depravity and the wicked world? As individuals the patrician councillors must have faced the same question, and wrestled with it in the innermost privacy of their hearts. How they did this it is impossible to know. Few of them committed their reflections to writing, and those who did recorded only external things. None put down his intimate thoughts and feelings. However, it seems plausible that, in their efforts to come to terms with the Lutheran creed as it was being put to them in the early 1520s, the councillors were most powerfully impressed by the correspondence between the Lutheran insistence on the need to accept the consequences of the Fall and their own conventional ideas of the political and social character of their fellow men. In fact, the Lutheran image of the sinner accords perfectly with contemporary political views of man as seen from the top down, and the preachers' rhetoric about human profligacy, evil thoughts, and the will inclined to no good thing gave precise formulation and substance to notions and principles formerly only dimly grasped and left undefined.

Much greater stress was laid on the corruptness of human nature in the early years of the Reformation than modern historians like to acknowledge. To be sure, this was a general cultural phenomenon at the time. In all quarters voices were raised to lament and deplore, though the tones of gloom were necessarily darkest around the pulpit. In Nuremberg, exhortations to accept the gospel of human wickedness were no less insistent than elsewhere. Perhaps they were more so. The air was certainly thick with them. Johann Staupitz sounded the call forcefully in his sermons of 1516:[12] Man created true and good, but misled by free choice to question, doubt, argue, from which proceeded the Fall. Since then "man fails in everything he attempts to do".[13] Staupitz dwelt on the contrast between natural man and man regenerated, and he illustrated it with much citation and exemplification. His own subject — and he never lost sight of it — was the promise of divine grace, the love of God and Christ for man despite his sins. But the local preachers blurred the theme of love

---

[12] They were translated into German by the Council's legal adviser Christoph Scheurl: *Ein nutzbarliches büchlein von der etlichen volziehung ewiger fürsehung, wie das der wirdig vatter Johannes von Staupitz . . . zu Nurmberg gepredigt hat* (Nuremberg, 1517), printed in *Iohannis Staupitii . . . Opera*, ed. J. K. F. Knaake, i (Potsdam, 1867), pp. 136 ff.

[13] *Ibid.*, p. 148.

46

in order to expose the more ruthlessly the dark corners of man's unregenerate nature. Not all men of good will were agreed that this emphasis was a good idea. Erasmus, for one, feared the effect of such a harsh doctrine on untutored minds. "Do not tell the multitude", he advised, "that everything man does ends in sin. In a certain sense this is true, but unlearned persons are bound to interpret it in a way that does them no good".[14] But Erasmus and the Lutheran preachers spoke different tongues. Preaching was education, and ministers felt it to be their duty to come down hard on the baseness, the self-deception, the fickleness, the procrastination, and all the other instinctive traits impelling natural man. One could not open a religious book without having the matter leap to one's eyes. Spengler's little tract on the nature of the Christian faith, for example, starts from the declaration that

> Man's heart, reason, temper, sense, and power, in other words his entire nature, have been so corrupted by the primal serpent poison of our first parents that no deed he performs out of his own resources can be anything but sinful.[15]

In 1524 the point was put directly to the Council, in a lengthy memorandum submitted by three prominent preachers, Osiander acting as their spokesman.[16] What should be the Council's position in these perilous times of strife and confusion? Drawing their advice from Scripture itself, the preachers warned against following human teachings at the expense of God's doctrine. Scripture contains two bodies of teachings, law and Gospel, the one to kill, the other to bring to life. Law commands us to do what we are incapable of doing naturally; it also compels us to face, and detest, our human failings. The Gospel, in turn, reveals God's goodness, grace, and mercy and leads our hearts to the knowledge of God. We need law because of our corrupt nature. Men — natural men, that is — love not God but themselves. They seek not God's ways but pursue their own. Before God can give us eternal life, all brutish greed and ambition, all false confidence in reason must be annihilated. This is the function of law. For God's law demands love, and whoever has not love cannot fulfil the commandments. "All that man does, or

---

[14] *De sarcienda ecclesiae concordia* (Antwerp, 1533), p. 97.
[15] *Ain kurzer Begriff und underrichtung aines gantzen warhafften Christenlichen wesens* . . . (n.p., 1522), A ii r.
[16] *Ein Ratschlag aus heiliger göttlicher Schrift, wie und wes man sich in diesen färlichen zeiten* . . . *soll halten und trösten. Einem Erbarn weisen Rat zu Nürnberg durch ire prediger beschriben und überantwort* (Nuremberg, 1524). For a discussion of the theology of this document, see Emanuel Hirsch, *Die Theologie des Andreas Osiander und ihre geschichtlichen Voraussetzungen* (Göttingen, 1919), §2-6.

does not do, is sin and hypocrisy". It is not a happy predicament. Law, the preachers contend, reproves transgressors, thus revealing God's wrath. Therefore law creates anger, for man, fearing damnation but unable to escape it and convinced that he has earned it, rebels against God's law. He turns against God. The result is ill feeling and anger on both sides, for God is vexed with us as transgressors and we, injured by God's wrath, resent God for the unbearable burden he has placed on us. Consumed with rancour, man gains such hatred of himself that his self-confidence, the spring of all his former actions, is utterly broken. Thus, by crushing self-love and self-trust, law annihilates the natural man.

These were familiar arguments, of course. Luther spoke in the same vein at the time.[17] But the point is that they were put straight to the Council and as a matter of great civic urgency. There was need for action, and soon. It is difficult to imagine that the councillors could have pondered this long and subtle theological exposition without first transposing it into a more familiar setting. Law, to them, meant laws, positive laws, their city's concrete body of legislation, that fine mesh of do's and don'ts which had welded 20,000 wilful individuals into a tolerably peaceful community. The preachers could not have been ignorant of this equation, for they never failed in their arguments to refer to secular authority and its responsibilities. Less than a year later, the same issues were aired publicly in the Religious Disputation which turned Nuremberg formally Protestant. Article 6, for example, on "How the Old Adam is to be Killed", elicited a vigorous discourse on the criminality of human nature and the need for crushing the natural instincts.[18] Catholic rebuttal was discursive and equivocal on this point, as on others. In fact, Catholic spokesmen displayed a rather condescending attitude towards the gathering. They had prepared a statement, they said, "wherein we have shown sufficiently all that laymen need to know about salvation". This could not have gone over very well with the councillors, nor the priests' frequent protests that complex questions could not be answered in so short a time and so few words. Lutheran preachers never seem to have found it difficult to simplify their

---

[17] Cf. sermons on Luke xix. 41 ff., printed in 1524 (Weimar Ausgabe [WA] xv, pp. 662 ff.), on 1 Tim. i. 8-11 (WA xvii¹, pp. 121 ff.) and on Acts xv. 1 ff. (WA xv, pp. 578 ff.). The two latter sermons were printed in 1525.

[18] "For inasmuch as the nature of man is corrupt and inclines toward all that is evil, as it cannot help itself, is capable only of sinning, there must first occur an annihilation from within, effected by God Himself and by His Spirit which dwells in us . . .": *Handlung eines Ersamen weysen Rats zu Nürnberg mit iren Prädikanten* (Nuremberg, 1525), Article 6.

48

theology. Their talent for concise, vigorous utterance was surely one of the main reasons for their success with the crowds, as it was with the Council.

Success did not bring an end to the talk about human depravity. In fact, the strongest formulation ever given to the subject came in the early 1530s, and it was addressed to the most impressionable of minds, those of young children. The preachers had been urging the Council to draw up a uniform catechism, "for catechism is Christian primary teaching, and all Christians must learn and memorize it from childhood". Luther's *Enchiridion or Small Catechism* served as the model, but Osiander and Schleupner, the two authors, went far beyond the Reformer. In 1533 the *Nuremberg Catechism or Sermons for Children* was printed,[19] a useful textbook not only in Nuremberg, but in about a dozen other German cities as well.[20] Sin and wickedness are emphasized throughout, in strong words and dramatic figures. We are all children of sin. Our parents impregnate us with sin as a plague-ridden mother infects the child in her womb.[21] Everything we do and experience serves to make us worse. Being wicked we cannot follow the word of God, and

> he who does not obey the divine word is obstinate and ever inclined to disobedience, rebellion, murder, adultery, theft, lying and deceit, which lead to a bad conscience, to fear, sadness, dismay, and depression. A man who suffers these cannot live long. He declines from day to day, eating his heart out as he broods on his disagreeable nature. He feels hunger, thirst, heat, cold, fatigue, and weakness, and these conditions bring in their train every sort of sickness, and ultimately death. And because each of our fellow men is as bad as we are, none better — excepting only the truly faithful — we are surrounded on all sides by envy, hatred, wrath, bickering, deceit, robbery, theft, assault, murder, war, and all sorts of corruption. God observes this state of things and cannot let it go unpunished. He therefore sends down poisoned air, dreadful storms, fire, floods, madness, and a thousand agonies so that people fall into despair. And all these calamities we suffer because we have sinned.[22]

This is but one paragraph out of many. Sin is everpresent and continuous. Baptism may introduce the Holy Ghost into the heart, but evil inclinations overcome piety again and again. "Therefore man must ever be fearful of falling victim to sin". The office of

---

[19] *Catechismus oder Kinder-Predig, wie die in meiner gnädigen Herrn Marggraven zu Brandenburg und eines ehrbaren Raths der Stadt Nürnberg Oberkeiten und Gebieten allenthalben gepredigt werden* (Nuremberg, 1533). Reprinted in Johann Michael Reu, *Quellen zur Geschichte des kirchlichen Unterrichts*, i (1) (Gütersloh, 1904), pp. 462-564.

[20] It was reprinted in Wittenberg the same year, and new editions came out in 1534, 1536, 1539, 1556, 1564, 1566, 1591, and 1592. It was translated into English in 1548.

[21] Reu, *op. cit.*, i, p. 513.

[22] *Ibid.*, i (1), pp. 545-6.

preacher was instituted to console us in our despairing confusion. The preacher's every word is to announce to us forgiveness of sin as the promised reward of penitence and faith. But if we are not penitent, if we do not cease sinning, do not truly believe in the Gospel, then the preacher is to hold our sins up to us and, "if we are stubborn in sin, threaten us with damnation".[23]

Thus doubt and fear remained. For despite the words of hope, trust, and promise, it was the picture of the unremittingly sinning human being that stood out, set down in the most pungent phrases and the most memorable images. But even if the message of hope had been stated more forthrightly, so much remained vague about man's ability to reform himself (a point on which all the reformers contradicted themselves at times),[24] about the efficacy of baptism, the promise inherent in Christ's sacrifice, about that shadowy borderland where man's effort and God's power coincided — so much remained ambiguous about all this that suspicion, uncertainty, confusion were bound to persevere.[25] According to Osiander's Augustinian theology, baptism remits a part of the guilt incurred by the individual in his inheritance of original sin; but concupiscence itself remains to oppose and frustrate and degrade him. Could the layman be expected to understand this distinction? It is doubtful if he did. Osiander was not unopposed in the rigour of his Catechism. Johann Eck

[23] *Ibid.*, i (I), p. 556.

[24] See, for example, the contrast between Lazarus Spengler's tract on the nature of the Christian faith, printed 1522, cited in note 15 above, and his *Ermanung und Unterweisung zu einem tugendhaften Wandel* (Nuremberg, 1520), written two years earlier and dedicated to Albrecht Dürer. In the latter work the emphasis is all on self-help and the assumption is that a man can, by his will and exertion, avoid the vices and attain the virtues. Even Osiander was guilty of ambiguity. See, for example, his *Predig, wie man umb zeitlichen frid unnd ruw unnd andere notturfft dises zergengklichen lebens, Gott bitten soll* (n.p., 1527). Parts of this sermon seem to sound a call to voluntary self-improvement ("we can recognize our errors and improve our lives, if we are willing to do so": B iiii r.), while other parts speak of prevenient grace (e.g. B iiii r.). There is, of course, no doubt about Osiander's theology on this point. But what the layman heard from him was not always clear.

[25] E.g. the following passage from the *Catechism*: "Every sinner, though he have the Holy Spirit in him to help him struggle against sin, will be defeated at times and will fall into sin. ... He must therefore be ever in fear lest he be too weak to defend himself against sin, or while defending himself, that his faith may prove insufficient to gain right standing in the judgement of God, as, in truth, no one gains right standing in God's judgement (Wer ein sünder ist, ob er schon den heiligen geist hat, der im wider die sünd hilft streiten, so wird er dannoch je zu zeiten überwunden und felt wider in sünde. ... Darum muss er immerdar fürchten, er wird sich der sünde nicht können erweren, oder wann er sich schon erwere, so sei doch sein fromigkeit zu schmal and zu unvolkommen, das er damit vor gottes gericht nicht bestehen kann, wie dann in der warheit vor Gottes gericht niemand besteht)": Reu, *op. cit.*, i (I), p. 551.

challenged him on the sinfulness of children and Melanchthon thought he might have been less severe.[26] Moreover, infant culpability violated a traditional legal principle (and one which, incidentally, remained in force in Nuremberg) that youthful offenders cannot be held accountable "because children cannot sin", as it was stated specifically by the jurists.[27] But Osiander knew better. Even the babe in the cradle, he wrote, is guilty:

> This is something we all know and experience: from the moment of their birth men are full of evil lusts. For men crave what is pleasing to the flesh while they seek to avoid all pain and discomfort. Even the babe in the cradle is lustful. Let a child lie uncomfortably or feel hunger or thirst, and he will kick and cry. Show him a pretty toy and then take it away, or withhold something he wants, and he will scream. Is this not clear evidence that the infant in his cradle, even in his mother's womb, is full of evil lusts? For we see him acting against the ninth and tenth commandments: thou shalt not covet.[28]

Osiander admits that reason cannot grasp this. "But", he goes on, "it is not for us to judge by reason, but according to the word of God".[29]

The word of God, one feels compelled to add, as interpreted by Saint Augustine. Osiander's boundless idealization of the pristine condition of man, his equation of sin with concupiscence and cupidity, passed on to every human being in the act of generation and constituting not only sin itself, but also guilt, leading to dreadful consequences on earth and to perdition in the hereafter, his conviction that his doctrine is the only true and orthodox reading of the Christian creed — all these are faithfully, indeed rigorously Augustinian.[30] Like

---

[26] Johann Eck criticized the Nuremberg-Brandenburg *Kirchenordnung* in his *Christenliche Unterricht ... wider die ... angeber vermainter newer Kirchen-Ordnung* (Ingolstadt, 1533). Osiander defended himself in print, and the controversy between the two waxed hot for some years. In 1539 Eck sent the Nuremberg Council his *Schutzred kindlicher Unschuld wider den Catechisten Andre Hosiander* (Eichstätt, 1539). For Melanchthon's opinion see his letter to Veit Dietrich, 26 Oct. 1539, *Corpus Reformatorum*, ed. C. G. Bretschneider, iii, 802. The argument between Osiander and Eck is reminiscent of St. Augustine's polemic against Julian of Eclanum in the fifth century.

[27] *Nürnberger Ratschlagbuch*, no. 2, f. 70 v., a case taken up in December 1518, involving a mental defective who had stabbed and killed a citizen. The lawyers concluded that fools, like children, are not considered responsible: "In law, children and fools are to be taken as alike, in the sense that neither knows sin. For the child is exculpated by his childhood, and the fool by his misery".

[28] Johann Reu, *op. cit.*, i (1), p. 500. The German translation from the Hebrew is "Du sollst dich nicht lassen gelüsten".

[29] *Ibid.*, i (1), p. 501.

[30] For a scholarly, though tendentious, exposition of St. Augustine's doctrine of sin, see Julius Gross, *Geschichte des Erbsündendogmas*, vol. i: *Entstehungsgeschichte des Erbsündendogmas von der Bibel bis Augustinus* (Munich and Basel, 1960), especially pp. 295-376.

Augustinianism, Osiander's teachings were sharpened by controversy and made intolerant by opposition.   His doctrine was not, of course, found in its own time as extraordinary as it is by us today.   But all the same it was a departure from time-honoured premises of practical ministering.   The contrast with Catholic popular teaching is interesting.   Take for example a booklet on confession, or *Beichtspiegel* as it was called, written for laymen to prepare them for the sacrament of penance and published in Nuremberg in 1510.[31]   Amid the basic instruction in religious knowledge common to such books, the *Beichtspiegel* offers the following explanation of the cause of sinful acts:

> Nine motives[32] reside in the soul of man.   From these, as from a root, spring all our sins and all evils and wickednesses, and also all the virtues, piety, and good works.   Now mark this: If, acting on one of these nine motives, you will keep God before your eyes as your objective and goal, your deed will be pleasing to God and counted meritorious to you.   But if, on the other hand, you pursue your own material profit in your actions, against the commandments of God, your deeds will be reckoned sinful and worthy of reprobation.   Therefore, consider well the intentions of your heart.

It is all up to the individual.   He can turn this way or that.   He can learn from experience.   He can improve his chances.   Such meliorism is in sharp contrast to Osiander's dismal misanthropy.   Nor will it do to associate Lutheran sin-consciousness[33] with the *de contemptu mundi* literature which was so much in vogue throughout the late Middle Ages.   These tracts about the misery of the human condition and the false and wicked world scatter their charges so broadly that they condemn nothing at all.   Vanities and corruptions are itemized with perfunctory pedantry, as in a catalogue, and neither the writing nor the reading of them could have been more than a ritualistic act.   At most, their aim was to produce Stoic indifference to material things, a balanced sense of life, serene detachment.   The accusing finger pointed at the world at large, not at the individual.   How different

---

[31] *Peycht Spigel der sünder* (Nuremberg, 1510).   The passage quoted is on B iiii v.

[32] The German word is *Beweglichkeit*, a translation of Latin *mobilitas*, drive or motive.

[33] John T. McNeill, *A History of the Cure of Souls* (New York, 1951), p. 160, puts the contrast between Lutheranism and Catholicism this way: "Perhaps the most regrettable phases of the medieval man's religious experience were connected with his approach to the problem of sin.   For long centuries the emphasis had been not on sin as a state of the soul from which repentance and divine grace would emancipate it, as upon sins in the plural that swarmed in great numbers and must be confessed in great detail".   For Luther's own ideas on confession, see his *Kurze Unterweisung, wie man beichten soll* of 1519 (WA ii, pp. 57-65); also *Von der Beicht* . . . (1521, WA viii, pp. 129-85), and *Ein Sermon von der Beichte* (1524, WA xv, pp. 481 ff.).

this was from Protestant denunciations! There the accusations fell straight upon the individual sinner. Their object was not *ataraxia* but disgust and self-hatred. Even today one cannot read such a production as Osiander's *Catechism* without feeling distinctly uncomfortable. Contemporary listeners (and it is easy to imagine how lugubriously the catechists intoned their dark phrases) must have squirmed. Later on, in the 1550s and 60s, Nuremberg theologians abandoned the extreme position on sin as the very substance of man. But in the 1520s and 30s Osiander's rigid views dominated the discussions and defined the creed.

Now, I do not think it is reasonable to doubt that the councillors of Nuremberg absorbed this creed by seeing it in the image of their own civic world of administrative responsibilities. These patricians were practical men. They took a strictly functional view of things; they were literal-minded, not very imaginative, utterly conventional in outlook and habits. Their interests and abilities were confined to business and government; these they handled very well, but everything else was secondary to them. They would not have accepted the Lutheran creed had it not been presented to them as the best and most ancient Christian tradition and had it not fitted so well into the civic setting as they saw it from the Council Chamber and from their watchposts in the streets and squares of the city. For this doctrine with its suspicion of human motives and its negation of the natural instincts was the theological counterpart of what municipal politicians assumed, and occasionally said, about the individual and what they asked of him as citizen: denial of the self-seeking drives of his natural proclivities, and submission to a larger purpose and greater power than his own. Neither in religion nor in politics could the natural man be justified. To curtail the natural man and to make him socially useful, or at least harmless, the city had devised a proliferation of laws: statutes, regulations, injunctions to peg the individual in his proper social, economic and political place and tell him what to do and what not to do.[34] No human activities were left out of this legislative mesh except the most intimately personal ones — and not even all of those. Every shoemaker had his legal patterns, every pork butcher his specifications. Rules determined the number of wedding guests and the fare at funeral meals. Even the parting of hair was covered by a statute. A swarm of inspectors, tasters, probers moved in wherever something was made, sold or stored. In his *Early*

[34] For a collection of these, see Joseph Baader, *Nürnberger Polizeiordnungen aus dem XIII. bis XV. Jahrhundert* in *Bibliothek des litterarischen Vereins in Stuttgart*, lxiii (1861).

Democracies in the Low Countries Henri Pirenne asserts that this "municipal socialism", as he calls it, "is as logical in its principles, as coherent in its parts, and as rich in its details as the finest monuments of Gothic architecture, or as the great *Summae* of the scholastic philosophers".[35] The analogy strikes me as inept, not because municipal legislation was not coherent, or rich in details, or even logical in its way — it was all of these — but because there is nothing imposing or grand or wonderful about it. It was all based on suspicion and fear, on a narrow, nagging distrust of human nature, and on the most resolute determination to expect nothing but the worst of men.

Therefore the laws. Society could function only if every instant of public and private conduct was covered by its directive. Men were ruled not by appeals to civic loyalty or good sense or enlightened self-interest, but by laws issued as commands, telling them what to do, where, when, and how. "Ought" meant nothing, only "must". Transgressors faced punishments which in their severity and — in the case of physical inflictions — barbarity, demonstrated a determination to uphold the social order at all costs. Let the wretches remain in the city "so that others may see what has been done to them and have a good fright from it", wrote Christoph Scheurl in a memorandum on some poor culprits whose fingers had been hacked off.[36] Mercy rarely tempered justice where punishment was meant to be exemplary. To the men at the top, society must have seemed like a teeming hive of headstrong creatures, mutable and fickle, tending to excess and extremes, driven by narrow self-interest and swayed by passion, excitable, volatile, kept from crossing the brink to chaos only by their confinement in a comprehensive order of laws. It is an attitude reflected in the texts of many of the city's statutes.[37] Their tone suggests a kindly but stern parent, admonishing his wayward brood but sadly aware of the frustrations in store for him in his thankless task. Indeed, one does not get the impression that the councillors enjoyed the privilege of governing. They seem to have borne it as a heavy and joyless burden. Most of their working days were spent writing laws, but all the time they realized that "in their hearts men remain as wicked as ever".[38] Reiterations of laws often carried a sad and petulant preamble complaining that earlier prohibitions had proved

---

[35] Henri Pirenne, *Early Democracies in the Low Countries: Urban Society and Political Conflict in the Middle Ages and the Renaissance* (New York, 1963), p. 86.
[36] *Nürnberger Ratschlagbuch*, no. 6, 15 r.
[37] E.g., Baader, *op. cit.*, pp. 42-3; *Nürnberger Ratschlagbuch*, no. 5, ff. 43 v.-44 r., 92 v., 207 v., 213 v.
[38] *Ibid.*, f. 92 v.

54

of no avail.[39] This was especially true of clothing ordinances, a matter on which the Council saw no alternative but to give way grudgingly to fashion trends it deplored.[40] Innovations — new products, new habits, new ways of doing things — were immediately suspect as the creations of men's fickle instincts. Usually they were outlawed, at least for a time. Regulatory laws often began with a reference to the eagerness of men to take advantage of each other.[41] The councillors knew that nothing good could be expected of men, and events tended to confirm the assumption. They kept themselves poised for every sort of trouble. Elaborate police precautions were in readiness to crush the first symptoms of unrest. Heavy iron chains could be pulled from their drums to block the streets and impede the movement of crowds. Whoever broke the peace or abused his privileges or was derelict in his duties felt the full weight of the law. Leniency was worse than useless; it was a positive evil, for it encouraged men to think that they could transgress with impunity. "The harsher the penalty the longer the memory of it", was the advice offered to the Council by its lawyers.[42]

This was how the councillors saw the motives and consequences of human action. Suspicion defined their world, the real world of palpable human deeds that confronted them every day in the Council Chamber. It was, for the most part, a petty world of trivial derelictions, requiring constant admonition, censure, punishment, above all unremitting vigilance. We can read the record of it in the minutes of Council sessions and of the meetings of the Committee of Elders. This was day-to-day reality to the councillors. And on this point their practical wisdom coincided with the salient element of the Lutheran creed as it was being presented to them. It often happens that out of a complex and subtly integrated system of ideas one or two items are plucked because they happen to agree with experience and make the whole system intelligible, meaningful, true. This, I think, is what happened in Nuremberg. To be acceptable, to be comprehensible, the Lutheran creed must not only be shown to be true metaphysically. It also had to make sense when placed in the

---

[39] E.g., Baader, *op. cit.*, pp. 41, 53.

[40] E.g., *ibid.*, p. 101. Another vice that convinced councillors of the incorrigibility of men was the use of profanity. Councillors and their advisers were outraged by this and inflicted ever harsher penalties; but it was no use. Cf., e.g., *Ratschlagbuch*, no. 5, f. 92 v.

[41] E.g., Baader, *op. cit.*, pp. 134, 136-7.

[42] ". . . je ernstlicher der gestraft, sovil lenger werde der gedacht, und andern Scheu gemacht sich vor dergleichen lastern zu hüten": *Ratschlagbuch*, no. 5, f. 214 r. See also f. 213 v.

councillors' own frame of reference.   And the line of contact where Lutheran theology touched the councillors' real world of experience was its fundamental theme of human depravity and wilful dereliction, because this illuminated much that had formerly been unexplained and offered a theory where formerly no one had even asked a question.

Needless to say, this was not the only reason for the acceptance of Lutheranism in Nuremberg.   To escape charges of crass over-simplification, it might be well to say how I think this acceptance came about.   It is certain that initial sympathy for Luther and his cause was brought on by a long-standing antipathy to the Roman Church, its administrative and legal apparatus, its financial practices, its distant centres of control, its taint of parasiticalism, its abstruse and protean theology, its alien Latin culture (and our term "Latin" does not begin to convey the multitude of associations that crowd the German's mind when he hears his word for it, *wälsch*).   This dislike existed long before the Lutheran alternative.   It was bound to assure Luther of a sympathetic hearing.   The stature of Luther's early adherents in the city helped further.   Their prominence made the creed respectable, while the contrast between articulate, passionately committed Lutheran preachers and their much more casual Catholic colleagues made the creed intellectually attractive and created an exciting atmosphere of rhetorical controversy.   By 1523 the Lutheran preachers had come to dominate the city's counsels.   Even the college of legal advisers recommended that only they be consulted in matters of religious policy.[43]   They extolled the virtues of a single creed based on one source of truth.   Osiander and his colleagues never ceased to contrast their singleness of purpose and the compactness of their doctrine with the manifold and mutable opinions of Roman theologians and their scattered sources of authority.   Unanimity and uniformity were much prized by the Council, diversity thought to be perilous.   Osiander knew that his words would strike home when he waxed heatedly on the subject of human doctrines, "those manifold and mutable human words and thoughts, sown by the lying devil and raised up by men with their natural inquisitiveness".[44]   When the

[43] *Ratschlagbuch*, no. 24, ff. 531 v.-534 v.   Christoph Scheurl recommended soliciting opinions from Osiander, Schleupner, the other Lutheran preachers in the city, and from Melanchthon in Wittenberg.   A colleague suggested that the universities also be consulted, but this proposal was rejected violently by Scheurl and the majority of the college of legal experts.

[44] "das mannigfaltig und unbestendig menschenwort und gedunken, das der teufel durch sein lügen . . . gepflantzet hat": *Ein Ratschlag . . .* (1524). Spengler, in his *Schutzrede und Christenliche Antwort eins erbarn libhabers götlicher warheit . . .* (Leipzig, 1520) also spoke (A ii v.) of the many and often contradictory opinions of non-Lutheran preachers, each citing his own authorities.

56

Council sent a detailed note of explanation to other governments following the Disputation of 1525, it emphasized this point as the reason for its action and spoke of the perils of multiple opinions, especially in preaching.[45] Where a single truth existed, it alone must be heard. This consideration determined action. All non-Lutheran preaching must be stopped. This decision had been reached by 1523. Numerous entries in official books show the councillors' preoccupation with religious matters and their growing determination.[46] They began to intervene frequently and more aggressively in internal church affairs. No open break with Rome was contemplated. The Council proceeded at all times most cautiously and deliberately. It knew exactly what it was doing; no step along the way was taken without exhaustive discussion, based on copious advice from the legal experts who were joined, whenever the question touched religion, by the preachers, who tended to be hard-liners while the lawyers often vacillated.[47] Careful planning prepared the way for action. When the time was ripe for that, it came with only slight discomfort to opinion and institutions.

But these are external facts and they do not explain very much. To repeat the central question, then: what was there about the Lutheran creed as presented in Nuremberg in the early 1520s that made it seem so convincingly true to the councillors? I think it was

---

[45] "...ungleichen und ungeschickten predigten", *Nürnberger Briefbuch* (Staatsarchiv, Nuremberg), no. 89, ff. 31 v.-36 r. As far as the Council was concerned, the object of the Disputation was to change the orthodox preachers' minds: "to lead them, by means of a friendly and patient discussion, to right preaching...and to a correct and unanimous understanding of Scripture": *Ratsbuch* (Staatsarchiv, Nuremberg), no. 12, f. 393 r. The same intention is communicated to Johann Poliander of Würzburg, one of the judges of the Disputation, *Briefbuch*, no. 88, f. 226 r. and v. Again, in 1533, the preachers urged the Council to cause a uniform catechism to be written "so that in every place and by no matter what teacher it be taught in one and the same way": Johann Reu, *op. cit.*, i (1), p. 419.

[46] The *Ratschläge* show this too. The lawyers' tone, when writing about the monasteries, was, as early as 1522, sharp and truculent. Cf. *Ratschlagbuch* no. 4, f. 17 r.

[47] Deliberation of lawyers and preachers together occurred at least as early as April 1524. See the case in *Ratschlagbuch* no. 4, f. 121 v., where the formula "prediger und doctores" is used. In judging offenders, particularly moral offenders, the preachers tended to recommend blanket penalties to apply to all culprits and all cases. They liked to cite the Old Testament (cf. *Ratschlagbuch* no. 5, f. 187 v., for example), while the lawyers always advised the Council to judge each case on its own merits and consider extenuating circumstances where they existed (cf. *Ratschlagbuch* no. 5, f. 43 v.). The preachers also effected a change in the language of the *Ratschläge*. While these had always been dry, matter-of-fact, business-like in style, from about 1525 on frequent reference is made to things as they ought to be done "according to the word of God", or "for the honour of God".

its resolute insistence on the weaknesses and deformities inseparable from the natural human being. For on this point theology and secular knowledge agreed, rhetoric met common sense, and theory was borne out and illustrated by observation. Struck by the correspondence between what experience and sense had taught them about political man and what the Lutheran preachers now expounded to them as the theological doctrine of man, the councillors accepted the latter as the explanation of the former and adopted the Lutheran creed as a most suitable ideology for their city state.

Ideology was something new. No one in the city — neither patrician councillors nor Roman lawyers nor civic chroniclers — had heretofore felt the need of a theory to explain civic purposes, or to defend them. But, as often happens, when an ideology is offered, it is most eagerly embraced where none had existed before. So much could now be explained; so many scattered details fell into place. Nuremberg's policy makers had never been a reflective lot. No norms, theories, ideals had been before them as they laboured to govern. Citizens were not expected to match an ideal type. Laws had not been designed to perfect men, or even to improve them, only to govern them as they were. No one tried to justify the laws, or the assumptions on which they were based, except to point to the security and comfort they had brought, and to the alternative, which was chaos. It had never been asked, were men necessarily as they were, and why? Would a different set of assumptions and other laws work just as well, or better? And yet, these were obvious questions — that is to say, they were questions that sprang to mind the moment answers to them were suggested. And the Lutheran creed did supply the answers; more than that, it provided the city with a comprehensive ideology to explain, justify, and sanction what it was doing and to raise its dreary business of manipulating men and affairs to the exalted plane of divine purpose.[48] Argus-eyed government and severe laws were necessary and right, for was not the citizen the Old Adam? Injunctions, prohibitions restrained him and revealed his natural inclinations, to others and to himself. True, there was nothing intrinsically good about these laws, indeed about government itself. Laws did not turn men into good men. Only the individual himself could do that, though whether this reformation of his nature lay within his own resources or depended on the intercession of a higher

---

[48] On this point, see also Bernd Moeller, *Reichsstadt und Reformation* (*Schriften des Vereins für Reformationsgeschichte*, no. clxxx, Gütersloh, 1962), a discussion of the reciprocal effects of the medieval city's dual character as a political and a sacral community.

power was never made very clear. Eventually, so the ideology suggested, society will transcend the "Jewish" epoch of prescriptions and proscriptions. Old Adam having been killed, the new man will break from his chrysalis, filled with the spirit of love, gentle and co-operative where his earlier self had been mean and grasping. "We can say with Paul, 'Yet I live, and yet no longer I but Christ liveth in me,' . . . that is to say, we no longer live according to the flesh, but the spirit of Christ is and dwells in us". Thus Osiander, in his memorandum to the Council in 1524. Translated into the Council's workaday language this meant that the new man, having shed the slough of his brutish condition where Draconian laws had kept him from working havoc upon himself and others, would emerge from his conversion right-thinking and understanding, self-controlled, self-motivated by regenerated instincts to seek those social ends sanctioned by his community. This happy state of affairs lay in the future, the very distant future most likely. But in the meantime the laws helped Old Adam by subjecting his rebellious nature to an unrelenting discipline, which was for his own good.

What the preachers held out to their government was a high doctrine that linked political objectives to the divine cause. It combined a practical Machiavellism in the management of men with a grand and sacred purpose. It offered a compact theory of man. It justified the present and indicated the future. At its essential points it agreed with observed reality. What more could one ask of an ideology?

V

THE RELIGIOUS POLICIES OF DUKES WILHELM AND LUDWIG OF BAVARIA IN THE FIRST DECADE OF THE PROTESTANT ERA*

On the seventh of October, 1528, late at night, agents of Dukes Wilhelm IV and Ludwig X of Bavaria came to the home in Abensberg of Johann Aventinus, the distinguished historian and pedagogue, and arrested him, "ob evangelium," as he notes the occasion in his diary.[1] The Dukes' action was not unexpected. Aventinus recorded arrests of acquaintances and associates in May and July, also "ob evangelium." He had been away from home much of the time, possibly to avoid the same fate. He spent the summer in Regensburg[2] where the Bavarian government had no jurisdiction, but where prolonged residence, at a time when both Lutheranism and Anabaptism seemed to be making rapid gains there,[3] could not but arouse suspicion in Munich. In early October Aventinus returned to Abensberg, his captors at his heels.

The charge against him listed several instances of non-compliance with ducal decrees concerning religious conduct—close association with known or suspected heretics, carelessness in observing fast-day rules, participating in discussions of forbidden topics—but overt action was hardly needed to arouse ill will against him. Aventinus was one of the most outspoken men of that blunt age in which he lived. Although none of his major historical works had as yet been put into print, his strong critical views and savory phrases circulated widely,[4] and they stung where intended. Resentment and alarm over his attacks on the clergy and his apparent espousal of the Lutheran heresy were intense in the Bavarian hierarchy,[5] and there must have been strong pressure on the Dukes, particularly after 1526, when he produced the most unrestrained of his anti-clerical writings,[6] to proceed against him. This, however, could not have been an easy decision for Wilhelm and Ludwig. Aventinus was among the most illustrious of the community of German humanists whose members the Dukes could ill afford to alienate. He was a renowned Bavarian patriot. He was closely tied to the ducal family: official historiographer since 1517, and before that tutor to Ludwig, now co-sovereign with Wilhelm, and to his younger brother Ernst, now Administrator of the bishopric of Passau. His relations with his princes had been excellent, and expressions of high gratitude had not been lacking. Only the weightiest of considerations could have persuaded the Dukes to order his arrest.

What were these considerations? What was the chain of events

*Much of the material on which this study is based was gathered during a research trip financed by a grant from the Research Committee of the University of Alabama.

V

which led to the incarceration of a man whose work added so much luster to the reign of the young Dukes? Only a detailed investigation of the religious policies of Wilhelm and Ludwig in the first decade of the Protestant era can answer these questions. As always, however, when one holds the magnifying glass to processes of statecraft, the individual strands of policies and implementing actions merge into a tissue which tends to cover, rather than expose, underlying principles. The Bavarian policy makers were not committed to any fixed purposes. As we watch them at work, we catch a glimpse of a government first reaching out for an understanding of the new teachings, perceiving their relations to the political realities that must determine policies, finally girding itself for action against what assumed, more and more as time went on, the appearance of a dangerous foe.

Aventinus' confinement, incidentally, was of short duration. He had supporters in high places. On the eighteenth of October Leonhard von Eck, the powerful ducal Chancellor, secured his release.[7] He stayed out of religious controversy after that and was not molested again.

I

In 1517 Bavaria had just emerged from a troublous period of political and dynastic dissension. Thirteen years earlier Upper and Lower Bavaria had become reunited under the Dukes at Munich, after the death of Georg of the Landshut line and the defeat of his son-in-law Rupprecht of the Palatinate in a brief but violent war of succession. The victor, Albrecht IV, a skillful and rational ruler, capped the success of his arms with a political triumph, the institution of primogeniture in his Duchy.[8] Thus the new century had opened auspiciously; but the primogeniture decree failed its very first test. Albrecht died prematurely in 1508, leaving three minor sons, Wilhelm, Ludwig, and Ernst. For three years there was a regency, provided for in Albrecht's will and exercised by his brother Wolfgang and, fully equal with him, six representatives of the Bavarian Estates. In 1511 Wilhelm, turned eighteen, took the reins himself. Soon after that his brother Ludwig reasoned that the decree could not apply to him since he had been born before its promulgation, and demanded co-rule or a third of the Duchy. Ludwig had timed his challenge well. Since 1508 the Estates had been urging a clarification and augmentation of their traditional liberties.[9] Now came demands for greater participation in the administration of the Duchy. Wilhelm had to retreat on all fronts. At a dramatic session in 1514 of the Estates, the two young Dukes (Ernst was still in Aventinus' care and preparing for a study journey to Italy), and their advisers, a general reconciliation took place: Wilhelm and Ludwig to rule jointly but with separate administrations, the Estates to maintain a standing committee for close cooperation with the Dukes.[10] Still unsolved was the question of what independent income might be found for the youngest brother, now approaching majority. A career in the Church seemed inescapable for him. The financial condition of Bavaria was far from sound after a century of division and intermittent warfare. There was further cause for grave anxiety in the expansionist moves of the Habsburgs whose lands surrounded Bavaria on three sides. Wilhelm's and Ludwig's official relationship with the great figures of their time, Emperor and Pope above all, was therefore determined by a multiplicity of concerns vital to the status of their ancient territory.

These concerns rested in the capable hands of the ducal Chancellor, Leonhard von Eck, one of the great Realpolitiker of his time. This career politician, whose astuteness had so impressed the representatives of the Bavarian Estates that they demanded—unsuccessfully—his permanent dismissal,[11] saw in the precarious situation of Bavaria a supreme challenge to his talents. The principle of his policies was simple enough: might and prestige of the Dukes was to be increased; they must be masters in their own house, they must fill a position of influence in the Empire. It was the virtuosity of his means which won him his reputation, favorable or abhorrent, depending on the critic's allegiance. In 1520 there arose an opportunity to display the flexibility of statesmanship for which he became famous. Wilhelm's victory of the previous year over his irascible brother-in-law, Ulrich of Württemberg,[12] had been turned to frustration by Habsburg diplomacy. In February 1520 the Duchy of Württemberg came into the control of Charles V. Eck at once recognized the futility of Wilhelm's inclination to sulk. Some months previously he had recommended a wait-and-see attitude toward the new Emperor. Since Charles had so far shown himself well disposed, he counselled, close attachment to him was indicated. If, on the other hand, it should turn out that greater advantages were to be gained by joining Charles' opponents, then no scruples must stand in the way of such a move.[13] In 1520 Charles had got the upper hand; he could not now be resisted. Eck therefore urged both Dukes to attend the diet called to meet at Worms, and to attend with great show, in order to fix attention on their position among the German princes, and to use their presence to enhance their influence.[14]

If at this time either the Dukes or their Chancellor were troubled over the movement that had begun to spread from Wittenberg, they feared its implicit threat to established law and order. Eck was quick to detect the social and political implications of the new teachings. To him the momentous transformation which the astrologers had been announcing for the year 1524, a prognosis which he took very seriously, could be but one thing: a fusion of the religious revolt with the social groundswell whose tremors his fine senses detected. He prepared a memorandum for the Dukes accordingly, warning them, in January 1520, that the great conflagration which was leaping up everywhere could not burn itself out without grievous damage.[15] Later he was to refer to the unduly long period of tolerance which the new teachings enjoyed in Bavaria.[16] As a matter of fact, the first reactions of the Dukes had been at least non-committal, if not benevolent. They were aware of the various failings of the church organization in their lands, and they knew how these enfeebled the entire state. They had themselves refused to permit the sale of the indulgence of 1517.[17] It was known to them that Luther's theses were being passed about in their territory,[18] but they were not disposed to take immediate action. When the Ingolstadt professor Johann Eck returned from Rome with the Bull *Exsurge Domine,* Wilhelm reminded the bishops in his lands that the Emperor had granted Luther a safe conduct to Worms, there to hear him. Until the Emperor's decision was announced the parish clergy should not use the pulpit to condemn the man and his writings.[19] Developments were to be awaited.

Wilhelm and Ludwig arrived in Worms at the end of January, in splendid style, as Leonhard von Eck had recommended.[20] Wilhelm had some conferences with the Emperor and apparently succeeded in impressing Charles favorably, for which he received a pat on the back from his Chancellor. ("I am well aware of Your Princely Grace's competence," Eck wrote him, "when Your Princely Grace has decided to buckle down and not loaf."[21]) Late in February he left to proceed to Augsburg in the affairs of the Swabian League. Ludwig remained in attendance at the diet to await the appearance of Luther. Letters which Wilhelm wrote to Leonhard von Eck while at Worms show that he did not abandon his moderate position toward Luther. He maintained that his writings should not be burned.[22] The Venetian ambassador Gasparo Contarini, who saw him in Augsburg on April 9, reported a conversation in which Wilhelm averred that all Germany would rally to Luther if he restricted himself to criticism of religious abuses.[23] Ludwig's reports from Worms describe Luther's appearance before the Emperor in objective words with no opinions recorded.[24] There is no reason to think that the deliberations at Worms, or the events leading to Worms, touched the religious convictions of the Dukes with either doubt or decision. But they were not likely to forget Eck's warnings that however justified Luther's protest, its consequences could not be foreseen and were bound to be troublesome.

II

Considerations of high politics were not the only ones which dictated a close alliance with Charles in 1521. An issue in which the support of the Emperor would prove invaluable was the candidacy of Duke Ernst for the coadjutorship of the bishopric of Eichstädt. Finding an adequate source of income for this youngest of the three Dukes was a vital domestic matter. Wilhelm and Ludwig had first occupied themselves with it in 1513, shortly after their reconciliation, when Ernst had just turned fourteen. The brothers were naturally fearful lest Ernst raise demands for co-rule similar to Ludwig's. The Duchy could not afford a third court. Even payments on existing debts could not be met without new loans and mortgages.[25] For Ernst there seemed to exist no alternative to a career in the Church, but to find prebends which would support him in the proper manner did not prove easy. At the Imperial diet held at Worms in 1513, Ludwig went before the Emperor Maximilian and implored him in the most urgent terms to help procure the coadjutorship of Salzburg or at least that of Passau for the young Duke, who even now, he said, displayed great aptitude for the clerical life.[26] Ludwig made as strong a plea as he could. He stressed the heavy debt faced by the older brothers, the eagerness of the chapters at Salzburg and Passau to have Ernst, the many bonds uniting the Houses of Austria and Bavaria, and the Emperor's influence with the Pope who would surely issue the appropriate orders. A petition from the Dukes' mother, Maximilian's sister, was added. The matter was kept before the Emperor through letters and emissaries.

Salzburg proved unobtainable at the time, but in 1517 Ernst got to be Administrator at Passau. It was not long, however, before the able and ambitious prince showed open disdain for the life which his brothers had marked out for him.[27] Only fat revenues would keep him in the Church, and the debt- ridden bishopric of Passau did not provide them. When, therefore, an opportunity to obtain the coadjutorship of Eichstädt arose in 1521, Wilhelm and Ludwig once again made their plea. Neither the Dukes nor their Chancellor were blind to the great strategic value of this piece of territory north of the Danube. "A good fortress wall," Eck called it.[28] This, of course, complicated the problem of procurement which was already grave because of the rules concerning pluralities, and because Ernst had not taken Holy Orders.[29] Furthermore, the Dukes still had their minds set on Salzburg for Ernst. Not until 1540 were they able to win that prize for him, and not without protracted and difficult negotiations,[30] but Ernst's distinguished subsequent career at Salzburg, though not noted for its spiritual character, never gave them cause for regrets.

It is clear from all this that whatever personal impressions the Dukes may have carried to and from Worms, a policy in accordance with the decisions made there was mandatory for them. Still they hesitated to take decisive action against the heresy at home, perhaps because the outcome of certain important negotiations which were being conducted at Rome late in 1521 was awaited. In February 1522 a group of professors from the University of Ingolstadt, led by Dr. Johann Eck, Luther's famous opponent, petitioned the Dukes for a special decree to enforce the Edict of Worms in Bavaria.[31] The Chancellor supported the request. He urged the promulgation of such a mandate on the Dukes and he urged it on the other members of the Swabian League which was then meeting in Ulm. He also supplied rough drafts of the decree to be issued. The Dukes now complied and, in early March, sent two draft versions of the decree to Munich where the Councillors were to make the choice between the shorter and the longer. A second letter from Ulm, a few days later, emphasized the need for haste. The mandate was to be released at once and dated back to March 5.[32]

The Councillors deliberated and decided to publish the briefer of the two drafts, the other containing too much theological argumentation with Lutheran beliefs to be effective. The shorter version assumed the theological issues to have been settled by papal condemnation, restricted itself to a brief history of the heresy, and announced steps to be taken toward its extirpation.

> As is surely known to all [the Edict begins], Martin Luther has published certain writings which have been declared by Pope Leo and his learned advisers to be suspect, obnoxious to Christian teaching, and heretical. Such warnings not having proved sufficient to cause Luther to desist, the Emperor recently ordered him to appear before him at the Imperial Diet at Worms. There the Emperor graciously and with fatherly concern reminded, besought, and begged him to consider well the consequences of a possible split in the Christian Church. But Luther was not to be turned from his stubborn path. The Emperor and Estates therefore caused an Edict to be published against him, his supporters and comforters, and all their books and writings. This Edict has been posted in all Our cities. Now, whereas it appears to Us that Luther is not merely guilty of insubordination, but that his shocking teachings will result in nothing more certain than a tearing asunder of all divine and human laws, customs, and regulations, which, as loyal servants of Pope and Emperor, We may not condone, We therefore order all Our subjects to reject each and all those articles of the Lutheran creed which have been or will be condemned, and not to engage in disputations over any such article. We further instruct all Our officials to be vigilant in their respective districts, and to take into custody every person, of whatever estate he may be, who is suspected of association with the Lutheran heresy. He is to be held until We ourselves, having been apprised, can make disposition of the case. This Decree is being printed and posted throughout Our lands, so that no one may claim ignorance of Our wishes and commands.

The Edict did, in fact, reach every town and hamlet in Bavaria,[33] but its immediate effects were slight. In mid-March the *Pfleger*[34] in Ingolstadt reported a priest named Bardian for having participated in a discussion on Communion under both forms. Wilhelm ordered an investigation. The man's action was judged to constitute Lutheranism and he was asked to explain and recant. This he did, promising henceforth to observe the Edict, and that was the end of the matter.[35] Only one other case of arrest is known.[36] Such lack of action certainly does not mean that the new teachings had, in 1522, made no progress in Bavaria. But the Dukes apparently could not bring themselves to a systematic exposure of the heresy. Leonhard von Eck knew that severe measures would have to be employed if the Edict were really to be implemented, but for the moment he counselled moderation until its deterrent effect could be observed.[37] The wording of the Edict itself precluded general persecution by obliging local officials to make immediate report to the Dukes of every action taken. The power of ducal agents did not go beyond temporary arrest and notification.

Obviously Wilhelm and Ludwig were still marking time. Their deeds as well as their omissions still lacked conviction. They had aligned themeslves with Pope and Emperor, but they retained full freedom of action. Events elsewhere, however, now intervened to make more determined steps advisable.

III

The religious crisis of the early sixteenth century presented the Dukes with a unique opportunity to affirm their sovereign rights over the regular and secular clergy in their lands by assuming the sponsorship of ecclesiastical reform in the Bavarian Church. In pursuing this policy the Dukes and their advisers could claim the support of tradition. Bavarian rulers had often taken an active role in the supervision of clerical propriety. Conditions which invited the reformer existed in Bavaria as elsewhere; visitation records[38] reveal a wide range of abuses: the sale of monastic property, simony and commercialism, pawning Church treasures to Jews, offering manuscripts to collectors. Serious breaches of discipline seemed to be general. Concubinage was a universal practice, but we also hear of the abandonment of other vows, of disobedience and insubordination, coarse behavior and even murder within monastery walls.[39] In order to arrest the spread of this decay there arose in the various orders reforming sects like the Community of Observants and the Martinians among the Franciscans, and the Kastl and Melk movements among the Benedictines.

The Bavarian Dukes not only encouraged this restoration, they often took matters into their own hands. Albrecht III personally visited monastic houses and chapters in order to observe conditions and learn

V

to correct them where necessary.[40] The same ruler sought to join the various observances into a common reform front.[41] Ludwig the Rich ordered the Franciscan houses in Landshut and Ingolstadt occupied by Observants. Albrecht IV, Wilhelm's father, acting against the determined opposition of the bishops, even appointed a commisson of prelates and jurists to visit and improve the monasteries in his lands.[42]

An increase in ducal prestige and power was a not unwelcome by-product of these early attempts at centralized reform. In the early 1520's the need for reform was more obvious than ever, and the Bavarian rulers were in a better position than their forebears to relate it to their political plans. But this was a far-reaching ambition, and it required delicate negotiations at Rome.

That such negotiations were in fact taking place with agents of Pope Leo X is attested by the existence of the draft of a papal bull, dated November 14, 1521, which was to extend to the Bavarian Dukes the right of visitation in their territories.[43] But Leo died in December 1521, and the project came to nothing. The passing of the great Medici pontiff, however, gave to the whole issue of reform a new aspect. Early in January 1522, the deadlocked Cardinals chose Adrian of Utrecht, former tutor of the Emperor Charles and, at the time of his election, Bishop of Tortosa and Viceroy of Spain. Adrian was the first non-Italian pope in a century and a half. Widespread surprise and dismay greeted the announcement; the Emperor's pleasure, on the other hand, was apparent. Adrian, who took the name of Adrian VI, was known for his deep piety, for the simplicity of his tastes, for his dislike of show and flattery. Italy resigned itself to the worst from this German. A reform papacy was in the offing.

Adrian entered Rome in August, and the expected changes were not slow in coming. Adrian's grand design, the reunion of western Christendom for more effective opposition to the Turks, required a thorough housecleaning, which was to commence in Rome and to proceed to all the limbs of the Church. Such rulers as had something to gain from the papacy were therefore forced into a speedy reappraisal of their religious policies. In Bavaria, too, the new regime in Rome was reflected in certain decisions that were now taken. Not only the coveted rights of visitation and correction, but the future of Duke Ernst, who was still sulking at Passau, depended on the good will of the new pope. When, therefore, Dr. Johann Eck made ready to go to Rome to attend Adrian's coronation, Wilhelm commissioned him to be his representative at the Throne of St. Peter's.

In Johann Eck the Dukes had an invaluable asset in their relations with the earnest Adrian. A learned and articulate man, theologian and jurist, well thought of in academic circles, even among the practitioners of the humanist disciplines, faithful and conscientious in all his duties,[44] passionately attached to his religion, Johann Eck became the symbol of the quick but constructive resistance to the spreading heresy which he advocated. His labors on behalf of the bull against Luther and the Leipzig disputations had gained him a wide renown whose reflection Wilhelm and Ludwig were now eager to catch. Eck, however, did not reach Rome at this time. The plague had broken out afresh there in September, and he was forced to return. In December a letter from Adrian reached him. The Pope expressed his regrets over the mischance which had prevented their meeting, spoke warmly of Eck's work, and implored him to use all his skill and all his strength with his territorial lords to persuade them to favor determined action against the Lutherans at the Nuremberg diet which was then in progress.[45]

To that same end Adrian had ordered his Nuntius in Germany, Francesco Chieregato, to Nuremberg. Ludwig had a talk with Chieregato there, and the Bishop was diplomatic enough to speak in kind words of the measures already taken in Bavaria to exclude the heresy.[46] Ludwig, in his report of the conversation to his brother, points out that this good will must be at once exploited. Powers of visitation, of investiture of abbots and their removal without the consent of the bishops —these may be gained now if their cards are played right. Adrian himself turned to the Dukes early in 1523 with a request for cooperation.[47] But the outcome of the Nuremberg meetings was a sharp disappointment to the Pope. Adrian's sincere confessions of grave irregularities in the Church organization and his plea for time to correct them, which Chieregato had read to the diet with unprecedented candor, had been heard, but had not produced the desired result.[48] The Edict of Worms was not ordered enforced. The assembled Princes and Estates could not be moved to anything more than some tentative decisions respecting preachers and printers.[49] In Bavaria, however, now for the first time there appeared some evidence of a serious determination to carry out the terms of the imperial and ducal edicts.

The first indication of the changed spirit was a new ducal order, dated February 25, 1523, and despatched to all administrative officials:

> Once again we inform you that it is Our earnest command, decision, and wish that, under threat of serious penalty and Our high displeasure, you are to be relentlessly watchful and make active inquiry concerning those infected with the Lutheran heresy.[50]

Upon this order followed letters of admonition to responsible local officers where incidence of the heresy had been reported. The *Pfleger* and Council of Aichach were told to arrest certain citizens who had been openly goading the priest.[51] In March, a tailor's apprentice, who was overheard in a criticism which was judged to be heretical was expelled from the land, having beforehand been examined by a committee of

Ingolstadt professors.[52] But there was trouble at the University itself. Two members of the faculty were denounced to the Dukes for having ignored Scripture in their lectures and read instead Erasmus' *Colloquia* and the Epistles of St. Paul. One of them was taken into custody. He was Arsacius Seehofer, a native of Munich, alumnus of Wittenberg and former student of Melanchthon's, now a master at Ingolstadt. It was also said about him that he denied freedom of the will. Wilhelm considered this a serious matter, as a dissemination of heterodox ideas at the university would be difficult to contain. He himself handled all the correspondence in the case, as well as its final disposition.[53] Seehofer was repeatedly interrogated. When letters of an incriminating nature were found in his rooms his twelve students were called up for examination. Finally he was forced to recant before the assembled University, then consigned to a safe monastery.[54]

Another case which came up in March involved two apprentice bookbinders, one Valentin and one Hans Löffer. Both confessed to a number of specific charges of Lutheran heresy. The minutes of their interrogation were sent to Duke Wilhelm for his information and adjudication.[55] Valentin was examined first. What did he think of the Pope, he was asked. Pope, priest, Luther—they were all the same to him, he answered; no priest could save his soul for him. What did he think of indulgences? He cannot imagine of what use they are. Has he eaten meat on fast days? Yes, on Fridays, in Wittenberg, for his master there served nothing else. Finally, what did he think of Luther? He can say nothing bad of the man. When the questioning was done, witnesses were heard. One remembered a slighting remark about the Pope's power of excommunication, another an allegedly obscene joke about a sermon. Then Valentin was led from the room while the other defendant was interrogated. Both men were eventually expelled from Bavaria and forbidden to return.

Later in the summer some arrests took place in Burghausen, and there too expatriation was ordered.[56] In September action was taken against one of the most fearless members of Luther's advance guard, Argula von Grumbach, who had challenged the theologians of Ingolstadt to a debate on the question of Seehofer's guilt. Johann Eck sent her a distaff for an answer, but that did not end the matter for her. She warned the Duke himself of the consequences of his persecution and, for good measure, proposed that the surplus wealth of the clergy be confiscated to finance a Turkish campaign.[57] Wilhelm could hardly have been shocked at this suggestion, which had occurred to him too; but he reacted by relieving her husband, who had little sympathy for his wife's convictions, of his duties as *Pfleger*. Argula herself had to leave Bavaria.

Thus the year 1523 saw some determined attacks on the spreading heresy, though individual punishments were in no case severe,[58] and no disposition to annihilate the movement root and branch can be detected. All this was in accordance with the terms of the Religious Edict of the preceding year. An expression of papal pleasure came from Rome in June,[59] and this itself was a source of satisfaction to the Dukes, for negotiations for the visitation rights had now reached the critical stage. In March Dr. Johann Eck once again journeyed south to continue the talks with the Pope which had been interrupted by Leo's death, and he urged the Dukes to keep him posted on "what is currently being done at home in the Lutheran matter" in order to improve his bargaining position at the meetings.[60] Eck had been given detailed and specific instructions.[61] He was, if possible, to obtain all of the following:

1. Freedom of action for the Dukes where the responsible bishops had not within a reasonable time proceeded against priests guilty of misdemeanors or crimes.

2. Ducal jurisdiction over clerics who committed reprehensible acts while disguised in lay clothes.

3. Appointment of a papal commission of two or three prelates in each of the four administrative Circles of the Duchy "to be judges and investigators in the name of His Holiness, possessing full powers to hold in prison all such clerical persons as shall have been delivered to them by Our officials, to defrock those who are found guilty and to hand them over to secular judges who will deal with them according to Imperial and Bavarian law." A list of prelates acceptable to the Dukes—native Bavarians all—was attached.

4. A declaration that no member of the clergy may hail a lay person under ducal jurisdiction into an ecclesiastical court for debt or other minor matters.

5. A curtailment of the passing out of sentences of excommunication for trivial offenses.

6. A Papal Bull empowering the Dukes to order visitations of monasteries by certain selected prelates and ducal officials for the purpose of correcting abuses and removing and replacing unsuitable abbots and priors.

None of these was an exorbitant request, and all had been previously granted to one or another territorial sovereign, as the Dukes pointed out in their comments. A more delicate matter was barely touched upon in the instructions: the current annual income of the bishops in and adjoining Bavaria (i.e., Salzburg, Augsburg, Passau, Freising, Regensburg, and Eichstädt) together with that of their clergy was said to ex-

V

ceed that of Princes, nobility, and citizenry combined.[62] The financial distress of the Duchy being well known to the Pope, Eck was to negotiate a tax on the Bavarian clergy.

Eck, after a lengthy delay caused, he wrote home, by Adrian's refusal to delegate any part of his duties,[63] began the presentation of his claims. He would not have been acting in character had he not exceeded his ambassadorial duties to speak in his own behalf of the larger issue of Church reform in Germany. For this latter purpose he composed during his stay in Rome a number of memoranda for the Pope's perusal.[64]   In these, and, presumably, before the Pope, Eck minced no words in his condemnation of the decrepitude which had overtaken the Church in Germany. To revive it he suggests not a general Church Council, which would be rendered powerless by bickering among its national components, but instead a reactivation of the practice of holding annual diocesan and triennial provincial synods. The first provincial synod was to be convoked in Bavaria under the auspices of Duke Wilhelm. Meanwhile far-reaching and ruthless correctives were to restore the curia and the Church as a whole. Every effort was to be made to prevent an irrevocable split between the Church and the Lutherans—the real purpose of reform being to win them back.

The death of Pope Adrian in September once again changed the entire situation, but Eck was able to return to his sovereigns with papal permission to tax the Bavarian clergy up to one fifth of their income for the purposes of the Turkish campaigns, as well as with authorization to set up a Commission of Visitation on the Dukes' terms.[65]   In Munich a sense of relief and elation must have prevailed. There was certainly every reason to be satisfied with the policy pursued so far.

IV

But still the Lutherans or suspected Lutherans multiplied in Bavaria. Their preachers and their books came from places where the Dukes had no direct power: the imperial cities of Augsburg and Regensburg, and the little principalities Haag, Ortenburg, and Miesbach-Hohenwaldeck which were under imperial jurisdiction. Regensburg especially was a thorn in their flesh. A determined band of Lutherans steadily gained strength there,[66] and the City Council was openly sympathetic.[67] Luther's sermons were reprinted and distributed by Regensburg booksellers.[68]   In the summer of 1524 the ambassador of Electoral Saxony saw some Lutheran writings sold openly on the streets of Munich.[69]   There was no concealing the unpleasant fact that the control measures so far undertaken had not checked the spread of the revolt. Evidence of anxiety at Rome came from Cardinal Campeggi who reminded the Dukes in May that they were still delinquent in their enforcement of the papal and imperial edicts.[70]

Campeggi was on his way to Regensburg where the Archduke Ferdinand had called a meeting of princes and prelates in the territories surrounding Austria for the purpose of joining in more effective measures against the Lutherans.[71]   The sessions were held in late June and early July, 1524.   Wilhelm and Ludwig attended for only five days, and not until October did they decide to publish their own orders implementing the agreements which had been reached.[72]   But their conversations with the papal legate and with the Archduke must have convinced them of the advisability of common action.   Referring to the comprehensive papal reform program for Germany announced at Regensburg by Cardinal Campeggi,[73] the Dukes now stated their firm resolve to stand by Pope and Emperor, and in a general directive, charged their officials again to carry out all papal, imperial, and ducal mandates which had come to them.   In order to dispel any remaining uncertainty, there followed a number of specific decrees:[74]

> No printer is henceforth to publish any book or pamphlet without previous official examination and approval.   Nor may any of the forbidden heretical writings be bought, sold, given away, or otherwise distributed in the ducal lands.
>
> All Bavarians now studying at Wittenberg are to depart from there within three months,[75]   No person who has studied at Wittenberg may hold ecclesiastical office or a university appointment in Bavaria.[76]
>
> No one is to be permitted to preach in any church without having been examined and pronounced sound by his Bishop, and holding a written certificate to that effect.   No soap box preachers will be tolerated.
>
> Escaped monks who have taken wives are to be expelled forthwith.
>
> No change is to be condoned in the celebration of Holy Communion. No one is to receive Holy Communion without having first confessed and obtained absolution.   Fast days are to be held as prescribed by the Church.

In accordance with Campeggi's recommendation and the decisions made at Regensburg, the Dukes appointed a number of special commissioners who were, in association with regular administrative personnel, to keep the whole land under surveillance and to take malefactors into custody.   Bavaria either had then, or developed in response to this challenge, an effective system of internal security, an organization which proved its value in 1525 when the borders were quickly sealed and budding agrarian revolts suppressed efficiently.[77]   Once again the Dukes explicitly reserved to themselves alone the right to decide on proceedings and declare punishments.   They agreed not to give asylum to any person expelled as a heretic from the territories of another signatory; however, notable through its absence from the promulgation was that provision of the Regensburg agreement which sought to oblige signatories to aid each other when endangered by rebellious subjects. We see again that Wilhelm and Ludwig, prompted no doubt by their prescient chancellor, insisted on retaining the utmost freedom of action. A Bavarian religious policy implementing political, if not confessional, principles was in process of formulation, but it was one based on purely indigenous considerations.

Wilhelm's correspondence reveals him busily occupied with the handling of cases that were referred to him through administrative channels. He kept in touch with his officials and gave prompt acknowledgement to their reports.[78] Voluminous dossiers piled up. Most interesting about these records is what they tell us about Wilhelm's methods of investigation. There was no witch hunting in Bavaria; no one was condemned without a careful evaluation of all the evidence. The affair of Bernhard Tichtl, or Tichtler, a judicial officer at Starnberg before his dismissal, is a case in point.[79] Late in 1524 Tichtl was denounced by an Ingolstadt professor to whom he had made some unguarded remarks about the plight of Lutherans in Bavaria. He was arrested and placed in the Falkenturm in Munich. The charge was itemized and declared true by Tichtl. He also admitted to several discussions and a disputation on Lutheran articles (both forbidden by the Religious Edict of 1522, it will be remembered). Examination of witnesses to these discussions yielded a transcript of long conversations, repeated in detail and from an apparently fresh memory. The report was then analyzed and heretical articles laid to Tichtl by the witnesses extracted. Thirty-six of these were placed before Tichtl who admitted and recanted them one by one. Meanwhile, Wilhelm's father-in-law, the Margrave of Baden, had addressed Wilhelm with an entreaty for Tichtl's release which was promptly answered, and Tichtl himself petitioned the Duke with three compendious writings. A final brief of the proceedings was drawn up. Wilhelm was now ready to pass judgment, and on February 13, 1925, less than two months after his internment, Tichtl was released after payment of a fine of 1,000 florins.

Recantation was the major prerequisite for release from the ducal prisons. The Augsburg patrician Georg Regel got himself and his family off for 2,000 florins after admitting his lapse.[80] One Georg Vogel and his wife Anna confessed contritely to having eaten meat on fast days and to having received Communion under both forms. Their sentences were revoked by Wilhelm.[81] Another, Erhard Gugler, a twice-convicted heretic, recanted once more, and again the pleas of his wife and children moved the Duke (as Gugler recalls in a lachrymose letter of gratitude) to commute his sentence to expulsion.[82] Leonhard Pirckheimer, a preacher in Otting, confessed to having included Lutheran articles in his sermons. He too was let go after pronouncing the formal declaration of renunciation: He had accepted the Lutheran and new teachings against all the commands of the true Christian religion and the papal, imperial, and ducal mandates. For this he has been put in prison. He now condemns his own action, renounces his adherence to a vile heresy, and vows his steadfast intention to be true to the venerable Christian traditions. Furthermore, he agrees to leave Bavaria and never to return to within ten miles of her borders, nor enter the territory of any of those princes and prelates who support the decisions of the Council of Regensburg. So help him God.[83]

Reckoned quantitatively, the number of men and women expelled from Bavaria in 1524 and 1525, or otherwise disciplined, is not significant.[84] But it is likely that through careful and deliberate detection and prosecution most of the potential trouble makers were isolated. The absence of organized and influential groups of religious dissenters certainly contributed to the relative calm which persisted in Bavaria during the peasant uprisings which broke out all around the Duchy in Swabia, Franconia, Upper Austria, Salzburg, and Tirol in 1525.[85] To most contemporaries of these unhappy events there was only one interpretation of the ideological roots of this rebellion.[86] "All this has no other cause than that Lutheran heresy," Chancellor Eck assured his Dukes,[87] though other voices were not lacking which counselled Wilhelm to meet the peasants' wishes half way.[88] Had Aventinus' *Bavarian Chronicle* been available to him then, it is not likely that Wilhelm would have remained untouched by his official historian's evocation of the monotony, degradation, and hopelessness of peasant life in Germany. But Wilhelm listened to Eck, and there is no doubt that determined action was called for if the spreading revolt was to be kept out of Bavaria, though Eck's plan for demonstrative cruelty in dealing with captives—his policy of deterrent effect—[89] seems excessive now. Eck's contempt for his lowly adversaries was such that he was convinced that a stout heart and a firm front were sufficient to defeat them.[90] The social gospel of the peasant movement and, he assumed, of Luther's, was detestable to him. "I want nothing of their brotherly love," he declared. "I have never been tempted to share my possessions with my next-of-kin, to say nothing of strangers and peasants."[91] There is little chance, he comments sarcastically, that Mr. Fugger will be so brotherly as to divide with him. Before long every one, even peasant oafs, will see from the fruits of the Lutheran heresy what kind of tree it is they grow on.[92] "Then we will snuff out their hellish gospel!"[93]

It is likely that Eck saw in the peasant uprisings the turning point of the whole Lutheran rebellion. He had always warned of the inescapable political consequences of an individualistic religious creed. Here now was the proof. Johann Eck, too, had been arguing this position,

V

and, to support it, had culled a number of anti-authoritarian remarks from Luther's writings.[94]   When the peasant wars came to an end and Bavaria had been spared the devastation of neighboring lands, all concerned could congratulate themselves on the determination with which rebelliousness had been resisted. It is customary to cite in this connection the taunt of the controversialist Johann Cochlaeus to Luther: "Had all our Princes been as diligent as the Bavarian Dukes in driving out your books and your disciples, their peasants would have remained as peaceful as those in Bavaria."

In Bavaria's relations with the papacy this diligence continued to be played as a trump card in the diplomatic game for control of the monasteries. Beyond this there now commenced an attempt to recover some of the financial losses sustained in the pursuit of the Dukes' and Eck's political schemes by charging them to the struggle against the Lutherans.[95]   But the years 1525, 1526, and most of 1527 showed little drive toward "the extirpation of heretical practice," which Wilhelm had promised Rome.[96]   Even a priest who, in March 1526, was indicted for having told his peasant congregation in Sielenbach that the relic at a near-by shrine was really the bone of a hanged criminal,[97] was set free by Wilhelm with no other penalty than the loss of his parish. A little nest of Lutherans at Wasserburg was cleared out,[98] a renewed effort to hunt down illicit preachers and gospel interpreters was made,[99] and a more permanent foundation for the control of heresy was laid by the announcement of a plan to improve primary and secondary education.[100] The Dukes watched with some concern the growing Lutheranization of Regensburg,[101] but they refused to stand against the tide, even when requested to do so by the Administrator.[102]

It is probable that once again high political considerations intervened to bring about a relaxation in prosecution, though not in vigilance. In the course of 1526, the uneasy relations between the Dukes and their Habsburg cousins broke into open hostility, and the Dukes could not, in a time of shifting policies and alliances, afford to destroy all their bridges to the other camp. With Chancellor Eck it was axiomatic that possibilities of approach and detachment must always be open. Eck had convinced himself that the Emperor, and more especially his brother Ferdinand, were intent on keeping Bavaria encircled, squeezing at every point where pressure could be brought to bear.[103]   "If ever a Prince of Austria has had designs on our Duchy, he is it," Eck warned Wilhelm of Ferdinand.[104]   But mere defense went against Eck's grain. The struggle he waged challenged the Habsburgs on the major political battlefields. In September his agents were bargaining in Prague, where the crown of Bohemia might be procured for Ludwig;[105] simultaneously he pursued what he regarded as the climactic objective of his stewardship, the election of Wilhelm as King of the Romans. The pillage of Rome by Charles' troops in May of 1527 improved Wilhelm's chances, and Eck undertook far-ranging negotiations. Both attempts turned out magnificent failures, but both necessitated the kind of agile diplomacy in which a zealous and unswerving religious policy could have no part. Also, since Wilhelm insisted on handling all religious investigations himself, a lull during these busy and tense months was natural. In any case, the surviving records inform us about no more than a handful of cases of heresy exposed and judged until the autumn of 1527.

V

It was the appearance of the brotherhood of Anabaptists on Bavarian soil which abruptly ended this period of inaction. From then on, until the menace from this new Hydra-head of the rebellion had been terminated, persecution, not only of extremists, but of all persons of doubtful loyalty, became incisive, thorough, and merciless. For the first time one senses conviction behind the Dukes' acts.

Since the summer disquieting news of the gathering of Baptists in neighboring regions, especially in Augsburg and Salzburg, had come to Munich. On the subject of the internal threat posed by these "garden brethren," as they were called from their clandestine nocturnal meetings in the gardens beyond the city walls, there was no disagreement among governments. It is most probably this awakened consciousness of danger which explains three executions of heretics, not necessarily themselves Anabaptists, which took place in Bavaria in February, June, and August, the first capital punishments which can be documented. One Leonhard Käser, or Kaiser, a fugitive priest who returned to Bavaria for his father's last illness, was arrested and later burned at the stake by order of Duke Wilhelm. Another, Georg Wagner, refused to let his new-born child be baptized, and, when challenged, maintained further that he saw no value in the Eucharist. He too was burned.[106] At about the same time a cutler named Ambrose created a disturbance in the Frauenkirche in Munich, shouting that "God Almighty is not in this bread and cannot be put into it. It is nothing but a piece of bread." He was at once put under lock and key, condemned to the stake, but "went into himself, renounced his sin, and begged for clemency." His sentence was commuted to beheading. Soon afterwards he was seen being led to the block, calm and at peace with himself. He traced a cross on the ground, knelt on it, and offered his head.[107] The sentences applied in these three cases soon became standard: the stake for unregenerate heretics, beheading or, if a woman, drowning, for those who recanted.[108]

In November 1527 the persecutions began in earnest. Early that month, according to the ever-alert Johann Eck,[109] some Baptist apostles had arrived at the Bavarian borders. They apparently found a fertile field for their labors. On November 6, Eck reports, a Baptist group of eleven men and sixteen women was discovered in a farm house half a mile from Salzburg. The Cardinal, who, according to Eck, still had not grasped the seriousness of the peril, allowed twenty-one who recanted to go free, though the others were shut inside the house, which was then burned to the ground.[110]   On the 10th, the Cardinal offered a general amnesty, of which twenty-five women and sixteen men took advantage. In the territories of the Dukes, however, there was now no disposition to be soft-hearted. Eck reports with approval that as early as November 4 two men were burned to death and two beheaded, that a certain Leonhard Spörle, who had been sent from Augsburg to make converts in Bavaria, was quickly caught and sent to the block, and that of eighteen men imprisoned in Burghausen all were beheaded. One of the latter was a castle guard who had been drunk and out of his senses when he submitted to his second baptism. Still he was ordered executed, for, Eck adds in a telling comment, "my gracious Lord is of the opinion that no one becomes a Baptist who has not previously become a Lutheran. Nor do the Anabaptists approach anyone but a Lutheran." The last is surely an admission that Lutheranism had been far from annihilated in Bavaria.

But by now Wilhelm was thoroughly aroused. His Chancellor's warnings of the ultimate forms which the Lutheran revolt would take appeared to have come true: "a corruption, rejection, and destruction of all sacraments," and the corrosion of civic law and authority; a denial, above all, of those virtues of rectitude, order, and respectability so honored by Bavarians. He resolved to declare war on the heresy in all its guises. On the 15th of November, a sternly worded Second Religious Edict issued from Munich.[111]   In order to establish continuity of policy, it repeated some essential passages from the Religious Edict of 1522 and the general directive of 1524,[112] and then identified the present danger:

> For now a new sect of men, called Anabaptists, have come within our borders, and with them a corruption, rejection, and destruction of all sacraments, as well as numerous other evil, unchristian, and inhuman practices.

The methods announced for detection and apprehension reveal the no-nonsense mood which now prevailed; rewards of 32 Gulden for denunciation leading to the capture of a Baptist, and of 20 Gulden for a Lutheran, and the most severe penalties to follow conviction. Simultaneously Wilhelm had authorization sent to ducal officials, permitting them to hold investigations of all persons accused of Anabaptism.[113]

Imprisoned Baptists were to be held in separate cells so that none would find support or encouragement from others.[114] Anyone found sheltering a suspected sectarian must be arrested. Immediate written notification was to be made to the Dukes of all action taken.

That Leonhard von Eck was behind these stringent measures is shown by a letter which he drafted for Wilhelm to send to his brother Ludwig, whom the Chancellor found not nearly effective enough in driving heretics from his administrative districts. "Do not fail to realize," Wilhelm duly wrote on November 17th, "that a creed which allows each man to interpret his faith according to his taste and will must breed civil disobedience and ultimately rebellion and bloodshed."[115] Rumor has it, Wilhelm goes on, "and perhaps it is the truth, that Lutheran and other teachings find ready entry into Your Grace's districts and towns. . . . Wherefore I would ask Your Grace to be henceforth more observant . . . so that with patience and determination we may keep our land and our people free from misfortune." Eck's studies of the role of the Anabaptists among the peasant insurgents elsewhere must have convinced him that he now faced an organized conspiracy. When, therefore, some time later, groups of Baptists were discovered sailing down the Danube on rafts, there was devised a more systematic method of investigation, a part of which consisted of a questionnaire (*Fragstück*)[116] to be answered in writing by each prisoner:

Who is he (or she), where does he come from and what is his destination? How did he come to Bavaria, and why? What is his position on infant baptism? Who converted him to Anabaptism, and where and when? Has he himself made converts? What is his opinion of the Mass? Has he received Holy Communion within the year? What are the customs of his sect; particularly, how do Baptists arrange for the community of all possessions? Does he know of any secret Baptists in Bavaria? Are other individuals or groups following his trail? Is he resolved to resist or to undermine law and authority? Does he advocate the overthrow of government by force and violence?[117] Is his group planning to meet other members of their sect, and if so, where? Does he know that Bavarian laws forbid the existence of his sect, and is he aware of the penalty for non-compliance? Has he been punished or expelled elsewhere?

Enforcement of the decrees and laws now came swiftly and with the utmost severity. At the time of issue of the new Edict three men and three women were in detention at Burghausen; all were executed.[118] On Sunday, December 23rd, 1527 nine men were beheaded in Landsberg.[119] Two teamsters were put to death in Munich, one by the sword, the other at the stake.[120] Around the first of the new year the Emperor issued his own Mandate against Anabaptists from Speier.[121] Charles' interpretation of the true object of the sect was that of the Dukes: "Many of these people have no other ambition than to use their false religion as a cloak from under which to carry on the most monstrous ravage and destruction of civil law and order, of authority, indeed of all propriety." The pace of persecution was stepped up. In January alone a citizen of Munich might have observed twenty-nine men being drowned in the Isar, six steadfast artisans burned after a secret trial, and two of their wives, unswerving as their husbands, condemned to the stake, but permitted to suffer death by drowning before being burned.[122] Further executions were ordered elsewhere in the Duchy. Even the chronicler of the Anabaptist persecution in Bavaria, Andreas Perneder, lost count. "A great multitude of persons was tried and condemned," he merely writes of the later months of the year 1528.[123] In some cases special circumstances led to a full pardon, but these were rare for convicted Baptists.[124] A persistent effort was made to keep on the trail of preachers sent to proselytize,[125] for example one Augustin Tucher, who used his brother's butcher shop in Landshut as a front for his missionary work. Tucher escaped to Regensburg and was executed there in October upon insistent demands of the Dukes.[126]

Meanwhile there was no slackening in the campaign against real or alleged Lutherans. To Wilhelm these were, as we have seen, pliable subjects for the Baptist agents. Special measures were ordered against itinerant Lutheran preachers who slipped across the borders from Augsburg, Ulm, and Regensburg. Now at last the Dukes decided to cooperate with the Administrator of Regensburg in his efforts to suppress the Lutherans there,[127] the city itself not having taken adequate measures against the Anabaptist danger. It was there that Aventinus sought asylum in August after the arrest of two of his Bavarian associates. Aventinus had been under surveillance since the spring when he opened his home in Abensberg to Erhard Zänkl, the first monk in Regensburg to discard his robes and take a wife, and a notorious person to the orthodox.[128] Soon after that two of his acquaintances were seized, in May Georg Fabri, Duke Ludwig's court chaplain, in July Christoph Achster, a priest in Kelheim. Both were charged with Lutheran sympathies. In Regensburg Aventinus apparently participated in colloquies among various advocates of the new faith.[129] In October, following a temporary abatement of prosecutions in Bavaria, he returned home. On the seventh the Dukes, who now no longer were willing to take chances, had him arrested.

Thus ended the first decade of Protestantism in Bavaria. To the Dukes and their industrious Chancellor it was surely a source of deep satisfaction that their land had been spared the divisive and debilitating consequences of a territory rent by religious strife. In retrospective contemplation of the ten years just concluded they could reflect with pleasure that their cautious and far from immoderate measures had brought them success on many fronts. The cost of all this, to be sure, had been high, and the ducal treasuries were near exhaustion. In 1549, not long before his death, Wilhelm was compelled to turn to the Pope for aid, extending an offer of his personal jewelry for purchase.[130] For twenty-eight years, he writes, his government has been in a constant state of mobilization against the enemies of the faith. The cost of this preparedness he estimates at 25,000 gold gulden yearly.[131] Was this too high a price for what had been achieved? It is improbable that Wilhelm thought so in 1528. His Duchy was entire. The administrative powers in his hands had been strengthened. Revolution and dissension had been averted. The prestige of his House stood high. The future could be faced with confidence.

1. Aventinus, "Haus-Kalender," *Johannes Turmairs genannt Aventinus Sämmtliche Werke*, VI (Munich, 1908), 45.

2. *Ibid.*, 44-45.

3. Leonhard Theobald, *Die Reformationsgeschichte der Reichsstadt Regensburg* (Munich, 1936), 164 ff.

4. Between 1526 and 1529 he himself sent the manuscript of the most anti-clerical of his writings, the booklet on the Turkish wars, to various authorities in the hope of arousing them to concerted military action. Cf. "Türkenkrieg," *Aventinus* I (Munich 1880), 218.

5. Cf. Aventinus' own statement, *Ibid.*, 186.

6. *Ein warnus und anzaigung der ursach, warumb got der her dem Türken . . . so vil sigs wider uns christen gebe . . . . Aventinus*, I, 171-242.

7. Cf. entry in the "Haus-Kalender," *Aventinus*, VI, 45. Cf. also Leonhard von Eck's letter to the Dukes, *Ibid.*, I, 2 page L.

8. On the approval by the Estates of this rule, and its endorsement by the Emperor Maximilian, see Sigmund Riezler, *Geschichte Baierns* III (Gotha, 1896), 641 ff.

9. Franz von Krenner, *Baierische Landtags-Handlungen in den Jahren 1429-1513*, XVII (Munich, 1805), 9 ff. On the period generally see Sigmund Riezler, *op. cit.*, volumes III-IV.

10. Actually it was suspicion of the motives of their uncle, the Emperor Maximilian, which ultimately prompted Wilhelm and Ludwig to end their quarrel. Cf. Riezler, IV, 9-27 on the Emperor's influence and on the settlement worked out by the brothers.

11. See the detailed but unfriendly study of Eck's career by Wilhelm Vogt, *Die bayrische Politik im Bauernkrieg und der Kanzler Dr. Leonhard von Eck* (Nördlingen, 1883), chapter 1.

12. This was the war of the Swabian League, of which Wilhelm was Ober-

feldherr, with Ulrich of Württemberg, precipitated by Ulrich's attack on the member city of Reutlingen.

13. See the series of memoranda from Eck to Duke Wilhelm, discussed by August von Druffel, "Die bairische Politik im Beginne der Reformationszeit, 1519-1524," *Abhandl. d. hist. Cl. d. kgl.-bayer. Ak. d. Wiss.*, XVII, Abt. 3 (1886), 611-612.

14. See letters of 17 November and 7 December 1520, *ibid.*, *Dokument* No. 4.

15. Wilhelm Zimmermann, *Geschichte des grossen Bauernkrieges* (Naunhof and Leipzig, 1939), I, 247.

16. Eck to Wilhelm, 25 February 1525; Vogt, 395-396. See also Wilhelm's letter to Ludwig of November 1527; note 115 below.

17. Correspondence of the Dukes with Albrecht of Brandenburg, 1517-1518; *Bayerisches Hauptstaatsarchiv*, Munich (from now on cited as *BHM*) *Fürstensachen 338*. The Dukes pleaded two recent indulgences in Bavaria as well as an increase in the cost of living.

18. Matthias Simon, *Evangelische Kirchengeschichte Bayerns* I (Munich, 1942), 161-162.

19. Communication to the bishops of Salzburg, Freising, Regensburg, Passau, and Eichstädt, 11 March 1521; Vogt, 46. Cf. also August von Druffel, "Über die Aufnahme der Bulle 'Exsurge Domine' — Leo X gegen Luther — von Seiten einiger süddeutschen Bischöfe," *Sitzb. d. philol.-hist. Cl. d. Akad. d. Wiss.*, (Munich, 1880), 575 ff.

20. Wilhelm describes their reception in Worms in a letter to Eck; Druffel, *Dokument* No. 5.

21. ". . . ich wais E. F. G. schicklichkeit wol, wenn E. F. G. sich der hendl annemen und nit faul sein wollen." Eck to Wilhelm, February 1521; Druffel, 678.

22. *Ibid.*, 620.

V

23. Franz Dittrich, *Regesten und Briefe des Cardinals Gasparo Contarini* (Braunsberg, 1881), 253.
24. Druffel, *Dokument* No. 11.
25. Wilhelm to Ludwig in 1513. See note 26.
26. Instructions for this plea were drawn up for Ludwig by Wilhelm. *Geheimes Hausarchiv*, Munich, *Korrespondenzakten* No. 583.
27. Cf the statement in Ernst's testament: "'. . . aber nichtte unser will und mainung gewest, Briester zuwerden, oder in disem standt zu pleiben.'" *BHM Fürstensachen* No. 319. Cf. also Karl August Muffat, "'Die Ansprüche des Herzog Ernst . . . auf einen dritten Teil und an die Mitregierung des Herzogthumes Bayern,'" *Abhandl. d. hist. Cl. d. kgl.-bayer. Ak. d. Wiss.* (Munich, 1867), 190 ff.
28. Vogt, 279.
29. Druffel, 622. At the time the Dukes were able to obtain only the provostship of Eichstädt. The election as Bishop came in 1526 through the offices of Clement VII. Cf. Gustav Wolf, "'Die bayerische Bistumspolitik in der ersten Hälfte des 16. Jahrhunderts . . . ,'" *Beiträge zur bayerischen Kirchengeschichte* VI (1899-1900), 146. In 1523 the attempt to gain the coadjutorship was renewed when Johann Eck was asked to intercede with the Pope. Cf. Wilhelm's letter to Eck, 6 February 1523, printed by Theodor Wiedemann, *Dr. Johann Eck,* (Regensburg, 1865) 659-660.
30. The way to the election was cleared by a secret agreement between the incumbent, Cardinal Matthäus Lang, and the Dukes during and after the peasant insurrection in Salzburg in 1525. Cf. Albert Hollaender, "'Studien zum Salzburger Bauernkrieg 1525 mit besonderer Berücksichtigung der reichsfürstlichen Sonderpolitik,'" *Mitt. d. Gesellsch. f. Salzb. Landeskunde* 72 (1932).
31. Carl Prantl, *Geschichte der Ludwig-Maximilians-Universität in Ingolstadt* (Munich, 1872), I, 148.
32. Druffel, 625 ff. Eck's draft with additions and corrections in *BHM Staatsverwaltung* 2778, 45 recto-46 verso; 48 recto. Of the published *Religionsmandat* there are many exemplars. Druffel printed one among his *Dokumente,* page 689 ff.
33. Simon I, 206.
34. A *Pfleger* was an official whose duties combined judicial and administrative functions.
35. Documents of the case in *BHM Staatsverwaltung* 2778, 26.
36. Druffel, 634.
37. *Ibid.,* 633-635.
38. Romuald Bauerreiss, *Kirchengeschichte Bayerns* V, 42-44.

39. Cf. Johann Eck's suggestions for Church reform in Germany, made to Pope Adrian VI in 1523, for a discussion of corruption and irregularities. Eck's notes were published by Walter Friedensburg, "Dr. Johann Ecks Denkschriften zur deutschen Kirchenreformation," *Beiträge zur bayerischen Kirchengeschichte* II (1896), 159 ff.; 222 ff.
40. For a contemporary account of these visits of Albrecht in the 1440's cf. Lorenz Westenrieder, *Beyträge zur vaterl. Historie . . .* (Munich, 1788-1817), V. 38 ff.
41. Simon I, 153-154.
42. Bauerreiss V, 68-71.
43. Vitus Anton Winter, *Geschichte der Schicksale der evangelischen Lehre in und durch Baiern* (Munich, 1809), II, 325; Vogt, 50.
44. He never failed to arrange for a colleague to take over his lectures when his many undertakings required his absence from Ingolstadt. Letter to Wilhelm, 14 April 1526; *BHM Staatsverwaltung 2778*, 42.
45. Druffel, 630 ff.
46. Ludwig to Wilhelm, 21 October and 6 November 1522; *BHM Staatsverwaltung 2719,* No. 5; Druffel, 637.
47. Adrian to Dukes; *BHM Staatsverwaltung 2719,* No. 3. Answer from Ludwig, 16 January 1523; *ibid.,* No. 4.
48. On the Nuremberg Diet cf. *Deutsche Reichstagsakten,* Jüngere Reihe, III (Gotha, 1901).
49. *Ibid.;* Carl Theodor Gemeiner, *Reichsstadt Regensburgische Chronik* (Regensburg, 1800-1824) IV, 480-481.
50. Draft and printed copy in *BHM Staatsverwaltung 2778,* 40.
51. Simon I, 173; Druffel, 641.
52. Druffel, 644.
53. His draft letters and some other documents pertaining to the case in *BHM Staatsverwaltung 2778,* 38-39, 34.
54. A "'versperrt, reformirt closter.'" It was Ettal, from which Seehofer later escaped to become a Lutheran minister in Augsburg.
55. The documents relating to this case are in *BHM Staatsverwaltung, 2778,* 34-36.
56. *Ibid.,* 5-6, 44.
57. The letters and related documents were printed by Felix Joseph Lipowsky, *Argula von Grumbach* (Munich, 1801), *Beilagen* I, III, and VI.
58. Winter I, 174, reports the beheading of a baker's apprentice, accused of Lutheranism, in Munich in July. But it is not likely that the offense was purely religious.
59. Letter to Dukes, 15 June 1523; *BHM Staatsverwaltung 2719,* No. 2.
60. Eck to Dukes, 1 May 1523; *Geheimes Staatsarchiv,* Munich, 311/12. The

Dukes responded, but too late for Eck to make use of the information in his talks with Adrian. Cf. Wilhelm's letter to Eck, 1 November 1523, printed by Theodor Wiedemann, *Dr. Johann Eck*, 664-667.

61. ''Verzaichnus, was Doctor Johann Egkius . . . an stat unnd zu namen unserer gn. herrn, H. Wilhelm unnd H. Ludwig in Bairn bei Babstlicher Heiligkeit hanndlen sol,'' BHM *Oefeleana 26*, 33 recto—43 recto.

62. *Ibid.*, 34 recto and verso.

63. ''Es gen wol alle ding langsam und verdriesslich zu, dass menigklich drob klagt: ursach, das der babst lutzel hat, damit er alle ding aussricht: braucht sich keins cardinals, seien ir allain 4 die das kleinst und das grösst ausrichten: so wil der babst alle ding selbst sehn. Bei Babst Leon hat man ain wochen viel ausgericht, das jetz viel zeit darf dazu.'' Eck to Wilhelm, 1 May 1523; *Geheimes Hausarchiv*, Munich, 311/12.

64. Published by Friedensburg. Cf. note 39 above.

65. Wilhelm and Ludwig to Eck, 1 November 1523; printed by Wiedemann, 664-667.

66. Theobald, 109.

67. *Ibid.; Gemeiner IV*, 471 ff.

68. Theobald, 110 ff. By 1523 the printer Paul Kohl had reprinted twelve of Luther's sermons. The booksellers Kaspar Schreiber and Hans öttl handled these and others.

69. Gemeiner IV, 510.

70. Letters to Wilhelm and Ludwig, 8 May 1524; BHM *Staatsverwaltung 2778*, 51, 53.

71. For a full account of the meeting see Gemeiner IV, 513 ff.

72. *Lanndpot im hertzogthum Obern unnd Nydern Bayrn wider die Lüttheranischen Sect*, dated Munich, 2 October. The corrected draft of this decree is in BHM *Staatsverwaltung 2778*, 89-112.

73. This was printed and circulated in the territories of those who attended the council. A copy is in BHM *Staatsverwaltung 2778*, 65 recto—72 verso. As read by Campeggi, it was to be the most exhaustive attempt at reform yet undertaken. It included Johann Eck's suggestion for provincial and diocesan synods.

74. These were given in the *Lanndpot* and also separately. A collection of them is in BHM *Staatsverwaltung 2772*.

75. In 1518 thirteen Bavarian students matriculated at Wittenberg, in 1519 thirty-four, in 1520 sixty. Simon I, 164. After 1520 the number fell. *A l b u m Academiae Vitebergensis* (Leipzig, 1841). Other territorial governments had begun to recall their students in 1522. See the Instruction

from the Elector Frederick of Saxony to Johann Oswald, 26 February, 1522, *D. Martin Luthers Werke* (Weimar edition), *Briefwechsel*, vol. II, p. 450.

76. In primary and secondary schools, Wittenberg graduates were distrusted, but not removed unless they showed definite Lutheran proclivites. The records of the great Bavarian visitation of 1558-1560, printed by Georg Lurz, *Mittelschulgeschichtliche Dokumente Altbayerns* . . . (Berlin, 1907-1908: *Monumenta Germaniae Paedagogica*, XLI-XLII) I, 251 ff., reveal many former Wittenberg students teaching in Bavaria.

77. Vogt, 135 f.

78. BHM *Staatsverwaltung 2778*, 123 recto—124 recto; 125, for a typical case.

79. *Ibid.*, 124 verso—146 recto.

80. Simon, 177.

81. BHM *Staatsverwaltung 2778*, 121.

82. *Ibid.*, 177.

83. *Ibid.*, 162-166.

84. Due to the scattering of the material from this period among the various Bavarian archives, it is difficult to arrive at a reliable quantitative estimate of the prosecutions. But because the investigations had to be supervised by Wilhelm personally it is likely that the great majority, and certainly the most important, of cases have come down to us.

85. On the general subject of the peasant wars in Bavaria see the works by Zimmermann, Vogt, and Riezler already cited. Also Franz Ludwig Baumann, *Akten zur Geschichte des deutschen Bauernkrieges aus Oberschwaben* (Freiburg i. B., 1877).

86. Vogt, chapter 3.

87. Letter from Eck, 25 May 1525; *ibid.*, 456.

88. The Bavarian Councillor Sebastian Schilling was one. Cf. Schilling to Wilhelm, 13 March 1525; Zimmerman I, 252.

89. Letters to Wilhelm of 29 April, 3 May, 25 May 1525; Vogt, 448, 452, 454.

90. Letter of 13 April 1525; Vogt, 431. Again, 29 April; *ibid.*, 448.

91. Eck to Wilhelm, 9 March 1525; *ibid.*, 408.

92. Eck to Wilhelm, 22 February, 1525; *ibid.*, 393.

93. Eck to Wilhelm, 9 March 1525; *ibid.*, 408.

94. BHM *Staatsverwaltung 2778*, 86 recto and verso.

95. Cf. the drafts of two letters of Wilhelm to Clement VII, 15 and 16 December 1525; *Geheimes Staatsarchiv*, Munich, 311/12. Also Wilhelm's letter to Johann Eck, 19 October 1523, written upon receipt of the news of the death of Adrian VI, in which the Duke indicated his hopes for finan-

cial support from the new pontiff. Printed by Wiedemann, 667-670.

96. Letter of 15 December; *Geheimes Staatsarchiv*, 311/12.

97. Confession and recantation of Wolfgang Hackenschmitt, 6 March 1526, *BHM. Staatsverwaltung 2778*, 169.

98. Wilhelm mentions this in his draft letter of 15 December to Clement.

99. Decree signed by Wilhelm and Ludwig in 1526; *BHM. Staatsverwaltung 2772*, No. 20.

100. 1526 saw the first ducal mandate on inspection of schools and compulsory school attendance. See Lurz, I, 206-208. School reform continued to be one of Wilhelm's concerns. Cf. Lurz, especially I, 234-236.

101. Gemeiner IV, 533 ff. *BHM Staatsverwaltung 2729* is a collection of letters and reports to Wilhelm and Ludwig relating to the spread of Lutheranism in Regensburg and Ulm.

102. Theobald, 173-174. During the disturbances of 1525 the City Council had compelled the clergy to accept taxation and the imposition of some civic duties. In September 1527 the Administrator called on certain ecclesiastical and secular rulers to meet with the Council in order to persuade its members to revoke these burdens. The Bavarian Dukes refused to attend.

103. According to Vogt, 357, Ferdinand's occupation of the city of Füssen was the turning point for Eck. On the politics of the entire period, cf. Andreas Sebastian Stumpf, *Politische Geschichte von Bayern* I (Munich, 1813).

104. Vogt, 362.

105. Stumpf I, 39 ff.

106. Andreas Perneder, *Verzaichnus, was sich sonderlich in Bayern von 1506 bis aufs 1529. jar, besonders im Baurn Krieg, Türkisch Zug, und das wider tauffern begeben*. Bayerische Staatsbibliothek, Munich, *Cod. germ. 1594*, 47 verso. See also Simon I, 209.

107. Perneder, 48 recto and verso.

108. Women were ordinarily sewn into a sack, thrown in the river, and held under by the executioner with a long pole. Cf. Gemeiner, IV, 442 for a description.

109. Johann Eck to Duke Georg of Saxony, 26 November 1527; Simon I, 198 ff.

110. *Ibid.* Cf. Joseph Schmid, ''Des Cardinals und Erzbischofs von Salzburg Matthäus Lang Verhalten zur Reformation,'' *Jahrb. d. Ges. f. d. Gesch. d. Protestantismus in Oesterreich* XXIX (1898).

111. Draft in *BHM Staatsverwaltung 2778*, 179-181.

112. Cf. note 72 above.

113. *BHM Stattsverwaltung 2778*, 184.

114. *BHM Staatsverwaltung 2843*, no signatures on leaves. This is perhaps of a slightly later date.

115. The letter is given by Perneder, 25 recto—26 recto. Perneder identifies Leonhard von Eck as the author, 26 recto.

116. *BHM Fürstensachen 34*, 7-8.

117. ''Ob sy mit verstand oder anschlag wider die Obrigkhaiten mitainander fürgenommen oder Auffruer und emperung bewegen.'' In 1534 another question read: Have you any contact with the Anabaptists of Münster, and do you carry letters or messages from them? *Ibid.*, 8 recto.

118. Perneder, 25 recto.

119. *Ibid.*, 26 recto and verso.

120. Simon I, 200.

121. A copy from the ducal archives in *BHM Staatsverwaltung 2778*, 185.

122. All these in Perneder, 27 recto and verso.

123. *Ibid.*, 27 verso.

124. Perneder mentions some: 27 verso, 28 recto.

125. Vitus Anton Winter, *Geschichte der baierischen wiedertäufer im sechzehnten Jahrhundert* (Munich, 1809), 5-6.

126. Simon I, 201 ff.; Theobald, 182 ff.

127. Theobald, 174 ff.

128. Cf. entry in Aventinus' *Haus-Kalender* under 22 March 1528. Cf. note 1 above. On Zänkl see Gemeiner IV, 547.

129. *Haus-Kalender*, under August 1528.

130. In spite of careful administration, Wilhelm's personal finances were in desperate state at the end of his reign. See the documents in *BHM Fürstensachen 322* and *352*.

131. Winter, *Wiedertäufer*, v-vi.

VI

Luther as Barabbas

I T is common knowledge that Cochlaeus's *Septiceps Lutherus* fails
as propaganda.[1] Hastily compiled and written with distaste for its
subject evident on every page, it falls considerably short of realizing the promise of its ingenious and appealing form. But Cochlaeus's central theme, Luther at odds with himself, does remain
with the reader as a lasting impression. To that extent at least, his
tract finds its mark. Dialogue was nicely suited to dramatizing the
inconsistencies palpably present in Luther's published opinions.
1528, the year of the *Septiceps*, was also the date of the Saxon
territorial visitation. Like most other Catholic controversialists,
Cochlaeus interpreted this event, and especially the *Instruction of
the Visitors* appearing that year over the names of Luther and
Melanchthon, as the supreme contradiction of the libertarian
strains that had sounded in the first decade of the Reformation.
Luther as visitation official makes a natural counterpoise to the
earlier enthusiast and freedom fighter, an ironic juxtaposition the
polemical possibilities of which were not lost on Cochlaeus. For
the *visitator* in his dialogue, he wrote some of the most telling lines
coming from the seven 'heads' among which the disputation is carried on, and in several crucial passages touching the basic question
of law and obedience, the 'visitor's' antagonist is 'Barrabas', the
archetype of the headstrong and reckless destroyer of established
order who—as a psychological type even more than as a present
menace—was a source of genuine alarm to the magistrates of
Catholic and Protestant Church and State. Of the irreconcilable
conflict between these two symbolic figures, Cochlaeus makes
very clever use. What they signified was obvious to every reader:
autonomy and self-righteousness versus constituted, externally-
controlled authority. The winner of the struggle would determine
whether there was to be order or discord in the land. In every age
and place, 'Barrabas' and *Visitator* stood in opposition. If Luther
was both, the outlook for society was at best uncertain; at worst it

---

[1] Martin Spahn, *Johannes Cochläus* (Berlin, 1898; Nieuwkoop, 1964), p. 148.

was hopeless, as master and rebel took turns spinning the world in a vicious circle of self-destruction.[2]

Luther–Barabbas is the character of the anarchical activist. 'Barrabas will knock you down with his club', Cochlaeus writes, differentiating the insurrectionary and killer mentioned briefly in the New Testament[3] from the six other *personae* keeping Luther and Lutheranism for ever off balance. He is always ready to come to blows, never mind the consequences [*S K*, b. iv, verso]. Whatever the law, he will disobey it. It matters little what it says: as long as a rule has been laid down by human authority, Barabbas is on the attack. Let a Church Council make a law respecting the taking of the sacrament under one or both forms, and Barabbas will do the opposite of what is commanded. 'Even if some Council were to put it out now that we should use the sacrament in both forms, I won't do it. Rather, I'll defy the Council and its statutes, and will use one form, or no form at all, and I'll curse those who, submitting the Council's power, are using both forms.' [*S K*, E., verso.] 'When a human being orders something done', he declares, 'that's enough reason for me not to do it. If he hadn't ordered it, then I would do it. I only obey my own wishes and ideas, and I won't let myself be conformed to human laws.' [*S K*, D. iv, recto]. Christians are free agents, Barabbas holds. Human laws can mean nothing to them [*S K*, a. iv, verso—b.i, recto]. 'Let us be so certain of our cause and so confident of its rightness that we can disregard the whole world's judgement as no more than empty straw.' [*S K*, a. iii, recto]. 'Isn't it disgraceful and slavish that free Christians should be subject to any laws other than God's?' [*S K*, b. iii, verso]. But Barabbas's way is not that of passive resistance. He is a destroyer. 'Let's go, dear brothers,' he cries, 'we'll pull down all man-made rules and statutes!' [*S K*, b. iv, verso.] Having written this, Cochlaeus does not fail to point the obvious moral that this battle cry, if it should be taken up, will mean the end of organized society. 'You are not a god', he tells Duke Johann of Saxony, in the dedication of a German version of the *Septiceps*. 'If human laws are

---

[2] In this article, quotations from Cochlaeus come from S[*ieben*] K[*öpffe*] Martini Luthers. Vom hochwirdigen Sacrament des Altars ... Part I (Leipzig, 1529), Part II (Dresden, 1529).

[3] Ibid., Aii, recto. Luther's New Testament gives *Mord* and *Mörder* in Luke 23: 19, John 18: 39, and Mark 15: 16–7. Cf. Luther's comment *WR, DB* 6, 125.

to count for nothing, all your lordly commands will be ground into the dirt and your officials and visitors will invoke your authority in vain. No one will pay them heed.' [S K, D. iv, recto] Give Barabbas an audience, and respect for government is at an end. He knows how to turn people against their legitimate rulers. 'Even pigs and donkeys can see how blind and dumb our leaders are in all they do, how they lie, cheat, and issue bad and harmful laws.' 'German beasts, that's what they are, as savage as wolves and wild boars.' [S K, b. i, recto] The fury of this verbal onslaught reflects the truculence of the Luther–Barabbas temper, a violent spirit expressed in his image among the seven heads of Cochlaeus's title-page with rough beard, wild hair, and deadly-spiked club ready to hand.

Barabbas's ravings are countered by the *Visitator*, who is the dialogue's figure of lawful and beneficent authority, the counsellor of voluntary submission to the ways things are [cf. S K, a.iv, verso; b.i verso, b.ii, recto, and b.iii, verso]. 'We must recognize the will of God in all worldly laws and statutes', he asserts [S K, b.iv, verso], explaining that people must learn what they are to believe before they can decide what they may do [S K, A.iv, recto, cf. d.iv, recto]. There is, of course, no common ground between the visitor's magisterial principle of compliance and docility and, on the other hand, Barabbas's exultation in his own moral autonomy, and his eagerness to act on it. Cochlaeus drew the contrast as sharply as he could. How is it possible, he asks, that one and the same person can hold such contrary views on so vital a matter of public and private life? No wonder Lutheranism has brought only chaos! This is the conclusion he wished to leave with his readers.

Cochlaeus was too close to his subject and too much the creature of his passions to see the problem clearly, although his image of Luther and Lutheranism must reflect with some accuracy contemporary anxieties about the future of religious and civic life—fears that he was doing his best to fan. Today we should be able to judge more fairly, given our long view, the full record, and our detachment from the old hatreds and loyalties. What was Luther's authentic voice on the vital matter of law and obedience? Was he 'Barabbas' or was he the 'visitor'? Or was Cochlaeus correct in charging the Reformer with a fatal and fateful ambivalence on this central issue of religion and politics?

It is true that Luther's many pronouncements on law and its uses were ambiguous. A selective reading of them can yield contradictory lessons. It is possible to gain the impression that good and honest men owe no obligation to the codes that define their social lives or to the functionaries who enforce them. Or the opposite conclusion can be drawn that obedience is all. Granted the theological basis of Luther's legal thought, law and lawyers were, for him, the consequences and expressions of God's distrust of men.[4] 'Politics and law', he said, 'don't follow from grace: they arise from anger.' [*WA* 49, 316. Sermon of January 1544] While he distinguished formally between *lex*, *Gesetz* (theology) and *jus*, *Recht* (government and jurisprudence), the two concepts interpenetrated each other as he counselled men on their rights and duties. 'These three: law, sin, death are inseparable', he argued, casting a dark shadow over the entire realm of *jus* as well as over *lex*.[5] In his *Kirchenpostille* (1522), he defined the purpose of law for Christians in such a way as to make a very close connection between religious and civic objectives.

> The first purpose is that it maintains discipline among us and compels us to an honest way of life externally, so that we can live together and not devour one another, as would happen if there were no law, no fear of punishment. . . . The second function is that man learns through the law how false and evil is his heart, how far he is still from God.

This view of law as arising from man's corrupted condition is explicitly joined to the political use of the law and the work of the worldly sword through which order is maintained in sinful human society.[6] Writing against the antinomians in the late 1530s, Luther

---

[4] From the considerable literature exploring Luther's relationship to law, the following are particularly valuable: F. E. Cranz, *An Essay on the Development of Luther's Thought on Justice, Law, and Society*, Harvard Theological Studies xix (Cambridge, Mass., 1959); J. Heckel, *Lex charitatis. Eine juristische Untersuchung über das Recht in der Theologie Martin Luthers*, Bayerische Ak. d. Wiss: Abhandlungen, philosophisch–historische Klasse, N. F., Heft 36 (Munich, 1953); K. Köhler, *Luther und die Juristen. Zur Frage nach dem gegenseitigen Verhältniss des Rechtes und der Sittlichkeit* (Gotha, 1873); Hans Liermann, 'Der unjuristische Luther', *Luther–Jahrbuch* 24 (1957), pp. 69–85; and Hermann Wolfgang Beyer, 'Glaube und Recht in Denken Luthers' *Luther–Jahrbuch* 17 (1935), pp. 56–86.

[5] *WA* 39¹ 354, quoted by Gerhard Ebeling, 'Zur Lehre vom triplex usus legis in der reformatorischen Theologie', *Theologische Literaturzeitung* 75, No. 4/5 (1950), pp. 243–4.

[6] Sermon on Galatians 3: 23–9. *WA*, 454, quoted in F. E. Cranz, op. cit., pp. 99–100.

made this link stronger still;[7] but the connection was in his mind from the beginning. 'God gave the imperial laws [i.e. Roman, or 'general' law] for the sake of the wicked', he wrote in the *Preface to the Old Testament* (1523). 'They are laws to defend ourselves with, not laws that can instruct us in anything.'[8] This is the negative view of law, and Luther maintains it vigorously. In its origin and purpose law is man's recompense to the Fall. Moses, the classic lawgiver, is 'a minister of sin; his office is that of death.'[9] In its exercise, law is naked power. 'Whoever has the law in his hand', Luther urged, 'wields power, and only God knows whether such power is right.' 'Law rests on the fist', he added. 'Turn the word *ius* inside out, and it spells *vis*, might.'[10] The uses of power, and the uses of law, can be justified only if there are good motives at work in the minds of those who employ them. A magistrate should do more than merely follow law. The law by itself teaches nothing. If his heart is not good, his enactments will only increase misery and his might spread corruption. 'That is why I have no laws to suggest to a ruler. I wish only to reform his heart.'[11]

As for lawyers and jurists, they live and work in the grubby world of 'mortal, transitory, wretched, earthly things',[12] a career that, Luther is clear, makes them singularly unfit for the prominent places in Church and State to which they aspire. Like many of his contemporaries, Luther spoke with annoyance of the apparently irresistible usurpation by lawyers of positions of influence and power. 'With God's help, I'll defend my Church against them', he said, but knew it was a losing battle [*WA, TR* 4, No. 4382]. The gradual take-over of ecclesiastical and political offices by lawyers and legally trained bureaucrats represented to Luther the fatal closing of the gulf between the world of affairs and administration on the one hand, and the realm of truth and justice on the other. His slashing attacks on lawyers combined with his largely negative view of legislation to create the impression that the worldly network of man-made rules and obligations operated on some lower

[7] Ibid., p. 104.   [8] *WA* 8, 16–17.
[9] From his *Preface* to the Old Testament (1523 and 1545), *WA* 8, 20–1. Cf. Ibid., 8.26–7.
[10] *WA,TR* 6, No. 7016; cf. *WA, TR* 3, No. 3793.
[11] *Von weltlicher Oberkeit* (1523), *WA* 11, 273.
[12] *An die Pfarrherrn, wider den Wucher zu predigen* (1540), *WA* 51, 342–3.

plane of morality where the true Christians's restored conscience should preserve its inviolability from the touch of corruption.

What Luther had against the law and its practitioners was that they seemed to him to care little for the substance of the matters they handled; that they held nothing to be certain; that they lacked firm principles; and that they were rigid formalists, approaching every question in a spirit of mechanical literalness. 'Lawyers deal with words', he said, 'they don't go to the heart of anything, seeking truth. Show me a single jurist who has studied law with the aim of learning truth and finding out what is right and what is wrong.' [*WA, TR* 1, No. 349]. 'Jurists have nothing to do with conscience' [*WA, TR* 1, No. 320]. They are not able to prove anything; circumstances govern all matters of law, and these call the substance itself of things into question [*WA, TR* 1, No. 349]. By contrast, theology recognizes no exceptions, no accidents. 'A theologian must be utterly certain that a thing is thus and not otherwise; that is why theology is certain truth' [*WA, TR* 1, No. 349]. Lawyers, for their part, 'run the world with their whims and opinions' [*WA, TR* 3 No. 3622]. They are like organists who, 'if one pipe doesn't sound, they'll play another' [*WA, TR* 1, No. 134]. Worst of all, lawyers are now preparing to 'intrude on our Lord Christ's own spiritual government, stretching their hands out to take over everything' [*WA, TR* 6, No. 7029], and make all people live according to their laws, 'with which they will once again shake and confuse the conscience of men, which we have only just begun to build up.'[13] 'It makes me angry', Luther told his congregation, warning them of the lawyers in their midst, 'that they go about confusing your consciences. That's the cause of my fury against them.' [*WA* 49, 316.] The violence of some of his diatribes was so great at times that he felt bound to explain himself. 'You must forgive my outbursts against the jurists', he said. 'It's because of my zeal for God and my great wish to increase his honour and affirm his Gospel!' [*WA* 49, 299.] The type of lawyer-bureaucrat was to Luther always the antithesis of that of the preacher and teacher which he felt himself to be. 'An eternal fight wages', he said, 'between jurists and theologians, just as law and grace are forever opposed to each other.' [*WA, TR* 6, No. 7029.] Speaking

---

[13] Sermon of January 1544, *WA* 49, 298.

as a pastor, he vowed that 'as long as I live, I will keep this Church pure against all you jurists.'[14]

Given the profusion of such expressions and the hot aggressiveness of their tone, Luther's followers might be forgiven for supposing that so rare a being as the true Christians ought to be, and in fact was, immune from the reach of the law. Luther's early treatise *Concerning Worldly Government* (1523), could be read a supporting this surmise. Those Christians who are of God's kingdom, he declared, 'require neither sword nor law, and if the whole world were peopled by genuine Christians—that is to say, by believers—there would be no need or use of princes, kings, sword, or law.' [*WA* 11, 249–50.] Christians, he continues, 'should always conduct themselves so as to show that they have no need for law. They have heaven to guide their steps; they should not depend on the law to goad, restrain, terrify, or punish them' [*WA* 11, 259]. 'A good tree', Luther writes in what could be taken as his strongest charter of the Christian's independence from normative and positive law, 'needs neither doctrine nor law to teach it how to bear good fruit. Its nature guarantees it: that without either rule or instruction it brings forth what is natural to it. Thus Christians are so constituted by the spirit and by their faith ... that they need for themselves neither statutes nor laws.'[15] Luther at once limits the relevance of this declaration by admitting that the majority of men and women are not 'Christians'. Most people, he maintained, belong to the far-from-saintly crowd, the rabble or *Pöbel*. With their fickle ways, they need strong-armed government by magistrates, law codes, and law-enforcement agents. But as no sure signs were available for identifying the genuine Christians among the many false ones, a strong incentive must have existed for individuals to assume the best, rather than the worst, about their condition. Such individuals might well interpret Luther's words as a tempting invitation to see themselves as standing in some way above the degrading scene where laws were imposed and regulations enforced. And once the laws were perceived as pernicious, and the enforcers as tyrants, the stage was set for the appearance of a Barabbas.

But all this, while true as far as it goes, is far from being the

---

[14] Sermon on 2 Corinthians 6: 1 (1539), *WA* 47, 670–1.
[15] Quoted by Köhler, op. cit., p. 85.

whole story. Luther also held a very positive view of the law, its uses and powers, and its agents; and he gave vigorous expression to this side of the argument as well. All was not lost when Adam fell. Even sinful humanity harbours God's natural law in its heart. Its spiritual purpose may be obscured by man's depraved state, but a sense of right and wrong remains. Its divine purpose may tend to be neglected in favour of mere earthly felicity; none the less it can instil a sense of the common good in men.[16] Wherever man-made laws reflect and transmit the spirit of this divine natural law they are beneficial. Thus political legislation is a blessing for mankind.

The model of such law-giving is the Roman Law, for which Luther (granted his apparent detestation of the legal mind and profession) expresses some enthusiasm.[17] The old pagans have much to teach us concerning secular government, which is, he writes, an image on earth of eternal bliss and the heavenly realm— 'something like a distorting mirror or a carnival mask', but a reflection none the less [WA 51, 241]. The Imperial Roman Law 'is nothing other than a piece of that pagan wisdom the like of which we shall never see again. . . . Whoever wants to be wise in politics, therefore, let him read the pagan writings', especially the old books of law whose authors were as much God's prophets and theologians as the wise men of Israel [WA 51, 242–3]. Thus the laws must be allowed to stand. Altering them always spells trouble. 'Before you could make a new constitution in Germany, the country would be wrecked three times over.' True, there is a great deal wrong in politics and society. Law and politics are in desperate need of a Luther. But they will not get one. What they will get is a Müntzer instead; in other words, not a reformer but a destroyer [WA 51, 258]. Don't be a know-it-all who thinks he can meddle in the established polity. 'We'll see no new government in the Roman Empire for the rest of its days, David tells us that.' [WA 51, 258.] And the government we now have will not function unless its laws are maintained, 'not with fist and armourplate, but with brains and books'. For this reason 'we must learn and know the laws of our worldly realm.' A jurist, therefore, as long as he is pious and not false, is not merely a worthwhile

---

[16] J. Heckel, op. cit., pp. 70–8.
[17] See esp. his *Auslegung des 101. Psalms* (1534–5), WA 51, 200–64.

citizen, but 'a prophet, a priest, an angel, a saviour'.[18] And by this I mean, Luther elaborates, not only jurists as such, 'but also all others in the trade of politics, namely chancellors, secretaries, judges, advocates ... and also those important personages who are called Court Councillors, for they, too, do the work of law and the office of jurist.' [WA 30², 559] God sees his will done by all these officials, and he approves of what they do. Thus 'secular government is the cornerstone, rock, and foundation of a people and a land. It makes human beings of wild beasts and keeps them from becoming animals again. It is a necessary estate and office, instituted by God himself.'[19] All men owe it their support. None dare oppose it.

In short, the dialogue between 'visitor' and 'Barabbas' is not confined to the pages of Cochlaeus's pamphlet. First one, and then the other surfaces in Luther's published works; at times, to be sure, both of them speak from the pages of a single one. In the informal remarks of the Table Talk they coexist in profusion. 'Barabbas' is more strident before 1525 than afterwards; the 'visitor' speaks with greater force from 1528 when—it has been pointed out—Luther seems in the course of his responsibilities as a Saxon visitation officer, and under the impact of the desperate state of the Church as this was brought to light during the visitation, to take on many of the characteristics of the territorial bureaucrat.[20] Circumstances thereafter multiplied the·opportunities for his official side to assert itself. The apparent decline of schools and universities prompted Luther in 1530 to give lavish public praise to the study of law and the career of politics.[21] The death of John the Steadfast in 1532, and the succession to the Saxon state of a young duke of unproven quality, caused the Reformer to reconsider the need for sound, stable laws to guard against princely caprice. It was also the occasion of the commentary on Psalm 101 [WA 51, 200–64]. The Protestant movement's problems of survival and defence in the 1530s brought him to what Wolfgang Günter has called 'a new understanding of the *ius politicum et imperiale* that led him to appreciate the significance of positive law for the constitu-

[18] *Eine Predigt, dass man Kinder zur Schule halten solle* (1530), WA 302, 557–8.
[19] Quoted by J. Heckel, op. cit., pp. 109–10.
[20] Gerald Strauss, *Luther's House of Learning. Indoctrination of the Young in the German Reformation* (Baltimore and London, 1978), pp. 250–1.
[21] *Predigt, dass man Kinder zur Schule halten solle*, WA 30².

tion of the empire'.[22] But the Reformer's responses to these political cries only gave developed expression to concepts long
embedded in his mind, concepts rooted in the basic distinctions
inherent in his theology of the two kingdoms, of true and false
Christians, and of pious rulers and tyrants. Depending on the
given historical circumstances and their interpretation, either
Barabbas or the visitor could appear as the more persuasive guide
to right conduct in the world.

Thus Luther himself nullifies the proposition that a human
situation can ever be so closed as to relieve the individual of the
need for judging and choosing. To judge and choose is to draw on
empirical knowledge of the world, on a sense of right and wrong,
or conscience. This is man's autonomy. It is the impulse that
moves Barabbas, though he follows the blandishments of his legitimate self-reliance far beyond the bounds set by the limits of human knowledge and ability. Lacking a sense of man's frailty, and
therefore of restraint, Barabbas never heeds. He cannot recognize
the merits of conventional wisdom, accumulated experience, age,
and tradition. The visitor, for his part, lacks the passion to share
his antagonist's anger and exultation. The creature of institutions,
he sees society from the top where individual men and women
seem to fuse into a featureless mass to be protected from its own
appetites, and to be kept safe by a network of rules. His problem
is logistic and managerial. Barabbas's problem is psychological,
dealing in imagination and emotion. Neither figure is entirely
wrong; but neither right by himself. Their opposition—in
Luther's terms an irreconcilable opposition—illuminates the tension generated by the double need to accept discipline and authority in life while, at the same time, judging them for their validity
and their practical consequences. Luther recognized the existence,
as well as the psychological and social authenticity of both needs.
As the leader of a new Church he wore the visitor's hat more often
than he would have wished. But he lacked neither fellow feeling
nor sympathy for Barabbas, of whose sense of outrage he understood too much himself to reject the type. He did not wish to see
Barabbas silenced; he only wanted to take away his club.

---

[22] Wolfgang Günter, *Martin Luthers Vorstellung von der Reichsverfassung*, Re-
formationsgeschichtlich Studien und Texte No. 114 (Münster, 1976), p. 125. On
the issue of resistance and political thought see Quentin Skinner, *The Foundations
of Modern Political Thought* (Cambridge, 1978), ii, pp. 189–224.

VII

The State of Pedagogical Theory c.1530: What Protestant Reformers Knew About Education

The urge to persuade, present in us all, is most active in reformers. In the 1520s Lutherans seized the opportunities offered by pulpit and press to propagate their faith, releasing an unprecedented flood of spoken and written words to a society ill trained to receive them. Fearful of their movement's prospects, they resolved to prepare the ground for a more understanding response in the future. A great educational enterprise was launched and plans made for the systematic indoctrination—in no pejorative sense of that word—of the young.

The decision to embark on an experiment in mass education was heavy with difficulties, not the least of which arose from ambiguities inherent in the Lutheran creed then taking shape. When men were invited to join in the excitement of eschatological expectations imminently to be realized, what was the use of building for the future? When Luther's theology made it clear that mortals cannot enlighten themselves, much less each other, by their own efforts, why make elaborate designs for schools and teachers?[1] Most likely these inconsistencies are more apparent to us now than they were to the first generation of Protestants. In any case, they vanish as impediments when set against the opportunities for educational organization present in the intimate alliance with political authorities to which the emerging Lutheran churches owed their structures and their strength. Backed by the legal and financial power of territorial and municipal states, the reformers could plan an education system equipped with all the features they thought desirable, the absence of which from medieval schools they had deplored: order, control, clearly perceived and pursued objectives, a coherent pedagogy, uniform curricula, skilled teachers with professional qualifications, above all a sense of religious purpose to give meaning to the endeavor.

After 1525 needs and opportunities converged in a crisis mood. The unhappy events of the early 1520s convinced the reformers that they must lose no time in taking steps to gain some measure of control over the minds of men and, thus, over their actions.[2] Deploring the general indifference to learning and the decrepit state of schools, and highly sensitive to charges that the disturbances following the

Copyright © 1976 by The Johns Hopkins University Press. All rights reserved.

appearance of the Lutheran movement were accelerating the distressing decline in intellectual culture,[3] the reformers turned emphatically to matters of education. Beginning in 1528, wherever Lutherans were in authority, they produced a host of school ordinances establishing school systems in cities and territories.[4] Consisting of concrete, specific provisions for curriculum and instruction framed in statements of general purpose, these ordinances set the pattern for school organizations for centuries to come. While only moderately important to the development of German universities, they are of quite extraordinary significance in the history of secondary and elementary schooling, in both its Latin and its vernacular streams. In an attempt to reach the masses, and to reach them at an impressionable age, school ordinances (which were nearly always parts of church constitutions imposing ecclesiastical organization on a region or a city) established networks of popular schools and provided for religious teaching through catechism instruction. Notwithstanding his serious doubts concerning the wisdom of allowing formal schools to cater to popular interests,[5] Luther concluded that the decades ahead offered no grounds for hope if attempts were not made to exert some influence on the young. As early as 1517 he had told his parishioners that "if the Church is ever to flourish again, we must make a beginning by teaching our children." After 1525 the need to make a beginning had become all the more urgent.[6]

In view of the magnitude of this undertaking, it is interesting to ask, What did these men know about education and about those to be educated? It will not come as a surprise to anyone familiar with the sixteenth century to learn that what they knew was what they had read. Not that interest in real-life youngsters was lacking. Luther himself can be quoted for a great number of acute, and often very touching, observations on his own and other people's children,[7] and it would not be difficult to cull from contemporary autobiographical and other writings the evidence to show that adults regarded children with concern and affection.[8] The growing corpus of pediatric books also suggests that the young were being studied with something like the care which we feel they deserve.[9] Empirical attention given to children was never systematized, however. It remained fragmentary, occasional, and—except for medical writings—subjective. The literary tradition, on the other hand, supplied a ready-made and coherent set of assumptions about the nature of children and young people. It also offered apparently reliable predictors of their behavior and responses in each stage of development. Given the receptive attitude of sixteenth-century intellectuals to written authority, it is not surprising to see them turn to literature for their general ideas about the young, for clues to the possibilities and the limits of education, and for tangible suggestions on how to train them to good purposes. A rich and prolific body of writings on education reaching back to Plato carried a cumulative weight of conviction which was hard to resist, even where written dicta could not easily be reconciled with observed or sensed reality. In any case, in the context of their culture it was an obvious move for the reformers to depend on the distant and recent past for usable answers to their many conceptual and technical questions concerning the education of the young.[10]

In order to answer our question, What did sixteenth-century reformers know about education? let us assume that they were familiar with the entire body of pedagogical literature from Plato to Vives and Erasmus. This is not as absurd a supposition as might appear at first glance. The sixteenth-century intellectual was a voracious reader. He took pleasure in fullness and reiteration. He had a professional interest in the study of books on special subjects. He kept himself informed of the appearance of new editions of the works of distinguished authors. He knew that the subject of education had occupied most of the great minds of pagan and Christian antiquity and of the philosophical schools of the Middle Ages. He also knew—and here we come perhaps closer to the realm of the feasible—that older writers had, for their part, drawn inspiration from books available to them, much as he proposed to do now. When he read Vincent of Beauvais he also came to know Hugh of St. Victor, Jerome, and Quintilian. In Wimpheling's *Adolescentia* he could find a veritable mosaic of educational bits and pieces gathered from earlier writers.[11] Otto Brunfels' *Catechesis puerorum* of 1529 made an effortless introduction to Quintilian, Cicero, Plutarch, and a wide assortment of fifteenth-century Italian writers. Our reformer could also, if he wished, obtain anthologies of educational classics which would give him a speaking acquaintance with the pedagogical tradition,[12] an acquaintance often indistinguishable to the modern reader from familiarity with the true sources. No one in the sixteenth century needed to be ignorant of what the great thinkers had said on the subject of education. For browsers there was plenty to read in digests, and for the scholar who wished to go back to the sources there were convenient editions, and innumerable references to them.

In any case, the men charged with the awesome task of consolidating the tentative gains and reversing the incipient failures of the Lutheran movement in Germany had a deep interest in educational questions. Sustaining this interest was an implicit trust in the power of education to achieve desired ends. This confidence could not have arisen from Luther's faith, which permitted scant hope of men's ability to mend their ways. Nor could it have been drawn from observed reality, for reformers tended to be inveterate pessimists when it came to judging the behavior of their fellow men. Confidence in the ability of some to teach and others to learn could have come only from the many writers who in the previous millennium and a half had speculated on some of the great questions now occupying the reformers. These lessons from the past were by no means unambiguous. The pedagogical tradition did not speak with one voice. It was not a program to be adopted but a critical discussion to be confronted. But on two points, at least, there was substantial agreement among the authors: that men could and should be taught, and that one must begin with the young. It was a matter of common knowledge among the reformers that their own generation was too far gone for help. But in the young there was still hope. "Don't bother with the older generation; they are a waste of time. Instead let us, with God's help, try it with children."[13] Or, "When we have begun to train our foolish, tender youth to Christian doctrine and discipline we may expect to see a beneficial evangelical change among us and a better Christian society. This is our only hope for restoring corrupt Christendom."[14] Such expressions of trust abound in the prefaces to the catechisms and schoolbooks of early Lutheranism.

It follows that reformers lacked neither incentive nor opportunity to steep themselves in the literature of the pedagogical tradition. Let us now examine this literature in order to discover what principles men could extract from it and to what actions they were likely to be moved.

II

At the root of all that was said and done on the subject of education lay two contradictory sets of convictions about the child's essential nature. The affirmation of human instincts, and their adoption as effective and beneficial impulses to learning, was most attractively summarized by Quintilian, whose observations on children and their upbringing exerted a lasting but not unequivocal influence on sixteenth-century pedagogues. "Nature brought us into the world that we might attain to all excellence of mind"[15] can stand as the motto of the optimistic school, which accepted the fundamental soundness of human nature, at least to the point of denying its inescapable corruption. Most children are intelligent by endowment and eager to learn by instinct.[16] The function of education is to deepen and extend this promise.

An equally eloquent opposing view rejected nature as a basis of trust and severely limited expectations and scope of education. Corrupt from birth, or corrupted within a few years of it, human impulses exist only to be restrained, not to be aroused and encouraged to unfold. This pessimistic view, firmly anchored in the Old Testament (Genesis 8:21: "because [man's] heart contrives evil from infancy"), was given powerful momentum by the compelling assertions of Augustine on the subject of infants and children and by a large assemblage of pedagogical writers from Gerson to Wimpheling and Vives who had fallen under Augustine's spell. Their position is epitomized by Augustine's introspections on the motives underlying the childish pranks and petty deceptions of his own childhood. "Is this childish innocence?" he asks. "It is not, Lord, it is not. . . . These are the same things, the very same, which as our years go on . . . are done with regard to kings and governors, business and profit."[17] Among the Protestant reformers this pessimistic strain struck a lasting echo. In a large part of the pedagogical literature of Lutheranism it is the dominant theme.

Augustine's position is far from simple. Quite apart from the polemical purpose of much of his writing (of which his sixteenth-century readers need not have been aware), and from the serious internal inconsistencies which have often been pointed out, the Bishop of Hippo harbored ambivalent and shifting attitudes toward the early stages of life and their influence on adult behavior. For the purposes of our inquiry, however, it is not so important to discover what he really meant—this question has been meticulously examined[18]—as to know how he was read in the sixteenth century.

Looking back from the literature written for children in that age we can see

Augustine looming as the apostle of unmitigated pessimism. From his *On the Merits and Forgiveness of Sins and on the Baptism of Infants* later readers could, if they wished, extract passages to prove the rottenness of the babe in his cradle: "Seeing that the soul of an infant fresh from its mother's womb is still the soul of a human being, . . . I ask why, or when, or whence it was plunged into that thick darkness of ignorance in which it lies? If it is man's nature thus to begin, and that nature is not already corrupt, then why was not Adam created thus? Whereas [the infant], although he is ignorant where he is, what he is, by whom created . . . is already guilty of offense."[19] Augustine is here at pains to prove against the Pelagians that original sin is inherited and that baptism makes no sense without assuming this, and that sin does not have to be committed; it is our human heritage. In the *Confessions* the same point emerges, sharpened by the author's self-portrait as a natural sinner: "It is the physical weakness of a baby that makes it seem 'innocent,' not the quality of its inner life. I myself have seen a baby jealous: it was too young to speak but it was livid with anger as it watched another baby at the breast."[20] Augustine shows that the young child, the infant even, displays the signs of human depravity, greed, envy, lust, the insistent will, and the *amor sui* which is the heart of sin. Without grace the infant remains in the "thick darkness of ignorance," incapable out of his own powers to surmount his animallike condition. He is all instinct, and his behavior reveals the direction of his infantile drives.[21]

But Augustine does not have to be read quite so dismally. Jean Gerson, whose influence on the religious strain of early modern educational thought almost equaled the Bishop of Hippo's,[22] while also rejecting the innocence of infants as a Pelagian heresy and pointing to evidence of *concupiscentia* as proof, insisted on a basic natural goodness in the child which, he says, renders him capable of yielding to influence and instruction. Gerson denied that every human instinct was depraved, preferring to speak of an inclination, or a susceptibility, to concupiscence, a tendency which could be counteracted.[23] As a pedagogue—which he was with a passion—Gerson built on the existence of germs of goodness and reason in the child which, with careful cultivation and protection by a "wall of discipline," could grow into virtues.[24] Gerson believed in restraint, particularly in matters relating to the senses, and he worked out rules for exerting beneficent influences on children.[25] His writings show that the Augustinian position on inherited sin did not necessarily lead to total educational pessimism. His arguments persuaded many who found Augustine himself too hard to take. Jacob Wimpheling, who was much influenced by his older French colleague, worked up Gerson's suggestions into a comprehensive (though incoherent and not very profound) theory of pedagogy.[26] Although the young are full of undesirable inclinations, Wimpheling states, four means exist for reaching the residue of virtue in each child, and these make training possible. They are the efficacy of divine grace, the influence of intelligent parents, good examples, and direct appeals to mind and character. Small children, being least corrupted by life, offer the best chance of success through restrictive, if necessarily coercive, action on the part of educators charged with creating favorable conditions around the child, conditions in which every influence tends toward the desired end.[27] Only within this all-enclosing pedagogical environment, Wimpheling suggests, can the slender shoots of virtue prevail against the proliferating weeds of the natural vices.

In the Reformation the Augustinian position was most often cited as an argument for the systematic use of severe restriction and enforced conditioning in the education of the young. One naturally wonders whether this was a case of theology leading to educational ideas or, conversely, an empirically based feeling seeking a principle on which to rest a determination that the young must be kept down. No matter. The fact is that the question of the natural innocence or natural depravity of children, remote though it seems from the everyday world of practical teaching, had a profound impact on the form and content of religious and secular instruction in the sixteenth century. Arguments were available to show that the young would inevitably misuse even the slightest extension of freedom to give in to the self-destructive urges in which concupiscence manifests itself in all men. The only correctives were restraint and control.

Other arguments existed, however, to supply a different set of guiding principles. Little was made of theological affirmations of the natural innocence of infants and young children,[28] nor of the exceedingly positive appreciation of the child implied in Jesus' injunction (Matthew 18: 1–6) to ''become as little children.'' Childlike qualities exalted in these and many other passages[29] were invoked as correctives to adult proclivities—constantly in sermons, frequently in pedagogical writings—but they supplied nothing in the way of concrete suggestions for educating the young. Much more promising as a starting point was the idea of ''crude matter,'' which pictured the infant at birth as a neutral entity and placed on the educator the burden of fashioning the raw substance into something good and useful. Taken from Quintilian into the sixteenth century, and acquiring in the passage a mildly Augustinian overtone, the *rudis massa* concept is prominent in the educational thought of Erasmus, especially in his *De pueris instituendis*, his pedagogical best seller which was first published in 1529 and had great influence on Reformation pedagogy. ''Nature'' was to Erasmus simply the ability to be taught. It does not incline children to wickedness. Men accuse ''nature,'' he says, when they should blame themselves ''for ruining the minds of children by allowing faults to be acquired before directing them to the good.''[30] This position explains Erasmus's emphatic insistence on early childhood training which is the chief purpose of his treatise. Education molds the unformed mass into the shape of a man (''in hominis speciem''). Left to itself the substance would turn ''naturally'' into the image of a beast.[31] Erasmus is not free of latent pessimism. But he has confidence in the power of instruction. As dogs are born for hunting and birds for flying, man is put on earth for the recognition of truth and virtue. Every creature is capable of learning that for which it is born. The human child, when properly taught with purpose and industry, is quick to acquire good discipline. Without such teaching he is speedily corrupted, for humans are always readier to choose the bad than aim at the good.

It is easy to see how Erasmus failed to give a satisfactory answer to the contradiction posed by his classical and Christian sources. While rejecting—often indignantly—rigorous Augustinianism, he was enough of a pessimist to agree that education should be more than helping natural abilities to unfold. Unremitting vigilance is indicated, for the young are driven by desires, not by judgment. "Indeed, the good is more quickly forgotten than the bad, which we remember much longer."[32] The fact that children succumb instantly to corruption from external influences had been unquestioningly accepted since antiquity. It was, moreover, common knowledge that the young were an unruly, naturally rebellious, shiftless, and fickle lot. There was no disagreement with Plato on this ("Of all the animals the boy is the most unmanageable, since the fountain of reason in him is not yet regulated"), nor with his corrective: "When he gets away from mothers and nurses, he must be under the management of tutors."[33] This conclusion could be buttressed with comments from Augustine to the effect that the young were naturally lazy and irresponsible, capable of effort only when placed under constraint.[34]

Such basic convictions about human nature tended to be applied indiscriminately across the age span from infancy to adolescence. But this does not mean that authors failed to make distinctions among the obvious stages of biological development. Divisions of childhood and youth into the periods of *infantia, pueritia,* and *adolescentia* were ancient. Pagan as well as Judeo-Christian sources could be consulted on this tripartite division, as well as on finer discriminations, based upon observed behavior within each phase.[35] Thus Augustine distinguishes between the nursing and the learning-to-speak phases of infancy, and between the *puer loquens,* who has just emerged from childish helplessness, and a later condition of *pueritia,* just preceding puberty, when reason begins to be active.[36] Far from being periods of mere physical growth, the stages of youth leave profound and lasting experiences in the psyche. With the development of memory in infancy comes the retention of impressions. Augustine maintains that all early impressions are stored and become the formative experience which shape the adult man.[37] When the power of will first asserts itself, also in infancy, the child begins to notice the outside world, but sees it as an object of resistance to his instinctive wishes. Taking his will to be a command, he responds violently if denied. Thus the will is established early on as the driving faculty it is in adulthood.[38] Augustine's psychological perspicacity is unusual among the sources of the pedagogical tradition, but the importance he attributes to development itself is a matter of general agreement. Human life was lived in stages, the onset of each of which signaled an important physical and mental transformation.[39]

There was no doubt about the significance of one such stage, adolescence, coming at age fourteen.[40] It would be difficult to improve upon the picture of the inner storms and pressures, the restless longing and seeking for something not clearly perceived which is conveyed by Augustine in his *Confessions* (II, 2 and III, 1). A similar impression, though a much cruder one, emerges from the books of Vincent of Beauvais and Aegidius Romanus on the education of young princes, where the adolescent's rampant pride, arrogance, and rebelliousness are stressed.[41] All authors clearly identify the source of these tensions and excesses as sexual. Unrestrained by experience of consequences and with no care about the future,[42] adolescents, in the first flush of their physical powers, are driven to "natural" vices: lying, blaspheming, violence and cruelty, theft, disobedience of parents and disrespect toward their elders, idleness, gambling, recklessness and lack of shame, and—to come to the point—"voluptuous desires which consume the body and mind," namely masturbation and sexual advances ("contactus sui ipsius in locis abstrusis aut aliorum eiusdem sexus"). Catalogues of this sort were frequent in the pedagogical literature. The one just cited comes from Wimpheling's *Adolescentia*,[43] but Wimpheling takes it mainly from Gerson who, as is well known, was fixated on the apparently irrepressible sexual proclivities of adolescent boys, the gravest peril to their souls, as he saw it.[44] Sensuality had to be suppressed to the extent it was possible to do so by influencing youthful minds. No sexual stimulus was permitted in the seeing and hearing of young boys; Gerson never ceased to plead with secular and religious authorities for help in guarding the young from corruption. At the very least, he thought, these safeguards would delay sexual maturity until the boy had acquired some self-control.[45] All authors agreed that a more or less rigorous system of control was needed to keep boys of from fourteen to sixteen from destroying themselves for life. Even those who, like Erasmus in his *Colloquies*, make no attempt to conceal the unabashed sexuality which seems to have existed among the young in the early modern period deplore the effects of it on character and fortitude. Few writers, incidentally, addressed themselves more than cursorily to the problems of female adolescence, although when Vives, writing on the education of girls, quotes Jerome's "neither the burning of Etna, nor the country of Vulcan . . . boils with such heat as the bodies of young folk inflamed with wine and delicate meats,"[46] it is clear to everyone what he is saying.

All that was written on adolescence, then, pointed to the conclusion that in this, as well as in the earlier, even more impressionable phases of young life, nothing beneficial to the individual and to society could be achieved through any means other than restrictive ones. All authors advocated kindness and understanding. But the idea that the young might be allowed to develop with a minimum, rather than a maximum, of coercive authority was—if discussed at all—declared to be abhorrent. In any case, childhood and adolescence were seen as stages to be transcended, as a segment of life the sooner surmounted the better. Early life was obviously important to the educator. But it was understood as a period of privation, a stage leading, if correct educational means were employed, to something better. Child into man was a passage from imperfection to—if not perfection[47]—then at least to something less imperfect. Adulthood, or the change in status from *adolescens* to *iuvenis*, signified success in having learned to overcome the traits of childishness rooted in the instinctive, untaught, unrefined nature of man. To be a child meant saying whatever came into one's head, craving none but frivolous things, giving thought only to the cares of the moment, being unclean and enjoying it, being unreliable and fickle, reacting to the world with superstition and fear, desiring everything one saw and wanting it all at once, showing lack of consideration for others, and being thoughtless and self-centered.[48] Such enumerations of childish traits were common in the literature. No one idealized the young.[49]

Everything said so far relates to the *nature* of the young—that is to say, to the instinctual, emotional, and biological drives which equip the basic human personality with its natural impulses and impetus. Against nature, seen in this way, was set mind, intellect, *ingenium,* the seat of intelligence and reasoning power. Nature was force, mind was retraint, holding the reins and, if resourceful and skilled, able to guide impulses and control drives. The training of the mind is the first important task of the educator, for (to quote Augustine in a less pessimistic vein) in the child "reason and intelligence somehow slumber, as if non-existent, but ready to be roused and developed with the increase of age, so as to become capable of knowledge and learning. . . . Thanks to these faculties it may imbibe wisdom and be endowed with the virtues so as to struggle . . . against errors and the other inborn vices and conquer them."[50]

What enables the mind to know? The question may be narrowed at once. Pedagogues had mundane concerns. They worked toward the inculcation of practical disciplines the possession of which defined the useful member of church and society. True knowledge, knowledge of metaphysical and religious truth, did not enter their province, for they generally accepted Augustine's distinction between two kinds of knowing or, rather, two levels of knowing: the grasping of essential truth, which is a matter of illumination and not available to all, and ordinary knowledge, useful information. The distinction does not affect the work of practical teaching through which the usual disciplines are communicated by means of language and other "signs."[51] Sixteenth-century pedagogues were for obvious reasons unable to adopt the ideal tutoring situation portrayed by Augustine in his book on the teacher, a situation—in the sixteenth-century context a Utopian idyll—where mentors guided and suggested while pupils "consider within themselves whether what has been said is true . . . by gazing attentively at that interior truth, so far as they are able."[52] In the 1530s practical teaching faced different problems. But the educators of this period must have shared Erasmus's conviction that "there is no branch of learning for which the human mind is not receptive," for without embracing this innate capability as a starting point of their endeavors, they would at the very outset have reduced themselves to mere drillmasters (a task many did, in fact, accept later on when disappointing results cast a shadow on earlier expectations). Erasmus added a proviso to this optimistic assessment of the mind: "As long as we do not fail to supply instruction and practice."[53] This, indeed, was the province of the pedagogue. Instruction and practice "depend entirely on our industry," Erasmus said.[54] Here solid work could be done.

Nearly all authors agreed that three elements were necessary to effective learning: natural endowment ("the ability to grasp easily what they hear and to retain firmly what they grasp"),[55] practice (usually called *exercitium* or *exercitatio*), and discipline. If learning was the development of potentiality into actuality, as suggested by the useful scholastic model,[56] practice and discipline were the means by which the transition was effected. The teacher himself was the efficient cause of the knowledge engendered in the pupil. Thomas Aquinas saw the mind working naturally by the method of "discovery" (inventio). Good instruction imitates this method: "Natural reason by itself reaches knowledge of unknown things; this way is called 'discovery.' In the other way someone else aids the learner's natural reason, and this is called 'learning by instruction,' [disciplina]. . . . For the teacher leads the pupil to knowledge of things he does not know in the same way that one directs himself: through the process of discovering something he does not know."[57] Natural learning proceeds by turning into concrete and particular knowledge concepts at first only indistinctly grasped ("by sense we judge of the more common before the less common"). In the same way, teaching moves from the general to the particular, aiming at orderly arrangement.

What was learned was stored up in memory through an activity sometimes called "gathering" (colligere). Thomas, who was not very much interested in practical educational questions, said nothing about this, but other writers told how it was accomplished: "Reducing to a brief and compendious outline things which have been written and discussed at some length."[58] The faculty of memory had since antiquity been regarded as a prime indicator of the ability of a mind to learn easily and well. Quintilian said so, and what he said was restated by nearly every educational writer who came after him.[59] The capacity of the human mind which so excited Quintilian—"so swift and nimble and versatile that it cannot be restricted to doing one thing only"[60]—depended in the first instance on memory. In Augustine's persuasive presentation (De Trinitate, books 9–14) memory is pictured as the scene where thought takes place; understanding (intelligentia) works with the materials found there and subjects them to imagination and reasoning; the will acts as catalyst, gets the thought process under way, and gives it direction and purpose.[61] Memory, intelligence, and will, while affected in their qualities by inborn endowment, are subject to training. Innumerable mnemotechnic manuals and devices attest to the conviction present throughout medieval and early modern history that a good memory was, at least in large part, the result of practice. With memory trained and subject matter well arranged, learning was not much of a problem. Only occasions had to be provided, and able instructors, and some form of compulsion to overcome inertia.

Some authors went very far in their efforts to present the activity of learning as an orderly and essentially simple procedure. Rudolf Agricola, for example, a widely read humanist and pedagogical writer whose De formando studio was written in 1484 and first printed in 1518, having asked rhetorically, What distinguishes the scholar's mind from the books he reads? replies, There is very little difference, except that the human mind is more efficient and—if equipped with a keen memory—quicker in its operation than a book, even a well-designed commonplace book. Able minds have swift recall. More important, the mind can use the stored material for new purposes not originally foreseen when information was placed in the memory. Unlike books, the mind works with general governing concepts to which facts are related as we learn them. These enable us to have new thoughts.[62]

This kind of reductionism, which pictured the mind as an efficient engine with discrete parts and a tidy division of mechanical operations, simplified matters enormously for pedagogues. While nothing could be done about the pupil's *natura*, his talent, much might be accomplished by working on *ratio*, his thinking faculty, and *exercitatio*, the practiced discipline with which he employed it. (The Latin words are Erasmus's; terms differ slightly among the various authors but refer to the same faculties.) Teaching procedures and materials in the sixteenth century reflect this prevailing model of the mind and its operations. Intellectual differences among children were recognized, of course,[63] and the gifted were quickly spotted and advanced to special schools. But there was also the conviction, and a sense of rightness in holding it, that instruction can, to a considerable extent, level the gifts unequally bestowed by nature.[64] Erasmus enjoyed telling Plutarch's story about Lycurgus and the two puppies, one a highly bred but ill-trained animal, the other a mongrel but carefully drilled. Not surprisingly, Lycurgus discovered that the latter performed better. "Nature can do much," comments Erasmus, "but instruction is superior because it can do more" ("efficax res est natura, sed hanc vincit efficacior institutio").[65] Education was mainly training, and every child could be trained. The modest expectations held by Reformation pedagogues for all but their brightest pupils were thought to be attainable by all minds in good working order.

This conviction was supported by another set of assumptions about the pupil's responses to learning situations. It was believed that the human being exhibits certain basic psychological impulses affecting his interaction with his fellow men. If presented in the form of appeals to these impulses, learning is not simply a possible result, but a highly likely one.

At the most rudimentary level there was the pleasure-pain principle. Plato had written that this was responsible for the initial impetus to all actions,[66] and educators made use of this principle in many ways. Erasmus argued at length that learning should be fun to the young child—make it a game, he said[67]—but he was only restating what had often been said before. It was, after all, mere common sense, verified by experience, that children always seek delight and avoid pain.[68] Hence the many injunctions to "make play a road for learning" and to offer frequent rewards "so that [the child] may love what [he] is forced to do, and it be not work but pleasure, not a matter of necessity but one of free will."[69]

Sterner pedagogues could draw from the same principle a more rigorous physiological interpretation and employ it to create situations where positive and negative reinforcement techniques produced desired responses. Plutarch's popular treatise on the education of children suggested how this might be done. Counseling against the use of corporal punishment as unfit for freeborn youngsters, Plutarch recommended instead the use of methodical praise and rebuke: "It is well to choose some time when children are full of confidence to put them to shame by rebuke, and then in turn to cheer them up by praises, and to imitate the nurses who,

VII

when they have made their babies cry, in turn offer them the breast for comfort.''
He concludes: ''These two things—hope of reward and fear of punishment—are,
as it were, the elements of virtue.''[70] There were other ways, too, some not so
gentle as Plutarch's. In view of generally prevailing notions that early educational
thought was a set of variations on the theme of corporal punishment, it should be
said at once that the weight of traditional authority was emphatically against this
device. Quintilian, Plutarch, Maffeo Vegio, Battista Guarino, Wimpheling, and
Erasmus were quoted in condemnation of this inhuman practice,[71] and explicit
rules against it in the school ordinances of the sixteenth century show that this
advice was accepted. On the other hand there existed in many minds an irrepressible, nagging suspicion that natural wickedness required unnatural punishment.
The Old Testament supplied a wealth of vivid passages to prove that punishment
administered by parents and educators was a good and godly thing; indeed, it has
been pointed out that the very word for education in Hebrew came from the term
for chastisement.[72] These passages exerted a certain influence on sixteenth-
century teachers. There is, however, hardly an educational writer of the medieval
and early modern periods who fails to point out that severe and frequent punishment is counterproductive. Vives, for example, who tended to disagree with the
rejection on principle of all corporal punishment, regarded corrective blows as
effective only if held in abeyance, as a threat. In any case, as with pleasure-
oriented stimuli, the use of the human inclination to avoid pain suggested itself by
way of common sense and observation. But if authorities were consulted on this
point, the arguments against harsh punishment as a stimulus to learning were not
only more eloquent, but also more practical than those arguments recommending
it.[73]

Beyond simple reactions to pleasure and pain—but of course not independent of
them—there was the innate urge to compete for success. Appeals to this impulse
were highly recommended in the literature, but for Reformation pedagogues the
principle of competitiveness was a two-edged weapon, as easily turned against
their best efforts as it was likely to advance them. Their image of the desirable
man, the new man, was of a being freed from the ultimately self-destructive ego
drives of ambition. Nevertheless they recognized competition as a fact of life and
made use of it for—they hoped—good purposes.

The principle of competition was said to depend on the instinctive operation of
two urges, the positive desire to excel, to win fame and honor, and the equally
pronounced negative wish to avert disgrace and avoid shame. The possibility of
appealing to these desires had, of course, long been recognized. The literature
furnished abundant proofs of their effectiveness and many illustrations of their use
in practical teaching. Writers who, as Christians, deplored the persistence of the
deadly sins among men nevertheless endorsed the sense of pride as a beneficial
impetus to good scholastic performance. Jerome was often quoted: ''Let her [the
girl Pàula about whom he was writing] have companions in her lessons, so that she
may seek to rival them and be stimulated by any praise they win. . . . Let her be
glad when she is first and sorry when she falls behind.''[74]

The writers of the Italian Renaissance supplied most of the arguments for using the urge to excel as the psychological ground of successful teaching. Battista Guarino denied even the possibility of teaching where the desire to excel is lacking. This, he says, was recognized by his famous father Guarino da Verona and made the starting point of his practice.[75] Maffeo Vegio suggests a number of devices for awakening feelings of honor and ambition in young boys.[76] The judicious and sparing bestowal of praise, he says, produces a "noble contest" among pupils. Boys may be seated in ranked order, each according to his performance. Let the brightest boys always display their attainments before the whole group. Never hesitate to give preferential treatment to achievers; this will not fail to spur the rest to greater efforts, which is a good thing not only for performance, but for character as well. Few writers troubled to explain the inconsistency between their adoption of the principle of competitive ambition on the one hand and their Christian values on the other; some, indeed, made the incongruity obvious. Thus Wimpheling says that the signs of a good disposition in the young are the striving for praise and the desire for honor and fame ("studio laudis excitari incendique amore gloriae").[77] This he takes from Piero Paolo Vergerio's *De ingenuis moribus,* where it is asserted that a sound nature is one that is stimulated by praise. Upon this stimulus rests emulation, "which may be defined as rivalry without malice."[78] On the other hand Wimpheling concludes his treatise with a set of cautionary maxims taken from Petrarch (alphabetized for ready reference), prominent among which is the reminder that fame is an empty bubble: "Fama ventus est, fumus est, umbra est, nihil est."[79] Wimpheling may never have reflected on the incongruity between the two attitudes demanded by these contrasting pieces of advice. He was not much of a thinker. But he was a useful purveyor of wisdom gathered from others. And the received wisdom accepted ambition, and relied on it. Only Vives among early modern pedagogues was consistent to his religious values in rejecting ambition. But Vives looked at the world with a much colder eye, and he had seen too much havoc done by the search for fame and glory to accept it as a guiding principle for the education of the young.

As effective as the wish to be praised was the fear of being put to shame. Most pedagogical authors advise reliance on this as an alternative to physical punishment. Inflicting pain and humiliation is not needed where the dread of failure and the sense of shame are utilized.[80] These fears are innate in human nature; it is the teacher's job to bring them into the pupil's consciousness and establish them as impulses to action. The teacher who does this well is a good teacher.[81] A visible manifestation of the sense of shame is the tendency to blush. Boys who blush readily reveal their susceptibility to this appeal.[82] *Pudor,* the "fear of deserved censure," is an effective internal control and obviates the use of the rod in all but desperate cases.[83]

By playing on the child's inborn senses and feelings the knowing teacher could thus begin to shape his pupil's mind and mold his personality. He had every confidence that instruction early in life would determine the entire direction of an individual's existence. The pedagogical tradition sustained him in this conviction.

Plato's system of compulsory training, prescribed and supervised by a board of philosophers in accordance with fixed norms and rules, was too distant from recognizable reality to be of specific use, but it did make available a powerful argument for systematic indoctrination in the service of an idea. Where the ideal mandated a renovation of the human personality—as it certainly did in the Reformation—Plato's *Republic* was a relevant text. But the entire pedagogical tradition could be summoned to supply evidence that such renovation could really be done, that the child, at a young and tender age, could in fact "be molded to take the impression one wishes to stamp on it."[84]

The extreme position on this point is given by Plutarch's lapidary "character is habit long continued."[85] Christian writers ought not to have accepted this assertion in principle. They should have known too much about sin and its effects to be tempted into regarding the moral character as a neutral substance shaped by habit. But Plutarch's observation is never explicitly challenged, and it is very often repeated. In its weakened form—"youth is impressionable and plastic, and while such minds are still tender, lessons are infused deeply into them"[86]—it is certainly unexceptionable. A more moderate and feasible position on early childhood education therefore expected of the teacher nothing more than the successful inculcation of right ideas, sound purposes, and good habits which, even if the child's nature tended to wickedness, would set him on a straight path. Thus, Aegidius Romanus advocates religious indoctrination for all children at an early age. Since the Christian faith cannot be proven by reason, he says, and is best accepted in a spirit of simple credulity, it is most efficaciously imbued in childhood.[87] This is true also of habits of civility and morality. Let children be trained "not to see" objects catering to base instincts. For what they absorb early in life they will remember always.[88] Jean Gerson, as has been seen, spent much effort in arguing that children should never be subjected to sense impressions that would make them lifelong slaves to passion.[89] More important, he had practical suggestions on how to shape the little ones into good Christians. The confessional, he thought, offered the best means of sound indoctrination. He speaks of rooting the habit of confession in children. But public instruction and preaching are also vital to the creation of the proper environment.[90] In a social setting very different from the one Gerson had in mind, Maffeo Vegio proposed the creation of a complete environment for the young child, in which he might develop a forceful character, a good disposition, and habits appropriate to the pursuit of worthwhile aims.[91]

Like all writers, Maffeo used the plastic argument. You can make the child what you wish. It is like soft wax. Bend the twig and the tree will incline as you wish. Even more revealing of how pedagogical writers imagined the process of molding is the constantly drawn analogy to the training of animals.[92] Erasmus has the most to say on this, and he says it very divertingly in his little book on early education. You train a puppy from birth; why not a child?[93] He multiplies examples from the animal kingdom until he has covered it from parrots to elephants. His *declamatio* is, in fact, of all pedagogical treatises the most emphatic on beginning the conditioning process in infancy, almost from the moment of birth, not only the indoctrination of behavior, but of learning too. To fail to do this is to waste the most receptive years and to miss the best chance of making a lasting impression. Without the shaping hand of the educator, Erasmus says, the child will grow into a wild creature, not a man. Teaching is everything. The crude mass of life must be molded to shape. There is no use deploring the effects of sin. This is empty posturing. It is we who are at fault if a child turns out badly, for we have allowed him to take on faults before directing him to the good. It is impossible to unlearn bad habits, but easy to be trained in good ones, so long as training comes early in life.[94] Basic nature may be impervious to mutation; but the evil to which man is inclined may, as Vives writes, "be amended by education" ("disciplina emendatur").[95]

It would be otiose to quote passages from the literature to show that Erasmus's and Vives's arguments for early conditioning were the received wisdom. Pedagogical writers spoke with one voice on this, and they prove the contention by citing the young child's pliability, his innocence and trusting openness, and the facility with which he absorbs and remembers what he is taught.[96] In any case, early learning is mere rote work, for which the child, even the infant, is especially well suited.[97]

How does one get him started? There was agreement on this point too: Utilize the child's natural love of imitation to get his physiological and psychological impulses under way. The *imitandi libido* exists even in infants. You may see it, says Erasmus, in the signs of joy they give when they have succeeded in imitating something. They are like monkeys. It is this eagerness to imitate which makes children "docile," ready to be taught.[98] The knowing educator will use this readiness methodically, moving from imitation of simple acts and words to emulation of complex ones. As Quintilian said, "Repeated imitation passes into habit" ("frequens imitatio transit in mores").[99] Quintilian is at pains to point out that no more than a learning technique is suggested here. Imitation is not enough. The object of study is not rote imitation. It is to reach inventiveness and independent judgment.[100] But it remains a rule of life that "it is expedient to imitate whatever has been invented with success."[101] For the first years of life this is the cardinal rule. It shapes the personality. Directed imitation passes by frequent repetition into habit, and—as we have seen—"character is habit long continued."[102]

"If one were to call the virtues of character the virtues of habit," Plutarch continues, "he would not seem to go far astray."[103] This generally accepted assertion gave educators much confidence in their labors. Over habits they had some measure of control. If, in his actions and reactions, the finished person was indeed the sum of the habits instilled in him, they had some hope of success in their attempts to shape him to conform to their standards. Plutarch's dictum did not need to be taken literally for educators to devote the most careful attention to that part of their activity which dealt with the formation of habits.

The fundamental importance of habit training had been pointed out by Aristotle when he cautioned against establishing in the young person behavior and thought patterns uninformed by reason and good purpose. Once firmly set, habit was all but ineradicable. "It is possible for man to be wrongly trained through the habits," he warned; we can prevent this only "if the most perfect harmony [is created] between reason and habit." Since the body develops before the soul, habituation must precede the training of understanding.[104] Man shares with all animals the propensity for modifying his nature by means of acquired habit (an argument favored by Christian writers confronting rigorous Augustinian pessimism).[105] Understood as a way of acting and thinking with sufficient frequency and regularity to have become unconscious, habit turns into a kind of second nature. "Consuetudo est quasi altera natura" was a commonplace among medieval and early modern educational writers.[106] If bad habits learned early in life are inextinguishable,[107] good habits may be as firmly rooted. It takes practice and endless repetition. Stoic philosophy reinforced the point: the mind, Seneca said, can "by practice make mercy its own" ("usu suam faciat").[108] Seneca was speaking of adults, who knew what they were doing, and why. But the method worked even better with the young. Accustom the child to do and think by rote habit what reason tells you he should do. Don't confuse him with explanations and justifications. Unpremeditated response is enough at this stage of life. Understanding will come later and with it his acceptance, as right and good, of rules the compliance with which has already become automatic.[109]

Extravagant claims were sometimes made in the sixteenth century for the power of habit. Vives encouraged mothers to think that their intimate control over young children's lives empowered them "to form [their] disposition. For she may make them what she will—good or bad."[110] Supporting evidence could be found in pediatric literature from Galen[111] to the medical popularizers of the sixteenth century, who asserted that good habits, inculcated early on, were capable even of changing a child's "complexion."[112] Few words turn up with greater frequency in the educational regulations of the Reformation than "habituation" (*Gewöhnung, consuetudo, usus*). No other pedagogical idea is more confidently accepted as a good thing and more insistently applied as the only way. It was hoped, of course, that comprehension would come later, and with it internalization of rules and doctrines first imposed by drill: "For the young cannot grasp our teachings unless they are first habituated to them by means of verbatim repetition."[113] Events would show that this was a vain hope. Little or no understanding seemed to come to most men. But in the end educators could at least console themselves with the thought that as long as habits stuck, their work had not been entirely futile.

III

Nature, impulses, responses, habits—the pedagogical literature had much to say on these. It had accumulated a large body of pedagogical assertions and reflections which—profound or not, empirically verifiable or not—generated confidence by showing agreement on many important problems, and by frequent reiteration of arguments advanced by writers of unassailable authority.

To what general educational purpose were pedagogical ideas harnessed? What specific goals of education were implicitly assumed and explicitly advocated in the literature? Let us first state some underlying propositions about educational activity itself. It was generally agreed that education must proceed in accordance with a governing purpose. The definition of this ideal was not, of course, the function of educators; but unless they accepted it, they labored without purpose. Secondly, education cannot limit itself to one part of the human personality or to one side of life; it must instruct the young in religion, in the arts, and in civility, and it must instruct them in these simultaneously. Finally, educational activity must be not only high minded, but also competent. The pedagogical literature set high standards for the teaching profession; it also furnished some practical directives on techniques. But all this was rudimentary, and it hardly needs to be said that a wide gap separated expectations from the ability of educators to fulfill them.

Specific educational goals were various, but not often clearly defined, at least not clearly enough to permit tidy classification. There seem to have been three groups of objectives. The first describes educational goals as an aspect of civic well-being, society being the general object of education, the citizen's place in society its particular goal. As its most grandiose the end is the creation of the ideal state, or the rigorous reform of an existing less-than-ideal one, by means of the education of its citizens. More modestly considered, education aims at the inculcation in the individual of a code of civic ethics likely to make him a useful member of the commonwealth.

Plato's state—the ideal state of the *Republic* and the model state of the *Laws*— was a compelling instance of the harmony of education and politics.[114] In the sixteenth-century context Plato's propositions had no practical application, but Lutheran theologians and pedagogues would have been well advised to mind Plato's demonstration of how an ethos established as the guiding principle of a society may be transmitted by means of education to the new generations who are to uphold and practice it in the future. There is no doubt that many of the leading proponents of the Reformation hoped that this could now be done. At the very least they recognized the relationship between religious and civic virtues and advocated early indoctrination in both. It was a truism to say—and nearly every writer in the pedagogical tradition did say it—that the commonwealth flourished only while its citizens accepted its principles as their own, or at least acted as if they did. The culture of the community defines the normative values of the individual. It must determine the pattern of his education. Education therefore was a public concern, and nearly every writer from Plato and Quintilian to the Renaissance said so.[115] Few Lutheran pedagogues evinced much interest in the particular civic virtues on which the educators of the Italian Renaissance placed such emphasis.[116] But they knew that peace and prosperity in the community depended on the good behavior of its members, and they quoted the "Christian" humanists on the important place to be given in pedagogy to civic education.[117]

A second objective was predominantly religious. At the maximum it sought to create in the individual person, insofar as it could be done by human effort, those dispositions which were the preconditions of salvation. The moral and religious restoration of Christendom was to be the aggregate result of this effort in individual reform. Augustine defined the problems and indicated the possibilities of this endeavor. The origin of sin lies in man's natural pride (*superbia*). Pride is expressed in thoughts and acts of egotism (*amor sui*). Only grace can deliver man from this condition, but hope of grace is open only to those who have faced up to their predicament and entered the state of humility in which they come to recognize themselves as sinners, as a *massa peccati*.[118] This image of man and his condition defines the role of education: Destroy the "old man," the "old Adam," and raise the "new man." Augustine states the aim of Christian education most explicitly in *De vera religione* (which argues that Christianity grasps fully what Platonism had seen but dimly). He passes before us the ages of man: infancy and the purely nutritive existence; childhood, when memories are stored; adolescence and the onset of sexual power; manhood with its responsibilities; and lastly the calm of old age. "This," he concludes the review, "is the life of man so far as he lives in the body. . . . This is the 'old man,' the 'exterior or earthly man.' " Among these old men some are reborn: "With their spiritual strength and increase of wisdom they overcome the 'old man' and put him to death and bring him into subjection to the celestial laws. This is 'the new man,' 'the inward and heavenly man.' "[119] The aim of all education, then, is to augment the qualities necessary to the inward creation of the new man. With the *humilitas Christi* as his paradigm, the educator selects specific goals and procedures toward the restructuring of the sinner's personality, insofar as it is amenable to human manipulation. Augustine did not raise very much hope on that score. But he did reject passivity and resignation, encouraging men instead to be energetic in the endeavor to supplant the self-seeking impulses of the old man with the humility and charity of the new man.

Obviously, Augustine's design is too schematic to be a prescription for teaching anyone or anything. His ideal types are as abstract as are Plato's concepts. They are about Man, not men. They can be usefully tested only as theology. Still, the enormous religious and moral force pulsating in his phrases exercised a strong hold upon sixteenth-century theologians and pedagogues, who succeeded in bringing Augustine down to earth by translating the abstract qualities that defined his old and new men into concrete vices and virtues, recognizable to every observer of the human scene and largely congruous with the traits enumerated by secular-minded pedagogues as the attributes of citizenship. The overwhelming majority of Christian writers on pedagogy described their desired objective, the product of right education, as a young man exhibiting habits of obedience, humility, modesty, submissiveness, a bland passivity of behavior, and lifelong docility.[120] Vives thought that human faculties could stand a bit of blunting. Not that he wanted boys made dull or stupid; but at the end of their education they ought to be simpler, more honest, less cunning, above all less self-seeking persons than the "natural" creatures they had been at the beginning.[121] This product was a long way from the exuberance and precocious self-confidence of Quintilian's ideal youngster, who "runs riot in the luxuriance of his growth."[122] Christianity is not the only explanation of the distance between the two types. It was also that the Christian writers of the early modern period saw the violence and tensions of their age as being in large part the result of the indifference and permissiveness with which parents, as well as society as a whole, allowed the young to develop and give free play to their natural impulses. In the days of antiquity, Erasmus notes shrewdly, pedagogues could count on the homogeneity of their culture to do their educating for them. Alas, such conditions prevail no longer.[123] The young must be taken in hand. They cannot be left to themselves, or to society at large. They must be taught. There is no other way to individual reform, nor to social renovation.

The third group of educational writers concerned themselves less with social objectives than with the individual person's drive to self-fulfillment. It will be obvious that this group had least to say to sixteenth-century reformers, who lacked sympathy with the implicit assumptions of Renaissance humanism. On the other hand, the liberal and often very eloquent pleas on behalf of the intellectually, emotionally, and physically growing young person could be taken as a corrective to the many suppressive tendencies in Lutheran education. To enlarge the mind,[124] to direct the growing person toward "virtus et gloria" as the only worthwhile pursuits,[125] to create in him resources for becoming the "vir probus atque perfectus" or the "homo virtuoso,"[126] to build a foundation for self-respect by encouraging methodical examination of conscience[127]—these were noble objectives. They were beyond the reach of all but the select few for whom pedagogical writers in the classical tradition had always written.[128] They related to a social and political setting increasingly alien to the conditions for which Reformation theologians were legislating. Above all, they offered no concrete suggestions for solving the most vexing of the problems facing reformers in the 1530s. But as reminders of a humane tradition they never lost their force. As sentences from the works of the great authorities they continued to command respect. And in Erasmus's eloquent and reasonable fusion of these ideals with the cause of religious reform, Lutheran pedagogues could, if they wished, find justification for tempering their theoretical and empirical pessimism with the benign gentility of classical humanism.[129] Erasmus's goal of a "sapiens et eloquens pietas" could be cultivated as common ground. It was, in fact, an attainable goal for that part of Reformation pegagogy which concentrated on the training of a professional elite. But Lutheran pedagogues also wished to cast a wider net. And to the purposes of mass indoctrination in the rudiments of religion and in the minimum requirements of useful and peaceful citizenship, the humanist ideal had no practical contribution to make.

IV

The Pedagogical literature spoke not only on fundamental questions relating to guiding purposes and methods. It also offered suggestions on a host of corollary issues on which sixteenth-century reformers ill prepared by experience to make decisions sought the counsel of tradition. Is education best accomplished in public institutions or in the home? This question answered itself in the 1530s, but it was comforting to know that the pedagogical tradition spoke overwhelmingly with the reformers in urging the creation of a system of public schools. Who has authority to establish and control such schools? Again, the answer was clear: the lawgiver, the state. Erasmus's uncompromising phrase "opportet scholam aut nullam esse aut publicam"[130] epitomizes the discussion reaching back to Quintilian and brings it up to date with an excoriation of teaching by monks and unskilled privateers. Should learning and teaching be rigidly structured, or should they be informal? Arguments existed on each side of this question, but writers whose concerns coincided most closely with those of Lutheran reformers recommended formalized curricula and instruction. These were adopted. The role of the family in education was an important consideration for the reformers, specifically the training given in infancy and the responsibilities of fathers and mothers toward their children's formal schooling. On these points, too, the tradition was informative, as also on questions concerning the education of girls—whether or not, how much, to what end. The literature abounded with detailed suggestions on practical methods and instructional devices. Curricula were, of course, entirely conventional in the sixteenth century. Only the introduction of the catechism as an instrument of mass education offered opportunities for new departures. These were very rarely grasped, however; and innovational teaching, in the sense of experimenting with methods not recommended in the classical and medieval literature, was unknown. Persuasive arguments existed for setting standards of professional skill for teachers; indeed teacher training, to the extent that this could be carried out in the sixteenth century, owes something to the idea that formal education should be so systematically organized that, as Quintilian wrote, if anyone fails to learn, "The fault will lie not with the method but with the individual."[131] To these and other concerns the pedagogical literature made solid contributions.

In general the pedagogical literature gave powerful support to ideas and assumptions already firmly lodged in the reformers' thoughts. Few pedagogues could have approached the problems of education with an open mind. They came to them with their guiding concepts intact. The literature supplied pedagogues with a battery of arguments to present their case for a reorganization of the educational structure according to the principles of the Reformation. It convinced them that the learning process was a simple mechanism which could, without great difficulty, be set in motion and given momentum. It lent them the confidence of knowing that behind their own efforts stood an ancient and intellectually unimpugnable tradition. And this tradition sustained them in their sense of being engaged in a profoundly important enterprise on whose success or failure rested the shape of the future.

Less fortunately, the literature encouraged them in their unwillingness or inability to consider educational questions from the point of view of the child. Granted, this is a criticism of doubtful historical validity. But one is almost forced to make it by the insuppressible and, to us, irritating inclination of pedagogical authors to discourse upon the nature and behavior of children without giving much evidence of having studied them. It has already been said that there was no lack of interest in children. Nor is a certain warmth and sympathy absent from the literature about the young. Many passages could be quoted to convey the human feelings aroused by their subject in most authors. But these natural responses to the affective appeal of the theme of education did not prompt writers to increase their familiarity with real children. They did not ask what flesh-and-blood, true-to-life children were like, what their needs were, what it felt like to be subjected to educational methods drawn from their theories.

In the end, what mattered to the reformers, as it had mattered to older pedagogical writers, was the objective result obtained by their procedures. The Lutheran theologian cared for the faith he preached and for the religious disposition of the society which did or did not live by this faith. Similarly, Erasmus and Vives showed genuine concern only for the fate of the learned disciplines they loved, not for the child who was expected to acquire them. Few if any authors were much interested in the individual youth, except as the recipient of their ideas and the respondent to them. Sixteenth-century educators thought in abstractions. The "natural" child was one such abstraction; a second was the finished, educated product seen as a model conceived on the lines of a biblical Tobias, an Isaac, or a Joseph. The good society peopled by such types was a third.

To say all this is merely to repeat a well-known fact. But it is one which goes a long way toward explaining another fact not so well known. The educational enterprise of the Lutheran reformers was a failure when judged by their own aims. It was a grand failure, perhaps even a tragic one. But a failure it was, nonetheless, and as such an important historical factor. The disappointing outcome of their fervently pursued educational endeavor affected the ways in which reformers understood and judged themselves. It forced them to reappraise their efforts and their talents. It gave them second thoughts about their mission. It may even have led them to doubt their cause. But this is a different story, which need not be told here.

NOTES

1. The sense of living at the end of time was implicit in much that was said and done by the first generation of the Reformation. On Luther's complex views concerning the possibilities and limits of education, see the stimulating discussion by Ivar Asheim, *Glaube und Erziehung bei Luther* (Heidelberg, 1961), esp. pp. 88ff. Also interesting is Edgar Reimers, *Recht und Grenzen einer Berufung auf Luther in den neueren Bemühungen um eine evangelische Erziehung* (Weinheim, 1958).

2. For a particularly striking account of the impact of the religious and political troubles of the 1520s on a reformer's mind, see Wilhelm Maurer, *Der junge Melanchthon*, 2 vols. (Göttingen, 1967–69), esp. vol. 2.

3. These arguments are acknowledged and met in Luther's *An die Ratsherren aller Städte . . . dass sie christliche Schulen aufrichten und halten sollen* (1524), W[eimar] A[usgabe] XV, pp. 9–53.

4. For a convenient list of these ordinances, in chronological order, see Georg Mertz, *Das Schulwesen der deutschen Reformation* (Heidelberg, 1902), pp. 162–65. Mertz prints the texts of many of these ordinances. Others are printed by Emil Sehling, ed., *Die evangelischen Kirchenordnungen des 16. Jahrhunderts*, 5 vols. (Leipzig, 1902–13).

5. See the warning against teaching in the German language in the *Unterricht der Visitatoren* (1528), WA XXVI, p. 236. At that time Luther was concerned mainly with ensuring the church of an adequate supply of trained ministers.

6. From *Decem praecepta Wittenbergensi praedicata populo* (1528), WA I, p. 494, comments on the sixth commandment. The sermons were given in late 1516 and early 1517.

90

7. See the many references to *Kinder* in the index to Luther's Table Talk, WA *Tischreden* VI, pp. 595–96.

8. For one example among many, see *Das Buch Weinsberg*, ed. Johann Jakob Hässlin (Munich, 1961), which contains childhood memories suggesting that parents and children were closely involved with each other.

9. A survey of sixteenth-century medical literature shows that from about 1520 physicians devoted more attention to the diseases of babies and children. A growing number of special treatises on pediatrics were published beginning c. 1540.

10. Very few of the innumerable general histories of education and of educational thought are of much use to the historian. Two exceptions: Josef Dolch, *Lehrplan des Abendlandes: Zweieinhalb Jahrtausende seiner Geschichte* (Ratingen, 1965); Karl Schmidt, *Geschichte der Pädagogik, dargestellt in weltgeschichtlicher Entwicklung*, 4 vols. (Cöthen, 1890), which is encyclopedic. There are, of course, numerous excellent works dealing with particular periods.

11. See Otto Herding's elaborate identification of Jacob Wimpheling's sources in his edition of Wimpheling's *Adolescentia (Jacobi Wimpfelingi opera selecta*, 1 [Munich, 1965]: 31–151).

12. For example, Antonio Mancinelli, *De parentum cura in liberos* . . . (Milan, 1504), a compilation of choice classical and patristic thought on education. Mancinelli gives a chapter each to Plutarch, Quintilian, Plato, Aristotle, Aulus Gellius, Xenophon, Cicero, Diogenes Laertius, the Plinys, the Book of Proverbs, St. Paul, Augustine, Jerome, Isidore of Seville, and Vergerio.

13. Johann Agricola, *Hundert und dreyssig gemeyner Fragestücke für die jungen kinder* . . . (Wittenberg, 1528), preface, Aii verso.

14. Johann Bader, *Ein Gesprächbüchlein vom Anfangk des christlichen Lebens mit dem jungen Volk zu Landaw* (Landau, 1526), quoted in J. P. Gelbert, *Magister Johann Baders Leben und Schriften* (Neustadt, 1968), p. 123. Bader's was one of the earliest Protestant catechisms.

15. Quintilian, *Institutio oratoria* XII, 11, 12. I use the Loeb Classical Library edition with the English translation by H. E. Butler. The *editio princeps* of Quintilian was Rome, 1470.

16. *Ibid.* I, 1, 1f.

17. Augustine, *Confessions* I, 19. Cf. II, 4, on the famous incident of robbing the pear tree. I use the Loeb Classical Library edition with the English translation of William Watts of 1631.

18. Joseph Hogger, *Die Kinderpsychologie Augustins* (Munich, 1937).

19. *De peccatorum meritis et remissione*, in *A Select Library of the Nicene and Post-Nicene Fathers of the Christian Church*, vol. 5, *Augustine's Anti-Pelagian Writings* (New York, 1887), chap. 67. For a particularly strong view of infant sinfulness and a colorful description of its symptoms, see Andreas Osiander, *Catechismus oder kinder Predig* . . . (Nuremberg, 1533), also printed in Johann Michael, Reu, *Quellen zur Geschichte des kirchlichen Unterrichts* . . . , 1 (Gütersloh, 1904): 542–564, esp. 545–46, 556.

20. *Confessions* I, 7, 11. Here I use the translation by Peter Brown, who quotes this passage on pp. 28–29 of his *Augustine of Hippo* (Berkeley, 1967).

21. Hogger, *Die Kinderpsychologie Augustins*, p. 48, remarks shrewdly about Augustine's explanations of his own childhood that "from a hoard of stored-up psychological knowledge he laid bare only such items as would carry a conscious or unconscious conflict into his philosophy of life."

22. See Klaus Petzold, *Die Grundlagen der Erziehungslehre im Spätmittelalter und bei Luther* (Heidelberg, 1969), chap. 2. The first of many editions of Gerson's works was published in Cologne in 1483–84. The Strassburg edition of 1502 was partly edited by Wimpheling.

23. Jean Gerson, *De innocentia puerili*, in *Opera omnia* (Antwerp, 1706), 3: 293–96.

24. For an excellent discussion of this, see Petzold, *Die Grundlagen*, chap. 2.

25. *Tractatus de parvulis trahendis ad Christum*, in *Opera omnia*, 3: 277–91, esp. 283.

26. The first edition of Wimpheling's *Adolescentia* was printed in Strassburg in 1500. Many others followed within a few years. I use the critical edition by Otto Herding (see n. 11 above). For Wimpheling's debt to Gerson, see Herding's introduction (pp. 110–32).

27. *Adolescentia*, Herding ed., pp. 206–40.

28. As advanced, for example, by Clement of Alexandria, *Paedagogus*, ed. H. I. Marrou and Marguerite Harl, 4 vols. (Paris, 1960–70), 1: 19–21.

29. For these, for an excellent discussion of the whole problem, and for a large bibliography, see Werner Jentsch, *Urchristliches Erziehungsdenken: Die Paideia Kyriu im Rahmen der hellenisch-jüdischen Umwelt* (Gütersloh, 1951), particularly pt. 2.

30. *De pueris instituendis*, in the critical edition by J. C. Margolin, *Opera omnia Desiderii Erasmi*, I, 2 (Amsterdam, 1971): 39–40.

31. Ibid., p. 33.

32. Ibid., p. 50.

33. *Laws* 808d.

34. *Confessions* I, 9–10, 12–13.

35. For the immense literature on the subject of the ages of human life see Franz Boll, "Die Lebensalter: Ein Beitrag zur antiken Ethologie und zur Geschichte der Zahlen," *Neue Jahrbücher für das klassische Altertum, Geschichte und deutsche Literatur* 16 (1913): 89–154; and Adolf Hofmeister, "Puer, iuvenis, senex . . . ," in Albert Brockmann, ed., *Papsttum und Kaisertum . . . Paul Kehr zum 65. Geburtstag dargebracht* (Munich, 1926), pp. 287–316. Boll stresses the numerological sources and significance of the division of the life span into three, four, six, or seven stages.

36. For passages, mostly from the *Confessions* and *De peccatorum meritis et remissione et de baptismo parvulorum,* see Hogger, *Die Kinderpsychologie Augustins,* pp. 63–165.

37. Augustine further distinguishes between the merely nutritive stage of early infancy, when all impressions are quickly forgotten, and the memory stage, when they are retained.

38. Hogger, *Die Kinderpsychologie Augustins,* pp. 88–89. Pedagogical material exists in astonishing profusion in Augustine's works, but it is scattered, some of it in his early writings, much in his late works. While the sixteenth-century reader could not have drawn a coherent system of educational thought from Augustine, he would certainly have been profoundly impressed by the acuteness and psychological force of many of his observations.

39. See Hofmeister, "Puer, iuvenis, senex," for examples from Varro, Isidore of Seville, and others whose writings might have influenced sixteenth-century readers.

40. The legal literature agreed with this: e.g., Ulrich Tengler, *Layenspiegel: Von rechtmässigen ordnungen inn bürgerlichen und peinlichen Regimenten . . .* (Strassburg, 1544), x recto; Justin Göbler, *Handbuch . . . kayserlicher und bürgerlicher Rechten . . .* (Frankfurt am Main, 1564), I, title 12.

41. Vincent of Beauvais, *De eruditione filiorum nobilium,* ed. Arpad Steiner (Cambridge, Mass., 1938), chap. 35. The book was printed in 1477 and 1481. Egidio Colonna (Aegidius Romanus), *De regimine principum,* ed. S. P. Molenaer (New York, 1899), pp. 220–24 (the thirteenth-century French version). This work was printed frequently after 1473.

42. Maffeo Vegio, *De educatione liberorum,* written 1444, printed frequently from 1491. I use the German translation by K. A. Kopp in Bibliothek der katholischen Pädagogik, vol. 2 (Freiburg i.B., 1889), p. 121.

43. Herding ed., pp. 198–99, 242.

44. Jean Gerson, *Doctrina pro pueris ecclesiae Parisiensis,* in *Opera omnia,* 3: 717–20; *Expostulatio ad potestates publicas adversus corruptionem juventutis per lascivas imagines,* in ibid., 3: 291–92; *Tractatus de pollutione diurna,* in ibid., 3: 335–45.

45. Gerson may have been on the right track. Hans Heinrich Muchow, in an interesting study *Jugendgeneration im Wandel der Zeit: Beiträge zur Geschichte der Jugend* (Vienna, 1964), argues that while the onset of biological sexuality occurs at about the same age in all periods and among all peoples in history, "psychic-sexual maturity," the psychic acceptance of sexuality and the readiness to employ it, comes later. The length of this lag is determined by cultural and social factors. Repression means a longer lag. See esp. p. 26.

46. Vives, *De institutione feminae christianae,* bk. I, chap. 7, in *Joannis Ludovivi Vivis . . . opera omnia,* vol. 4 (Valencia, 1783).

47. This scholastic argument was presented by Aegidius Romanus in *De regimine principum* (see n. 41 above).

48. *De eruditione principum,* in *Sancti Thomae Aquinatis . . . opera omnia,* vol. 16 (New York, 1950; reprint of the 1852–73 Parma ed.), opusculum 37, bk. V, chap. 48. This anonymous book was attributed to St. Thomas throughout the late Middle Ages and the early modern period. On the authorship question see Wilhelm Berges, *Die Fürstenspiegel des hohen und späten Mittelalters* (Leipzig, 1938), pp. 309–13.

49. I leave out of consideration here the matter of eugenics, although a number of early modern writers stressed it, notably Vegio, *De educatione liberorum,* Kopp trans., p. 37 ("The physical and moral condition of the father at the moment of conception is transmitted directly and inexpungeably to the body and mind of the offspring"), and Erasmus, *De pueris instituendis,* Margolin ed., p. 43. Most authors did not advise eugenic practices consonant with those in plato's *Republic* but confined themselves to counseling continence and abstemiousness before intercourse. In any case, such advice did not enter the province of the sixteenth-century pedagogue.

50. *City of God* XXII, 24.

51. *De magistro*, 45, in *Saint Augustine, The Teacher* . . . , trans. R. P. Russell, The Fathers of the Church: A New Translation, vol. 59 (Washington, D.C., 1968).

52. Ibid.

53. *De pueris instituendis*, Margolin ed., p. 45.

54. Ibid., p. 46.

55. Hugh of St. Victor, *Didascalicon* III, 6. I use the critical edition by Charles Henry Buttimer, *Hugonis de Sancto Victore, Didascalicon* . . . (Washington, D.C., 1939). The translation is by Jerome Taylor, *The Didascalicon of Hugh of St. Victor* (New York, 1961).

56. Thomas Aquinas, *De magistro*, Article 1, Reply (Quaestio XI of *Quaestiones disputatae de Veritate*, trans. James V. McGlynn as *The Disputed Questions on Truth*, 2 vols. [Chicago, 1952–54], 2: 77–101). Cf. John W. Donohue, *St. Thomas Aquinas and Education* (New York, 1968); Mary Helen Mayer, *The Philosophy of Teaching of St. Thomas Aquinas* (New York, 1929). In this treatise Thomas seeks to prove that man *can* teach, against the view, ascribed by him to Augustine, that only God teaches.

57. *De magistro*, Article 1, Reply.

58. Hugh of St. Victor, *Didascalicon* III, 11: "Opportet ergo ut, quae discendo divisimus, commendanda memoriae colligamus. Colligere est ea de quibus prolixius vel scriptum vel disputatum est ad brevem quandam et compendiosam summam redigere." The translation in the text is that of Jerome Taylor.

59. Quintilian I, 3, 1: a good memory has two characteristics; it is "quick to take in and faithful to retain." Cf. Augustine, *Confessions* X, 8–19, where Augustine gives voice to his delight at the workings of the mind, particularly of memory. For another example see Vives, *De disciplinis* (1531). I use the German translation by Rudolf Heine, *Johann Ludwig Vives: Ausgewählte pädagogische Schriften* (Leipzig, n.d.), pp. 55–56.

60. Quintilian I, 12, 8.

61. *De Trinitate* X, 10–11 (*A Select Library of the Nicene and Post-Nicene Fathers* . . . , vol. 3 [Buffalo, 1887]). On this see the comments by Charles Trinkaus, *In Our Image and Likeness: Humanity and Divi⸱ in Italian Humanist Thought* (Chicago, 1970), vol. 1, pt. 2, chap. 4.

62. *De formando studio* (Freiburg, 1539), pp. 75–90.

63. The pedagogical tradition speaks with one voice on this point. From Quintilian and Augustine to Vegio, Vergerio, Wimpheling, and Erasmus, authors maintained that intellects differ in natural endowment.

64. E.g., Erasmus, *De pueris instituendis*, Margolin ed., p. 45.

65. Ibid., p. 29. Cf. Plutarch, *De liberis educandis*, 4.

66. For the clearest statement see *Laws*, bk. V, 732e–734e. See also R. C. Lodge, *Plato's Theory of Education* (London, 1947), pp. 193ff.

67. *De pueris instituendis*, Margolin ed., p. 53 and passim. Also *De ratione studii*, in Margolin, ed., *Opera omnia* I, 2: 111–151 passim, with reference to Quintilian I, 1, 20.

68. Aegidius Romanus, *De regimine principum*, Molenaer ed., pp. 195–96.

69. These quotations from Jerome, Ep. 107 and 128, respectively (*Select Letters of St. Jerome*, ed. and trans. F. A. Wright [London, 1933], pp. 347 and 469).

70. Plutarch, *De liberis educandis*, 12; 16. Plutarch is probably not the author of this treatise, but throughout the early modern period it was attributed to him. On the authorship question see Daniel Wyttenbach in his edition of Plutarch's *Moralia*, vol. 6, *Animadversiones* (Oxford, 1810), pp. 29–64. Many Latin translations of this work were published in the fifteenth century, including one by Guarino da Verona.

71. Quintilian I, 3, 13–18; Plutarch, *De liberis educandis*, 12; Maffeo Vegio, *De educatione liberorum*, Kopp trans., pp. 52–56; Battista Guarino, *De ordine docendi et studendi*, in *Vittorino da Feltre and Other Humanist Educators*, trans. William Harrison Woodward (New York, 1963), pp. 162–63; Wimpheling, *Isidoneus Germanicus*, in *Jakob Wimphelings pädagogische Schriften* . . . , trans. Joseph Freundgen (Paderborn, 1898), p. 170; Erasmus, *De pueris instituendis*, Margolin ed., p. 61.

72. For this, and for references to passages advocating corporal punishment, see Jentsch, *Urchristliches Erziehungsdenken*, pp. 85–139.

73. For an especially eloquent, as well as sensible, argument against harsh punishment see Erasmus, *De pueris instituendis*, Margolin ed., pp. 61–62.

74. Ep. 107, Wright ed., p. 347.

75. *De ordine docendi et studendi*, Woodward trans., p. 162. His treatise, says Battista, "represents the doctrine of my father Guarino Veronese; so much so that you may suppose him to be writing to you by my pen" (ibid., p. 161). Battista's treatise was first printed in Heidelberg in 1489 and reprinted several times thereafter.
76. Vegio, *De educatione liberorum*, Kopp trans., pp. 78–82.
77. *Adolescentia*, Herding ed., pp. 194–95.
78. Pietro Paolo Vergerio, *De ingenuis moribus* (edition in Princeton University Library, n.p., n.d., but probably 1472), 3 verso–4 recto. Vergerio's treatise had twenty or more editions before 1500.
79. *Adolescentia*, p. 368.
80. Guarino, *De ordine docendi et studendi*, Woodward trans., p. 163.
81. Vegio, *De educatione liberorum*, p. 78.
82. Wimpheling, *Adolescentia*, p. 195, taken from Vergerio.
83. Erasmus, *De pueris instituendis*, Margolin ed., pp. 62–63.
84. *Republic*, bk. II, 377b.
85. *De liberis educandis*, 3A (F. C. Babbitt, trans. Loeb Classical Library). A more accurate translation of Plutarch's ἠθικὰς ἀρετὰς would be "moral virtue." Latin translations of the Greek phrase usually read "cum mores ipsi Graeco sermone nihil sint quam assuefactio diuturna" (*Plutarchi . . . moralia . . .* , trans. Guilielmus Xylander [Basel, 1572], p. 4). Plutarch's phrase is a Peripatetic commonplace; see the references by Stobaeus in his Anthology (*Ioannis Stobaei Anthologii libri duo priores*, ed. Curt Wachsmuth II [Berlin, 1884]), pp. 116–17).
86. *Plutarchi . . . moralia . . .* , trans. Xylander, p. 4.
87. *De regimine principum*, Molenaer ed., pp. 193–94.
88. Ibid., pp. 206–7.
89. See n. 44 above.
90. Jean Gerson, *Tractatus de parvulis trahendis ad Christum*, in *Opera omnia*, 3: 277–91. The reference is to pp. 283–84.
91. *De educatione liberorum*, Book I, Kopp trans., pp. 41–45.
92. Ibid., pp. 57–58.
93. *De pueris instituendis*, Margolin ed., p. 29.
94. Ibid., passim. The same arguments are made in Erasmus's *Education of a Christian Prince*, trans. Lester K. Born (New York, 1968), p. 140.
95. *De officio mariti liber*, in *Opera omnia*, 4: 322.
96. On this last point, see Quintilian I, 12, 8–9.
97. Ibid. I, 12, 11; also I, 1, 19.
98. *De pueris instituendis*, Margolin ed., p. 48.
99. Quintilian I, 11, 2.
100. Ibid. X, 7, 1.
101. Ibid. X, 2, 1.
102. See n. 85 above.
103. "Neque abs re morales virtutes dixeris virtutes consuetudinis eorum lingua." See n. 85 above.
104. *Politics* VII, 13, 21–23.
105. Ibid., VII, 12, 7; Vives, *De officio mariti liber*, in *Opera omnia*, 4: 322.
106. Aegidius Romanus, *De regimine principum*, Molenaer ed., p. 195.
107. "Mala enim consuetudo, diu inroborata, est inextinguibilis." This phrase is quoted by Nonius Marcellus, *De compendiosa doctrina ad filium* (ed. L. Quicherat [Paris, 1872], p. 137), who attributes it to Varro's *De liberis educandis*.
108. Seneca, *De clementia* I, 3.
109. Vives, *De disciplinis*, Heine trans., p. 44.
110. Vives, *De institutione feminae christianae* (1523), in *Opera omnia*, 4: 258.
111. Galen, *De sanitate tuenda libri sex* I, 12, 5f.
112. E.g., Otto Brunfels, *Weiber und Kinder Apoteck . . .* (Strassburg, 1535), xliii recto.
113. Dan die iugent fast die lehre nicht, so sie nicht zu ausdrücklichem nachsprechen gewehnet wird" (visitation articles for Electoral Saxony, printed in Karl Pallas, ed., *Die Registraturen der Kirchenvisitationen im ehemals sächsischen Kurkreise*, Geschichtsquellen der Provinz Sachsen [Halle, 1906–14], 41 [Allgemeiner Teil]: 91).
114. For all relevant citations see Lodge, *Plato's Theory of Education*, chap. 4.
115. Quintilian I, 2; for the Renaissance, see, e.g., Vergerio, *De ingenuis moribus*, 7 verso.
116. For a good discussion of this subject and references to authors, see Gregor Müller,

94

"Educazione morale-civile," *Bildung und Erziehung im Humanismus der italienischen Renaissance* (Wiesbaden, 1969), esp. pp. 204–10 on Francesco Filelfo.

117. E.g., Wimpheling, *Adolescentia*, Herding ed., pp. 188f., 208; idem, *Isidoneus*, Freundgen trans., pp. 82f.; Vives, *De disciplinis*, Heine trans., p. 26.

118. For a discussion of Augustine's theology with reference to education, and for relevant passages, see Rudolf Strauss, *Der neue Mensch innerhalb der Theologie Augustins* (Zurich, 1967), particularly pp. 52–55.

119. *De vera religione*, trans. J. H. S. Burleigh, Library of Christian Classics, vol. 6 (Philadelphia, 1953), pp. 48ff.

120. *De eruditione principum*, in *Sancti Thomae Aquinatis . . . opera omnia*, 16: 287–93; Vegio, *De educatione liberorum*, Kopp trans., pp. 137–59; Wimpheling, *Adolescentia*, Herding ed., pp. 209ff; Erasmus, *Pietas puerilis* (also called *Confabulatio pia*) in *Colloquia familiaria*, in *Opera omnia* (Leiden, 1703), vol. 1, cols. 648–53; Vives, *De disciplinis*, Heine trans., pp. 56–57.

121. Vives, *De disciplinis*, p. 33.

122. Quintilian II, 4, quoting Cicero, *De oratore* II, xxi, 88.

123. *De pueris instituendis*, Margolin ed., pp. 50–51.

124. E.g., Quintilian I, 8, 8.

125. Vergerio, *De ingenuis moribus*, 11 recto.

126. For references to the large number of Italian writers who saw this as the object of education, see Müller, *Bildung und Erziehung*, pp. 321–22.

127. Vegio, *De educatione liberorum*, Kopp trans., pp. 159–63.

128. This fact is too evident in all these writings to require proof. Even Erasmus, despite his talk about the ploughboy, concerned himself almost exclusively with the well-born, hoping that ordinary mortals would be beneficially influenced if they observed the children of prominent men working hard at their studies ("si conspexerint heroum liberos a primis statim annis dicari studiis"); see *De civilitate morum puerilium* (1529), in *Opera omnia* (Leiden, 1703), vol. 1, col. 1033.

129. See the discussion of the Erasmian ideal as put into action by Johann Sturm in Walter Sohm, *Die Schule Johann Sturms und die Kirche Strassburgs . . .* (Munich and Berlin, 1912), pp. 31ff.

130. *De pueris instituendis*, Margolin ed., p. 55. As usual, Erasmus can be quoted in self-contradiction. In his *De ratione studii*, Margolin ed., p. 125, he recommends domestic tutoring as superior to public education. But this is so only for the well-to-do. Erasmus insisted on public control over schools for ordinary boys.

131. Quintilian I, 1, 11.

VIII

The Social Function of Schools in the Lutheran Reformation in Germany

One of the most interesting aspects of the German Reformation for us to ponder is that of the educational reconstruction attempted in all Lutheran states in the sixteenth century. Churchmen and politicians acted in close collaboration, first in response to the reformist zeal charging the Lutheran movement in its heroic years, later in meeting the procedural obligations laid down for officials in the established Reformation's institutional structure. They agreed on fundamental objectives and shared a coherent body of pedagogical suppositions. They had high hopes for the power of education to direct thought and mold behavior. In the new church–state symbiosis they recognized unprecedented opportunities for reform and were eager to act on them. For a time, religion and politics moved in unison toward the enactment of a program of schooling intended in its overall purpose to conform the young to approved patterns of evangelical and civic rectitude.

Our questions concerning a past system of schooling are no different from those we ask about one in the present. What does a society wish its schools to accomplish, and what is, in fact, being accomplished? Who speaks for society in establishing goals? Have those who set the objectives formulated a policy? A program? A feasible program? One to be implemented by schools adequate to the purpose? A purpose representing concrete interests? Of identifiable social groups? With what responses from these groups? And with what consequences—in the short and in the long term—for society itself?

The first thing to note in approaching the sixteenth-century Lutheran schooling scene with these questions is that the evidence is available for supplying answers. (This essay's focus on Lutheran regions should not be taken to imply that Catholic and Reformed Germany pursued educational goals essentially different from those of the evangelicals.) Our sources may not suffice for a fully differentiated social history of early Protestant education; but about objectives and performance, and about the evaluation of these, we are very well informed.[1]

Who, then, spoke for society in the making of educational policy in sixteenth-century Germany, and who acted in the implementation of it? Governing authorities did, and the administrative bodies appointed by them. In other words—to use the correct terminology—*Obrigkeit, potestates*, as in *Jedermann sey unterthan der Oberkeit, die gewalt über jn hat* and *omnis anima potestatibus sublimioribus subdita sit*,[2] that is to say, sovereign rulers possessing *Herrschaft*, dominion and power, and the executive agents and agencies appointed by them to exercise dominion and power. With respect to schools and schooling, the purview of territorial and urban governments in Germany was fixed at an early juncture in the chain of events leading to the established Reformation. This assignment, or self-assignment, happened because governments, in the decades following the late 1520s, took on the job of directing ecclesiastical affairs in their respective domains, and education had traditionally been included among ecclesiastical responsibilities. But this assumption of control did not happen without due consideration being given to the problems at issue in this turn of events.

In principle, instructing the young was the duty and the right of parents. By necessity, however, this obligation now fell to the state. This was because individual parents could only in exceptional cases be relied upon to perform competently the vital—indeed, it was thought to be a fateful—task of child rearing. Luther was his usual emphatic and uncompromising self on this point. "The common man can do nothing," he wrote in 1524, as he urged magistrates to maintain and govern schools. "He [the common man] doesn't have the means for it, he doesn't want to do it, and he doesn't know how."[3] The experience of the early 1520s, particularly the failure of the community of Leisnig to appropriate sufficient funds—and Luther seems for a time to have held high hopes for Leisnig as the model for a reformation on a communal base—had per-

---

[1] For a general bibliographical introduction to this subject see Gerald Strauss, *Luther's House of Learning: Indoctrination of the Young in the German Reformation* (Baltimore, 1978), especially the notes to chapter 1.

[2] From Luther's German translation of the New Testament and revision of the Vulgate, *D. Martin Luthers Deutsche Bibel* (*D. Martin Luthers Werke: Kritische Gesamtausgabe* [from now on WA]) 7: 69 and 5: 645.

[3] *An die Ratsherren aller Städte* (1524), WA 15: 44.

suaded Luther that voluntary, participatory procedures were inadequate to the gigantic task of reform.[4]

Ordinary people being unqualified to undertake their own children's upbringing (Luther included *auffzihen* among the tasks for which he held people generally unsuited) and instruction, government was the only existing alternative. Hence Luther's exhortation in 1526 to his prince that he must act as "guardian-general of the young"—*"oberster furmund der jugent"*—in holding citizens to the support of schools,[5] a formulation later sharpened by Melanchthon to "government as a common father."[6] In 1530 Luther came out in favor of the use of political force to ensure general school attendance,[7] and this is the position adopted officially in the *Kirchenordnungen*—ecclesiastical constitutions or ordinances— through which governing authorities in Lutheran territories and cities regulated for their respective domains all aspects of church and religion, including schooling. In these immensely prolix documents we see church and state acting jointly, with the temporal part clearly dominant. As early as 1528, Bugenhagen's ordinances for Braunschweig and Hamburg were confirmed and authorized by the town councils of these cities,[8] and subsequent ecclesiastical constitutions were always published under the names of the territory's reigning prince: "Christoph, by the Grace of God Duke of Württemberg, our declaration of doctrines and ceremonies as they must be believed, kept, and obeyed in the churches of our principality."[9] *Schulordnungen*—enabling charters setting up the schools in a given realm—were in nearly all instances appended to these church constitutions. They placed the supervision of all educational institutions firmly in the hands of prince and magistrates, who were the owners and wielders of the instruments of public power.

It is only when seen from the vantage point of a much later period of conflicts between church and state, and between individual rights and state power over the control of education, that this amalgamation of schooling and political sovereignty seems ominous.[10] The sixteenth cen-

---

[4] For citations of all relevant documents on this point see Werner Reininghaus, *Elternstand, Obrigkeit, und Schule bei Luther* (Heidelberg, 1969), 5.

[5] Luther to Elector Johann, 22 Nov. 1526, WA *Briefwechsel* 4: 134.

[6] *"Die obrigkeit als gemeiner vater."* Quoted in Werner Reininghaus, ed., *Evangelische Kirche und Elternrecht* (Lüneburg, 1961), 19.

[7] *Eine Predigt, dass man Kinder zur Schulen halten solle* (1530), WA 30 II: 586.

[8] Reinhold Vormbaum, *Die evangelischen Schulordnungen des 16. Jahrhunderts* (Gütersloh, 1860), 8, 18. Cited from now on as Vormbaum.

[9] Ibid., 68.

[10] For the German debate on this issue from about 1800 see Erwin Stein, Wilfried Joest, and Hans Dombois, *Elternrecht: Studien zu seiner rechtsphilosophischen und evangelisch-theologischen Grundlegung* (Heidelberg, 1958).

tury recognized no *Elternrecht*, no right—statutory or customary—of parents to have their children instructed in private, as opposed to public, schools or to have in some other important way a voice in what their offspring were to learn. Lacking legal grounds on which to challenge state and church control of schooling, opponents had no position from which to wage resistance—except, of course, passively, by indifference and apathy, the traditional weapons of the weak. In any case, nothing written by the educational theorists of the day suggested that formal learning was, or could be, anything other than a blessing bestowed by an *Obrigkeit* upon those privileged to receive it. This is how it was represented in official pronouncements, notably in a host of *Schulpredigten*, sermons preached in church to remind fathers and mothers—I quote the words of Werner Reininghaus—"of their parental responsibility and to awaken in them an attitude of grateful acceptance of the opportunities created for them by the governing authorities."[11] Without posing it explicitly, the question of who should bear primary responsibility for the child's education—family or state—was being answered definitively in the early years of the Lutheran era. Moving together toward what Gerhard Oestreich, anticipating the seventeenth- and eighteenth-century German state, has called *Sozialdisziplinierung*,[12] Reformation church and Reformation state seized upon the control of schooling as an efficient and effective way of acting directly on individual subjects for the purpose of instilling in them a lasting sense of their places and duties in the well-ordered society.

Lutheran churchmen and theologians heartily collaborated in this effort. Although the final word always belonged to the temporal authorities, it was to the offices and activities of the ecclesiastics that the actual operation of schools was entrusted. They saw in this assignment a powerful opportunity to put the evangelical Reformation into place. Hence their full-throated affirmation of existing arrangements, as when a group of Rostock University professors, urging the dukes of Mecklenburg to take a stronger hand in the governance of schools, addressed them in the—creatively interpreted—words of Psalm 24: "ye princes lift up your gates, that is to say your churches, schools, cities, and entire governments, that the king of glory may come in, meaning that Christ may be known and honored by the multitude through the doctrine of

---

[11] Werner Reininghaus, *Elternstand* (see note 4), 5.
[12] Throughout in his *Geist und Gestalt des frühmodernen Staates* (Berlin, 1969); and in "Policey und Prudentia civilis . . ." in *Strukturprobleme der frühen Neuzeit* (Berlin, 1890), 367–79. On the concept of *Sozialdisziplinierung* in Oestreich's work see now Winfried Schulze, "Gerhard Oestreichs Begriff 'Sozialdisziplinierung in der frühen Neuzeit,' " *Zeitschrift für historische Forschung* 14 (1987): 265–302.

the holy gospel." The professors did not fail in this connection to quote Isaiah 49:23 to the effect that "Kings shall be your foster fathers" (*deine pfleger*, in Luther's translation),[13] an echo, perhaps, of Melanchthon's view of "government as a common father."

The eager and—despite the frustrating job of finding the needed cash—sustained response made by all governments to such open invitations suggests that rulers and their advisers sensed the role schooling might play in the extension of public power over the populace. The results of their efforts were, to be sure, a long way from the virtually absolute administrative control later exercised by eighteenth-century German states through their *Landschulordnungen*, most notably Prussia's *General-Landschul-Reglement* of 1763. However, looking back in time from this point of observation—in my opinion the correct perspective—one can see things definitely tending in that direction. The clearest evidence of this trend is found in the texts of *Schulordnungen*, many of them long and punctiliously detailed programs declaring the regulations for every level and for every aspect of teaching and learning. The most important of these *Ordnungen* are conveniently available for study in three volumes of texts edited by Reinhold Vormbaum.[14] But a vast number of additional school plans, schedules, and related documents may be found in state and municipal archives, all of them, in their anxious concern for regulating everything and leaving nothing to whim and chance, giving confirmation of the sixteenth-century governing mind's predisposition to arrange things in a definitive order, to stipulate, regulate, and control.

Organizationally at least, this endeavor must be counted a success. In every German state, primary and secondary schools were built up, enlarged, equipped, ably staffed (more or less), tied together in sequence, and given fully articulated teaching programs and a clear sense of mission. This part of the story of Lutheran education has been told often. By the 1560s and 1570s, something like an integrated school system existed, or was coming into existence, in most of the Lutheran states in the Holy Roman Empire—integrated in the sense that its levels and streams were linked in a coherent structure, and that the educational apparatus as a whole was closely tied in its stated aims and assigned functions to the objectives and operations of the ecclesiastical and political organs of the state.[15]

What purpose did this apparatus serve? Luther's call for *Christliche Schulen* to replace the "donkey stalls and devil's dens" of his own

---

[13] *Monumenta Germaniae Paedagogica* (from now on MGP) 38: 253–54.
[14] *Evangelische Schulordnungen*, 3 vols. (Gütersloh, 1858–64).
[15] Evidence for this development is given in Strauss, *Luther's House of Learning*, chap. 1.

childhood[16] set a goal without much specificity beyond the exhortation that boys and girls should be trained to play their several parts in upholding God's spiritual and temporal realms.[17] Luther's language and choice of examples on the occasion of this appeal suggest that he was thinking primarily of well-placed townsmen with ambition for their offspring and the means and social connections to speed them on their careers: "the men to govern land and people," as he wrote, "the women to manage the house, children, and servants."[18] From among these circles young men would be taken to staff the proliferating bureaucracies of the expanding Reformation state and church.

Melanchthon's 1528 school ordinance for Saxony made this the official aim of schooling. Schools, he wrote, are "for raising up people who are skilled to teach in the church and govern in the world."[19] Announcing this aim more formally, the *Schulordnung* of Württemberg of 1559—taken as a model by many subsequent ordinances[20]—makes a preamble of the proposition that "honest, wise, learned, skilled, and God-fearing men are needed to serve in the holy preaching office, in worldly governments, in temporal posts, in administrative offices and households, and . . . schools are God's chosen and rightful instruments for raising up such men."[21] A rigorous selection process—at least, it was intended to be rigorous—advanced the more clever, or perhaps simply the more compliant, pupils to the upper forms and, from there, to elite schools such as the Saxon *Fürstenschulen* or the Stuttgart *Gymnasium*, and thereafter to university. Instructions to "pick out the most gifted"(*die geschicktesten auswählen*) appear in every *Schulordnung*,[22] while "dull heads and slow talents" (*ungeschickte köpfe und ingenia*) are ordered demoted to the vernacular benches at the bottom of the educational edifice, where all lessons were given in German.[23]

What was learned in these common schools catering to the undifferentiated pre-teen children of ordinary folk was rudimentary indeed, even when judged by the period's own standards. Württemberg's *Schulordnung* summarizes the German-language curriculum as "prayers and catechism, and in addition some writing and reading for [the pupils'] own use and the public good, also psalm singing and Christian con-

[16] *An die Ratsherren*, 31.
[17] Ibid., 44.
[18] Ibid.
[19] Vormbaum, 1.
[20] E.g., the *Schulordnung* of the Duchy of Braunschweig 1569; that of Saxony 1580.
[21] Vormbaum, 68–69.
[22] E.g., Saxony 1528. Ibid., 8.
[23] Duchy of Mecklenburg school ordinance for city of Güstrow. MGP 38: 472.

duct."[24] Regulations called for conscientious teaching in these popular schools ("let the schoolmaster teach German writing and reading with as much diligence as is given to the teaching of Latin"[25]); but the substance of what was taught was very thin, as it was in what learning was imparted to girls: "reading and writing, and if both of these can't be mastered, at least some writing, the catechism learned by heart, a little figuring, a few psalms to sing," and "stories from the German Bible."[26] As the Mecklenburg *Schulordnung* summed it up in 1552, "Habituate [girls] to the catechism, to the psalms, to honorable behavior and Christian virtue, and especially to prayer, and make them memorize verses from Holy Scripture so that they may grow up to be Christian and praiseworthy matrons and housekeepers (*Christliche und lobliche matronen und haushälterinnen*)."[27] Needless to say, female pupils were kept out of schools offering the kind of learning that fitted a young person for a place in the public world. Poor boys, on the other hand, if born with good heads and agile minds, were—when things went according to plan—marked by observant teachers and, with financial aid from their government, sent to Latin schools to prepare them for careers in the church or the state. The clerical profession seemed especially suitable for boys of modest background. Every territory opened one or several boarding schools for the nurturing of such otherwise wasted talent.[28]

The greatest effort was given to monitoring the curriculum of the Latin School, the plan of studies designed to bring to maturity the type of man considered most useful to, productive in, and representative of the well-ordered Christian polity. The Latin course was the track laid down for all who were expected to play a leading role in making it work. Several aspects of this rigorous academic shaping process are worth mentioning here. In its contents and in its teaching practice, it was the humanist program, taken over virtually without change except for the inclusion in it of the catechism. But for this addition, the Reformation's pedagogy appears taken straight from the educational tracts of Vives,

---

[24] Vormbaum, 71.

[25] Baden-Durlach school ordinance of 1536. Ibid., 31.

[26] *Jungfrauen-Schule* in Wittenberg, 1533. Ibid., 27–28; Braunschweig school ordinance of 1543. Ibid., 50–51.

[27] MGP 38: 215.

[28] Urban schools generally admitted poor children free of charge "*um Gottes willen*," e.g., Rostock, 1534. MGP 38: 122. For the care with which poor boys were selected for the pastorate, see the regulations in the Württemberg school ordinance, Vormbaum, 104. It was often stated that *gute und fruchtbare ingenia* are found among the poor as well as the rich: e.g., Vormbaum, 70, 102.

Erasmus, and Johann Sturm.[29] Begin serious formal education early in life. Concentrate on language, especially on Latin, which is "a tongue sacred to the learned." All learning depends on correct pronunciation and on fluency in writing and speaking—Latin, of course. Speech is the best index to the quality of a mind, memory the clearest sign of its power. Superior results are obtained by close imitation of classical models. As Roman and Greek authors offer the best preparation for an intelligent and active life, ancient literature must be the pupil's steady mental diet.[30] The right technique for feeding it to him is by means of ephemerides or commonplace books in which each pupil's growing stock of knowledge is to be stored for lifelong utilization. Dialectic and rhetoric prepare the mind for putting this accumulation to purposeful use. Method is the key to all effective learning; every step along the educational way must be governed by rules and by close surveillance of the pupil's—and the teacher's—adherence to them. When this is done, learning will build in the able pupil to form a mental culture composed in equal parts of *eloquentia*, *sapientia*, and *pietas*.

The finished products of this learning process were men equipped to play leading roles in the organized society emerging out of the turmoil of the early Reformation. To say it in a vivid phrase used by Walter Sohm: "the fully educated graduates of the Latin school were the offerings brought by humanism to the state and to the church."[31] In their mentality—a mental cast patiently cultivated during ten or more years of schooling—and in their speech and bearing, they exemplified the intellectual and civic posture deemed appropriate for members of the ruling social group: they embodied the culture of the elite. Their activities in the world were expected to transmit this culture to those destined, like them, to rise to topmost positions in ecclesiastical and political administration. Among those who were not so destined, they would engender

---

[29] Desiderius Erasmus, *De pueris statim ac liberaliter instituendis declamatio* (1529) (*Collected Works of Erasmus* 26 [Toronto, 1985], 295–346); *De recta latini graecique sermonis pronuntiatione dialogus* (1528) (ibid., 365–475); Juan Luis Vives, *De tradendis disciplinis libri quinque* (Antwerp, 1531; English translation by Foster Watson, *Vives: On Education* [Totowa, N.J., 1971]). Johann Sturm's pedagogical treatises are discussed in Walter Sohm, *Die Schule Johann Sturms und die Kirche Strassburgs* (Munich and Berlin, 1912). Ultimately these treatises are all based on Plutarch's *De liberis educandis*, translated by Guarino in 1411, and Quintilian's and Cicero's books on the education of the orator, the former published by Poggio in 1417, the latter recovered in 1422. An argument for a sharp break between Lutheran curricula and late fifteenth-century humanist educational reforms is made by John N. Miner, "Change and Continuity in the Schools of Late Medieval Nuremberg," *Catholic Historical Review* 73 (Jan. 1987): 1–22.

[30] Latin and Greek authors and titles given in Vives, *De tradendis disciplinis*, book III, especially chapters 6 and 7.

[31] Walter Sohm, *Die Schule Johann Sturms*, 92.

respectful esteem and willing deference. In this way—and this is saying only the obvious—schooling operated in the interest of the dominant groups, as an instrument of acculturation.

Without overextending its relevance to the sixteenth century, one can elaborate this line of interpretation and arrive at a number of general propositions concerning education in a hegemonic setting. Schools reflect social divisions and replicate them. They accomplish this stabilization of social stratification by means of streaming. In every stream and at every level, though in varying forms and ways, the reigning ideology is presented as universally valid knowledge, value, and truth. Teachers are trained to accept their role in this system of cultural reproduction. Their success is measured by the pupil's unquestioning adoption of the dominant culture's stock of ideas, as expressed in sanctioned formulae. Access to governing ideas, style, and speech is not restricted to a particular social class; but acculturation to this code promotes a young man, whatever his birth, to the ranks of those who are called to represent it in the larger society. A set of mutually reinforcing pedagogical assumptions links the code to techniques of transmitting it. Education works because all human beings are educable. Its essential purpose is to mold the young into a desirable form, this form being determined by society. The educational process must begin in childhood and must be well advanced before the onset of puberty. Its early phases consist largely of breaking the child's will and setting restraints to his natural inclinations. To do the job properly, all schooling must be public, private education being destructive of common goals. Equally destructive are habits of questioning, criticism, ambivalence, suspended judgment; they must be inhibited. Schooling, therefore, must purvey certainties.[32] In its formal procedures, it reflects the existing social order (modified somewhat by desires for its amelioration) and promotes it by accustoming the pupil from the start to hierarchy, authority, and the sanctity of the status quo. Everything done in school serves this purpose in one way or another.

Take grammar as an illustration. Grammar was present from first to last in the classical program, pervading all classes and all subjects. In his *Instruction of the Visitors to the Pastors in Saxony*, which includes a lesson plan for Saxon Latin schools, Melanchthon warns that where boys are not "pressed and driven" (*gedrungen und getrieben*) to the study of grammar, "all learning is lost and in vain. For," he continues, "no greater harm can be done to the arts than to fail to accustom the young to grammar."[33] The essence of grammar is, of course, rules—normative

---

[32] For a discussion of the application of these educational aims to the pedagogy of the Reformation, see Strauss, *Luther's House of Learning* chaps. 2–4.

[33] Vormbaum, 7.

and prescriptive rules—and drill. In all the years of a boy's academic development, grammar was therefore his daily routine. When you get to the end of etymology, syntax, and prosody, Melanchthon tells teachers, "start over again, from the beginning."[34] One wonders, what was the real object here: deep knowledge of grammar as "the mother and nurse of the other arts,"[35] or internalization of a rule-bound discipline as the paradigm of a rule-bound life? Both of these objectives were aimed at, it seems to me, with high hopes and expectations for the second one. The pattern of grammar being fixed and regular, its implantation as the individual's armature of thought was expected to guard against the temptations of whim and will and to recall the imagination to correct and authorized rules so that its tendency to free-wheeling speculation might be counteracted.

As for mastering the content of the curriculum's reading list, this was largely a matter of filling the blank spaces in commonplace books and ephemerides, an easily acquired and—once it was learned—habitual technique of organizing knowledge, and a method useful equally to pedagogues and pupils: to pedagogues trying to control their pupils' comprehension of literature, and to pupils whose future careers in religion, law, and administration demanded a constant recycling of the pieces of excerpted wisdom taken from the canon of authors and filed under approved rubrics.[36] Teachers inspected notebooks at regular intervals to ensure that no illicit opinions crept in and no authorized truth was omitted. Uniformity was the salient virtue. "The same books in all schools," directed the Württemberg school ordinance, "none changed or altered in any way, and each to be read at the appointed time as shown in our ordinance, and when finished to be read again from the beginning."[37] This regularity was an axiom of humanist pedagogy. It was made explicit in Vives's definition of art as "a collection of universal rules brought together for the purpose of knowing, doing, or producing something."[38] Later it was carried to its extreme by the Jesuits. "Nothing maintains the entire discipline so much as observing the rules," says the *Ratio* of

---

[34] Ibid. Repeated many times in other ordinances, e.g., Schleswig-Holstein 1542. Ibid., 36.

[35] Valentin Trotzendorf in the school ordinance for the Goldberg Gymnasium, 1563. Ibid., 54.

[36] For a discussion of this technique see Anton Schindling, *Humanistische Hochschule und freie Reichsstadt: Gymnasium und Akademie in Strassburg 1538–1621* (Wiesbaden, 1977), chap. 5, especially 180–95.

[37] Württemberg school ordinance 1559, Vormbaum, 72. For similar sentiments: Hessen 1537 (Ibid., 33), Braunschweig 1569 (MGP 8: 25–26), Pomerania 1563 (Vormbaum, 168), and many more.

[38] Vives, *De tradendis disciplinis* I, 3.

1599,[39] and this could stand as the motto of the Reformation's whole educational enterprise. "For God is a God of order" it was said, "*ein Gott der ordnung*, who demands that, in school no less than in the other walks of life, all things must be done in the correct and orderly way."[40]

For another example, let us consider religious instruction. To my mind, nothing illustrates better the overall aims of Reformation schooling, and the assumptions on which they stood, namely, that education inculcates certainties and that teaching assures the perpetuation of the status quo by accustoming coming generations to a voluntary acceptance of it. Notions of a conflict between learning and piety never occurred to Reformation educators, who saw no need to raise again the humanists' question whether "arts and erudition hinder the progress of religion."[41] The conviction that they were, in fact, perfectly complementary was implicit in every stated aim of schooling in the Reformation: to teach "learning, the fear of God, and good discipline," to give instruction "above all things in the fear of God and good behavior [*Gottesfurcht und gute Sitten*] and also in the liberal arts and languages,"[42] to imbue the young with "spirituality, the liberal arts, and honorable manners" (*geistlichkeit, gute künste und ehrliche sitten*).[43] "And this is best accomplished," the school ordinance for Mecklenburg directs, when, "along with instruction in liberal arts and languages, pupils memorize the catechism and selected psalms and verses from Scripture."[44] What was meant in these pronouncements by "fear of God" and "spirituality"? The Württemberg ordinance informs us. "As for the implantation of the fear of God in the boys," it says, "let them sing every morning before lessons, and again every afternoon, the first and last verses of the hymn *Veni Creator Spiritus*, in Latin, and reverently. And before going home at noon and again in the evening, let them recite from memory a portion of the catechism." These exercises were accompanied by "daily practice in catechism," a weekly catechism exam on Fridays, and attendance at all services followed by a quiz on the sermons heard in church.[45] An essentially mechanical routine, this regime was expected to lead boys to a

---

[39] "*Disciplinam omnem nihil aeque continet atque observatio regularum.*" *Ratio studiorum* (1599) in MGP 5: 395.

[40] "*Denn Gott ist ein Gott der ordnung, welcher will, dass es wie in allen Ständen, also auch in Schulenstand, mit Unterweisung der Jugend recht und ordenlich zugehe.*" From school regulations for the city of Wismar, 1644, MGP 44: 84.

[41] Vives, *De tradendis disciplinis* I, chaps. 4, 6.

[42] From school ordinances for the Duchy of Zweibrücken, 1575, MGP 49: 122; 1581, ibid., 142; 1602, ibid., 159.

[43] From visitation ordinance for Mecklenburg, 1541, MGP 38: 141.

[44] Ibid., 214.

[45] Vormbaum, 91–92.

godly disposition, which, the Württemberg ordinance explains, is the prerequisite for *eusserlich Disziplin und Zucht*. Procedures were the same in Saxony[46] and—or nearly so—in most other Lutheran states. Memorizing scriptural texts was relied upon above any other instructional method, and apparently it was not unusual for model pupils to have a repertoire of fifty or sixty psalms ready for recitation.[47] Great faith was placed in repeated verbal performance: declaiming aloud, in unison as well as individually and in small groups, prayers, hymns, verses from the New and Old Testaments, above all questions and answers from the catechism.

By the 1530s, in large part owing to the prestige gained by Luther's own catechisms, the catechism had become, certainly the chief, and virtually the sole, instrument of religious instruction in the schools of the German Reformation. From first grade in elementary school, where ABC primers fed straight into the Shorter German Catechism,[48] to the uppermost class of the *Gymnasium*, where preceptors lectured on the catechism in Greek and Latin, it dominated the curriculum as the pupil's authoritative source of theological knowledge and fixed frame of religious reference. Why this was so is not difficult to understand. Established religion requires experienced, informed guidance: the catechism gave it. The Bible is complex and far from unambiguous: the catechism offered reliable interpretation. It asked all the necessary questions and supplied the correct answers. It made first-hand occupation with Scripture practically unnecessary. The Bible itself became an adjunct to the catechism. This is why so little encouragement was given in the pupil's formal education to individual Bible reading. Most school plans make no mention of it at all. Pupils regularly attended services, of course, and heard the Scripture preached there. But this is the point: preaching was authoritative. Private reading, even when championed as part of a carefully drawn program of studies, was unpredictable in its consequences. This was the lesson responsible Lutherans drew from the events of the mid-1520s. They were determined thereafter to do all that lay in their powers to prevent a recurrence.

Every *Schulordnung* issued during the sixteenth century reflects this resolve. The best hope for prevention of future trouble rested with the catechism. "Because schoolmasters stand *in loco parentis*," states the ordinance of Brandenburg of 1573, "they must devote the greatest care

---

[46] Ibid., 247 (1580).
[47] See the description given by pastor Georg Zeämann of Kempten, in his *Schulpredigten* of 1618 quoted in MGP *Beiheft* 1 (Berlin, 1916), 10.
[48] E.g., Saxony 1580, Vormbaum, 237.

to our young people and instruct them with the utmost earnestness in the catechism and, for the rest, in the liberal arts and the singing of hymns."[49] In Hanover, "so that young people may learn the fear of God no less than the liberal arts," the Latin school taught them "catechism, grammar, good behavior, and also languages." In the upper forms, where the New and Old Testaments formed an integral part of the curriculum, the emphasis in the teaching of Scripture was placed on language and grammar.[50] In Mecklenburg, in 1552, "upper form boys read the gospel in Greek, and it must be expounded to them by giving them easy topics, making clear their meaning and letting the topics be declined and conjugated."[51] In Württemberg, Scripture seemed mainly to serve as a means of gaining proficiency in Hebrew and Greek, so that—to quote the 1559 ordinance—"through the study of these texts [pupils] may advance to careers in theology, in the other arts, in governing posts, offices, and in householderships.[52]

Preparing pupils for high office was always the salient objective. Superior schools in Saxony "instruct the young in languages, arts, and most of all in Holy Scripture, so that, in time, we will suffer no lack of pastors and other learned men among us."[53] Scripture seems to have functioned here—and elsewhere[54]—mainly as a vehicle for language training,[55] and little ingenuity seems to have been devoted to creating a learning atmosphere in which the deeper significance of Holy Writ might be understood. The teaching of Scripture did not seem to vary much from drill in catechism. Here is what the *Schulordnung* of Pomerania said in 1563 about Bible study in the third form of that duchy's Latin school:

> To accustom the boys from earliest youth to Holy Scripture and divine doctrine, the schoolmaster must, on Wednesdays or Saturdays, expound to them the Gospel According to St. Matthew or the Epistle of Paul to Titus or to Timothy, and also several selected psalms. . . . But he must not attempt learned interpretation. Let him explain the text plainly, that is to say grammatically, and let him implant the right understanding of it by teaching the boys definitions, asking them repeatedly *Quid Deus? Quot personae divinitatis? . . . Quid lex? Quid peccatum? Quid evangelium? Quid gratia? Quid fides? . . . Quid ministerium? Quid magistratus?* And above all things he must exercise the

---

[49] Ibid., 227.

[50] Hanover 1536. Ibid., 32.

[51] MGP 38: 210. Similarly Mecklenburg 1552, Vormbaum, 64.

[52] Vormbaum, 69.

[53] From regulations for the *Fürstenschulen* in Meissen, Pforta, and Grimma, ibid., 268.

[54] E.g., in the regulations for special boarding schools for talented poor boys in Württemberg, ibid., 102.

[55] On the advisability of teaching the Bible in the ancient languages, see Bugenhagen's memorandum of 1531 in MGP 38: 116–17.

students with all diligence in Latin speech and style, and to this purpose schoolmasters must speak only Latin in class, and never fall into German.[56]

What had changed, then, in Bible study as a result of the Reformation? For most pupils, including those educated in the classics, the Bible was still a book to be heard rather than read. Most of those who did learn to read it learned it in the ancient languages, the better to expound it or apply it, in their professions, later. Of course, more attention than ever before was now given to effective preaching. But private reading was not fostered. Preaching and oral explanation were still the most highly valued path to Scripture, and this was the path given official sanction in the teaching programs of Lutheran schools. Even the young men chosen for the ministry encountered Scripture as a largely passive experience;[57] for the rest, exposure to the Bible was entirely inactive. In any case, it was not from the Bible but from the catechism that all were expected to take their religious knowledge.[58] There are exceptions to this pattern,[59] but they are rare. Most ordinary folk got their religious instruction not from the Bible but from the catechism, from religious hymns, and from prayers (*Catechismus, Kirchengesang, und Gebet*), along with regular admonitions to display their fear of God in the form of disciplined (*züchtig*) conduct in the world.[60] Professionally trained pupils enrolled in Latin schools read the Bible in the setting of a carefully constructed learning program, and mainly in the ancient tongues; they, too, relied on the catechism for what they needed to know about their religion.[61] To convey a glimpse of how the process of total catechization was intended to work in ideal circumstances, I quote David Chytraeus, a theology professor in the University of Rostock, as he outlined the duties of pastors, teachers, and householders in the Duchy of Mecklenburg in 1578:

> Pastors in their churches, schoolmasters in their schools, and heads of household at home among their children and servants must practice the catechism with the utmost industry. Preachers will take their Sun-

---

[56] Vormbaum, 172–73.

[57] Cf. Walter Sohm, *Die Schule Johann Sturms*, 109–18 on the essentially passive exposure to Scripture given in Johann Sturm's pedagogical program.

[58] E.g., Württemberg 1559, Vormbaum, 71.

[59] E.g., *Schulordnung* for the German-language school in Güstrow 1602, MGP 38: 473; *Schulordnung* for Darmstadt, 1594, MGP 33: 206.

[60] E.g., Württemberg 1559, Vormbaum, 160–65.

[61] For a very different approach to catechization, one that attempted to engender individual responses to the faith, see John Morgan, *Godly Learning: Puritan Attitudes towards Reason, Learning, and Education, 1560–1640* (Cambridge, 1986), passim, especially 186.

day afternoon sermons from no other texts than the catechism, and once they have brought it to an end, they will start over, from the beginning, without cease or letup. . . . In the same way must the catechism be taught in the schools, day after day, with the same words, in Latin or German, the school master saying it to the pupils, the pupils reciting it back to him. . . . And every housefather must do likewise at home, making his children and hired help recite the catechism before they go off to school in the morning or to work, or sit down to a meal. . . . And lest the young and simple be thrown into confusion by the addition, omission, or substitution of even a single word or syllable, let all this be done *auf einerley weyse allenthalben stetes und ewiglich*— in a uniform manner, always and forever.[62]

Of the three target sites mentioned by Chytraeus—church, school, and home—only the school offered a sufficiently dependable environment to give the process a chance to work. Traditional learning psychology— essentially Aristotelian in provenance—justified the hope that systematic habituation would produce desirable mental and behavioral dispositions in the learners.[63] As the *Schulordnung* of Hanover asserted in 1536: "we normally remain all our lives what we are taught to be in our youth."[64] More than anything else, schooling was designed to effect this lifelong habituation, and to do so in the most systematic way possible. Whether the system was successful in accomplishing this aim is, of course, open to question.[65] But the aim itself is not in doubt. Education works by inculcating habits, not only habits of conduct, but also—and more importantly—habits of thought, of attitudes, of inclinations. At the primary and secondary level, schooling was essentially habit training. The humanist's course of liberal studies and the churchman's catechism drill constituted a teaching program in which the acquisition of knowledge was promoted through a technique of habituation: everything divided into small units of study, memorized, endlessly repeated verbatim in oral recitation. Commonplaces arranged everything in quotable statements ready to spring to mind when the need arose. The well-educated schoolboy had a notebook *für alle memorabilia*—for everything worth remem-

---

[62] From David Chytraeus, *Der fürnembsten heubtstück christlicher lehr nützliche erklerung* (Rostock, 1578), quoted in MGP 38: 336–37.

[63] For a discussion of the psychology of learning utilized in the Reformation, see Strauss, *Luther's House of Learning*, chap. 4.

[64] Vormbaum, 32.

[65] The unceasing appeals made throughout the sixteenth and seventeenth centuries by Lutheran churchmen to parents, to send their children to school, suggests that popular response to educational opportunities was not always enthusiastic. And the evidence in visitation reports makes it possible to argue that schooling was less effective than had been anticipated in producing the hoped-for change in habits. For a discussion of the problem of response to Reformation pedagogy, see Strauss, *Luther's House of Learning*, chaps. 12–13.

bering in each subject.[66] Having completed his training, the pupil, when he spoke, fell readily into cadences not his own. His memory furnished learned phrases for every occasion. When reflecting on something, his mind came back with catalogued and labelled formulae. In such a system, learning was made useful, tidy, orderly, above all ideologically safe.

Actuality may not have been quite as bleak as this picture suggests. Results always fell short of intentions. On the other hand, the picture is essentially accurate as to the aims of pedagogues, school administrators, and the political and church figures who stood behind them. These men were not petty tyrants. Most of the time, most of them seem to have felt kindly toward their charges. But they were deeply worried about the state of the world, and twenty or thirty years of Reformation in Europe had done nothing to dispel their fears and allay their anxieties. The prospects seemed anything but favorable. In the Latin School these men saw a spark of hope because, as they believed, the new generations of leaders being trained up in them would, in the years of their intensive schooling, internalize the approved values and would thus be intellectually and psychologically prepared to exhibit and promote them in their lives. At the core of these approved values lay the structuring ideas of authority, hierarchy, and order, the prerequisites of a stable society. As the ministers of these ideas, Reformation schoolmen were anything but liberal educators, despite their devotion to the liberal arts. They were dismayed to see—as the preamble to one school ordinance put it—"the flower of our young men wasted by being allowed to live by their own will."[67] "Not to let them have their will" (*ihnen iren willen nicht lassen*) was the essence of education, a process in which natural wishes, habits, inclinations, and tastes were replaced by a higher volition, the will of society's cultural masters. To the extent that they helped bring about this substitution, the schools of the Lutheran Reformation functioned as instruments of acculturation.

---

[66] Visitation ordinance for the Darmstadt *Paedagogium* 1655, MGP 27: 135.

[67] From regulations for preceptors at the *Domschule* in Güstrow 1619, printed in H. Schnell, *Das Unterrichtswesen der Grossherzogtümer Mecklenburg-Schwerin und Strelitz*, MGP 44: 33.

IX

Liberal or Illiberal Arts?

Public Schools in Renaissance France. By George Huppert (Urbana and Chicago: University of Illinois Press, 1984. xvii, 159 pp.).

George Huppert's latest book is just the sort of effort one has come to expect from the author of *Les Bourgeois Gentilhommes* (1977) and *The Idea of Perfect History* (1970). It is interesting, richly detailed, deeply researched, elegant in its proportions and presentation. It tells an encouraging story on a subject we all care about: schools and schooling. It shows how in the course of the sixteenth century there came to flourish in secondary schools in a very large number of French cities and towns a spirit of audacity and questioning, a critical intelligence, a mood of secularism and reform. Before this spirit was subdued late in the century by clerical meddling, statist intervention, and schoolmasterly routine, a precedent had been set, and a paradigm created to guide and inspire progressive pedagogues in ages to come. In its tensions between laity and clergy, between forward-straining and reaction, trust and suspicion, education for life, and indoctrination for compliance, the story has drama and suspense. It has its heroes: above all the admirable company of *régens* to whom we are introduced in this book — able teachers, urbane Erasmians — but also the practical-minded burgher magistrates who supported them to the hilt. And there are villains: men of the cloth and of the robe, fighting to hold on to, or regain, their power over minds, unadventurous spirits whose educational priority it was to make learning safe. The brief history of this eventful encounter of opposing forces engages not only our interest, but our passions as well, for no one can be neutral where conflict turns on so fateful a social and generational issue as the forming of our children and the shaping, through them, of the future.

Professor Huppert draws an altogether positive picture of the educational experiment undertaken by French pedagogues and their bourgeois backers. More than in any other country in Europe, secondary schools in France developed independently of church and state, and for this reason were able to serve and advance secular and empirical values. From the late fifteenth century, French bourgeois had battled churchmen for the power to direct their children's education. Having won control over schools, they showed themselves willing to spend large sums of tax money on buildings and staff while holding administration and curriculum firmly in their own hands. With "good learning and good *moeurs*" as the end products of schooling, alumni were to be prepared for prominent places in the world of affairs. No attempt was made to hide the elitism spurring the promotion of municipal *collèges*, but a wider social purpose was not absent. Children of "honest people who cannot afford to pay tuition" could enroll free of charge and — in principle at least — all residents were eligible to attend. The curriculum reflected these aims. The "new conception of the goals of schooling" was built on the most solid of all intellectual foundations: the corpus of Roman and Greek classics. Teachers, many of them trained in Paris, fanned out over the land to offer the enlightenment of humanism to impressionable young minds, arousing in the French bourgeoisie "a gargantuan appetite for classical learning." The results, as Professor Huppert describes them, were brilliant. The sixteenth-century French *collège* was an oasis of modernism in a medieval desert. It offered its pupils a sane refuge in a folly-ridden world. In an irrational culture it encouraged the processes of enlightened reason and functioned as a social equalizer in a society stratified according to traditional notions of rank. Its *régens* − at least the outstanding men among them − were innovators in a time of hide-bound traditions. Literature was taught as an introduction to the adult world. Learning was intended to make the boy critically perceptive. In this way schooling was to break the cake of custom and prepare the way for a new society. Hard work was expected, discipline enforced; punctuality, a sense of order, and regular habits were instilled, and piety demanded. Professor Huppert does not conceal the rigidity and tedium at work in sixteenth-century pedagogy. But the object of the undertaking was not the taming of native inclinations or the throttling of natural impulses, but their direction toward wisdom, conceived as an informed, flexible, responsive, pragmatic capacity for leadership in urban society.

Not that the phenomenon was without its questionable side. Why the abiding devotion to classical authors − authors who certainly had not written in their own time, nor had been reintroduced since, for the likes of merchants, traders, and artisans? Professor Huppert emphasizes, as other scholars have done, the blending of bourgeois and gentle status in the sixteenth-century city. But the real answer to the question, why the classics as the curricular base, must lie in their perceived worth as products, and in turn as moulders, of the best human intellects. Professor Huppert does not use the term, but acculturation, or rather selective acculturation, is clearly what was going on in the sixteenth-century French city where a few carefully chosen boys from the lower orders were admitted to the company of the better born to be jointly socialized, by means of the classical curriculum, to the good learning and good manners deemed right, useful, and pious by their civic guardians. And this was a good thing. For, with its new-found attachment to secular culture, the civic outlook was a bright beacon in a gloomy landscape. This is why, in the dramatic structure Professor Huppert gives to his narrative, this outlook had to succumb to the forces of darkness still dominating the European scene around 1600. To the latter, the school was far too dangerous a social mechanism to be left to the practical and the critical, the innovative and the inventive. It, and they, had to be brought to heel.

There is much about the circumstances of French secondary education as told in *Public Schools in Renaissance France* that can be confirmed from my own vantage point on the other side of the Rhine. In fact, the school system set up in the German Reformation − and I mean both the Protestant and the Catholic Reformations in the Holy Roman Empire − could serve as a clinching case in point of the aptness of Professor Huppert's portrayal of the enemies of liberal education and critical thinking, and for their success in making learning intellectually and socially harmless. There is, to be sure, a major difference between the respective situations. It is a difference, however, that strongly reenforces Professor Huppert's severe judgments on the educational intentions of church and state leaders. The difference is that, beginning in the late 1520s in Saxony, the homeland of the Lutheran Reformation, state and church teamed up in a powerful (though of course not necessarily effective) ideological and bureaucratic combination to direct and regulate public life. Not that church and state agreed on everything. But on one thing they did see eye to eye from the outset, and that was schooling: that it should be uniform across each territory, that it should be pedagogically effective, above all that it must inculcate approved religious and civic values as these were then being formulated in a spate of official pronouncements issued by councils and consistories. The seamless integration of schooling into this grand design for what Gerhard Oestreich, a student of early modern political organization in the Holy Roman Empire, has called *totale Sozialplanung* is made graphically explicit by the official publication in every German state of *Kirchenordnungen*, comprehensive codes of church legislation regulating every aspect of approved doctrine and conduct.

In each of these constitutions, the *Schulordnung* — the right order and method of governing schools — occupies a prominent place. Some attention was given to popular education. But the organizers' most strenuous effort went to Latin schools and Gymnasia. For the shaping of these elite institutions, theologians and churchmen were primarily responsible. They chose the authors to be read and set the time to be devoted to each; they established the sequence of subjects, determined lesson plans, set examinations, regulated leisure-time activities, and directed every remaining aspect of schooling.

School programs produced in this manner were virtually indistinguishable from each other. They featured the classical canon in ascending order from the so-called Cato to Virgil, some Greek but mostly Latin, religion but mostly the catechism. Unlike the bourgeois educators of whom Professor Huppert writes, German preceptors did not conceive of these procedures as innovations. The questioning and criticism Professor Huppert finds in the French *collèges* were conspicuous only by their absence. The vernacular was scarcely used; in many places it was expressly forbidden, all instruction being in Latin. Bible reading took place only in the learned tongues. What *was* new was the systematic approach now taken to education, and the direction given to the whole enterprise from the center. From ABC's all the way to professional degrees at university, the educational process was conceived, designed, and supervised as a unit. Its purpose: above all to produce a trained cadre for state and church; secondly to standardize knowledge and secure it as an orthodoxy, and to distribute this orthodoxy in controlled dosages to the population at large, from merest literacy and rote catechization at the base of the intellectual pyramid to encyclopedic knowledge of the entire approved canon at its peak. I do not mean to suggest that these objectives were ever reached. But I have no doubt that they were the desired goals toward which educational policy makers in the German Reformation directed their energies.

Now, apart from religion (reduced to the catechism), the staple of the German curriculum was the corpus of classics, the very same classical texts studied by boys in Professor Huppert's France. As one goes through hundreds of surviving school plans devised by educators in the service of Protestant and Catholic states, one begins to gain a sense of the agreement — indeed the virtual unanimity — among pedagogues on what education should be and how it should be conducted. They shared a cluster of common presuppositions, perceptions, and guiding ideas concerning human nature, society, religion, the function of education in the attempt to fit people into their appropriate places in the order of things, and the use of psychologically-based pedagogical methods for transmitting the agreed-upon canon of subjects in the time available during the pupils' impressionable years. The core of this endeavor was the body of texts called the classical curriculum, an intellectual and pedagogical canon, training in which produced the educated man. And of these classics Professor Huppert maintains that they were "indispensable instruments for thinking about the real world," and that teaching them was "a permanent call for criticism."

But how can this be? The whole idea of a "classic" is that it enshrines. And the point of a canon is that it sets a rule, establishing and perpetuating an orthodoxy. Shrines and orthodoxies remove texts, and the ideas they contain, from the give and take of debate, making them objects of veneration, not of argumentation. Traditionally the classics had been taught for the main purpose of handing down from one generation to the next the perduring standards considered vital by society's opinion molders. This had been so in the school rooms of Roman antiquity, as H.I. Marrou showed us long ago in his splendid *History of Education in Antiquity*. And it was still so when I attended Gymnasium in Germany in the 1930s. That it is no longer so today is due entirely to the deep changes that have taken place in the social and political structures of our post-industrial civilization. It has little to do directly with the intrinsic worth of Roman and Greek literature. The kinds of questions students are now apt to ask — of an ancient author as of everything else — what does he have to say to *me*? What is he doing for *me*? were, quite literally, inconceivable then. When I was in school I didn't wonder how Cicero proposed to help me in my young life any more than I would have asked: what has gravity done for me? The classics simply *were*. They were *true*. They spoke of, and with, perfection. H.I. Marrou made this point in describing how Latin was taught to Roman boys, but referring as well to the entire classical curriculum: "A tyrannical classical ideal," he writes "dominated this teaching which ignored the fact that. . .words are living things. Latin *was*; it was there for all time in the great writers; the science of correct speaking. . .was based in the last analysis on *auctoritas*."[1] How, then, could there have been criticism and thinking about the real world going on in the French class room when it was the whole thrust of classical education to substitute the cult of a static intellectual ideal for an empirically derived sense of real life?

The distinguishing feature, as I see it, of the governing mind in state and city was caution and distrust: distrust of human nature (portrayed in alarmingly unattractive ways by the theologians), distrust therefore of the interactions of people in society, and immense caution in approaching the problems of governing them, especially the task of socializing the young. If there was an ideal or a model in the mind's eye of the sixteenth-century German magistrate, it was an image of a stable order frozen into a permanent disposition of all members in their proper places and duties. Legislation was intended to produce an approximation of this ideal. The fact that it always fell short was ascribed to the inevitable frustrations dogging the efforts of feeble humanity. Schools were part of this scheme of things. Indeed it can be argued that they were the essential part of it, because the notion of order — the *Ordnungsgedanke* — which was the paradigm idea governing all theological and political thinking at the time — was most successfully realized in the organization of schools. In all likelihood, schools were the only place in society where the right *Ordnung* of things could be not merely blueprinted, but also carried into action. No other institution was so amenable to regulation. The orderly sequence of classes, the ranked seating in each room, the rigidly regulated school day, prescribed and inflexible routines of teaching and learning, the daily demand for verbatim recitations, frequent examinations and ceaseless visitations and inspections, an inexhaustible flow of minutely detailed *Schulordnungen* — these features of the sixteenth-century German Latin school identify it as the desired *ordo* in nucleus. The aim was uniformity of instruction from identical texts and authors by carefully selected teachers under the eagle-eyed surveillance of state and church officials. Forbidding as it sounds, this was the reality of schools in the settings with which I am familiar. And I cannot imagine that things were very different in another country which shared with Germany the same traditions and faced many of the same problems.

It was the classical curriculum, along with the catechism, that enabled this rigid system to perform according to its plan. This aspect of the classics, or rather the teaching of them — namely as purveyors of static norms and as guarantors of conformity — has, to my mind, never been sufficiently acknowledged by historians of education. But consider this: At an age and state of immaturity long before his intellectual defenses were in place, the pupil was subjected to relentless drill in two languages in which expression was entirely contrary to the habits of his natural tongue, and whose stock of ideas was alien to the thinking processes of his familiar world. While learning these — for him — artificial languages, he was required to parrot with his lips and exemplify in his daily conduct a set of precepts handed down to him as embodying nearly the whole of discovered truth, requiring no demonstration and admitting of no argument.

Torn from the accustomed milieu of his family, where he had been in the company mostly of women, the boy was thrown abruptly into the cold rigors of a male society where the stern virtues of *gravitas, severitas,* and − above all − *auctoritas* reigned along with a generous dose of punishment considered good for him. An extraordinary procedure, this must seem to us. But not so strange, really, as soon as one remembers that this regimen was, and was meant to be, the beginning of a course of training for leadership, in the service of which the school and what it taught functioned as what Anton Schindling, who has written the social history of the Gymnasium in the city of Strasbourg, has called "a criterion of social selection." Schindling shows how this criterion, which was intended to identify and advance the ablest among the students (ablest, of course, as judged by an officially approved standard of values) served Strasbourg's political elite by not only providing their sons with relatively low-cost training for appropriate careers, but also, and more importantly, by establishing *Bildung* − mental cultivation − as a condition legitimizing the position of their class, by distributing social chances according to a fixed norm of achievement, and by putting into action a technique for suffusing society from its top with a disciplinary program.[2] This was the real agenda of sixteenth-century pedagogues. It explains why state and church contended so vigorously for the control of education, for much more was at stake than the choice of a text or the proportion of religion to literature in a school plan. It was a question of power: the power to shape individuals and through them the whole of society.

Every aspect of schooling reflects this overall social purpose. The best example is grammar, the heart of the classical curriculum and the center piece of the entire pedagogical enterprise. The essence of grammar is rules, normative and prescriptive rules, and the drill by which these rules are instilled. A few educational reformers − Sir Thomas Elyot for one − warned at the time against a near-exclusive reliance on grammar in the lower forms. But Elyot was ahead of his age. The "burden of grammar," as he called it, was not lifted from the shoulders of Latin schoolboys. Nor could pedagogues see any reason why it should be, for the method dated back to antiquity itself and carried the endorsement of the very best Greek and Roman experts. Learning the rules, and exhibiting them in one's speech, was what grammar was about. Learning the rules and exhibiting them in one's life was what membership in society was about. Grammar was therefore a paradigm of citizenship, or rather subjectship. One learned the norms and lived by them, punctiliously. "Nothing maintains discipline so much," declared the Jesuit *ratio,* "as observing the rules." This article can stand as the motto of the whole pedagogical enterprise.[3]

Literature was cut to the same pattern. Some works, and even a few authors, were read in their entirety in the upper classes. But mental habits for understanding them were established much earlier, in the lower forms, when bits and pieces of approved wisdom were converted into entries in books of commonplaces and ephemerides. In this procedure excerpts from authorized writers were culled under pre-established headings and then endlessly recycled without much regard to their original context: fragmented and segmented precepts yielding an almost inexhaustible store of neatly packaged definitions and judgments. This is how students first met the classics: as lifted quotations, disembodied adages, ticketed pearls of wisdom. A look at Leonhard Culman's *sententiae pueriles* or Camerarius's *praecepta morum* will convey an idea of how this spoon feeding worked in the lower classes. I do not think it is reasonable to doubt that the practice of reducing all thought to commonplaces formed the pupil's attitudes to Latin and Greek authors (and also to the Bible), and that by the time he was exposed to them directly, in the upper forms, his mind was safely set in the approved patterns. I cannot see how any other result could have been obtained, or was meant

366

to be obtained.

Now, is it likely that such a system, if conscientiously implemented, as the sources tell us that by and large it was, would fail to produce in all but a few exceptional cases a mentality as rigid as the operations by which it functioned? When the building blocks of the structure of thought were so carefully chosen and so meticulously put in place, is it likely that free and agile minds grew and imagination flourished? We cannot, of course, conclusively prove that they did not. We do know, however, that it was not the intention of sixteenth-century pedagogues to produce free spirits, but rather fettered minds — by which I mean intellects firmly and safely moored to established rules of thought or — changing the metaphor — running unswervingly on tracks laid down to guide the thinking process in a straight and narrow line from impulse to fully formulated utterance and action. Commonplaces arranged everything that was learned into memorizable and recallable assertions, ready to spring to mind when appropriate categories were triggered by the need to refer to something. Having finished his education, the pupil, when he spoke, fell readily into pre-formed cadences. His memory furnished appropriate phrases for every occasion. When he reflected on a problem his mind came back with catalogued and labelled topics. In this way thinking was made predictable, and therefore safe.

In other words, the pedagogy of the sixteenth century employed the classics as a means of intellectual, moral, and behavioral conditioning. In that sense they were instruments of wielding power. They gave little or no useful information. They did not train the imagination to respond inventively to the unexpected and unfamiliar. They did not, so far as one can tell, inspire an enjoyment of literature or a respect for genius. What they did do was to exalt authority, sanction imitation, and promote compliance. The right response to them was a model of good citizenship. And schooling was intended to put this model into effect, through the lives of selected individuals who were expected to think and act as *exempla*, examples to be faithfully imitated by the rest of us.

One final thought seems à propos. If it should be shown that the picture of schooling given here based on the German sources does not hold for other countries, and that teaching the classics in France and elsewhere did, in fact, encourage free-wheeling speculation, critical examination, and imaginative reflection, I would argue, in response, that this tells us little about the intellectual principles animating the larger society beyond the schoolhouse walls. For where schools do function as laboratories of intellectual experimentation and citadels of liberating learning, it is likely that they are given this role to play by a society that, while recognizing as natural human traits the urge to probe, explore, judge, venture, reject, and seek alternatives, fears these inclinations as potentially destructive instincts that must be confined and channelled. This channelling, too, is a social function of schools. In playing this part, schools provide a benign but controlled, and above all temporally bounded institutional environment where thought can range freely and where few limits are placed on what can be said and written: no idea so unconventional, no criticism so sharp, that it may not be allowed its advocates in classroom discussion. But this is because such discussion occurs in an artificial setting created for this very purpose. School is not life. It is school, or college, a place and a time to sow one's intellectual wild oats so that for the rest of one's life one may say, perhaps nostalgically, "I was a radical too, in my young days," implying that iconoclasm is a posture suitable to the young, something to be got out of one's system with the other traits of adolescence. Maturity is victory over the rebellious tendencies of tempestuous youth, and the knowledge that one is the safer from their blandishments for having indulged them to one's heart's content in the salad days of one's minority. Could this not be the real objective of schools wherever they permit the young to be free and spontaneous?

FOOTNOTES

1. H.I. Marrou, *A History of Education in Antiquity* tr. George Lamb (London, 1956), 277.

2. Anton Schindling, *Humanistische Hochschule und freie Reichsstadt. Gymnasium und Akademie in Strassburg 1538-1621* (Wiesbaden, 1977), 385-97.

3. See the enormous (in terms of space) emphasis given to grammar in the school plan attached to Philipp Melanchthon's *Unterricht der Visitatoren an die Pfarrherrn im Kurfürstenthum zu Sachsen. 1528* in Emil Sehling ed., *Die evangelischen Kirchenordnungen des 16.Jahrhunderts* I (Leipzig, 1902), 172-3.

X

Lutheranism and Literacy: A Reassessment

About a dozen years ago Professor Lawrence Stone published an influential article in *Past and Present* on the factors affecting the condition of education and literacy in early modern Europe. He gave a prominent place among these factors to religion, especially to Protestant religion, because, as a religion of the book, Protestantism encourages reading, and therefore tends to promote literacy in society. He writes:

> In the early sixteenth century the Catholics were fearful of heresy because of Bible study, whereas the reformers were fearful of superstition because of lack of Bible study ... At this critical turning point in history [that is, the first large-scale social repercussions of mass production printing] the Protestants seized on the new invention but the Catholic world, after initial encouragement, soon realized its subversive potential and turned against it.[1]

Professor Stone develops this argument primarily in relation to English Puritanism. But he advances his explicit association of Protestantism with Bible-reading, and hence with reading itself, as a generalisation on the whole age of the Reformation.

This argument will be recognised as a commonplace in the vast literature on the Reformation, as well as in the much smaller, and mostly recent, body of writing on early modern European literacy. Most scholars seem to have concluded, or seem to assume, that the Protestant Reformation greatly advanced literacy because Protestantism was, much more than Catholicism, the religion of the word, and therefore of reading, and because it insisted on every individual's right – indeed his duty – to experience the word for himself. Reading was promoted—so the argument goes—to allow people to exercise this right and fulfil this duty. Schools were established and vernacular Bibles made available. And all this happened first in Germany, where Martin Luther turned the New, and then the Old, Testaments into plain German, and where he and his fellow reformers encouraged men and women to discover the truth for themselves by encountering it at first hand in Scripture; where a flood of Bibles issued from the presses, and where schools were established or improved so that a condition of general literacy might be created and perpetuated in the population.

This, or something very like it, is the common view of things.[2] The emblem for it is the title page illustration in John Foxe's *Actes and Monuments* where a group of devout Protestant men and women holding their Bibles is contrasted with a circle of suspicious-looking Catholics fingering their beads.[3] The task I have set myself is to find out whether this picture is in fact true as far as Luther and the German Reformation are concerned. Did Luther's Reformation promote Bible-reading? Did it advance common education? Did it therefore and thereby extend literacy in the population? At issue is not so much the general question of education and literacy itself. It is a fact that schools of all levels, including popular German language schools, increased in number and quality in the age of the Reformation;[4] it is also true, though not so readily demonstrable and quantifiable, that literacy spread through the German population in the course of the sixteenth century.[5] These questions, I say, are not at issue here. What *is* at issue is the link between these phenomena in German social history and Martin Luther's Reformation as their efficient cause. *Was* Luther, was the Lutheran Reformation with its dedication to *sola scriptura*, really responsible for the expansion of schooling and literacy in the sixteenth century?

First a few words about this expansion. It may not be generally known that Germany experienced in the sixteenth century a large-scale growth of educational institutions. I am not now referring to such intellectual forcing houses as the classical Gymnasia, the elite boarding schools for the superbright, or the universities. The expansion I refer to is of common, elementary local schools where rudimentary teaching was given to the children of ordinary people. Most of the facts concerning this development lie buried in regional histories and specialised monographs, most of all in huge piles of documents in local archives. They show that in region after region in the Holy Roman Empire, in princely states and ecclesiastical domains and cities and towns, networks of schools were organised in the course of the sixteenth century, often building on older foundations, but in every case extending, strengthening what already existed, if not starting anew. The goal was a centralised system of general education controlled from the chancellery or the consistory, locally financed though supplemented, where needed, by government aid. Needless to say, this ambitious, modern-seeming aim was not always achieved. But as an objective it emerges clearly from the documents. Its purpose appears to have been twofold: to guarantee the production in the future of trained professionals for service in state and church; secondly, to equip the populace at large with enough reading and writing to enable them to function in their various stations in life. By and large these goals seem to have been met. Towns and cities had fine Latin schools, of course, many of them institutions of great distinction. But village schools, too, were common, though many of them seem to have led a shaky existence, frequently shut down for harvest work, or bad weather, or impassable roads or a bridge down, or owing to a great dying among the children, or because parents were too poor or tight-fisted to pay the trifling sum it took to keep the schoolroom heated and the teacher in bread and beer. Nearly always, however, they started up again to teach at least two of the conventional three Rs along with a little religion. As a result of all this, basic functional literacy does seem to have spread through the population.[6] I cannot prove it statistically, and I do not want to estimate percentages. But my work with the sources has left me with a definite impression that a considerable portion of the populace in towns and countryside was being trained to read and to write. For precisely what purpose, however, and with exactly what consequences, is not at all clear. The documents from which I take the evidence for the existence of schools and the relative prevalence of literacy tell me very little about the objectives to which these conditions related.

In the absence of a good answer to the question of purpose – why so much schooling for the populace, why literacy for the many? – it has been generally supposed that Lutheranism was the critical factor in the promotion of schools and the advance of public literacy in early modern Germany. This is the supposition I want to question. Let me begin to do so at the source: Luther himself. What does Luther say about the objectives of schooling, about reading, and especially about reading the Bible?

This question is easily answered. Luther said a great deal, and most of what he said favoured the school as a specialised institution for preparing a professional cadre, one that was capable of assuming positions of leadership in church and state: pastors and preachers, theologians and church administrators, lawyers and bureaucrats, teachers, doctors. This is the argument of his two most important pieces of writing on the subject: *An Admonition to the Councillors of All German Cities to Establish and Maintain Christian Schools* of 1524, and the sermon *Children Should Be Sent to School* of 1530.[7] Both are vigorous, indeed passionate, polemics for his conviction that academic learning – especially the languages and arts of the liberal curriculum – are indispensable in a Christian society. Luther aimed his fire at two quarters from which this conviction was just then under attack: spiritualists, *Schwärmer*, and others of that ilk, men who claimed for their ideas the authority of immediate divine inspiration, and to whom the study of Greek and Hebrew was therefore nothing but idle pedantry; secondly, a kind of vulgar bourgeois utilitarianism which – so Luther feared–was starving out the academic schools. Luther's own aims for schooling were both sharply focused and broad. He is for general education. He even favours obligatory school attendance.[8] All youngsters – girls along with boys, poor as well as rich – should learn to read and write. But these objectives have little to do with the benefits of a general education or with any attempt to raise the level of public virtue. Their chief purpose is to identify and select able pupils, to skim off the best and move them – only the boys, of course – rapidly through the better schools and Gymnasia to the university and on to their careers.[9] In this way no boy of talent would be lost to society, and church and state would never need to worry about their *Nachwuchs*, the steady supply of qualified young men to help manage state and church.[10] There is no doubt that this is what Luther had chiefly in mind when he wrote about education in 1524, in 1530 and to the end of his life. When the opportunity arose to put the principle into practice, he made it the foundation of public education in his own state of Saxony. In *The Visitors' Instruction to the Pastors in Saxony* of 1528, a comprehensive blueprint for the new state church, written by Melanchthon and with a preface by Luther, it was stated at the very beginning of the section on education that children must attend school 'so that men may be trained who are qualified to teach in the church and govern in the world'.[11] Nothing is said in this document, a model school and curriculum plan as it became, about general or popular education, secular or religious. Provision is made for 'Christian instruction',[12] but this, as everything else, is given only in Latin. Latin as a language and as a culture is the heart of the whole programme. Lessons and books were those of the traditional arts programme. The overriding aim of the procedure was to separate the able from among the many and complete the quality education of the former.

But this cannot be the whole story. If Luther and Melanchthon, and their colleagues in the movement, believed it to be the chief aim of schools to produce qualified public servants, they did not see this as their only aim. They acknowledged the existence below the network of Latin schools of a host of German vernacular schools where the rudiments of reading, writing and religion were given to a large, scattered, intellectually undifferentiated, urban and rural juvenile population. What should be taught in these schools? In view of the reformers' mostly disparaging remarks about the common crowd,[13] what kind of education, especially what sort of religious education, did they think the masses should receive? Ought *Herr Omnes* to be a fluent reader? Should the *Pöbel* read the Bible? Can one trust the *Haufen* to read it with the right understanding? Let us see what Luther has to say on the subject of common Bible-reading, a subject that would seem to go to the heart of the Reformation as a social and cultural event, as opposed to an event merely in the history of ideas.

A survey of Luther's words on this point shows him favouring the principle of 'Every man his own Bible-reader' until about 1525 – a year that was in many respects the great divide in the history of the Reformation – then falling mostly silent on the subject and, at the same time, taking actions that effectively discouraged, or at least failed effectively to encourage, a direct encounter between Scripture and the untrained lay mind. In 1520, in the *Appeal to the Christian Nobility of the German Nation* – a sweeping reform plan for church and society – he put it to his public that

> Above all other things, Holy Scripture must be the foremost and common subject in universities and secondary schools, and the Gospel in elementary schools. And would God that every town had a girls' school in which young girls were taught a daily lesson in the New Testament, either in German or in Latin, so that by the time a young Christian person had reached the ninth or tenth year, he would be familiar with the entire Holy Gospel.[14]

Even more explicitly revealing of Luther's intentions in these early years of the Reformation are the short prefaces he supplied for his 1522 German translation of the New Testament. It is my purpose in these introductory remarks, Luther says, to make sure that the common man 'will not be looking for commandment and law where he should instead look for Gospel and promise' – in other words, mistake the whole meaning of the Gospel.[15] There is so much confusion abroad now on religious matters, Luther says, unhappily, that the simple person needs a guide to the right understanding of Scripture. Clearly he meant his new translation of the Bible to be placed in the hands of the public at large. Of the Gospel According to John, and of Paul's Epistle to the Romans, he says that they are 'the true kernel and marrow of these books, and every Christian should read these first and foremost and' – he goes on – 'by means of daily reading make them as common and ordinary to himself as his daily bread'.[16]

But in later years Luther seems to have grown increasingly doubtful of people's ability to understand these essential distinctions. It is significant – it is certainly interesting – that most of the references to 'reading' the Gospel by ordinary people are dropped from the otherwise unchanged prefaces to the 1546 edition of his New Testament.[17] From the preface to the New Testament as a whole they were omitted altogether; only two indirect references to common reading remain, one in the preface to Acts, the other in the introduction to Romans.[18] Luther did not entirely abandon his view that the Bible is simple for the simple, difficult only for the subtle and devious – 'the smart alecs and wheeler-dealers in the world', as he put it in an after-dinner remark.[19] Nor did he let go of his basic conviction that all reform must be accomplished within the individual conscience, where the Gospel has to take root and produce an internal change, before external constraints – laws, regulations, and such – can work. But by the second half of the 1520s he no longer thought that this internal change could be effected by means of private Bible study. On the contrary; he seems to have antici-pated chaos and confusion as the results of such ungovernable personal relations with the Bible, and he could point to enough recent events to give substance to his fears. Expert guidance was needed now: above all, preaching by authoritative interpreters. He had hinted at this as early as 1524, in his appeal to city councilmen, where he asked rhetorically: Why bother with Latin, Greek and Hebrew when we have the Bible in German now? and answered: Because no one can know what the Scripture really says without first having studied it in the original tongues. Even among the church fathers, he goes on, those who didn't know Greek and Hebrew 'weren't sure of what it all meant'.[20] Later he grew adamant on the need for expertise. 'Nowadays everyone thinks he is a master of Scripture', he said, 'and every Tom, Dick and Harry imagines he understands the Bible and knows it inside out.' 'But', he went on, 'all the other arts and skills have their preceptors and masters from whom one must learn, and they have rules and laws to be obeyed and adhered to. Only Holy Scripture and the Word of God seems to be open to everybody's vanity, pride, whim and arrogance, and is twisted and warped according to everybody's own head. That is why we have so much trouble now with factions and sects.'[21] To counteract this trend he began to publish works of popular indoctrination, above all the two catechisms of 1529. As everyone knows, the catechism caught on marvellously, and before long catechism-teaching became everywhere the approved and authorised method of religious instruction. It carried Luther's own imprimatur – 'The catechism is the layman's Bible', he said; 'it contains the whole of what every Christian must know of Christian doctrine';[22] even more important, it served the interests of church and political authorities who came to depend on catechisation as by far the most effective, efficient and, above all, the safest means of instilling in the multitude a reliable knowledge of religion – that is to say, of the officially formulated and established creeds of the Lutheran state churches then in process of building.

The proof of this can be found in the school ordinances issued by every Lutheran state (and also by most Catholic states) from about 1530.[23] These ordinances are impressive documents. They are authoritative, being published as integral parts of comprehensive ecclesiastical constitutions which established the legal framework for the operation of church and religion in a given state. They set down explicitly, in detail and with the power of the state to back it up, what was to be taught, to whom, when, how, from what books, in what manner, to what purpose. Few of them say very much about the Bible as a text for religious study in class, or anything about individual Bible-reading as a practice to be developed in the populace or a habit to be instilled in the young. The overwhelming majority of school ordinances assign only the catechism as an instrument of religious instruction for the school population at large.

Take the *Schulordnung* of the Duchy of Württemberg of 1559 as an example: a good example, because this more than any other curriculum plan became the model of school organisation in German territories and cities in the second half of the sixteenth century.[24] The New Testament turns up among the assigned books only in the fifth and sixth forms of the Latin school curriculum, and then it is the Latin and Greek New Testament, taken up in conjunction with the *Aeneid*, with Isocrates and with the *Cyropaedia* of Xenophon.[25] The Bible is studied also in so-called *Klosterschulen*, boarding schools where future ministers were trained, but that goes without saying.[26] In other words: only where the ablest students had already been segregated does the Gospel make its appearance as a study text, and then only in the learned languages. As for German-language schools, where – as the ordinance puts it – 'the children of working parents ... learn to pray and do the catechism, and in addition are taught to write and read and sing psalms',[27] – in these popular schools no Bible is listed among the books, no New Testament.

Similar provisions are found in the school ordinances of Mecklenburg, 1552;[28] Pomerania, 1563;[29] Saxony, 1580;[30] and so on. When the Bible makes its appearance in the curriculum, as it usually does in the fourth or fifth form, always in Latin and/or Greek, its reception has been prepared by several years of catechism drill. In the lower forms, beyond which most children never advanced, and in the common German schools, Bibles were scarcely to be found, only the catechism.[31] There are some exceptions to this pattern.[32] I could not be wrong, however, in concluding from my reading of most of the published and many of the vast number of unpublished school programmes that the great preponderance of these plans neither included Bible-reading among the subjects taken up in school, nor seems to have regarded training in this as an obligation to the young. Stories from the Old Testament, yes; selected passages from the evangelists, yes; Psalms and Proverbs, yes. But consecutive Bible study, or efforts to develop in the young a habit of turning to the Bible, no.[33]

The reason for this shift in the official Lutheran attitude is not difficult to grasp. Relying on the catechism instead of the Bible was a way of playing it safe. Catechisms spelled out the approved text and meaning of all the essentials of the creed. Catechisms came in many forms and levels, for all ages, varieties of intelligence and stages of preparation. They were suitable for memorisation: Luther's own Shorter Catechism of 1529 established this as one of their chief purposes. Incessantly repeated, they rooted basic religious precepts in the memory and thus ensured habits of correct thought – at least this is what contemporary learning theory taught.[34] In their explicit application of divine commands to the obligations of civic life, catechisms shored up the pillars of society.[35] No catechism explanation of the fourth commandment therefore failed to underline, often heavily, the God-imposed duty to obey not only father and mother but, as well, all one's superiors in the ranked order of society. Luther himself recommended this use of the catechism as an instrument of socialisation. He said – in the preface to the Shorter Catechism of 1529, addressed to his fellow pastors – that, although no one can be forced to learn against his will, 'one must drive the common crowd until they know what counts as right and what counts as wrong in the land where they live and earn their bread'.[36] In other words, one must teach respect for, and loyalty to, prevailing social and political conventions. This goal could never be achieved by Scripture alone with its many ambiguities requiring informed explanation. The catechism, on the other hand, was safe, certain and – it was believed – effective. 'One single schoolboy can bring the catechism to a whole household', it was said. To its proponents, therefore, the catechism seemed a wonderful, self-proliferating device for effecting reform in religious and civic life, both in attitudes and in behaviour. Lutheran theologians and pedagogues really believed this.

Now, catechism teaching and catechism recitation were predominantly oral activities. They had to be if they were to have any chance of succeeding with a population still largely illiterate or at best minimally literate. Memorising and repeating the catechism was every child's duty; saying it back when required to do so was the adult's obligation at visitation time and occasionally in church. Fluent reading was not necessary to these tasks, nor, indeed, reading of any kind. Catechisation had a long oral tradition to fall back on and could flourish in a culture of non-readers. This is not a judgement about literacy itself, only about the linkage usually made between learning to read on the one hand and, on the other, Lutheran reliance on the Bible as a spur or incentive to reading. There was plenty of interest in the former. Governments fostered literacy in many ways,[37] and from below, too, demands were often raised for schools and effective teaching, especially teaching of reading and writing. The documentation for this is large.[38] But this documentation bears witness, above all, to the practical, utilitarian aims of a citizenry more and more alert to the importance of literacy as a precondition of keeping or raising one's place in a changing world,[39] and of governments apparently beginning to associate literacy with political loyalty. We do not yet know exactly what went on at these two levels. One *can* say, however, and I think we should say, that the evidence for claiming that Lutheran authorities wished to turn a whole population into a nation of Bible-readers, and for this reason promoted general literacy – that the evidence for this claim is exceedingly thin.

But what about all those Bibles that poured throughout the century from the publishing houses of Wittenberg, Augsburg, Basle, Zürich, Hagenau, Grimma, Leipzig, Nuremberg, Strasbourg, Erfurt?[40] Where did they go? Who read them? This question is not difficult to answer. Most of them went to parish churches and pastors' libraries, purchased by governments or bought out of church revenues, as directed by church authorities. Prices of Bibles were on the steep side in the sixteenth century: 2 gulden, 8 groschen for the first complete German Bible of 1534 – equivalent to more than a month's wages of an ordinary labourer at that time. The 1522 New Testament fetched from a half to one-and-a-half gulden. Half a gulden is what a mason's or carpenter's journeyman earned for four days' work. These were all folios. The quartos and octavos came later, but they were not cheap.[41] Not very many people could afford to buy them – and there were in sixteenth-century Germany no Bible-distributing agencies, as they did come into existence two centuries later among the Lutheran Pietists of Halle. In fact, most German Bibles printed in the sixteenth century were bought by parish churches out of public funds to be used by impecunious ministers, and by pastors and ministerial candidates, who were obliged, by law, to own them.[42] One example: the princes of Anhalt in Saxony purchased a quantity of the 1541 Wittenberg Bible, fearing, as they wrote,[43] that with Luther said to be ill and preoccupied now, this edition might well turn out to be the last authoritative text to appear in print. Similar action was taken by governments in every territory and city.[44] There were enough parishes in Lutheran realms, and enough young men preparing for the ministry, to account for most of the Bibles produced in Germany in the sixteenth century. The archives hold thousands of book lists submitted by Lutheran pastors to their superiors, most of them with two or more Bibles.[45] Of course I do not claim that no layman ever owned a Bible. We know of many who did, and many of these no doubt read it, although it has also been pointed out that household Bibles could serve several purposes other than reading.[46] Nor am I denying that men and women were apt to be moved by an eloquent preacher or by the touching words and affecting melodies of Lutheran hymns to turn to the Bible. One can imagine this happening, probably often. But if it did, this was not in consequence of, or because it reflected the intention of, Lutheran authorities. They favoured the catechism, at least for the great mass of their subjects.

To summarise: the facts as we can establish them do not substantiate the generally accepted supposition – which no one has ever felt obliged to prove – of a causal link between the Lutheran Reformation and popular Bible-reading. If one wishes to argue that Lutheran authorities promoted direct contact between people and Bible, one must first ask: what people, in what circumstances? I think it highly likely that Lutheran churchmen and magistrates distinguished between well set-up burghers expounding God's word at home to their wives, children, relations, apprentices, domestic servants and, on the other hand, the day labourer, the village tradesman, the farm hand and the lonely widow in her cottage at the edge of the hamlet.

Clearly the Bible was safer with the former than with the latter, not only because they were apt to be better educated, but also, perhaps mainly, because their social position shielded them from the host of hazardous ideas that a less established, less contented person might draw from his or her personal occupation with the sacred text. Lutherans never forgot the traumatic experiences of the 1520s when even trained minds had – so Luther thought – fatally misread the Bible. The acrimonious theological controversies of the second half of the century did nothing to lessen the overriding concern with orthodoxy. Confronting an increasingly pluralistic and unstable religious situation, Lutheran authorities were far too scared of heterodoxy to urge, or encourage, people to meet the Bible on their own terms. For a senior schoolboy to study the New Testament in the orderly sequence of a closely supervised school programme was one thing. To read it as a lay person, without guide or control, was quite another. This point is strengthened if we turn for the sake of comparison to one of the better-known advocates of unrestricted Bible-reading in the early sixteenth century, Valentin Ickelsamer, a distinguished grammarian and teacher in Rothenburg, Augsburg and various other places. In introducing his *Right Method for Learning to Read in a Short Time*, a teach-yourself manual printed in 1527, Ickelsamer declares that never has the ability to read been so precious as it is at the present time. Every person, he says, can now read the word of God for himself, not only read it but – he goes on – 'be a judge of it, all by himself' (*desto bass darin urteilen möge*).[47] Now, this is exactly what Lutheran authorities were afraid of: judging for themselves, by the unqualified. Why did Ickelsamer favour it? Because he was a partisan of Andreas Karlstadt; he was a *Schwärmer*, a spiritualist. He believed in direct inspiration. He attacked Luther for having broken with Karlstadt over this issue. He said that 'the Gospel gives us the freedom to believe and the power to judge',[48] and he meant it.

There, I think, is the crux of the matter. Sixteenth-century Lutherans never managed to dissociate Bible-reading from the spiritualist heresy, and in a world predominantly peopled by non-Christian worldlings (in Luther's two-realms terminology), the possibility for false inferences from ignorant or wrong-headed or deluded reading were legion, and their consequences terrifying. Hence the turn away from Scripture and towards the catechism, where there was nothing to judge, only to memorise and repeat.[49]

But this leaves us with the question: why, then, did governments support popular literacy? If the evangelical impulse was absent, or had been suppressed by fears of causing trouble, and if basic religion could be most effectively taught orally by means of the catechism, why bother to promote reading and writing in the population?

I do not claim to have a satisfactory answer to this question, but some hunches about it may be of interest to students of the Reformation and society in early modern Europe. Undoubtedly the primary motive was the principle of selection, which has been described. The expanding state and the aggressive church needed a large recruiting pool for their proliferating bureaucracies, at least the top echelons of which required specialised training in law, theology, letters, pedagogy, and so on. A strong elitist impulse was, therefore, at work from the base to the peak of the educational system.

But this does not mean that the great mass of ordinary people was seen only as so much dross to be discarded when the nuggets had been picked from among them. I think sixteenth-century rulers took their duties as Christian princes seriously. They never forgot that they would in time be called upon to justify their conduct to their maker. Their intentions towards their subjects – all their subjects – tended to be benevolent, however misguided some of their actions may appear to us now. They were not likely therefore to turn a deaf ear to the many requests for schooling reaching them from towns and villages across their realms. They knew of course that these pleas reflected entirely practical needs. People wanted to read and write so as to be able to hold their own or advance in the world. Petitions for school support make this quite clear, and there are thousands of such pleas in the archives.[50] This kind of pressure from below has been called the 'pull factor' in the growth of literacy.[51] Favourable governmental response, the 'push factor', was occasioned by sympathy with such popular requests, but also by independent calculations, and not only for the purpose of selecting the ablest to staff government bureaucracy. Rulers were told by their theologians that reading is a godly activity, a divine command; and as Christian magistrates they were not inclined to disobey it. This is why the preambles of so many school ordinances quote Paul, 1 Timothy 13: 'Continue with reading, admonishing, teaching,' (in Luther's version), and go on to comment that 'not for nothing is reading mentioned first in this passage'.[52] There was also the notion – to which Luther alluded in his 1524 tract to city councillors – that readers make good citizens.[53] Bucer pointed this out to the magistrates of Strasbourg. 'Practice in reading will make the common people more polite, peaceful, and disposed to the civic life', he said. The alternative was ignorance of law resulting in social chaos.[54] I think governments accepted this argument and for this reason, too, did what they could to broaden the base of literacy. There is a puzzle in this. We today would think that literacy makes people more independent-minded, but this could not possibly have been the objective of sixteenth-century governments. How, then, did rulers reconcile their benign accommodation to public desire for literacy with their conservative aims as heads of the Reformation state and the Reformation church? I think the replacement of the Bible by the catechism makes it possible for us to understand what happened. Once public education had been firmly set in the track of catechisation, with the catechism the single source of religious knowledge, authorities no longer needed to fear the spread of false ideas. In an approved Lutheran catechism one could not find a false idea. This was certainly not true of the Bible, and it was always from the Bible that deluded spirits in recent experience had drawn their destructive ideas. Thus, given the central position – virtually the monopoly – of the catechism in school and in parish education, there was no further need for anxiety about unpredictable consequences of common reading.

But I suspect that even in this indirect way via the catechism Lutheranism did not have much to do with the rise of literacy. We know, to be sure, of one famous instance in early modern Europe where the Lutheran Reformation appears to have achieved nearly total literacy in a population. This happened in Sweden where, beginning in the late seventeenth century and culminating in the eighteenth, the established church undertook to make all men and women in the country read the catechism and give proof of this accomplishment by passing annual examinations. Excellent parish records were kept of these examinations, and they tell the story which, on the level of literacy at least, appears to be a success story.[55] Swedish authorities were quite free in the use of techniques of negative reinforcement designed to make everyone conform and perform. They withheld communion and refused permission to marry to those who flunked the test. This method seems to have worked. Egil Johansson's tables drawn from Swedish parish records give impressive evidence of success. By the middle of the eighteenth century virtually 100 per cent of men and women in Sweden could read. But what sort of literacy was this? People couldn't write a line – they were obliged only to learn to read. And whether they understood what they read is a question to which statistics cannot supply an answer. I am inclined to doubt that they did.

In any case no comparable effort was made in Germany. German authorities did not use Swedish strong-arm methods for compelling people to learn their catechism. And without effective force there was no way in which catechism study could have led to a steady increase in literacy in Germany, for there was nothing about the catechism that made people wish to read it. If they read it at all, or even if they merely memorised it by rote, they learned words, not sense. This we know from what I take to be a highly reliable source: the record of parish visitations carried on annually in all German states from the middle of the sixteenth century on. The verbatim protocols of these visitations, which were conducted jointly by church and state officials who used printed questionnaires for gathering their information, reveal abysmal ignorance in the population on nearly every point of the creed.[56] I find it difficult to imagine, after going through most of these visitation protocols for the sixteenth and early seventeenth centuries, that ordinary people, even after a century of formal religious instruction by means of the catechism, had much of a sense of themselves as Lutherans or Catholics or, indeed, as Christians. They knew much too little religion. Many knew none at all. At best they could parrot a phrase or two from the catechism. Of what it meant, few could give an intelligent account. This being the result of catechisation, it is not possible to imagine that catechisms were much of an inducement to reading. Nobody learned them without being coerced.

Which brings me back to my earlier conclusion: For our explanation of how literacy came to grow in the sixteenth century we must look to mundane, pragmatic causes, not to the Lutheran Reformation. To suggest otherwise is to mark out a false trail. I imagine that people in the sixteenth century, as in other times, had a rather good idea of what mattered to them in life, and a doctrinaire orthodoxy imposed on them by an authoritarian church by means of a rigid catechism was no part of it. Protestant pastors and politicians could not understand this. They were truly mystified that

120

people should wish to resist the saving message. I have no doubt that these men were high-minded and selfless. That they failed in their evangelical endeavour is no reflection on the merit of what they tried to do, though it is, I think, a sign of the instinct people seem to have for protecting themselves from uplifting ideas forced on them from above. Whether we read this sign as a sad or a hopeful comment on human nature depends on how we feel about the idea.

Notes

1 L. Stone, 'Literacy and education in England 1640–1900', *Past and Present*, Vol. XLII (February 1969), pp. 77–8.
2 cf. H. G. Haile, 'Luther and literacy', *Proceedings of the Modern Language Association*, Vol. XCI (1976), pp. 816–28: 'From a secular viewpoint, surely the most far-reaching effect of Luther's activity was the radical increase in literacy from the early 1520's on through the rest of the century' (p. 817). Haile's article actually offers no evidence for an increase in literacy. It deals mainly with Luther's ability to stimulate the imagination and thus heighten the *quality* of literacy.
3 The Foxe illustration is cited by E. Eisenstein, *The Printing Press as an Agent of Change* (Cambridge, 1979), Vol. I, p. 415.
4 I summarise the evidence for this in my *Luther's House of Learning. Indoctrination of the Young in the German Reformation* (Baltimore, Md., 1978), ch. 1.
5 For arguments for this expansion of literacy, see ibid., pp. 193–202; also R. Engelsing, *Analphabetentum und Lektüre: Zur Sozialgeschichte des Lesens in Deutschland* (Stuttgart, 1973), chs 5–7; B. Könneker, *Die deutsche Literatur der Reformationszeit. Kommentar zu einer Epoche* (Munich, 1975), Introduction.
6 This paragraph is a summary of findings I describe in *Luther's House of Learning*, chs 1 and 9.
7 *An die Ratsherren aller Städte deutschen Lands, dass sie christliche Schulen aufrichten und halten sollen* (1524), Weimar edition of Luther's works (hereafter cited as *WA*), 15, pp. 27–53; *Eine Predigt, dass man Kinder zur Schule halten solle* (1530), *WA* 30[II], pp. 517–88.
8 *WA* 30[II], p. 545; ibid., p. 586: 'Ich halt aber, das auch die oberkeit hie schuldig sey, die unterthanen zu zwingen, ihre kinder zur schule zu halten.'
9 Luther to Margrave Georg of Brandenburg, 18 July 1529, *WA Briefe* (hereafter cited as *WA Br*), 5, no. 1452.
10 *WA* 30[II], pp. 520, 545–6, 557–67, 586. See also Luther's preface to Justus Menius's *Oeconomia Christiana* (1529), *WA* 30[II], pp. 60–3. Also *WA Tischreden* (hereafter cited as *WA Tr*), nos 4033, 5557, 7032 and many others.
11 *Unterricht der Visitatoren an die Pfarrherrn im Kurfürstentum Sachsen* (1528), *WA* 26, p. 236.
12 ibid., p. 238.
13 For example, Melanchthon, *Unterricht der Visitatoren* in *Werke in Auswahl*, ed. R. Stupperich, Vol. I (Gütersloh, 1951), pp. 228, 234, 246, 268; Luther, *Deutsch Katechismus*, *WA* 30[I], p. 126. On the use of the term *Pöbel* in the sixteenth century, see R. H. Lutz, *Wer war der gemeine Mann? Der dritte Stand in der Krise des Spätmittelalters* (Munich and Vienna, 1979), pp. 82–3.
14 *An den christlichen Adel deutscher Nation* (1520), *WA* 6, p. 461.
15 *WA Bibel* 6, p. 2.
16 ibid., p. 10.
17 ibid., pp. 3, 5, 7, 9, 11.
18 ibid., pp. 414–15 (Acts); Vol. 7, pp. 2–3 (Romans).
19 *WA Tr*, no. 5468 (1542).
20 *An die Ratsherren aller Städte* (1524), *WA* 15, p. 39.
21 *WA Tr*, no. 6008.

22 ibid., no. 6288.
23 The Protestant ordinances are collected in R. Vormbaum (ed.), *Die evangelischen Schulordnungen des sechzehnten Jahrhunderts*, Vol. I (Gütersloh, 1860). For examples of Catholic ordinances, see G. Lurz (ed.), *Mittelschulgeschichtliche Dokumente Altbayerns*, Vol. I, Monumenta Germaniae paedagogica, Vol. XLI (Berlin, 1907).
24 The Württemberg *Schulordnung* of 1559 is printed in Vormbaum, *Die evangelischen Schulordnungen*, pp. 68 ff.
25 ibid., p. 73.
26 ibid., pp. 102–27.
27 ibid., p. 71.
28 ibid., p. 64.
29 ibid., pp. 172–3, 177–8.
30 ibid., pp. 293–4.
31 For another example see the Lutheran theologian Johann Marbach's *Bedencken von den Schulen, wie die im Furstenthumb Zwaienbrucken antzurichten seien* of 1558 (printed in K. Reissinger, *Dokumente zur Geschichte der humanistischen Schulen im Gebiet der bayerischen Pfalz*, Monumenta Germaniae paedagogica [MGP], Vol. XLIX, Berlin, 1911, pp. 14–38). Marbach confines the Bible to the upper classes, where it is read in the learned languages. Lower classes study only the catechism.
32 For example, Hamburg, *Schulordnung* 1529: Vormbaum, *Die evangelischen Schulordnungen*, p. 21; Hessen, *Schulordnung* 1594: W. Diehl (ed.), *Die Schulordnungen des Grossherzogtums Hessen*, MGP, Vol. XXXIII (Berlin, 1905), pp. 206, 208.
33 L. C. Green, 'The Bible in sixteenth-century humanist education', *Studies in the Renaissance*, Vol. XIX (1972), pp. 112–34, agrees that 'there was much less direct teaching of the Bible in Protestant schools of central Europe than is commonly supposed by those who have not had access to the original sources' (p. 113), but seems also to accept at face value what he calls the 'Protestant principle that every baptized person, as a priest before God, must be able to read his own Bible ...' (p. 118).
34 On the uses of catechism and catechisation in Lutheran education, see my *Luther's House of Learning*, cited n. 4 above, ch. 8.
35 For a demonstration of this argument, see ibid., pp. 140–50, 169, 239–46.
36 'soll man doch den Hauffen dahin halten und treiben, dass sie wissen was recht und unrecht ist bei denen, bey welchen sie wohnen, sich neren und leben wollen': *WA* 30^{I}, p. 272.
37 I present the evidence for this in *Luther's House of Learning*, pp. 10–28.
38 ibid., pp. 195–6.
39 I base this assertion on my reading of local school documents in a number of German archives, particularly correspondence between village communities and territorial governments, mostly on financial matters. An especially rich source is Württembergisches Hauptstaatsarchiv Stuttgart, Series A 284.
40 On the printing history of Luther's Old and New Testaments, see the introduction by P. Pietsch to 'Bibliographie der deutschen Bibel Martin Luthers 1522–1546', *WA Bibel 2*, pp. xx–xxviii; J. Luther, 'Der Wittenberger Buchdruck in seinem Übergang zur Reformationspresse', *Lutherstudien zur 4. Jahrhundertfeier der Reformation* (Weimar, 1917), pp. 261–82; W. Walther, *Luthers deutsche Bibel* (Berlin, 1917); O. Clemen, *Die Lutherische Reformation und der Buchdruck* (Leipzig, 1939); H. Volz, *Hundert Jahre Wittenberger Bibeldruck 1522–1626* (Göttingen, 1954), pp. 17–93; id., *Martin Luthers deutsche Bibel. Entstehung und Geschichte der Lutherbibel* (Wittig, 1978); id., in *Cambridge History of the Bible*, Vol. III (Cambridge, 1963), pp. 94–102; L. Febvre and H.-J. Martin, *L'Apparition du livre* (Paris, 1958), pp. 442–3.
41 On the prices of the various editions of Luther's Bible, see H. Volz, *Hundert Jahre Wittenberger Bibeldruck*, pp. 19, 79–80; Clemen, *Die Lutherische Reformation*, p. 25.
42 This assertion rests on my reading of two kinds of sources: (1) Church constitutions (*Kirchenordnungen*) which mandated Bibles in churches and in the private libraries of pastors (these are published in E. Sehling, ed., *Die evangelischen Kirchenordnungen des XVI. Jahrhunderts*, Leipzig, 1902–11, continued by the Institut für evangelisches Kirchenrecht der evangelischen Kirche in Deutschland, Tübingen, 1963 ff.; (2) the protocols of Lutheran visitations throughout the sixteenth century, which, among other

concerns, investigated the contents of pastors' libraries. For a general discussion of visitation records, see my *Luther's House of Learning*, ch. 12.

43 Sehling, *Die evangelischen Kirchenordnungen*, Vol. II, pp. 547–8.

44 Some additional examples: *Gemeine Verordnung und Artikel der Visitation in Meissen und Voitland* (1533): Saxon officials are to see to it 'dass von einer jeden kircheneinkommen den eingepfarrten selbs zum besten und zu irer sel heil ... folgende pücher erkauft, eingepunden und in jede pfar verordnet sol werden...'; eleven titles are mentioned, including Luther's Latin and German Bibles (Sehling, *Die evangelischen Kirchenordnungen*, Vol. I, pp. 194–5; see also ibid., pp. 244–5, 314, 349; *Kapitelordnung* issued by Friedrich Margrave of Brandenburg for Brandenburg-Ansbach, 1565 (Sehling, op. cit., Vol. XI, p. 351: every pastor must own a German Bible; *Visitationsordnung* for Pfalz-Neuburg, 1558 (Sehling, op. cit., Vol. XIII, p. 123); also *Generalartikel* 1576 (ibid., p. 175); *Visitationsordnung* for Hessen 1537 (Sehling, op. cit., Vol. VIII, p. 98): all towns and villages 'nach des gemeinen Kastens Vermögen' must buy for one gulden every year 'rechte gute nutzlichen biblische und andere dergleichen pücher'; again, 1566 (ibid., pp. 223–4): every parish church to spend part of its income on buying for its pastors books, especially the Bible in several languages; also Sehling, Vol. XV, p. 81 for County Hohenlohe 1553; Sehling, Vol. III, p. 448: Liegnitz und Brieg in Silesia; Sehling, Vol. II, p. 194: County Mansfeld, 1554; Sehling, Vol. I, p. 620: Oelnitz, 1582.

45 On the contents and implications of one such book list, see my article 'The mental world of a Saxon pastor', in P. N. Brooks (ed.), *Reformation Principle and Practice: Essays in Honour of Arthur Geoffrey Dickens* (London, 1980), pp. 159–70. See also the rich information on pastors' libraries in B. Vogler, *Vie religieuse en pays rhenan dans la seconde moitié du 16e siècle, 1556–1619* (Service de reproduction des thèses, Université de Lille III, 1974), Vol. I, pp. 468–71.

46 D. Cressy, *Literacy and the Social Order. Reading and Writing in Tudor and Stuart England* (Cambridge, 1980), pp. 48–9.

47 V. Ickelsamer, *Die rechte weis, auffs kürtzist lesen zu lernen, wie das zum ersten erfunden unnd auss der rede vermerckt worden ist ... sampt dem text des kleinen Catechismi* (n.p., 1527; 2nd edn, Marburg, 1534), p. 53. Ickelsamer's treatise is reprinted in facsimile in H. Fechtner (ed.), *Vier seltene Schriften des sechzehnten Jahrhunderts* (Berlin, 1882).

48 'weil uns das Evangelium freyheit zu glauben, und gewalt zu urteyln gibt': *Clag etlicher Brüder an alle Christen*, 1525, reprinted in L. Enders (ed.), *Aus dem Kampf der Schwärmer gegen Luther*, Flugschriften aus der Reformationszeit X: Neudrucke deutscher Literaturwerke des XVI. und XVII. Jahrhunderts, no. 118 (Halle, 1893), p. 44. On Ickelsamer, see H. Noll, *Der Typus des religiösen Grammatikers im 16. Jahrhundert, dargestellt an Valentin Ickelsamer* (Marburg, 1935).

49 For a description of the methods of catechism teaching, see my *Luther's House of Learning*, pp. 165–75.

50 For example, Staatsarchiv Neuburg, Grassegger-Sammlung no. 1535[III], fol. 108 r (1584): 'So ist auch der nutz, so aus den schulen folgt, unaussprechlich, in dem oftmals eines armen Mannes kind durch Mittel eines so geringen anfangs zu hohen dignitet und ehren kombt.' In 1614 the Bavarian *Landtag* deputies resisted Maximilian I's attempt to abolish German schools with the argument that 'nicht alle Bauernkinder mögen bauern werden ... aber einer, der seine Muttersprache weder schreiben noch lesen kann, gleichsam schier wie ein todter mensch ist', quoted by A. Kluckhohn, 'Die Jesuiten in Baiern ...', *Historische Zeitschrift*, Vol. XXXI (1874), pp. 405–6.

51 Cressy, *Literacy and the Social Order*, p. 184.

52 For example, Mecklenburg *Kirchenordnung* 1522 in Vormbaum, *Die evangelischen Schulordnungern*, pp. 59–60; 'Und ist vom lesen ausdrücklich geboten 1 Tim 4, "Du solt anhalten mit lesen, trösten und lehren"'. In welchem spruch das lesen nit vergeblich am ersten genannt ist.'

53 *WA* 15, p. 45.

54 'Das volck wurdt zu burgerlicher beywonung uss erfarung und ubung des buchstabens dester geschlachter, freuntlicher und geneigter, so sonst uss unwissenheit, der groben natur nach, wütet mit unwurss färheit und kein achtung des rechtens und der billichkeyt geben mag': R. Stupperich (ed.), *Martin Bucers deutsche Schriften*, Vol. II (Gütersloh, 1962), p. 400.

55 E. Johansson, 'The history of literacy in Sweden in comparison with some other countries', *Educational Reports Umea*, Vol. XII (1977).
56 See my discussion of the evidence concerning mass understanding of religion in my *Luther's House of Learning*, chs 13 and 14.

XI
SUCCESS AND FAILURE IN THE GERMAN REFORMATION

A HUNDRED AND THIRTY YEARS AGO THE CATHOLIC HISTORIAN AND church politician Ignaz von Döllinger scored a polemical point by using the Protestant reformers' own words to prove his contention that the evangelical movement in Germany had failed in its objectives. The first of Döllinger's three volumes on the Lutheran Reformation consists almost entirely of quotations from eighteen reformers, led by Luther and Melanchthon, who speak of their defeat in explicit terms and vivid language. No change for the better had occurred in the hearts and minds of men. On the contrary, they said, all was worse now than it had been under Rome. Melanchthon's deep pessimism became evident as early as 1525. A decade or so later Luther began to vent his despair in increasingly gloomy outpourings of his bitter disappointment over public indifference to the Gospel and the absence of any visible effects of his work on the thoughts and lives of his fellow Germans. Assembled in Döllinger's book these utterances make a powerful argument for his case against the Reformation.[1]

Many of Döllinger's quotations turn up again in Johannes Janssen's *History of the German People at the Close of the Middle Ages*, where they help substantiate Janssen's contention that social and intellectual conditions quickly deteriorated in Germany on the introduction of the Lutheran heresy.[2] Janssen's book found a wide response which could not fail to provoke reaction from the Protestant camp. The most prolific of Lutheran spokesmen, Wilhelm Walther, began to reply in 1884;[3] in 1906 he published *For Luther Against Rome*, a systematic apology in answer to Catholic allegations.[4] Walther

---

[1] Johann Joseph Ignaz von Döllinger, *Die Reformation, ihre Entwicklung und ihre Wirkungen im Umfange des lutherischen Bekenntnisses*, i (Regensburg, 1846), pp. 1-408. Passages from Luther: *ibid.*, pp. 284-348. Döllinger's list is indiscriminate; it includes Erasmus as well as Luther, also radical dissenters such as Franck and Schwenkfeld.

[2] Johannes Janssen, *History of the German People at the Close of the Middle Ages*, trans. A. M. Christie, 16 vols. (London, 1896-1910). See generally iii, pp. 363-70, on Luther's complaints about decline; vii, pp. 141-3, on Melanchthon's despair. Cf. also Janssen's *An meine Kritiker* (Freiburg i. B., 1882), p. 122.

[3] Walther published a series of pamphlets entitled *Luther im neuesten römischen Gericht* in the Schriften des Vereins für Reformationsgeschichte, nos. 7 (Halle, 1884), 13 (Halle, 1886), 31 (Halle, 1890), 35 (Halle, 1892).

[4] Wilhelm Walther, *Für Luther wider Rom: Handbuch der Apologetik Luthers und der Reformation* . . . (Halle, 1906). Walther presents arguments against Heinrich Denifle, as well as against Janssen.

* This article first appeared in *Past and Present: A Journal of Historical Studies*, no. 67 (May 1975), pp. 30-63 (World Copyright: The Past and Present Society, 175 Banbury Road, Oxford, England).

rejects many of the passages quoted by Janssen and Döllinger as inaccurate or taken out of context. Others, particularly Luther's own, he acknowledges as genuine but tries to explain away. In any case, he argues, beside each despairing utterance can be set a passage in which Luther asserts confidently that the Gospel had wrought a beneficial change among men.[5]

There is little satisfaction nowadays in making one's way through these wordy and contentious volumes. Janssen's one-sidedness now appears evident on nearly every page. For his part, Walther — the author, incidentally, of a ferocious tract of the First World War entitled *Germany's Sword Consecrated by Luther*[6] — writes throughout in a strident tone which neither gives nor asks mercy. Today this aggressive bickering leaves one with a sinking feeling of energies wasted and talents misapplied. Is there anything to be gained from opening once again the question of whether the Reformation is a success story or the tale of a failure? Let us see.

I

I shall beg for the moment the question of what constitutes "success" in the Reformation. Let us first recognize it as a fact that most of the leading participants in the Lutheran movement during its first half century or so came to believe that they had been defeated. Given their resolutely pessimistic view of human nature any other conclusion would, perhaps, have been surprising. All the same, the chorus of disenchantment conveys a distinct sense of tragedy. Luther himself foresaw the demise of the evangelical movement, and his loyal followers did not fail to point to his prediction as the legitimation of their own disillusionment. Johann Aurifaber, who edited Luther's "Table Talk" in 1566, concluded that "[Luther's] teachings have grown and prospered up to our own time, but from now on they will decrease and fall, having completed their appointed course".[7] Luther had anticipated this outcome, Aurifaber said. He knew that "God's word has seldom tarried in one place longer than forty years", a prophecy sadly come true, "for [Luther's] teachings are now everywhere despised, and so many men have lost interest in them that his very name is held in contempt".[8] Aurifaber — and other loyal

---

[5] *Ibid.*, pp. 716-21, for these arguments and passages.

[6] W. Walther, *Deutschlands Schwert durch Luther geweiht* (Leipzig, 1914).

[7] Aurifaber's preface is reprinted in *Dr. Martin Luthers sämtliche Schriften*, ed. Johann Georg Walch, xxii (Halle, 1743), pp. 40-54; the passage quoted here is on p. 50.

[8] *Ibid.*, p. 51. Aurifaber's entire preface is drenched in a mood of bitter disillusionment, saved from cynicism only by his conviction that the events he witnesses are evidence of the imminent end of the world.

32

Lutherans — pointed to sectarianism as the chief symptom of this decline. But even more disturbing was the general indifference to Scripture, especially when it occurred "in Germany, a country blessed above all others with the pure word of the Gospel".[9] The ingratitude of men! "Good things that come to us are soon forgotten in this world, and no one gives thanks for what he possesses". Who remembers nowadays, Aurifaber asks, what life was like in the time of struggle against Rome?

> We ought to look back fifty years and recall how gruesome, how frightful and pitiful had been the state of religion and church government then. We were all in a dungeon under the pope. But who remembers this today? Young people know nothing about it, and their parents have forgotten it too![10]

It will be useful to remind ourselves at this point that speculations of a cosmic nature must have coloured this pessimistic assessment of the course of the Reformation. Men who had read Daniel and Revelation, who studied the stars and contemplated the senility of nature as they anticipated the approaching end of the world knew what to expect from their own time.[11] Nonetheless the many expressions of discontent[12] make a poignant contrast to the assertive optimism of the movement's early years when Luther could write exultantly of the reformation he had inaugurated: "I declare, I have made a reformation which will make the popes' ears ring and hearts burst"; and of "the substantial benefit, peace and virtue it has brought to those who have accepted it".[13] Against detractors, who at that time were still mostly in the Roman camp, he declared that "hardly one of them is willing to acknowledge the good which the Gospel has accomplished not only in the individual conscience, but also in public affairs and in the

---

[9] Andreas Musculus, *Vom Himmel und der Hellen* . . . (Frankfurt an der Oder, 1559), fo. aii[v].

[10] Aurifaber, *loc. cit.*, p. 50. For a popular version of these sentiments, see "Pasquillus zwischen einem Bair und Sachsen", *c.* 1556, printed in August Hartmann (ed.), *Historische Volkslieder und Zeitgedichte,* i (Munich, 1907), no. 8.

[11] For a very good example of this, see Justus Jonas, *Das siebend Capitel Danielis* . . . (Wittenberg, 1529), especially fo. B[v], where the images of Daniel 7 are applied to the advancing Turkish empire and this, in turn, is seen as a punishment of Christians, especially Lutherans, who do not heed the Gospel.

[12] A sampling of these: Wenceslaus Linck, preface to Leonhard Culman's *Ein christlich teutsch spil, wie ein Sünder zur buss bekert wird* (Nuremberg, 1539), in Julius Tittmann (ed.), *Schauspiele aus dem 16. Jahrhundert* (Leipzig, 1868), p. 110; Veit Dietrich, *Kinder-Postilla* (Nuremberg, 1549), fos. 44[r]-45[v]; Musculus, *op. cit.*, fo. Aii[v]; Caspar Huberinus, *Spiegel der geistlichen Hauszucht* (Frankfurt am Main, 1569), fos. cxix[r], ccxliii[v]; Simon Musaeus, *Catechismus* . . . (Frankfurt am Main, 1571), fo. 2[v].

[13] Luther in his preface to Stephan Klingebeil's *Von Priester Ehe* (Wittenberg, 1528): *D. Martin Luthers Werke. Kritische Gesamtausgabe* (Weimar, 1883-) (hereafter *Luthers Werke*), xxvi, p. 530.

quality of family and household life.[14]   It was generally agreed that the year 1530 marked the zenith of the Lutheran movement in Germany.[15]   Thirty years later its fortunes had begun to decline. Politicians were taking over, "the jurists and courtiers who now control our churches and pulpits".[16]   Evidently the spirit had gone out of the evangelical revival in Germany.

II

It has not usually been noticed that much of the reformers' early optimism rested on their conviction that they had found a way to implant evangelical Christianity in the minds of their fellow men, particularly in the minds of the young, who represented the movement's best hope of survival.   Religious instruction would root the principles of the faith in the impressionable minds and malleable characters of children and adolescents, with beneficial results inevitably to follow when the new generation came to adulthood.   In 1528 Luther apparently felt that this effort, just begun, was succeeding.   Expanding on the proud claim (mentioned in the preceding paragraph) that he had accomplished a true reformation, he asserts that

> nowadays a girl or boy of fifteen knows more about Christian doctrine than did all the theologians of the great universities in the old days.   For among us the catechism has come back into use: I mean the Lord's Prayer, the Apostle's Creed, the Ten Commandments and all that one should know about penance, baptism, prayer, the cross, how to live and how to die, and the sacrament of the altar, also about marriage, civil obedience, the duties of father and mother, wife and children, father and son, master and servant.   In short, I have established the right order and a good conscience for all estates in society, so that each will know how to live and to serve God in his appointed rôle.   And to those who have accepted it, my reformation has brought not a little benefit, peace and virtue.[17]

Luther's own catechisms, in preparation since 1523, were ready in 1529.[18]   Proving almost at once their merit as instruments for training pastors and for instructing the young and the ignorant, they generated countless emulations.[19]   In 1530 Luther took stock of

[14] From his lectures on the Song of Songs, given 1530-1, published in 1539 by Veit Dietrich: *Luthers Werke*, xxxi (2), p. 613.
[15] This is said by Aurifaber, *loc. cit.*, p. 50.
[16] *Ibid.*, p. 49.
[17] See n. 13 above.
[18] Cf. Georg Buchwald, *Die Entstehung der Katechismen Luthers* . . . (Leipzig, 1894).
[19] The only comprehensive attempt to survey the stupendous number of Lutheran catechisms produced in Germany in the sixteenth century was made by Johann Michael Reu, *Quellen zur Geschichte des kirchlichen Unterrichts in der evangelischen Kirche Deutschlands zwischen 1530 und 1600*, part 1, *Quellen zur Geschichte des Katechismus-Unterrichts*, 5 vols. (Gütersloh, 1904-24).

34

accomplishments. Writing to the Elector of Saxony, he boasted that

> there is no other land in the world to compare with Your Electoral Grace's territories for excellent pastors and preachers. Nowhere else do they teach so piously and purely and help maintain such serene peace among men. Our tender youth, girls as well as boys, are now so well taught in catechism and Scripture that my heart grows warm as I observe young children praying more devoutly, believing more firmly, and discoursing more eloquently on God and Christ than, in the old days, all the learned monks and doctors.[20]

The accuracy of this description is open to question; Luther was trying to encourage the Elector at a difficult moment. But Luther here illustrates the enormous trust placed by the early reformers in the educational — more properly indoctrinational — undertaking on which they were then embarking. According to what they knew about the young and the problems of teaching them (and what they knew they had, of course, read in books) there was every reason to expect good results from a soundly conceived pedagogy energetically applied in institutions established for that purpose. A vast literature on the education of children, dating back to pagan and Christian antiquity and tended as a living tradition by pedagogical writers throughout the centuries, supplied reformers with a body of theoretical evidence to show that all but a very few were capable of learning and that the learning process — providing it began early in the child's life, was pursued methodically, limited its aims to individual talents, and employed appropriate methods — was bound to produce lasting results.[21] That the older generations were too far gone in ignorance and corruption was a matter of general agreement among reformers. "Let them go to the devil", said Luther.[22] "Instead", said Johann Agricola, "let us with God's help try it with children".[23] The future evidently rested upon the young. "I believe with all my heart", said a Lutheran pedagogue, "that this is our only hope for restoring corrupt Christendom".[24]

This only hope could lead to some drastic experiments. Preachers in Strassburg, outraged at the deplorable conditions they had found

[20] Luther to Elector John of Saxony, 20 May 1530: *Luthers Werke, Briefwechsel* (hereafter *Br.*), v, no. 1572.

[21] I examine the pedagogical literature and its impact on Lutheran educational thought and policies in "The State of Pedagogical Theory *c.* 1500: What Protestant Reformers Knew about Education", which is to be published in a forthcoming volume on education and society edited by Lawrence Stone.

[22] Luther to Elector John, 22 Nov. 1526: *Luthers Werke, Br.*, no. 1052 (iv, p. 133).

[23] Johann Agricola, *Hundert und dreissig gemeiner Fragestücke für die jungen kinder* . . . (Wittenberg, 1528), fo. Aii[v].

[24] Johann Bader, *Ein Gesprächbüchlein vom Anfangk Lebens, mit dem jungen Volk zu Landaw* (Landau, 1526), quoted in J. P. Gelbert, *Magister Johann Baders Leben und Schriften* (Neustadt, 1968), p. 123.

in the city and in despair over the indifference of parents to pulpit
admonitions to send children to school, proposed to the council that
the city's young be declared to "belong to God and the religious and
civic community and not to their parents" so that they could then be
conscripted to their appointed lessons.[25]   The date was 1547 and
hopes for an immediate and whole-hearted response to the Gospel
had already been dimmed.   Twenty years earlier, discussions about
Christian education were not yet muted by fears of failure.   By 1528
reformers had worked out a compromise solution to the dilemma
inherent in the contradiction between their theological conviction that
education leading to faith was an impossibility, and their recognition
that at a worldly level training in religious and civic duties was not
only possible, but necessary.[26]   For the able — those suited by
intellect and character to be pastors, teachers, lawyers, and so on —
Latin schools (traditional institutions, but reformed and restaffed)
would be established.   Ordinary youngsters would receive religious
instruction in catechism classes and a modicum of useful learning in
"German schools" to be raised in a way not yet determined from their
present condition as private and local enterprises.[27]   In 1524, the
date of his tract *To the Councillors of all the Cities in Germany*,
Luther abandoned for all practical purposes his earlier notion that
fundamental Christian concepts of religion and citizenship could be
taught in the home.   As late as 1523 he had recommended as a model
(*eyn gemeyn exempel*) the constitution of the town of Leisnig, according
to which each householder was obliged to teach the Bible to his
children and domestic servants.[28]   But results of this procedure were
disappointing.[29]   By the later 1520s everybody knew that parents
were not doing the job of giving a Christian upbringing to their
children.   This was not for lack of exhortations to do so, nor of

[25] Strasbourg, Archives de la ville, Archive St. Thomas 84, carton 48, fo.
188ᵛ.   The council rejected the proposal, preferring to rely on persuasion.
[26] On Luther's complex views regarding the limits and possibilities of
education, see Ivar Asheim, *Glaube und Erziehung bei Luther* (Heidelberg, 1961),
esp. pp. 88 ff.   Also Edgar Reimers, *Recht und Grenzen einer Berufung auf
Luther in den neueren Bemühungen um eine evangelische Erziehung* (Weinheim,
1958).
[27] I deal with the objectives of Lutheran education in "Reformation and
Pedagogy: Educational Thought and Practice in the Lutheran Reformation",
in Charles Trinkaus and Heiko A. Oberman (eds.), *The Pursuit of Holiness.
Papers from the University of Michigan Conference* (Leiden, 1974), pp. 272-93.
[28] *Luthers Werke*, xii, p. 11.
[29] Luther noted shrewdly that "discipline taught in the home seeks to teach the
child by encouraging him to utilize his own experience (*eygen erfarung*).   But
before this can bring results, we are a hundred times dead".   *An die Ratsherren
aller Städte deutsches Lands* (Wittenberg, 1524): *Luthers Werke*, xv, p. 45.

36

assurances that in principle the home was the ideal place for Christian nurture and instruction.[30] But it was no secret that little or no Christian teaching was actually taking place in the home.[31]

The upshot of such painful reflections was that reformers willingly collaborated with political authorities in drafting school ordinances setting up educational systems in cities and territories wherever Lutheranism had become the established religion.[32] As is well known, these school ordinances, which are nearly always integral parts of comprehensive ecclesiastical constitutions, laid down detailed and explicit regulations covering teaching, curriculum and conduct. Specific rules were framed in statements of general purpose placing education in the grand design of a religious and political reformation of state, society and individual. The state being in nearly all instances the moving force behind the establishment of new schools and the reform of old ones, political ends came inevitably to be fused with religious objectives. Religious leaders, for their part, were gratified to know that the state was always prepared to intervene should pulpit persuasion fail to convince the faithful that schooling was necessary and good. School systems established in these circumstances could hardly fail to be "instruments of magisterial education", as they have rightly been called.[33] To the extent possible in an age of very imperfect centralization, educational procedures were made uniform and subject to enforcement. Municipal and territorial school authorities, composed of secular and ecclesiastical officials working jointly, wrote curricula, selected books, drew up lesson plans, appointed teachers, and controlled the enterprise by means of

[30] Asheim, *loc. cit.*, quotes passages in which Luther urges parents to take on the Christian training of their children. See also Bugenhagen's letter to the city council of Hamburg: Johann Bugenhagen, *Von dem christlichen Glauben und rechten guten Werken* . . . (Wittenberg, 1525; Nuremberg, 1527 edn.), p. 245. See also Justus Menius, *An die hochgeborne Fürstin, Frau Sibilla Hertzogin zu Sachsen, Oeconomia christiana* . . . (Wittenberg, 1529), fo. H iv[v]. The best synopsis of Luther's own view of the parental office is found in his explication of the Fourth Commandment in the Larger Catechism of 1529: *Luthers Werke*, xxx (1), pp. 156 ff. Asheim, *loc. cit.*, discusses the inconsistencies arising from Luther's recommendation of two possible courses of action, education in the home and education in schools. In the course of the sixteenth century a large *Hausväter-Literatur* sprang up, designed to train and assist householders in their responsibility to their children's upbringing.

[31] E.g. Veit Dietrich's statement in *Kinder-Postilla*, fo. 44[r-v].

[32] For a chronological list of school ordinances established in the sixteenth century, see Georg Mertz, *Das Schulwesen der deutschen Reformation* (Heidelberg, 1902), pp. 162-5. The texts of most *Schulordnungen* may be found in Reinhold Vormbaum, *Die evangelischen Schulordnungen des 16. Jahrhunderts* (Gütersloh, 1860).

[33] Wilhelm Maurer, *Der junge Melanchthon* (Göttingen, 1967-9), p. 463.

inspections and examinations. Apart from taking leading rôles in the drafting of school ordinances, reformers gave their formal blessing to the dominant rôle of the state in educational (and of course ecclesiastical) matters. Luther reminded the Elector in 1526 that "as supreme guardian of our youth (*oberster furmund der iugent*)" he had every right to force cities and towns to employ part of their wealth to build schools.[34] Elsewhere rulers and magistrates were addressed as "fathers of our youth" and granted the sweeping regulatory powers implied in this description of the nature and scope of their authority.[35]

By far the most promising instrument for religious and moral instruction was the catechism. Lutherans took justified pride in their development of the catechism as a means of teaching the elements of the faith to the young and simple, claiming its reintroduction into Christian practice as a distinctly Protestant contribution.[36] No other method seemed as suitable to the purpose.[37] Its aims were clearly stated in a memorandum prepared in 1531 by a group of Nuremberg theologians while that city's council was considering the establishment of public catechism lessons as a matter of policy:

> Catechism is Christian instruction for children. By this we do not mean only that such instruction should be given to children alone, but that all Christians must from the age of childhood learn and understand the catechism. "Cate-

[34] Luther to Elector John, 22 Nov. 1526: *Luthers Werke, Br.*, no. 1052 (iv, p. 134).

[35] In the Gengenbach *Kirchenordnung*: E.-W. Kohls (ed.), *Evangelische Bewegung und Kirchenordnung. Studien und Quellen zur Reformationsgeschichte der Reichsstadt Gengenbach* (Karlsruhe, 1966), p. 35.

[36] Cf. Melanchthon's assertion in Article 8 of the *Apology of the Augsburg Confession*: "Among our adversaries children receive no catechism instruction whatever". The most convenient reference to the Latin text and its English translation is: *Concordia Triglotta: The Symbolical Books of the Evangelical Lutheran Church* (St. Louis, 1921), pp. 324 (Latin) and 325 (English).

[37] This point is made too frequently for citation. One example: Johann Spangenberg, *Des kleinen Catechismi ... kurtzer Begriff* (Wittenberg, 1541), repr. in Reu, *Quellen ... Katechismus-Unterrichts*, ii (2), pp. 285-98: Nothing is as dear to God as pious, obedient, God-fearing children "and it is certain that no other ways or means exist for training children to piety and obedience than through the catechism". A popular rhyme ran: "Der Catechismus Luther klein/Das höchste Buch auf Erden,/das fast die ganze Schrift so fein/in kurtze summ zu lernen (Luther's Shorter Catechism is the best book on earth, for it gives us the sum of all Scripture so that we can learn it with ease)". Quoted in Friedrich Hahn, *Die evangelische Unterweisung in den Schulen des 16. Jahrhunderts* (Heidelberg, 1957), p. 66. There were, of course, several catechisms in circulation before Luther's. On these, see Ernst-Wilhelm Kohls, *Evangelische Katechismen der Reformationszeit vor und neben Luthers kleinem Katechismus* (Texte zur Kirchen- und Theologiegeschichte, pt. 16, Gütersloh, 1971), pp. 7-11. For an up-to-date bibliography on Lutheran catechism instruction, see *ibid.*, pp. 12-20. The older literature on all aspects of catechisms is cited in C. A. G. von Zezschwitz, *System der christlichen Katechetik*, 2 vols. (Leipzig, 1863-74).

chism" comes from the word "echo", which means reflected sound, for in catechism lessons we teach by saying aloud a sentence or two which the learner then repeats in the manner of the reverberation of the human voice in a great hall or in a forest. And this speaking out loud and repetition is to be kept up until the children can recite the entire catechism word for word without missing a syllable.[38]

The question-and-answer form adopted by Luther for his Shorter Catechism of 1529[39] proved ideal for purposes of rudimentary indoctrination and was never seriously challenged. For the sake of simplicity and orthodoxy authorities also stressed the need to keep always to the same text, to make no additions and attempt no innovations in content or wording. This, too, goes back to Luther's warning that young minds are easily confused by diversity.[40] In the course of time uniformity became a kind of fetish. In actual fact, however, there existed such a bewildering profusion of different catechisms in Lutheran Germany that a recent student of the subject can seriously suggest that "something like every third pastor drew up a substantial catechism of his own".[41] No figures are given, and the estimate is almost certainly exaggerated. But a glance through the far from complete collection of sixteenth-century catechisms in Johann Michael Reu's voluminous compilation[42] is likely to stun the reader with the sheer number of catechisms in circulation. At least until the general acceptance of the Formula of Concord in 1577-88 catechisms multiplied at a prodigious rate, the printed ones which have survived representing only a fraction of manuscript copies actually in use.[43]

It was a long time before control through territorial visitations reduced this profusion to something like the desired uniformity. In the meantime, however, catechism teaching was taking root, at least to the extent of making instruction mandatory in parish schools and

---

[38] Quoted in Klaus Leder, *Kirche und Jugend in Nürnberg und seinem Landgebiet 1400 bis 1800* (Einzelarbeiten aus der Kirchengeschichte Bayerns, lii, Neustadt an der Aisch, 1973), p. 54.

[39] Zezschwitz, *op. cit.*, ii (2), p. 36, argues that Luther got the idea from visitation examinations. But he also shows earlier uses of question-and-answer materials in popular devotional and confessional literature: *ibid.*, ii (2), chaps. i-ii.

[40] In *Der kleine Katechismus für die gemeinen Pfarrherren und Prediger* (Wittenberg, 1529): *Luthers Werke*, xxx (1), p. 268.

[41] Kohls (ed.), *Evangelische Bewegung und Kirchenordnung.*

[42] Reu, *op. cit.*

[43] I have seen few surviving MS. copies. No doubt these cheaply produced and flimsily bound booklets were read to pieces. Kohls (ed.), *op. cit.*, p. 35, quotes a statement to this effect by the preachers who produced the catechism for the city of Gengenbach. Even the printed catechisms do not survive in abundance. They too were used up, and their small format made them easy to lose.

churches as an obligation imposed by ecclesiastical constitutions.[44] For Latin scholars, particularly students in the upper forms, catechisms offered theologically demanding material to be learned and expounded. But for the common folk and the very young, contents and format of catechetical indoctrination were for the most part exceedingly simple. In rural areas, that is to say for the preponderance of the population, the sexton — called *Küster* in the north and *Messner* in the south, normally a rural artisan by trade — was responsible for catechism teaching. His emphasis was on plainness of instruction. Little was expected of common folk in the way of comprehension. But in cities, and in the hands of able preachers, catechisms could offer substantial food for thought. Some played rather heavy-handedly on the consciousness of inherited sin, evidently attempting to use induced sensations of shame and guilt as a means of exerting social control;[45] others made light of this.[46] Some catechisms confined themselves to basic religious instruction. Many others tried also to inculcate civic virtues and discipline. The Fourth Commandment generally served as the point of departure for disquisitions on social obligations and behaviour, while the Seventh — thou shalt not steal — often provided occasion for explicit affirmations of the right to property and to the rewards of one's labour.[47] Some catechisms were intended for use in the class-room, others for

[44] All *Kirchenordnungen* required this. For texts of these, see Emil Sehling (ed.), *Die evangelischen Kirchenordnungen des 16. Jahrhunderts*: vols. i-v (Leipzig, 1902); continued under the auspices of the Institut für evangelisches Kirchenrecht der evangelischen Kirche in Deutschland zu Göttingen, vols. vi (1955-7)-xiv (1969).

[45] Most notably Andreas Osiander's influential *Catechismus oder Kinder-Predig, wie die in meiner gnädigen Herrn Marggraven zu Brandenburg und eines ehrbaren Raths der Stadt Nürnberg Oberkeiten und Gebieten allenthalben gepredigt werden* (Nuremberg, 1533): repr. in Reu, *op. cit.*, i (1), pp. 462-564. Osiander's catechism, intended as a commentary on Luther's, was also introduced to Weissenburg (1533), Dinkelsbühl (1534) and elsewhere. On some of the political implications of Osiander's emphasis on sin, see my article "Protestant Dogma and City Government: The Case of Nuremberg", *Past and Present*, no. 36 (Apr. 1967), pp. 38-58.

[46] The best example I have seen of an approach emphasizing the sinner's ability to overcome his base inclinations through acceptance of the faith is Andreas Musculus's *Catechismus, Kinderpredig, wie die in Marggrävischer zu Brandenburgk und der Stadt Nürnberg Oberkeiten und Gebieten gepredigt werden* (Frankfurt an der Oder, 1566).

[47] A good example for the Fourth Commandment: Thomas Lindner, *Catechismus ... vor die evangelische Kirchen und Schulen zu Ravensburg ...* (Ravensburg, 1546; repr. in E.-W. Kohls, *Die evangelischen Katechismen von Ravensburg ... Ein Beitrag zur oberdeutschen Katechismusgeschichte* [Stuttgart, 1963]), pp. 53 ff. For the Seventh: Caspar Huberinus, *Der Catechismus. ... Allen frommen Hausvättern sehr nutzlich ...* (Augsburg, 1543), fos. Mviii[r]-Nv[r].

instruction in church.   A few were turned into primers.   Luther's Shorter Catechism usually served as the source for these.

If all this failed to produce results, it was not for lack of conviction, nor of methodical effort on the part of the reformers and their schoolmasters.   Teaching techniques in the early sixteenth century rested on certain generally held assumptions about the workings of the mind and the responses of the learner. A large body of received knowledge, dating back to classical and Christian antiquity and absorbed into the educational writings of the middle ages and the Renaissance down to Erasmus's comprehensive *de pueris instituendis* of 1529, assured sixteenth-century pedagogues that, given minimum natural endowment on the part of the child, successful teaching was almost entirely a matter of practice and discipline.[48]   The generally accepted model of the mind described the learning process as an essentially mechanical activity in which facts were stored in the memory for later recall, much as a scholar used the information, tags and sentences he had entered under appropriate categories in his commonplace book.[49]   To the sixteenth-century pedagogue the mind was an efficient engine with discrete parts and a tidy division of operations.   Outstandingly endowed talents (*ingenia*) were few, but nearly every human being was believed able to absorb and retain enough knowledge to allow him to be a useful member of church and society.   To make him learn what he needed to know, pedagogues concentrated on practice and discipline (*exercitatio*) as the means of implanting knowledge, habits and values. Plutarch's old story about Lycurgus's experiment with the two dogs, one highly bred, the other a mongrel but carefully drilled, was repeated by nearly every modern educational writer.   Since it was the trained dog in the test who performed better than the well-born but untaught animal, the story was taken to demonstrate that "nature can do much, but instruction is superior because it can do more".[50] Education was mainly training, and every child could be coached in right ideas, sound purposes and good habits, assuming only that the intellectual and moral conditioning process was begun in infancy[51]

[48] Erasmus, *de pueris instituendis*, critical edn. by J. C. Margolin, *Opera Omnia Desiderii Erasmi*, i (2) (Amsterdam, 1971), pp. 46-7.   For a discussion of the history of pedagogical literature and its influence on the educational thought of the Reformation, see my article cited in n. 21 above.

[49] This analogy was made explicitly by Rudolf Agricola, *de formando studio*, written in 1484, first published in Basel in 1518; I use the Freiburg, 1539 edn. The reference is to pp. 75-90.

[50] "Efficax res est natura, sed hanc vincit efficacior institutio": Erasmus, *op. cit.*, p. 29.   Plutarch, *de liberis educandis*, 4 (cf. n. 52 below).

[51] This is the main and pervasive argument of Erasmus's *de pueris instituendis*.

and was maintained throughout childhood and adolescence as a methodical and relentless programme of habituation.

No other word turns up as frequently in the school ordinances and visitation articles of the Reformation as "habituation" (*Gewöhnung, consuetudo, usus*). Plutarch was usually quoted on this point: "Moral virtue is habit long continued".[52] Formed early in life, habits are fixed in maturity and become second nature. *Consuetudo est quasi altera natura.*[53] This implicit reliance on the powers of habituation to effect a permanent conditioning of thoughts, values and habits goes a long way toward explaining the universal trust placed in catechism drill with its repetition of memorized questions and answers and its incessant, often life-long reiteration.[54] Thus when the dukes of Saxony declared in 1574 that "young people will not comprehend our teachings unless they are first accustomed to the practice of explicit repetition",[55] they were asserting the only pedagogical principle then thought capable of assuring success in their endeavours to create the conditions for a general reform in society.

III

Let us sum up. As we see the educational ideas and practices of early Lutheranism from the vantage point of institutions, curricula, instructional materials and methods, we can understand the original trust placed by the reformers in the promise of their movement. Where so much legislation had generated so many schools, where able pedagogues and theologians had written so many useful teaching

[52] *De liberis educandis*, 3A. Plutarch is probably not the author of this treatise, but it was throughout the middle ages and early modern period attributed to him. Many Latin translations of the work circulated, including one by Guarino da Verona. The Latin of the quoted phrase usually ran "cum mores . . . nihil sint quam assuefactio diuturna": *Plutarchi . . . moralia*, trans. Guilielmus Xylander (Basel, 1572), p. 4.

[53] This same point, that the adult person is the product of mental and moral habits acquired in early life, is made emphatically by Thomas More, *Utopia*, bk. ii: *The Complete Works of St. Thomas More*, iv, ed. Edward Surtz, S. J., and J. H. Hexter (New Haven, 1965), p. 228.

[54] On constant repetition, cf. e.g. Caspar Huberinus, *Vierzig kurtze Predig uber den gantzen Catechismum* . . . (Nuremberg, 1550), fo. iiii^r-v: catechism teachers should do nothing other than "take up one piece after another in the Catechism; and when you have finished with it and preached it all the way through, start again from the beginning, and this you are to make a constant, eternal custom (*in stetem ewigen brauch*)".

[55] "Dan die iugent fast die lehre nicht, so sie nicht zu ausdrücklichem nachsprechen gewehnet wird . . .". From the *Instructions-Artikel* for the 1574 visitation in Electoral Saxony, printed in Karl Pallas (ed.), *Die Registraturen der Kirchenvisitationen im ehemals sächsischen Kurkreise* (Geschichtsquellen der Provinz Sachsen, xl-xli, Halle, 1906-14), xli (Allgemeiner Teil), p. 91.

books, where such general agreement existed on the right techniques for imparting knowledge, and where political and ecclesiastical authorities were so eager to demonstrate their interest in the whole enterprise, it would appear that learning was bound to take place and that evangelical principles could not fail to come to permeate personal and social life.[56]

This confidence, and the enterprises on which it rested, suggest, it seems to me, a fair criterion for judging the success of the reformers' labours. Did their pedagogical effort bring about the anticipated results? Were men improved in some way as a consequence of the new education? Was society made better by the edifying instruction pressed upon the young? Had the adult population in Lutheran territories acquired some basic religious knowledge by the end of the sixteenth century? Had anything changed in the consciences and minds of men as a result of the Reformation?

I think that we do have in this point a means of assaying the success of the Reformation, using — it should be emphasized — as our touchstone the reformers' own criteria, which were of course not political but religious and moral. They are surely the criteria by which they themselves would have wished to be judged. We cannot do them an historical injustice by making them our own. If we agree that this is so, we can now proceed to an examination of the results of the Lutheran enterprise in mass education.

Fortunately we have in our grasp a suitable instrument for studying these results, for measuring them, and for judging their relation to the reformers' original purposes. Our instrument is the church visitation and the written record surviving in visitation protocols. Great quantities of these documents are extant; most still repose unprinted in the archives although some have been published.[57] Visitation protocols make absolutely splendid sources for the social historian, but they have never really been scrutinized from this point of view.[58]

[56] One example of an expression of this confidence: in Leipzig in 1539 Lutheran church officials recognized existing opposition to their religion among the people, but thought it would prevail only "until our doctrines have been implanted and rooted (*bis die lere eingepflantzt, eingewurzelt*) among the people and have won them over to a common and peaceful understanding". Stadtarchiv Leipzig, Tit. VII B.2.

[57] A convenient guide to the published and unpublished visitation records is Ernst Walter Zeeden and Hansgeorg Molitor (eds.), *Die Visitation im Dienst der kirchlichen Reform* (Münster, 1967).

[58] The editors of most of the published visitation materials were impelled either by purely local historical concerns or by an interest in the administrative and financial history of churches and monasteries. For a general history of visitations in one territory, see C. A. H. Burckhardt, *Geschichte der sächsischen Kirchen- und Schulvisitationen von 1524 bis 1545* (Leipzig, 1879).

Scholars interested in rural work and life, in folk customs and belief, in the prevalence of witchcraft, in attitudes to family, property, the village community, near and distant ecclesiastical and political authorities, the work ethic and the enjoyment of leisure, and so on, will find in the visitation records of the Reformation era enough material to engage them for years.

As is well known, the Lutheran reformers revived what they considered an ancient apostolic practice of periodic inspections of Christian life and manners in parish congregations. The political circumstances under which the Reformation was established strengthened the already firmly rooted medieval custom of associating secular and ecclesiastical authorities in the planning and execution of visitations. Luther's appeal in 1525 to Elector John to inaugurate such a visitation in Electoral Saxony, and Melanchthon's *Instruction of Visitors to the Pastors* of 1528 (with a vigorous preface by Luther) provided the programme for all subsequent territorial and municipal visitations.[59] Their purposes were, at the beginning, to discover conditions which the introduction of the Reformation was intended to correct; subsequently to investigate the population and its ecclesiastical and secular leaders in order to determine how firmly the — by now officially defined and established — Reformation was taking root.[60] It was the appalling general ignorance of religion revealed in the Saxon visitation of 1527-9 that prompted Luther to write his two catechisms. On many other substantive and procedural matters, too, the church visitations of the sixteenth century proved fruitful.

It is easy to see why the visitation scheme appealed to governments strongly committed to bureaucratic procedures: it offered excellent opportunities for supervision and control. Visitors themselves were given little freedom of action. Everything they were to say and do was precisely laid down for them in the *formula visitationis* issued by the authority mandating the visitation.[61] Interrogation formularies were drawn up, very long ones in some cases, with explicit, probing

---

[59] P. Melanchthon, *Unterricht der Visitatorn an die Pfarhern ym Kurfursten-thum zu Sachssen* (Wittenberg, 1528): *Luthers Werke*, xxvi, pp. 195-240. The 1528 visitation in Electoral Saxony is a model in every respect, including the documentary record. For the amazingly full and orderly protocols, see Staatsarchiv Weimar, Registrande I, nos. 1 ff.

[60] "We see a great need for conscientious inspectors to visit the parishes from time to time, in order to investigate the doctrines and habits of pastors and the Christian understanding and moral improvement of the common people . . .": Staatsarchiv Bamberg, c7/X, no. 1, fo. 91ʳ.

[61] A good description of the surviving documentation of Protestant visitations is found in Pallas (ed.), *op. cit.*, xli (Allgemeiner Teil), pp. 199-232: "Das urkundliche Material".

44

questions entering deeply into all areas of public and private life. Visitors were told exactly whom to interrogate: local officials (pastors, sextons, schoolmasters, mayors, councillors and so on), a stated number of private citizens including men and women in several age groups, children and adolescents, male and female servants, country people and town-dwellers. The deep-seated distrust of human nature which was then the hallmark of the governing mentality prompted authorities to oblige visitors to press parishioners for information critical of their clergymen and other officials, as well as of their neighbours. In gathering this information visitors could make little distinction between fact and rumour, and it does not seem to have disturbed them that their insistent prodding about public and private derelictions was bound to undermine respect for those local dignitaries whose authority they wished to strengthen. All respondents were urged to tell on each other. In Saxony every cleric was asked: "Can you report anything suspicious about the teachings of your colleagues?"[62] If a pastor was known to frequent the tavern, the locals were encouraged to describe his drinking habits. Recorded answers to such questions were often explicit enough to allow us to satisfy our curiosity about popular life at the village, hamlet and town level.

Armed with their questionnaire, visitors appeared at pre-announced places to which the official visitation mandate had summoned local worthies and citizens. Respondents were examined one at a time and their replies written down on makeshift pads formed by folding a folio sheet or two in four along its long side. These pamphlets, called *Kladden* (from *kladderen*, to scrawl or jot) hold the raw data of the visitations. Few of them survive. Respondents' replies were numbered to correspond to the questions in the questionnaire; thus visitors could simply write "Custor: Ad 1, affirmat; ad 2, negat; ad 3 . . ." — perhaps a lengthy response in German or Latin. The requisite number of individuals having been interrogated, the visitors moved on to the next place. Their tour completed, they retired to make clean copies of the collected information. One clean copy was despatched to the consistory, or whatever the central office of the territorial church organization was called; another went to the secretariat of the territorial ruler. The latter copy was confirmed by receiving the ruler's seal and became the official protocol of the visitation. Normally it is these protocols that survive in the archives. In making use of them the historian must, of course, remember that visitors may occasionally have altered data in accordance with what

<hr>

[62] *Ibid.*, p. 142. Also in Bavaria: Bayerisches Hauptstaatsarchiv München: Hochstift Literalien Passau 83, XI, fo. 16[r].

they wished their superiors to know, or with what they thought the latter might prefer to hear.   It is not clear, however, whether visitors would have wanted to make local conditions appear to be better than they found them, or worse.   An argument might be made for either of these temptations.   My guess is that attempts on the part of visitors to aggravate or gloss over the largely unpleasant information they had gathered tend to cancel each other out, and that the visitation protocols cast an accurate reflection of conditions as they were.

Ecclesiastical and political authorities took the information received with the utmost seriousness.   Protocols were closely examined and discussed in the synods and consistories charged with supervision of religious life.   Summaries of these discussions, with indications of action to be taken, were noted on the left-hand side of each protocol page which had been left blank for this purpose.[63]   These notes were then turned by secretaries into official instructions to superintendents, pastors, mayors, bailiffs, informing them of what was to be done. The territorial ruler's or magistrate's authority was, of course, behind these instructions.   Like the visitation procedures themselves, these instructions ignored the line between public and private affairs.   A village couple's habitual bickering, the failure of certain parents to make their children attend catechism, blasphemous language over-heard in someone's home, a farmer's failure to lay by enough grain for the winter — such matters were as disquieting to the authorities as a pastor's or schoolmaster's flagrant incompetence.   Visitors cultivated an air of benign *bonhomie* to encourage people to open their hearts to them,[64] while skilful questioning nearly always enabled them to check and double-check on a complaint or a piece of gossip.   These procedures left officials confident that they had at hand accurate information on which to base decisions, not only on the correction of individual abuses, but also on the matter of a general reform of moral and social conditions in the land.

General reform was clearly the overriding purpose of these visita-tions.   Most mandates announce this purpose explicitly as the objective to be attained.   In Württemberg for example, in 1557, the

---

[63] This custom was taken over from the method of drafting official letters, where the left-hand half of the page was allowed to remain blank for additions and corrections.   I describe a typical documentary situation.   Bureaucratic customs differed from region to region.

[64] "Let them [the visitors] take particular care that they and their assistants do nothing to cause distress to anyone.   Those who are to be examined, be they spiritual or secular, should be encouraged to open their hearts and reveal their thoughts.   This they will never do if they are given offence".   Bayerisches Hauptstaatsarchiv München: Hochstift Literalien Regensburg 34, fo. 7ʳ⁻ᵛ.

46

visitation was undertaken to accomplish "the imposition of good government and discipline, but first and foremost the planting among our people of God's saving Word".[65] In order to discover how broadly and deeply God's Word was in fact being planted among the population, every visitation instruction contained questions intended to test the religious knowledge and moral conduct of parishioners old and young. Most questions were taken directly from the territorial catechism, and respondents' replies allowed authorities to determine how well and how soundly people were being instructed. Thorough visitations — and by no means all visitations were thorough; they varied considerably from time to time and place to place — began by testing the local pastor on his religious knowledge and on his effectiveness as a preacher. In the duchy of Braunschweig-Grubenhagen, for instance, the Reformation had been established in 1532 and an Ecclesiastical Constitution promulgated in 1544; but a visitation undertaken in 1579 revealed generally unsatisfactory conditions among the town and country population. Church authorities thereupon examined all pastors in order to determine where the fault lay. Pastors were asked, first, what they had been studying during the preceding year (independent study was made an obligation for all clerics by Luther himself and by the first Saxon Visitation of 1528). Here are a few answers and follow-up questions, taken directly from the protocol:

> Genesis. How many chapters? Fifty. What subject is treated in the first chapter? Creation. Do you find reference to Christ in this chapter? Yes, for there is mention of Almightly God and His Word . . . . In which chapter do we read "Abraham believed in the Lord and he counted it to him for righteousness"? Chapter fifteen.
>
> [Another pastor]: Says he has read Genesis but remembers little of it. Says he took notes. Did not suspect he would be asked about it. Responded very poorly.
>
> [Another]: In John 16, Jesus says: "I leave the world". How, then, can he be in the Sacrament? Responded: Visibly Jesus left the world, but invisibly he has remained. For he also says: "I am with you until the end of the world". *Recte respondit.*[66]

Other questions related to preparation of sermons and the response of auditors, to the number of parishioners regularly attending com-

---

[65] ". . . zu anrichtung guter pollicey und äusserlicher zucht, zuvorderst aber pflantzung Göttlichs heilmachendes worts . . .". From the *Visitations-Ordnung* for the duchy of Württemberg, 1557: Württembergisches Hauptstaatsarchiv Stuttgart, A63, B21, fo. 1ʳ.

[66] Printed in Friedrich Spanuth (ed.), "Die Herzberger Synoden und Kirchengerichte von 1582 bis 1588", *Jahrbuch der Gesellschaft für niedersächsische Kirchengeschichte*, liv (1956), pp. 24-5.

munion and catechism instruction, and to suspected reasons for the deplorable moral standards found to prevail in the population.[67] Similarly, a general visitation held in Electoral Saxony in 1578 began with seventy-four questions put to pastor, sexton and schoolmaster. Many questions related to catechism instruction. "Do servants and children go regularly to catechism?" "Who [meaning what is the name of anyone who] fails to attend catechism lessons and examinations?" "Is the catechism being read in school and are all pupils regularly examined?"[68] School curricula and teaching practices were also investigated. "Visitors are instructed", the Mandate said, "to inquire into what is being taught in elementary schools in our towns and cities, especially whether children are well instructed in the principles of religion and what lessons they are given to learn".[69]

Following the examination of pastors, visitors turned to the general public. The Visitation Mandates ordered them to examine "the common people" in their knowledge of the catechism, but this did not always prove possible if time was short. In our example from Saxony in 1578 it was therefore decided to concentrate the questioning on children. In each parish a certain number of children were put through their paces. Where poor performance pointed to the failure of parents to compel their children's attendance at catechism lessons, the former's "insubordination" was reported to ducal authorities.[70] In Strassburg — to take a rare example of an urban visitation — visitors ordered parishioners to appear in church on a Sunday afternoon with their children, to whom it was first to be explained "in the friendliest and most patient manner", why it was that they were being examined that day. "Then the visitor goes among the children", the instructions continue, "asks the pastor about the forms into which they have been divided and what each group has learned, and then selects from each form several boys and girls to recite in a clear and loud voice, and before the entire congregation, what they have learned from the catechism".[71]

Such examinations took place at regular intervals in nearly all German territories, Protestant and Catholic, secular and spiritual. There can be no doubt that they produced comprehensive and

---

[67] Ibid., pp. 25-46.
[68] Pallas (ed.), Registraturen der Kirchenvisitationen, xli (Allgemeiner Teil), pp. 142 ff., questions 8, 16, 56.
[69] Instruktions-Artikel for the visitation of 1574: ibid., p. 95.
[70] Ibid., pp. 92-6.
[71] From a comprehensive memorandum written by Johann Marbach to the Strassburg council in 1533 on the virtues of visitations: Strasbourg, Archives de la ville, Archive St. Thomas 45, carton 21, 1, pp. 478-9.

elaborately detailed evidence on which to base considered judgements concerning the effectiveness of religious edicts, ecclesiastical constitutions, school ordinances, and previous visitations. By examining the evidence, we, like the governments of the Reformation era, can arrive at an independent opinion of what had been accomplished in the realm of religious and moral teaching. In fact we are more fortunate than sixteenth-century authorities, for while their knowledge was necessarily limited to the regional scope of their documents, we can see the whole picture.

It should be said at this point that our evidence is somewhat deficient in one important respect: it offers us little solid information on the state of religious knowledge in the larger cities. Visitations were not very well received in urban parishes. Territorial dignitaries found clergy and parishioners resentful of interference from above, and unco-operative to the point of sullenness. The general result of this was that authorities abandoned attempts to inspect cities through parish visitations. In Strassburg, for instance, Johann Marbach, the successor of Bucer, persuaded the council in 1554 to decree annual visitations of all city parishes. But he generated such opposition from the clergy that the visitation had to be cancelled in the following year, and none was undertaken again.[72] Owing to a similar situation in Saxony, the Visitation Instructions of 1578 stipulated that in the cities only domestic servants and children were to be examined, while in smaller towns, hamlets, and villages "the old as well as the young" faced the test.[73] The city of Magdeburg refused to admit visitors. So did Leipzig.[74] Exemption of urban parishes did not, of course, mean that rural churches in the territory under the control of the city escaped visitation. Visitations were as frequent and thorough in urban domains as in princely ones. It is the city population itself which remains just outside the light cast by the visitation documents.

Let us now look at the evidence gathered by territorial visitations from the 1530s to the end of the sixteenth century. Needless to say, what is presented here for purposes of demonstration is but a tiny sampling taken from a huge mass of documentation. I must ask the

---

[72] Johann Adam, *Evangelische Kirchengeschichte der Stadt Strassburg* (Strassburg, 1922), pp. 318-20.

[73] Pallas (ed.), *op. cit.*, xli (Allgemeiner Teil), p. 136.

[74] The visitation protocol for the archbishopric of Magdeburg for 1563 notes laconically: "The old city of Magdeburg refused to submit to visitation (Alte Stadt Magdeburg hat sich der visitation nicht unterwerfen wollen)": Staatsarchiv Magdeburg, Rep. A12, Generalia, no. 2434, fo. 1ʳ. For Leipzig: Stadtarchiv Leipzig, Tit. VII B. 3, fos. 160ᵛ-161ʳ.

reader to place his trust in my judgement: I have selected only such instances as could be multiplied hundredfold.

When the Electoral Saxon visitors informed Duke John Frederick in 1535 that the common people, following the bad example of nobles and burghers, "hold in many places of your realm the servants of God's Word in contempt",[75] the duke might well have reflected that seven years — the period since the first territorial visitation in Saxony — had not been enough time for the Gospel to be firmly implanted or for a new generation of effective pastors to be trained.[76]   Unfortunately the visitations of 1574 and 1577 showed that conditions had not changed forty years later.[77]   As before, pastors and sextons everywhere complained of poor church attendance and poorer attendance still of catechism sermons.   "You'll find more of them out fishing than at service", said the visitors.   Those who do come to church walk out as the pastor begins his sermon.   Parents withhold their children from catechism classes and refuse to pay school fees.   Domestic servants leave their jobs rather than let themselves be sent to service.   No wonder that blasphemy, fornication, adultery, drunkenness and gambling abounded.   Admonitions and threats are useless, the pastors note.   We warn them, reports one, "but they answer 'why pray?   The Turk and the Pope are not after us'!"[78]   Churches are half empty while taverns are full.   Sunday work, though forbidden, is openly carried on.   At Seegrehna a pastor testified in 1577 that he often quits his church without having preached the catechism because not a soul has turned up to hear him.[79]   In Grasso, a village in the administrative district of Schweinitz, only twenty out of 150 parishioners regularly attend church.   Many don't know their

---

[75] *Schreiben der Visitatoren in Chursachsen über die mancherlei Unrichtigkeit, Gebrächen und Mängel*, in Pallas (ed.), *op. cit.*, xli (Allgemeiner Teil), p. 30.

[76] The qualities and conditions of Lutheran pastors in Ernestine Saxony and Thuringia are examined in Susan Karant-Nunn's forthcoming *Luther's Pastors: The Founding of the German Reformation.*   See also Bernhard Klaus, "Soziale Herkunft und theologische Bildung lutherischer Pfarrer der reformatorischen Frühzeit", *Zeitschrift für Kirchengeschichte*, lxxx, no. 1 (1969), pp. 22-49. Klaus's assertion that the educational and theological level of the average clergyman rose significantly during the sixteenth century (pp. 48-9) is not borne out by the evidence.

[77] The following information is taken from the visitations of 1574 to the end of the century.   For the Saxon visitation of 1555, see Wilhelm Schmidt, *Die Kirchen- und Schulvisitation im sächsischen Kurkreise vom Jahre 1555*, pt. 1, *Die kirchlichen und sittlichen Zustände . . .* (Schriften des Vereins für Reformationsgeschichte, year xxiv [1], no. 90, Halle, 1906).   This is a summary description of the protocols.   Conditions in 1555 were no better than they had been twenty years earlier.

[78] Pallas, *Registraturen der Kirchenvisitationen*, xli (1), p. 129.

[79] *Ibid.*, p. 160.

50

prayers.[80]   Children perform poorly in catechism exams.[81]   They are being raised — the superintendent summarizes elsewhere — "like the dumb beasts of the field, without an inkling of the word of God".[82] Several reasons are suggested for this disgraceful state of affairs: the obtuseness of the population, addiction to drink and fornication so deep-seated that no preacher can hope to change it, the peasant's habitual tight-fistedness (when a child is sent to parish school his parents usually remove him before the end of the quarter to avoid having to pay the fee[83]), above all a deplorable lack of concern with religion, indeed with the state of their own souls.

Territorial rulers tried to counteract this lack of interest, but they could think only of using instruments which had already failed them: stricter mandates, longer sets of instructions to visitors, more systematic methods of inspection,[84] a six-stage method of dealing with offenders, from "fatherly admonitions in private" to the full ban proclaimed by the synod.[85]   But these steps did not help.   Visitations in Electoral Saxony continued to prove that even late in the seventeenth century no change had taken place.   Matters stood no better in the region of Saxony belonging to the princes of Coburg.   Visitations there in 1577 and 1589 brought to light a deplorable general disrespect for the church and its mission.   Nothing seemed to avail against widespread absenteeism from divine service and catechism sermons.   Nor could pleas or threats prevent congregations from stampeding out of church the moment the pastor began his sermon.   Groups of men continued to gather in the churchyard to drink brandy and sing bawdy songs while service was being conducted inside.   Malicious gossip spread through parishes touching pastors and other clerics.   And there was near-universal blaspheming, widespread sorcery, wife-beating and neglect of children, general refusal to fulfil congregational obligations, and so on.[86]   Again and again it was said plaintively that warnings, threats, even exemplary punishments brought no result.[87]   In some villages one could not find even a single person who knew the Ten Commandments.[88]

[80] *Ibid.*, xli (3), p. 580 (the year is 1602).
[81] E.g. 1578, parish Kleinrössen: *ibid.*, p. 591.
[82] *Ibid.*, p. 93.
[83] *Ibid.*, xli (5), p. 120.
[84] *Ibid.*, xli (Allgemeiner Teil), pp. 136-7.
[85] *Ibid.*, pp. 148-9.
[86] This sampling of abuses is taken from a detailed description of such conditions in Saxony-Coburg in 1589: Staatsarchiv Coburg, B 2492-3.
[87] *Ibid.*, B 2468, fo. 47ʳ.
[88] From 1569 visitation in Albertine Saxony: Staatsarchiv Weimar, Reg. I, i, no. 29, fo. 264ᵛ.

Visitations in the duchy of Brandenburg told the same story. Pastors in the villages and hamlets belonging to the bishopric of Magdeburg were discovered in 1584 to "have such a poor memory that they can't retain one passage from the Bible, in fact, most seem never to have looked at it at all".[89] These were not exceptional cases: "many of them are like this", a visitor's note explains, "the register shows it plainly".[90] Of course the flock was no better than its shepherds. "A great crudeness is among these people. Few of them can pray . . .".[91] "We could not find three people here who knew the whole catechism. Some could not recite even one section from it".[92] In one village the pastor confused the three persons of the Trinity.[93] His parishioners knew nothing at all. Things were not so dismal everywhere. A hard-working minister, a good school made all the difference. But even where the Brandenburg visitors could coax the words of the catechism from a few children and adults, how much of it was understood? In 1583 officials inspected villages "in which twenty, thirty, forty even fifty peasants could recite the whole catechism, piece by piece". But when a random group of men was invited to explain what it all meant, the result was disheartening. "We asked them how they understood each of the Ten Commandments, but we found many who could give no answer at all, who could not even say against which commandment a given sin offended. Moreover none of them thought it a sin to get dead drunk and to curse, using the name of God".[94] Visitors often found it difficult to persuade people to let themselves be examined. "No one wants to answer our questions. Therefore we must assume that they don't know their catechism . . .".[95] "Many say they have forgotten it long ago".[96] It is unnecessary to add that the visitors found everywhere evidence of prodigious drinking, horrible blasphemy, whoring, witchcraft and soothsaying, and widespread contempt for the clergy. The words chosen by the Brandenburg consistory to describe the situation: "a wild, disorderly, Cyclopic life",[97] would seem to err on the side of moderation.

It was possible, of course to find in regional and local circumstances the explanations for such behaviour. In some places Catholicism and

---

[89] Staatsarchiv Magdeburg, Rep. A2, no. 511, fo. 209r.
[90] *Ibid.*, fo. 211v.
[91] *Ibid.*, Rep. A12, Generalia, no. 2435, fo. 141r.
[92] *Ibid.*, no. 2436, fo. 40r.
[93] *Ibid.*, fo. 39r.
[94] *Ibid.*, Rep. A2, no. 511, fos. 105v-9v.
[95] *Ibid.*, Rep. A12, Generalia, no. 2445, fo. 160r.
[96] *Ibid.*, fo. 165v.
[97] *Ibid.*, no. 2545, fo. 2r-v.

Lutheranism had succeeded each other for a while with every change of ruler. The innumerable religious controversies dividing and inflaming Protestants against each other are likely to have contributed to the common man's religious confusion. Wars, natural catastrophes, epidemic diseases took their toll.[98] Relics of feudal obligations imposed labour service on some groups of peasants even on Sundays.[99] Chaotic social conditions in some regions made people reluctant to leave their homes on Sunday for fear of robbery.[100] The authorities knew all this, and no doubt considered it in their policies. But *tout comprendre* did not persuade them *tout pardonner*. In the matter of religion they could brook no compromise. A "horrible epicureanism" pervaded the land.[101] The records of their deliberations, the tone of their directives and mandates, show a deep dismay at deteriorating religious and moral circumstances and a nagging sense of frustration over the failure of corrective measures.

Frequent changes of religion may go some way toward explaining the unsatisfactory conditions discovered in the Brunswick duchies of Lower Saxony (*Niedersachsen*),[102] but they could not, in the eyes of the authorities, condone them. The duchy of Wolfenbüttel had been made Protestant during occupation by the Schmalkaldic League in 1542, re-Catholicized in the late 1540s, and turned Lutheran again by Duke Julius in 1568. A visitation of the duchy that year revealed incredible ignorance on all points of religion even on the part of the clergy. In the administrative district of Bockenem not one of the fourteen pastors examined could name the parts of the New Testament. No one knew the books of the Old Testament.[103] A decade

[98] In the hamlet and parish of Wahrenbrück in Electoral Saxony the 1577 visitation noted that while the parish had 1,127 communicants, only 12 boys attended school. This is so, the visitors remarked, because most pupils had been carried away by the plague during the previous year. Pallas (ed.), *Registraturen der Kirchenvisitationen*, xli (5), p. 170.

[99] E.g. Electoral Saxon visitation of 1577, parish of Dolien: peasants when questioned about staying away from catechism instruction on Sunday afternoons testified that they were obliged to do forced labour (*Frondienst*) at that time. *Ibid.*, xli (1), p. 116. In 1585 Margrave Joachim Friedrich of Brandenburg urged that peasants be let off on Sunday to hear the word of God "because even cattle and draught oxen are allowed to rest on the Lord's day": Staatsarchiv Magdeburg, Rep. A12, Generalia, no. 2442, fo. 98v.

[100] In 1577 some Saxon peasants said it was not safe to go to church because roaming *Landsknechte*, counting on empty houses on Sundays, stole people's pigs and chickens: Pallas (ed.), *op. cit.*, xli (1), fo. 116.

[101] Staatsarchiv Weimar, Reg. I, i, no. 45, fo. 71r.

[102] On this subject and its confusing geographical, political and dynastic ramifications, see Johannes Meyer, *Kirchengeschichte Niedersachsens* (Göttingen, 1939).

[103] The visitation records are published in Friedrich Spanuth, "Quellen zur Durchführung der Reformation im Braunschweig-Wolfenbüttelschen Lande, 1551 bis 1568", *Zeitschrift der Gesellschaft für niedersächsische Kirchengeschichte*, xlii (1937), pp. 241-88; the reference is to p. 284.

later no improvements were noted, though every effort had been made. Visitation procedures in the duchy of Wolfenbüttel were thorough and methodical. Visitors interrogated pastors and other clerical staff, inspected their books and investigated their private lives, asked leading questions about conditions in the parish, and examined heads of households with their wives, children and servants.[104] But the information compiled in the visitors' protocols has the familiar ring of general hopelessness. People stay away from service, at most two or three souls turn up for weekday catechism sermons, no children come to catechism class "and it is a pity to see the poor sexton stand there, all by himself in the empty church". No amount of pastoral admonition could persuade parishioners to cease their week-long drinking orgies. The visitors summarize:

> It is the greatest and most widespread complaint of all pastors hereabouts that people do not go to church on Sundays . . . . Nothing helps; they will not come. And the same obstinacy exists on weekdays when the catechism is preached. Only a small part of the population attends these sermons so that pastors face near-empty churches . . . . No wonder, then, that the people respond miserably in catechism examinations. Even if one finds a man or a woman who remembers the words [of the catechism], ask him who Christ is, or what sin is, and he won't be able to give you an answer.[105]

Not everywhere was the picture quite so dark. In the district of Salzliebenhall most children could recite their catechism pretty well in 1583.[106] But in Waldenburg in 1586, when,

> after the hymn had been sung and the congregation admonished to answer all questions to the best of everyone's ability, [the visitors] asked the people to repeat something from the previous Sunday's Gospel reading, they found not a single person among the grown-ups or the young who remembered as much as a word of it.[107]

Here too, however, the children could repeat their catechism. Four years later the parish of Liebe in the same district of Salzliebenhall could not produce even one parishioner to answer the question "who is our redeemer?" When the visitors turned in indignation on the pastor he vigorously denied blame for this unbelievable piece of ignorance. It's the people's fault, he said. They don't go to church. And where else were they to learn their religion?[108]

Even allowing for the religious shifts in Wolfenbüttel in the middle

---

[104] Wolters (ed.), "Die Kirchenvisitation der Aufbauzeit (1520-1600) im vormaligen Herzogtum Braunschweig-Wolfenbüttel", pt. 1, *ibid.*, xliii (1938), pp. 206 ff.
[105] This passage and the preceding remarks relate to Barum, visited in 1572, 1575, 1577 and 1579: *ibid.*, pp. 206-26.
[106] *Ibid.*, pp. 226-32.
[107] *Ibid.*, pp. 233-4.
[108] Wolters (ed.), *op. cit.*, pt. 3, *ibid.*, xlviii (1950), p. 84.

of the century, which older people would still recall in the 1590s, it is difficult to account for such abysmal ignorance except as the consequence of monumental public lack of interest in religion, at least in the doctrines of the established creed. Although Duke Julius took energetic measures to improve religious and practical teaching in his duchy, his best efforts failed in the face of such lack of concern. In the duchy of Grubenhagen, where the Reformation had been introduced in 1532 and institutionalized by the Ecclesiastical Ordinance of 1544, visitations in 1579 and 1580 tell the same sad story. Indeed, Superintendent Johann Schellhammer, who had charge of them, was moved to wonder whether "visitations themselves will not in the end become an object of mockery among the people".[109] Schellhammer reports that churches are largely empty on Sundays, that no one can be found who knows the catechism (one man, he says, could recite the Lord's Prayer in Latin, but when asked to explain it he hadn't an idea of what it meant) and nothing could be done to persuade or compel them to go to catechism sermons. Everywhere he found "that people over eighteen years of age are embarrassed to memorize the catechism and cannot be made to attend the lessons". The superintendent concludes with the usual recital of depravities among the common people: drunkenness, gambling, adultery and fornication, widespread witchcraft and sorcery — this latter practice very difficult to prove "because they won't tell on each other".[110] In the 1580s and in 1610 the basic situation had not changed, though a few parishes exhibited exceptions to the general rule.[111] Children could sometimes say their catechism tolerably well, but the pity of it was that "by the time they have grown up they have forgotten it all. In cases where we know that a certain child learned his catechism years ago, we discovered that by the time he becomes an adult he remembers not a word of it".[112]

In the duchy of Kalenberg, where Catholicism had been reestablished in 1543 and Lutheranism in 1568, the situation was so terrible[113] that Duke Julius of Wolfenbüttel, who inherited the

[109] Friedrich Spanuth, "Die Grubenhagensche Kirchenvisitation von 1579 durch Superintendent Schellhammer", *Jahrbuch der Gesellschaft für niedersächsische Kirchengeschichte*, lii (1954), p. 106.

[110] *Ibid.*, pp. 113-17.

[111] Spanuth (ed.), "Die Herzberger Synoden und Kirchengerichte von 1582 bis 1588", *ibid.*, liv (1956), pp. 35 ff.; "Die Generalvisitation in Grubenhagen von 1617", *ibid.*, liii (1955), pp. 49 ff.

[112] From visitation in Kalenberg-Göttingen 1646. Printed in Karl Kayser (ed.), "Die Generalvisitation des D. Gesenius im Fürstentum Göttingen 1646 und 1652", *ibid.*, xi (1906), p. 201.

[113] As revealed in the visitation of 1583: Hauptstaatsarchiv Hannover, Hann. 83, IV.

territory in 1584, ordered an exhaustive inquisition of all clerics to see what might be done.   The protocols of the sessions with each of the duchy's pastors are dramatic documents.   None of them was let off the hook if his answers were vague or evasive.   Only the totally ignorant were dismissed without further questioning.   Others were pressed hard on troublesome theological subjects, especially the Trinity: "Which person of the Trinity assumed human form?"   "The Father".   "Is it the Father, then, who died for us?"   Long silence, then "no".   "Prove that three persons are one".   No reply.   Original sin: few pastors were able to explain this adequately.   Mortal sin: "Is it mortal sin if a man gets dead drunk?"   "Yes, for God has forbidden it".   And free will: most pastors knew that the answer to this should be no, but they could prove nothing and were reduced to utter confusion by probing questioning.[114]   While turning the pages of these protocols in the archive, I was moved to sympathy as I felt the wretched men squirm under the onslaught of questions of considerable theological complexity and, in the case of poor respondents, distinctly unfriendly tone.   The ordeal to which they were being put seemed ludicrously incommensurate with the rudimentary pastoral duties these men had to perform among people who could remember no more than one or two of the Ten Commandments and barely knew the words of the Lord's Prayer.

Even where the church was organizationally and financially in good shape the religious attitudes among the public were often deplorable. In the duchy of Lauenburg, for example, visitors described a sound and smoothly functioning ecclesiastical apparatus.   But the reports on moral conditions and the admonitions contained in the visitation recesses reveal outright disrespect for the church among the population.   In Gronau in 1581 "the congregation behaved shockingly, refusing to answer a single question so that the examiner had to break off the visitation".[115]   An attempt to explain such insolence by the presence of "Anabaptists" in the community[116] carries little conviction when one reads of the universal drinking, whoring and other abominations detailed in the protocols.   Conditions in this duchy show how little even the most determined governments could do against lack of religious interest.   In the end the authorities contented themselves with the weak recommendation that every parent should "as much as he

---

[114] The entire protocol is *ibid.*, no. 101.   The examinations took place in 1588.

[115] Landesarchiv Schleswig-Holstein, Abteilung 218: Lauenburgisches Konsistorium Ratzeburg, no. 653, fo. 78ʳ.

[116] *Ibid.*, no. 654, fo. 119ᵛ.

is able" send his children to school *or* to catechism lessons.[117] No wonder that the visitation of 1614 registered no change in the dismal situation.

It needs to be stressed that the scenes depicted here are not the whole picture. Well endowed and expertly staffed Latin schools in towns and cities turned out soundly trained pupils. Visiting such institutions evidently gave officials much pleasure.[118] Village schools, too, were found on occasion to be functioning effectively.[119] As might be expected, the situation varied enormously from region to region. The point is, however, that while élite institutions produced able ministers, and while children and youngsters acquired in an occasional local school the rudiments of a religious education, very little of this transferred itself to the general adult population on whose everyday lives and thoughts the formal religion, Catholic or Protestant, seems to have made little impact. No sociologically revealing pattern — as, for example, between rich and poor — emerges from the records. Thus, in the county of Oldenburg the catalogue of ignorance and other outrages compiled during the visitation of 1609 did not vary between the ill- and the well-favoured agricultural sections of the land. Identical conditions prevailed in the Geest, where the soil was sandy and the population lived hand-to-mouth, and the Marsch, where farms were prosperous. In both sections of the county churches were largely empty, the catechism was ignored, and according to the visitors everyone led a scandalously godless life. In each place there were some exceptions. But the rule was the generally prevailing obtuseness.[120] Church officials never ceased to be scandalized by this. The superintendent of the district of Wiesbaden (in the county of Nassau-Wiesbaden) reported in 1619 that in many places no more than fifteen or so out of 170 householders went to church.[121] Among those who attend, he goes on, "there is such snoring that I could not believe my ears when I heard it. The moment these people sit down, they put

[117] *Ibid.*, fo. 43^{r-v}.

[118] For example, the visitations of schools in the towns of Grund, Lauental, Wildemann and Zellerfeld: Landeskirchliches Archiv Braunschweig, Voges 1926.

[119] For example in Württemberg: Staatsarchiv Stuttgart, A281, B 46 ff. (visitations of the duchy at the end of the sixteenth century). Each sexton or other person with teaching duties is characterized in these documents. See also Eugen Schmid, *Geschichte des Volksschulwesens in Altwürttemberg* (Stuttgart, 1927).

[120] Niedersächsisches Staatsarchiv Oldenburg, Bestand 73, II, pp. 170 ff. (for Geest), pp. 124 ff. (for Marsch). See *ibid.*, fos. 12^{r}-21^{v} for an exception, the parish of Stolhamme.

[121] Hessisches Hauptstaatsarchiv Wiesbaden, Abt. 137 Xa, no. 1, fo. 19^{r}.

their heads on their arms and straight away they go to sleep".[122]   They could not of course answer any of the questions put to them.   In one village the visitor discovered that sons and daughters of peasant house-holders were taking employment in Catholic regions for no other reason than to escape the Sunday catechism classes — "so as to be free to dance all the day".[123]   Children were found who could say the catechism, "but among the older youngsters, who no longer attend classes, there is the greatest ignorance you can imagine!"[124]

Matters stood no better in the territories of independent cities where means of surveillance, control and correction were more efficient.   The Strassburg territorial visitation of 1554 — which collected detailed data while the urban visitation of the same year elicited practically no information about the city population — revealed that people avoided church-going, especially on Sunday afternoons when they ought to have studied the catechism (rural pastors complained that city-dwellers walking in the country on fine Sunday afternoons were setting a corrupting example), that one could compel little girls to go to catechism lessons, but boys ran off to hide in the vineyards, and that nothing was being done to divest the people of "their native crude and sullen ways".[125]   Though an occasional improvement is registered in the course of the following years, the later sixteenth century showed no general rise in religious knowledge and morality.   In 1560 visitors acknowledged that even where the catechism was being taught, "as soon as boys and girls begin to grow into adulthood they turn from it as though it is beneath them to know it, and what they studied as children with such effort and diligence, they now forget in a moment's time".   And this, the visitors add, at a stage of life — they mean adolescence — "when it is most necessary for them to know the catechism".[126]   In 1598 a visitor noted plaintively that "as far as the catechism is concerned, things seem to go downhill from year to year".[127]   What he meant was that he could not get correct answers out of children and grown-ups, and where someone did know the words by rote, "ask him what does *Evangelium* mean in German, what is a sacrament, what do we mean by New Testament, and you will get the most ignorant, absurd, ridiculous replies you have ever heard".[128]

[122] *Ibid.*, fo. 72ʳ.
[123] *Ibid.*, fo. 11ʳ.   This was in 1594.
[124] *Ibid.*, Abt. 340, no. 1605a, fo. 174ʳ.
[125] Strasbourg, Archives de la Ville, Archive St. Thomas 45, carton 21, 1, fos. 535 ff.
[126] *Ibid.*, fos. 737 and 760.
[127] *Ibid.*, fo. 668.
[128] *Ibid.*, carton 21, 2, fos. 415-16.

58

Council decrees deploring and correcting year after year the same misdemeanours, abuses and nuisances tell the same story.[129] Scholars familiar with the history of Strassburg might argue that this city never cared sufficiently about the instruction of its general public. Educational concerns were limited almost exclusively to ensuring an uninterrupted flow of trained personnel into the clerical and other learned professions. In Nuremberg, on the other hand, where the council gave more attention than in Strassburg to rural schools and catechism lessons, the outcome as far as the general population was concerned was no different. In 1560-1 Nuremberg visitors complained of irresponsible parents who could not be persuaded to send children to school or sermons.[130] In 1626 we hear of grown men who could give no answer to such a question as "on what day of the year did our Lord die?" and of adolescents who had forgotten every one of the Ten Commandments.[131] The city of Ulm boasted an excellent gymnasium and a network of council-supervised German schools. But the countryside offered the same dim picture for inspection. Early visitations in 1532, 1535, 1543 and 1556 revealed stubborn resistance on the part of the Catholic country population to the imposition of the new creed; we hear of people kneeling before the stumps of sawn-off wayside crosses and shrines. But even at the end of the sixteenth century visitation protocols record near-total ignorance of religious matters. Although the Ulm catechism had been adopted as early as 1528 and had later been made mandatory in the city's entire territory, pastors reported that few of their parishioners knew even the words of the Lord's Prayer. Village school-teachers agreed when asked by the visitors that the fault lay with parents who could not care less whether their children received instruction or not.[132] In the city of Rothenburg visitors sent by Margrave Frederick of Brandenburg found in the 1550s that hardly anyone had learned his catechism;[133] despite repeated edicts to the contrary no change had occurred by 1618 when it was once again discovered that "neither grown-ups nor children know a word of the catechism".[134] In Hamburg visitors to the country discovered "unbelievable wickedness and contempt for preaching, for the holy sacraments, the Commandments, and for

---

[129] E.g. ibid., carton 48, fo. 576: a decree of 1573 outlawing everything complained of in former years back to the 1530s.
[130] Staatsarchiv Nürnberg, Kirchen und Ortschaften auf dem Lande, fos. 451-4.
[131] Quoted in Leder, Kirche und Jugend in Nürnberg, pp. 162-3.
[132] Stadtarchiv Ulm, A 9063, I, fo. 131. The date is 1605.
[133] Staatsarchiv Nürnberg, Reichsstadt Rothenburg Akten 2089.
[134] Ibid., 2096, fo. 83ᵛ.

sacred songs",[135] along with complaints about everyone being late for church, "making indecent gestures at members of the congregation who wish to join in singing the hymns", even bringing dogs to church "so that due to the loud barking the service is disturbed and occasionally even interrupted".[136]   Late in the seventeenth century we can read the same stories and complaints: Nearly everyone is ignorant of the main points of religion.   Many people "can't pray".   Children are kept out of school and from the catechism.   At best they know it by rote, and few examiners ever bother to ask them to explain what it means.   The plaintive note of one despairing visitor can stand as a general conclusion: "Pastors are doing all they can.   If people would only go to church!"[137]

IV

The evidence of the visitations speaks for itself; no comments are needed.   Lutheranism had not succeeded in making an impact on the population at large.   Early hopes for a renewal of religious and moral life in society were not fulfilled.   Experiments in mass indoctrination were stillborn or turned out not to work.   The Gospel had not been implanted in the hearts and minds of men.   An attitude of utter indifference prevailed toward the established religion, its teachings, its sacraments and its ministers.

To say this is not to argue that there were among Lutherans in Germany no men and women of serious, sincere and informed piety. Our evidence is inconclusive for the larger cities where we would expect to find such people.   We ought surely to suppose that things stood brighter there for religion than in the hamlets and villages of the countryside.   If not, who was it who responded to the beautiful hymns of the Lutheran service?   What would explain the loss of religious conviction by descendants of the guild members of Ulm whose names we can still read on the voting lists of 1530 where they recorded their overwhelming support of the Lutheran cause?[138]   What could have choked the religious spirit of the grandchildren of Nuremberg burghers who had crowded St. Sebald's and St. Lawrence's churches to hear the sermons of Dominicus Schleupner and Andreas Osiander?[139]   Cities

[135] This quotation is from the visitation of Amt Bergedorf in 1581: Staatsarchiv Hamburg, Cl VII. Lit. Hd., no. 8, vol. ic, fasc. 1.
[136] *Ibid.*   For an identical complaint about dogs in church, see Hessisches Hauptstaatsarchiv Wiesbaden, Abt. 137 Xa, no. 1, fos. 72-4.
[137] Landeskirchliches Archiv Braunschweig, Voges 1924.
[138] Julius Endriss, *Die Abstimmung der Ulmer Bürgerschaft im November 1530* (Ulm, 1931).
[139] See my *Nuremberg in the Sixteenth Century* (New York, 1966), ch. iv.

had abler pastors, more and better schools, and more effective means of control over conduct. But even if we assume, as I think we should, that city people went to church, paid attention to sermons, made their children learn the catechism, gave support to schools, and were responsive to the emotional appeals of their religion, we cannot tell much about their understanding of the faith they professed, nor about the ways in which this understanding affected their lives. The documents contain enough complaints from theologians and preachers to suggest that city people were no paragons of piety. Simon Musaeus, the orthodox Lutheran administrator and polemicist, mentions an encounter with a cloth-merchant during a visitation in the 1560s. Having failed in his attempt to elicit from the man a recollection of the previous Sunday's sermon, Musaeus inquired about the price of a bolt of cloth a year ago. To this the merchant gave a precise answer. Why was it, Musaeus wanted to know, that he could remember wool prices for a year and forget a Christian sermon within a week?

> To which the man replied that these are two entirely different matters. "Wool is my business" he said. "I must think about it day and night, because that is how I make my living. As for the sermon and the catechism — I don't worry much about them".

"Is this not horrible blindness?" Musaeus exclaims. "But that is how they all are!"[140] Despite obligatory drills in catechism and repetitive preaching on the articles of the creed, religious comprehension in cities is likely to have been much more shallow than the kind of understanding for which the reformers had worked and hoped in the years before 1530 when public enthusiasm for their cause ran so high. The exact nature of the faith of the urban citizenry has not yet been analysed. Much work can still be done on this subject, the sources of which remain to be exploited by students of *mentalités collectives*.

A fully coherent explanation of the phenomena described in this article would require more space than is available here. A few factors may however be suggested. It should first be noted again that the reporting procedures of sixteenth-century visitations differed among themselves. Some visitations gathered information on the basis of a "soft" questionnaire, and these would naturally fail to turn up the explicit data about the state of religious knowledge and behaviour compiled by visitations in other lands where "hard" techniques of investigative questioning were employed. Our general picture is therefore bound to be uneven. Generally speaking, however, the

---

[140] Simon Musaeus, *Catechismus. Examen mit kurzen Fragen und Antowrt . . .* (Frankfurt am Main, 1571), fo. 3ʳ. For a more sweeping judgement on the behaviour of burghers in Leipzig, see the visitation protocol in Stadtarchiv Leipzig, Tit. VII B. 3, fos. 59 ff.

more exhaustive the questions, the more disheartening the information brought to light. It also stands to reason that geographic and economic factors must have operated in the obvious way: isolated and poor parishes were more likely to persist in ignorance than well-to-do places in touch with urban culture. Still, as I have tried to show, the evidence does not suggest that religion was taken more seriously by the comfortable than by the poor. Occasionally an effective pastor or schoolteacher could overcome the general laxness, but the protocols, which are not self-serving in this respect, make it clear that the absence of tangible Christianity among the people was not usually due to lack of pastoral effort. The interminable theological polemics of the time must have had a deadening effect on people's religious interest. On the other hand there is also a strong possibility that visitation protocols occasionally confound religious indifference with confessional opposition to politically enforced creeds: Catholic to Protestant and vice versa, Zwinglian to Lutheran, and so on. One gets the impression that the most knowledgeable, serious and courageous Lutherans were to be found in hostile environments such as northern Bavaria under the rigorously Catholic régimes of Albrecht V and Wilhelm V.[141] In this as in so many other instances, strength of conviction seemed born of adversity. Where people had learned to adjust to the routine of officially sanctioned orthodoxy, on the other hand, their religious interest seems to have diminished. One might also take notice of the Marxist view that the lack of religious concern must have been the inevitable reaction of "progressive" groups to the collapse of the peasant rebellion and the suppression of urban independence movements. But I have found little in the documents to support this interpretation of religious indifference as a conscious withdrawal by the disaffected.

One other point seems worth making here. The evidence of the visitation protocols supports the view — much emphasized in recent years — that the operative religion of country folk, and perhaps of many city-dwellers as well, had much less to do with the doctrines of established Christianity than with the spells, chants, signs and paraphernalia of ancient magic lore and wizardry, the cult of which flourished unaffected by the imposition of new or old denominational

---

[141] This assertion is based on analysis of ample documentation in Bavarian archives. E.g. Bayerisches Hauptstaatsarchiv München: Staatsverwaltung 2784, fos. 189-97, 272 a-m: lists of persons in Ingolstadt and Wasserburg willing to be expelled rather than abandon their religious practices; *ibid.*, 2786, fos. 141-8, 155-9: lists of persons unwilling to conform to the Religious Edict of 1571.

creeds.[142]   To call the persistence of these magic practices a "counter culture" to the official culture of Christianity[143] is perhaps an over-reaction to our belated discovery of this fact of popular life.   But there can be little doubt that magic cults held the trust and engaged the interest of the majority of the populace at a time when the official religion as preached from pulpits and taught in catechisms became increasingly abstract, dogmatic and detached from the concerns of ordinary life.

Ecclesiastical officials knew that this was so.   Lutheran theologians never stopped warning against the plague of soothsayers.[144]   Visitors had standing instructions to probe for evidence of conjuring, wise women and cunning men, the evil eye, witchcraft, fortune-telling, spells and curses.   Although it proved difficult to extract solid informa-tion from the people (interestingly enough, villagers did not often tell on each other and accusations are rare) the clergy usually knew and told enough to convince officials that they had a problem on their hands. Magic was pervasive and deep-seated in popular culture.   One example will have to suffice here for the mass of evidence suggesting the penetration of popular culture by magic practices.   It comes from the visitations of the administrative district of Wiesbaden, in the county of Nassau-Wiesbaden, in 1594.   According to the visitors' report:

> The use of spells (*das Segensprechen*) is so widespread among the people here that not a man or woman begins, undertakes, does or refrains from doing anything . . . without employing some particular blessing, incantation, spell, or other such heathenish means.   To wit: in pangs of childbirth, when a babe is taken up or put down (so that no evil enchantment may befall him [*damit es nit bezaubert werde*]) . . . when cattle are driven into the fields, or are lost, etc., when windows are shut against the night, etc. . . .   Whenever an article has been mislaid and cannot be found, when someone feels sickly or a cow acts queer, they run at once to the soothsayer (*warsager*) to ask who has stolen it or put a bad spell on it, and to fetch some charm to use against the enchanter. . . .   Daily experience with these people shows that there is no measure or limit to the use of these supersititious spells, both among those who cast them, and among those who ask them to be cast, believing thereby

---

[142] See Keith Thomas, *Religion and the Decline of Magic* (London and New York, 1971); Alan Macfarlane, *Witchcraft in Tudor and Stuart England* (London and New York, 1970); H. C. Erik Midelfort, *Witch Hunting in Southwestern Germany 1562-1684* (Stanford, Cal., 1972); Friedrich Merzbacher, *Die Hexenprozesse in Franken* (Munich, 1970).   For a good *Forschungsbericht*, see E. William Monter, "The Historiography of European Witchcraft: Progress and Prospects", *Jl. Interdisciplinary History*, ii (1972), pp. 435-51.

[143] Lawrence Stone, "The Disenchantment of the World" (a review of several books on magic and witchcraft, including the volumes by Thomas and Macfarlane cited in the preceding note), *New York Rev. of Books*, xvii (9) (2 Dec. 1971), pp. 18, 24.

[144] E.g. Huberinus, *Spiegel der geistlichen Hauszucht* . . . , fos. ccxlv-vi; Christoph Vischer, *Auslegung der Fünf Heubtstück des heiligen Catechismi* (Schmalkalden, 1573), fo. cii^v.

to keep their lives and property from coming to harm. All the people hereabouts engage in superstitious practices with familiar and unfamiliar words, names, and rhymes, especially with the name of God, the Holy Trinity, certain angels, the Virgin Mary, the twelve Apostles, the Three Kings, numerous saints, the wounds of Christ, his seven words on the Cross, verses from the New Testament. . . . These are spoken secretly or openly, they are written on scraps of paper, swallowed (*eingeben*) or worn as charms. They also make strange signs, crosses, gestures; they do things with herbs, roots, branches of special trees; they have their particular days, hours and places for everything, and in all their deeds and words they make much use of the number three. And all this is done to work harm on others or to do good, to make things better or worse, to bring good or bad luck to their fellow men.[145]

Sixteenth-century theologians could not understand this. But to us, looking back, it should not appear astonishing that these ancient practices touched the lives of ordinary people much more intimately than the distant religion of the Consistory and the Formula of Concord. The deep current of popular life whence they arose was beyond the preacher's appeal and the visitor's power to compel. The permissive beliefs of medieval Catholicism had absorbed these practices and allowed them to proliferate;[146] but this accommodating milieu was now abolished. Hostile religious authorities showed themselves unbendingly intolerant of deeply ingrained folkways. The persistence of occult practices in popular life is therefore certainly a cause, as well as a symptom, of the failure of Lutheranism to accomplish the general elevation of moral life on which the most fervent hopes of the early reformers had been set.

---

[145] Hessisches Hauptstaatsarchiv Wiesbaden, Abt. 137, no. 1, fo. 9^r.

[146] The fusion of Catholic with ancient magic practices emerges clearly from the documents. An excellent example is the passage just quoted from the visitors' report on Wiesbaden in 1594.

XII

The Reformation and Its Public in an Age of Orthodoxy

How does an ideologically inspired movement pass from its beginnings in a time of struggle to a place of legitimacy and authority? The study of revolutions, and of other changes equally abrupt and sweeping, offers few more intriguing questions. How does the movement's leadership control the collective response of its followers? How may this response be sustained over time? All movements, it seems, tend to follow a similar course. Ideological emphasis shifts from guiding ideas, and the transcendent source of these ideas (God, History, or Nature), to institutions and the powerful human agents directing them. Reliance in the management of people and events passes from exhortation to surveillance. Long-range goals, originally set to accord with governing ideals, make way for short-term tasks necessitated by crises. As these begin to determine the making of policy, formerly inflexible norms are bent and adjusted. The ineluctable force is now exerted by reality, the real-world situation with which the movement has to contend. Ideals are relinquished to an indistinctly perceived future, their urgency attenuated by the press of immediate problems.

The very banality of this simple scheme endows it with historical verisimilitude. As an outline of how things change in the process leading from creative turmoil to settled order, it matches the world of ordinary affairs as we recognize it, making pattern fit observation in the way to which social history aspires. It also returns to its earthly base what has long been dressed up in unworldly spirituality. A sobering experience is in store for the historical scholar—especially the kind still drawn to the role played by great men—who charts the passage of a movement from its

Reprinted from Gerald Strauss, "The Reformation and its Public in an Age of Orthodoxy", in *The Germanic People and the Reformation,* edited by R. Po-Chia Hsia. Copright © 1988 by Cornell University Press. Used by permission of the publisher, Cornell University Press.

heroic to its established phase. My 1978 book, *Luther's House of Learning: Indoctrination of the Young in the German Reformation,* addressed itself to this transition, taking the sixteenth-century Reformation in Germany as a case in point. Although the book was not intended as a demonstration of how ideals succumb to reality, it became just that as my work moved from its original objective, the description of a vigorously pursued pedagogical enterprise, to an interpretation of the results of this undertaking.

Luther's House of Learning (the title is taken from Ecclesiasticus, a text much quoted in the pedagogical literature of the Reformation) made the following assertions and tried to offer some evidence for them. (1) An organized effort was made in Lutheran Germany in the first half of the sixteenth century to meet the challenge of the movement's future by imbuing young people with the essentials of Evangelical Christianity and civic morality (in using the term "indoctrination" to describe this effort, I had no pejorative innuendo in mind). (2) This effort represented the joint objectives of theologians and politicians, both groups having grown deeply worried over the unravelling of order in the early events of the Reformation. (3) The undertaking was well supported and systematic (always speaking relatively, of course) and was pursued with great vigor and dedication. (4) It rested upon the best available psychological evidence for the educability of the young and for the prospect of succeeding with the task of training them, provided that techniques of methodical habituation were employed, these techniques being fully explained in the writings of ancient authorities, notably Aristotle. (5) This technique was indeed utilized, most often in the form of catechism instruction, and a small army of pedagogues was kept busy writing catechisms, school texts, primers, readers—all of these incorporating Evangelical ideas. (6) From the very outset of the enterprise, governments monitored the results of their labors through parish visitations—again in a highly systematic fashion—and the unusually revealing written record of these inspections (visitation reports or protocols) told them, and still tells us, that their efforts were not succeeding. (7) On the evidence of these reports, the large mass of the populace exhibited after three-quarters of a century or more of Christian instruction a shocking ignorance of even the rudiments of the Evangelical religion and displayed disheartening apathy toward it. I drew the conclusion that the Reformation must be said to have failed *if* (and I stressed the *if*) it is understood as a serious endeavor to christianize people—all people or at least most—in a meaningful, as opposed to a merely perfunctory, way and if it is agreed that the Lutheran pedagogical enterprise was the heart of this christianizing mission. I suggested several explanations of this failure: the reformers' own ambivalence in pressing their pedagogy on the young—an irresoluteness grounded in large part in their pessimistic anthropology; the debilitating effect on the indoctrination program of the orthodox rigor into which the Lutheran movement settled in its established phase; confusions and doubts brought on by internal controversies about doctrine; and, last and probably most important, the enduring vitality of a popular counterreligion operating at the base of society that rendered the large mass of ordinary people virtually impervious to religious indoctrination from above.

The critical response to this conclusion was vigorous, most likely because the book was seen to be pushing a revisionist thesis in a field that needs no revision according to some of its most committed students but badly needs shaking up in the view of many others. Reviewers seemed to divide along a sharply drawn boundary of scholarly direction and personal engagement.[1] Heiko Oberman has identified this split. "Given the kind of Reformation history that regards the theological factor as a marginal phenomenon of merely circumstantial importance," he wrote in an essay on Luther and the Reformation for which *Luther's House of Learning* served him as a point of departure, "it is not surprising that this thesis has gained support."[2] Reaction to the book does indeed appear to have been governed by a writer's opinions on the place and weight to be given to theology in interpreting the Reformation. As this is also the issue on which the social historian parts company with the older scholarship, it will make a useful focus for this elaboration of my theme.

Most adverse criticism of my book has come from the traditional camp, although—it goes almost without saying—reviewers friendly to my own sense of how religion fits into a period and a culture have also found grounds for disagreement. From my own point of view it is unfortunate that critical comment has concentrated on the last fifty pages of the book, the part entitled "Consequences," in which I raise the question of the success or the failure of the pedagogical experiment and, by extension, of the Reformation itself. This emphasis is unfortunate because it creates the impression that the intent of my book was negative when, to my mind, its

---

[1]A sampling of reviews: Steven Ozment in *Journal of Modern History*, vol. 51, no. 4 (1979):837–39; Lewis W. Spitz in *American Historical Review*, vol. 85, no. 1 (1980):143; Joachim Whaley in *Times Literary Supplement*, March 21, 1980, p. 336; Jonathan W. Zophy in *Sixteenth Century Journal* 11 (1980):102–103; John M. Headley in *Catholic Historical Review*, January 1981, pp. 112–15; Mark U. Edwards, Jr., in *History of Education Quarterly* 21 (Winter 1981):471–77; Paul Rorem in *Princeton Seminary Bulletin*, vol. 3, no. 1 (1980):99; Kenneth Charlton in *History of Education* 10 (1981):150–52; Lawrence P. Buck in *Historian*, vol. 42, no. 4 (1980):673–74; Scott H. Hendrix in *Sixteenth Century Journal* 16 (1985):3–14.

[2]Heike A. Oberman, "Martin Luther: Vorläufer der Reformation," in E. Jürgel, J. Wallmann, W. Werbeck, eds., *Verifikationen: Festschrift für Gerhard Ebeling zum 70. Geburtstag* (Tübingen, 1982), p. 93.

chief purpose had been to call attention to an important though flawed and ultimately failed undertaking of great historical interest: the German reformers' experiment in mass pedagogy. Failure is no disgrace, although explanation of failure is often read as a judgment on those who tried. No such judgment was intended in my book, however. If we can see clearly now why the German Reformation's pedagogical effort was sure to falter, it is because our perceptions today are so unlike those with which reformers observed their scene. Our awareness of the central role of social reality in shaping every situation allows us to identify the impediments to the reformers' approach to religious and moral education. They, of course, saw things differently, as they were bound to do, given their presuppositions. To indicate that they failed is not, therefore, to dishonor them, nor does it detract from the significance of what they tried to accomplish.

A consideration of this failure should, however, persuade us to think in somewhat altered terms about the immediate and long-range impact of the Reformation on German society, and my argument has come under fire for having exemplified this thought shift. If my way of seeing things is correct, we must accept it as a fact that, for the great majority of men and women in the Lutheran territories of the Holy Roman Empire, the spiritual effects of the Reformation were neither deep nor lasting. Why should this conclusion be considered offensive? From my own perspective as a social historian, one reason suggests itself: because such an assertion undermines an old myth about the Reformation to which so many of us have long subscribed. In this myth, Luther's Evangelical message and its subsequent development in Protestant theology appear as the answer to everyone's prayer for a spiritual renewal. The superiority of the message is assumed, as is the eager acceptance of it by the great mass of the Reformation's loyal partisans. We do not ask: superior for what? Accepted for what reasons? How related to the lives of the men and women to whom it was preached? How understood by them in the context of their own places in the world? One has only to raise such questions to begin to see the conceptual gap dividing the older Reformation scholarship from the new. Practitioners of the latter sort remove their primary attention from the biographical and theological center in the person of Luther and the small circle of his fellow reformers. They direct their interest instead to the circumstances of the Reformation's differential reception in a vast number of distinct urban and rural situations. Inevitably, normative values in interpreting the Reformation make way for descriptive ones. It is this displacement that has aroused the greater number of misgivings.

The most serious objection made to my book is that it proceeds from a false premise. This premise contends that it was the Reformation's "central purpose to make people—all people—think, feel, and act as Christians, to imbue them with a Christian mind-set, motivational drive, and way of life." Wrong, it is charged by critics who find the book's credibility seriously weakened by a lack of familiarity with basic Lutheran theology. It is illegitimate, so goes the objection, to claim "for the Reformation a central purpose no Lutheran reformer ever entertained." "Christianization" was never the reformers' goal. Luther and his associates, it is argued, could not have expected people to live up to an ideal. Their religious persuasions made it impossible for them to develop such anticipations. Luther never imagined that "reformation" could take the form of a transformation of society. Reformation is God's doing, not man's. It comes at the end of time, not before. Luther himself is really a "prereformer,"[3] and categories such as "success" and "failure" are meaningless in testing the results of his work. They encourage a serious misreading of Lutheran intentions. Moreover, it is wrong to judge the reformers' actions by their high sense of mission. Doing so makes us overlook their many positive achievements, none of which encompassed the moral regeneration of their fellow men and women. It is true that Luther's own fundamental distinction between God's ultimate reformation and a—never attempted—temporal transformation was later dropped by Melanchthon, Zwingli, Bucer, and others of the second and subsequent generations of reformers. Still, they did not, any more than did Luther himself, confuse the however-much-to-be-desired elevation of tone and conduct in life with their real goal as Evangelical reformers, which was to lead people to a saving faith. As theologians, they did not greatly care how the world received the Gospel. None held much hope for the world. True reformation was in God's hands. Men accomplish little. "One trusts in God to rule the spiritual kingdom while doing the best one can in the affairs of the world."

Critics who follow this line of reasoning insist that, in judging the reformers' goals, I was misled by an occasional idealistic or ambitious assertion made by them. There is, of course, no shortage of these. Luther himself delivered an extraordinary one in 1528. In a buoyant mood that he found difficult later to recapture, he exulted:

I declare . . . I have made a reformation that will make the popes' ears ring and hearts burst. . . . By the grace of God I have accomplished so much that nowadays a boy or girl of fifteen knows more about Christian doctrine than all the theologians and universities used to know in the old days. For among us the catechism has come back into use: I mean the Lord's Prayer, the Apostles' Creed, the Ten Commandments, penance and baptism, prayer, the cross, living and

---

[3]Oberman, "Martin Luther," pp. 101, 104, 109. The other quotations in this paragraph are from the reviews cited in note 1, above.

dying . . . also what marriage is, and secular government, what it means to be father and mother, wife and children, parent and son, man servant and maid servant. In short, I have led all estates in society to their right order and have guided them all to a good conscience, so that each knows how he is to live and how he must serve God in his appointed place. And for those who have accepted this, the result has been more than a little benefit, peace, and virtue [*tugent*].[4]

This passage—and others could be quoted to the same effect—suggests what Luther had in mind for the "reformation" that he then believed was being embraced by his fellow men and women. All are to be firmly emplaced in their respective walks of life: "alle stende der wellt . . . zu . . . ordnung bracht," where *ordnung* refers to the external arrangements that establish duties and set boundaries. They are to be led to, and maintained in, this benign equipoise by being brought to good conscience ("zu gutem gewissen . . . bracht"), so that each will know ("das ein iglicher weis") how to conduct himself, both toward God and toward his fellow beings. The appeal, in other words, is by way of the Gospel to the individual's inner self. Its outcome is, personally, a virtuous disposition. Collectively, it is a right-living and right-serving human community.

At the end of the fateful 1520s, Luther was apparently still confident that such a community could be the result of reformation, though he claimed little credit for his own achievements, referring instead to "the good that the gospel has accomplished not only privately, in the individual human mind and conscience, but also publicly, in the conduct of political affairs and in household management" ("tum privatim in hominum animis et conscienciis tum publice in politia et oeconomia").[5] If any praise was due to him, it was for having helped to bring the Gospel to young and old, especially to the young. Luther did take pride in the evident success of his two catechisms. "Our tender young people," he wrote in 1530, taking stock of accomplishments, "girls as well as boys, are now so well taught in catechism and Scripture that my heart grows warm as I observe children praying more devoutly and speaking more eloquently of God and Christ than, in the old days, all the learned monks and doctors."[6] This, in Luther's view, was the hoped-for course of the reformation he was making. All men and women—but chiefly the young and the simple at heart—were to be imbued through the catechism with the sum and gist of Scripture, and the result would be a rightly ordered individual conscience, resulting in a human collectivity living in peace and virtue.

[4]Luther, preface to Stephan Klingebeil's *Von Priester Ehe* (Wittenberg, 1528), in *D. Martin Luthers Werke, Weimar Ausgabe* (=*WA*), 26:530.

[5]From Luther's lectures on the Song of Solomon, given 1530–1531, published 1539, *WA* 31², p. 613.

[6]Luther writing to Elector Johann, 20 May 1530, *WA* Briefwechsel 5, No. 1572, pp. 325–26.

The point to be made by the historian in judging this scheme is that, whatever its validity or feasibility in terms of Lutheran theology, it was the product of the reformer's increasingly direct involvement in the events activated by the Reformation. The overwhelming public response to his person and, apparently, to his message persuaded Luther of the divine favor shown to the movement whose acknowledged head he had become by the late 1520s. Second, the mass of practical problems created by the rejection of the old Church and brought to him for solution turned his attention increasingly to the worldly consequences of faith. The last of the passages quoted above occurs in a letter from Luther to his sovereign, the elector Johann. It offered the prince encouragement at a difficult moment in the political fortunes of Protestant states. In the mental world of Luther's day, religion and secular concerns interpenetrated seamlessly, for politicians and for ordinary people and for theologians as well. In making this pragmatic linkage of belief and its worldly manifestations, Luther was as little preoccupied as the layman with observing the tidy distinctions between the two kingdoms—God's and the world's—that are held so important in the modern discussion of Lutheranism. Riding the crest of his movement's success in gaining popular approval and political support, Luther was encouraged to look for substantial improvement in public morality as a consequence of the restoration of the gospel. Beset, at the same time, by the religious and social unrest of the Reformation's turbulent first decades, he turned increasingly to political means for actualizing his goal. Hence his close collaboration with Saxon statesmen in the building of a church government, the end product of a process in which the territorywide visitations of 1528 were the first decisive step.[7]

Luther never felt quite at ease with this trend. His many verbal protests against politicians and lawyers reveal his anxiety over the bureaucratic takeover of the church and over the debilitation suffered by civil society as a result of the destruction of its essential nerve, which is Christian love.[8] Still, although objections to the politicization of civic life—a process of

---

[7]The precise nature of Luther's involvement with the electoral Saxon state in the formation of the Saxon *Kirchenregiment* has been the subject of a vigorous controversy. For a discussion of this debate, see Hans-Walter Krummwiede, *Zur Entstehung des landesherrlichen Kirchenregimentes in Kursachsen und Braunschweig-Wolfenbüttel* (Göttingen, 1967), pp. 13–47; also Irmgard Höss, "The Lutheran Church of the Reformation: Problems of Its Formation and Organization," in Lawrence P. Buck and Jonathan W. Zophy, eds., *The Social History of the Reformation* (Columbus, Ohio, 1972), pp. 317–39.

[8]For a few examples of these protests, see *Eine Predigt, dass man Kinder zur Schule halten solle* (1530), WA 30², p. 566; Tischreden (=TR) I, No. 349 (1532); III No. 3622 (1537); preface to *Das fünffte, sechste, und siebend Capitel S. Matthei gepredigt und ausgelegt* (1532), WA 32, pp. 299–300; sermon of 6 January 1544, WA 49, p. 298. For an extended treatment of this issue, see my *Law, Resistance, and the State: The Opposition to Roman Law in Reformation Germany* (Princeton, 1986), chap. 7.

which Luther was keenly aware—fell easily from the reformer's lips, his actions did far more to support the trend than to oppose it. In any case, Luther's ambivalence on matters of politics and legislation soon gave way to a much more positive posture toward worldly laws, a posture associated, in Luther's own day, with Philip Melanchthon and, in later decades, with the controversialist theologians and ecclesiastical administrators who came to dominate the Lutheran establishment in the second half of the sixteenth century. A mere twenty years after Luther's death, the editor of his Table Talk, Johann Aurifaber, a loyal partisan of what he took to be authentic Lutheranism, noted sadly that "politicians, lawyers, and courtiers run the church now, directing religion like worldly affairs."[9] With this change in the direction—in both senses of the word—of the Lutheran movement in Germany, the question of whether a "moral transformation" of society could be reconciled with basic Lutheran theology became moot. The social turmoil of the 1520s had left a profound impression on ecclesiastical and political ruling circles. Above all other lessons, it had taught them that religious ideas could have revolutionary consequences. After 1525 it was no longer possible as a matter of practical politics to segregate faith from worldly affairs. If the latter were to be held stable, the former, too, must be placed under governance. Bracing authority became the paramount task of church and state, and anxiety over holding public belief in a condition of orthodoxy replaced the earlier zeal for spreading the word as a liberating message.

From about the middle of the sixteenth century, therefore, governments insisted on conformity in religion and practiced stringent supervision in order to obtain it. As the execution of religious policy became the business of the state, responsibility for putting it into effect passed from ecclesiastical to political personnel. This development received its most sweeping expression in the publication of *Kirchenordnungen,* comprehensive church constitutions through which the religious institutions of territories and cities were closely meshed in their operations with the politics of the territorial and urban state. An example will indicate the intent and range of these documents. A directive addressed by Duke Christian I to provincial administrative courts in Saxony, in 1587, declared that,

whereas a great contempt for God's word has been observed in many places, and people are lax and lazy in their attendance of church and their attention to God's word, and whereas governments are obliged to act against such contempt for God's word, it is ordered that one official person be appointed in every congregation . . . to make a weekly inspection in church, to see which chairs and pews are

[9]From the preface to Aurifaber's edition of Luther's *Tischreden* (1566), printed in Johann Georg Walch, ed., *Dr. Martin Luthers sämmtliche Schriften,* vol. 22 (Halle, 1743), col. 49.

unoccupied two or three Sundays in a row, and persons who have been absent and have not obtained permission for unavoidable cause shall pay a fine of six Groschen into the common chest, or, if they refuse, shall be put in prison for two nights and two days. And if a court shall be shown to be lax or recalcitrant in enforcing this order, it shall be accountable to the electoral district office for its failure.[10]

The same directive required that individuals found to be deficient in their knowledge of the Lutheran catechism be barred from "taverns, baptisms, church fairs and other such entertainments, nor is their presence to be tolerated at a carousing" until they could bring a clean bill in writing from their pastor.[11] Local officers were instructed to roam the village environs on Sundays to spot anyone standing or walking about during divine service. Such offenders, if they ignored the first warning, were imprisoned. If obstinate, they were put in the pillory. Blaspheming, "insulting remarks" about God, mutterings to the effect "that the Lord is not omnipotent or not just" were to be punished by death or mutilation. Careless cursing led the offender straight to the stocks. "And anyone in the village who hears such things, and does not report them, shall be punished more severely than the criminals [*verbrecher*] themselves."[12]

The pattern contained in this example of church legislation from Luther's own Saxony—vigilant political surveillance followed in cases of infraction by heavy-handed punishment—came to be adopted everywhere, and not only by the major states. Towns imposed such rules on their citizens, and even villagers found their religious behavior regulated by those who held jurisdiction over them. A Village Ordinance (*Dorfordnung*) issued by the counts of Castell for their village of Obereisenheim in Franconia in 1579, set a fine of fifteen pfennig for anyone missing adult catechism class and a much more substantial penalty of one pound for absence from Sunday service.[13] Nor was the surveillance/punishment sequence a monopoly of Protestants. Trying to cope with identical difficulties in advancing their own reformation, Catholic rulers adopted it in step with their Lutheran rivals. In Tyrol, for instance, beginning in the late 1570s, the government of Archduke Ferdinand II compelled parishioners

[10]*Ehegerichts Ordnung des Ambtes Stolbergk* (1587). Staatsarchiv Dresden Loc. 8832: "Ambt Stolbergks Acta," 63 recto and verso. *Ehegerichte* in Saxony were local courts situated in the electorate's administrative districts (*Ämter*) and in domains of landowners with administrative and legal jurisdictions.

[11]Ibid., 63 verso–64 recto.

[12]Ibid., 67 recto and verso.

[13]Printed in Emil Sehling, ed., *Die evangelischen Kirchenordnungen des 16. Jahrhunderts* (Leipzig, 1901–13), continued by the Institut für evangelisches Kirchenrecht der evangelischen Kirche in Deutschland (Tübingen, 1955–), XI[1], pp. 687–88. This collection will hereinafter be cited as Sehling.

to obtain "confession receipts" (*Beichtzettel*) from their priests. The names of recipients were transmitted to the local district chief, the *Pfleger*, who kept a list (*Beichtregister*) of them and sent a copy of it to the central administration in Innsbruck, where officials stood ready to go after slackers and resisters.[14] By such means did the archduke hope to raise the religious and moral temper of his duchy. Bavaria offers an even clearer example of a state girded to act on the proposition that reformation meant religious and moral rectification, and that this beneficial change could be achieved only by the joint forces of state and church. Unwilling to leave the supervision of religious life to the Bavarian church (even though this church was effectively linked to the state apparatus through "political" lay members sitting on its controlling organ, the Council for Spiritual Affairs), the duchy's zealously Catholic rulers empowered their provincial chiefs, the *Rentmeister*, to gather information (*aus-kundschaften*) about the populace's adherence to official religious man-dates during their annual circuit ride (*Umritt*) round their districts. As shown by the elaborate instructions issued to them (many such instruc-tions survive in the Bavarian State Archive in Munich[15]), no aspect of the enforcement of "true religion" escaped the vigilance of these exalted bureaucrats. Make certain, they were told, that town and village notables go regularly to church. Inspect booksellers' and bookbinders' shops for heretical volumes, and follow up all allegations and rumors by "visiting" (that is, by seeking out and interrogating) suspected householders. Trace to their sources all talk about people crossing "sectarian borders" (that is, from Catholic Bavaria to Protestant regions such as Regensburg and the Palatinate). Report all religious discussions said to have taken place among citizens (these had been banned). Question priests on their par-ishioners' loyalty, reliability, state of religious knowledge, and perfor-mance of religious duties. Compare this body of information with the delinquency reports that priests were required to make to the secular authorities. Inspect all monasteries, and "visit" the superiors and broth-ers, pressing each to divulge what he knows about his fellow members' offenses, such as breaking fasts and keeping concubines. Although the supervision of religious behavior was only one of the Rentmeister's many obligations, it was, in the age of Reformation and Counter-Reformation, given top priority. Catholics and Protestants were in rare agreement on this point.

But what aspect of religion mattered most to the authorities? What

[14]Joseph Hirn, *Erzherzog Ferdinand II von Tirol: Geschichte seiner Regierung und seiner Länder* (Innsbruck, 1885–88), 1:177–79.

[15]Bayerisches Hauptstaatsarchiv, Munich, G.R. 1262, No. 4, from the year 1584 on.

mattered to them above all other things was a condition of general orthodoxy, uniformity, and collective loyalty. Outward behavior was bound to count more heavily in the practice of these virtues than belief and inner conviction. For this reason, the Lutheran insistence on salvation by faith alone began to cause some concern among observers of the many social problems arising from the theological devaluation of works. Christoph Scheurl, for example, a prominent jurist in Nuremberg, no Lutheran himself, but nonetheless a trusted legal adviser to his Protestant city, warned his magistrates that, although the *sola* in *sola fide* was still being disputed by the experts, people seemed to be all too eager to act on it. "How devoid of works we have become now," he noted, "is, alas, plain for all to see."[16] To counteract this perceived decline in public commitment to moral action, church and state leaders put their trust in social discipline, the instruments of which were catechism training and systematic visitations. No theological scruples kept authorities from trying to impose "Christian discipline" (*Zucht*) on young and old, although their definition of "discipline" now included articles of belief as well as norms of conduct. Examples from the Old Testament served as precedents for this endeavor. King Josiah abolished idolatry and brought the religious practice of his state into harmony with its laws. Nehemiah cleansed religion of all foreign contamination. King Jehoshophat enforced the law upon the people of Judah. Citing these, and others, as examples for emulation, the *Kirchenordnung* of the County of Hohenlohe (for example) takes "visitation" to mean the institution of godly doctrine ("die lehr gotlichs worts") and the imposition of *Christliche Zucht* on all subjects. "In these last and perilous times," the document declares (it was published in 1558), with Satan gaining strength every day, only a government-promoted effort could keep civic life and religion from disintegration.[17] A law-and-order mentality thus combined with eschatological expectations to explain the transfer of religious initiative from individuals to institutions and to justify the passage of religious voluntarism into social control. Churchmen and statesmen joined hands in promoting this shift.

Although they were not fully articulated until after Luther's death, the developments described on the preceding pages certainly owe something to the reformer's own frequently voiced sense of frustration. The euphoria

---

[16]Scheurl in a 1530 memorandum on the projected Nuremberg-Brandenburg church constitution, Germanisches Nationalmuseum Nuremberg, Merkel-Handschrift 129, 5 verso.

[17]For the text see Sehling XV[1], pp. 120–32, especially pp. 129–30: "Von der oberkeit als beschützerin der kirchen." See also Gunther Franz, *Die Kirchenleitung in Hohenlohe in den Jahrzehnten nach der Reformation: Visitation, Konsistorium, Kirchenzucht und die Festigung des landesherrlichen Kirchenregiments, 1556–1586* (Stuttgart, 1971), pp. 40–41.

of Luther's early years as a reformer did not long outlast the troublesome 1520s. By 1530 it was gone, as dejection became the dominant mood in which Luther contemplated the worldly scene. For years now, he wrote in 1541, we Germans have been allowed to hear the precious word preached without falsification. "But how gratefully and honestly we have received and kept it is a dreadful thing to see." Only a few (*gar wenig*) want to accept it gratefully (*danckbarlich annemen*). The greater part shows itself to be impudent, licentious, faithless, lazy, thieving, given to consorting with evil sects and wicked heretics and "all this under the name and appearance of the gospel" while their real gods are Mammon and greed. "Thus Germany is ripe and rotten with all manner of sins against God," he concluded, which is why the Turk has been sent to punish us.[18] Luther took much of this dismal picture of Germany's moral condition from data newly brought to light by government visitations, in the planning for which in his own state of Saxony he had played a prominent part. The widespread apathy and ignorance discovered by the visitors convinced authorities, Luther and Melanchthon foremost among them, that "discipline" was now required above all other needs. As the chief theoretician of the Wittenberg movement, Melanchthon developed a doctrine of positive law that encouraged Protestant governments to overcome the earlier Lutheran ambivalence on the use of law, and to undertake, through legislation, the indoctrination of men and women in morality and *pietas*.[19] Such legislation was doing God's own work.[20] Hence the many mandates and directives concerning religion, the proliferation of which is the characteristic expression of politics in the second half of the sixteenth century.

Decrees and directives, however, tell us little about their impact on society. They may persuade us that "moral transformation" by way of a system of discipline was, indeed, the objective of both ecclesiastic and secular administrators, but they are silent on the results of this undertaking (although the ceaseless reissue of them in subsequent decades suggests that their results were less than perfect). For this reason visitation reports are an especially vital source for judging the social consequences of reformation in Germany. Visitations were designed to test the effectiveness of religious policy. They are, of course, official documents too, but they contain direct information obtained at first hand on the site, revealing the responses of ordinary people to government policy. Visitations were held frequently—at least annually, in most places—and carried out me-

---

[18]*Vermahnung zum Gebet wider den Türken* (1541), WA 51, pp. 585–89.

[19]Melanchthon, *Loci communes theologici* (1521), trans. L. J. Satre, in Wilhelm Pauck, ed., *Melanchthon and Bucer*, Library of Christian Classics, 19 (London, 1969), pp. 50, 53.

[20]Melanchthon, *Oratio de legibus*, printed in Guido Kisch, *Melanchthons Rechts- und Soziallehre* (Berlin, 1967), p. 196.

[206]

thodically. They were called "church visitations" (*Kirchenvisitationen*) not because churchmen alone conducted them (they did not) but because the unit of inspection was the church parish. Teams of ecclesiastical and lay officials passed 'from village to village and town to town (although they did not go to the larger cities, where magistrates were too jealous of their autonomy, and too powerful, to subject themselves to surveillance). There they put questions, taken from printed questionnaires, to local officials (pastors, schoolmasters, mayors, bailiffs, and council members) and to a selection of ordinary folk (women and men, old and young, rich and poor). Answers were written down by scribes at the site; later they were transcribed verbatim or in detailed paraphrase to fair copies. These were then gathered in volumes for use by appropriate government agencies. Most of these copies have survived, many in excellent condition. They may be read in state, municipal, and church archives throughout Germany. A few have been published.[21] They hold invaluable—and so far largely unexploited—evidence for discovering both the facts and the quality of life at the grass roots of society.

This claim, first made in my 1978 book, has been disputed. Many critics have asked whether, by their very purpose, the visitation reports do not overemphasize abuses and shortcomings. Were visitors not instructed to find faults? Were they not "intended to ferret out problems, not successes"? Clerical informants, in particular, must have had a "tendency to see sin everywhere." Taking the visitation reports at face value, it has been suggested, is like writing the history of our time from the police blotter. Still, I do not think that these are fatal objections, though they are valid cautions. Visitation reports, like all other historical documents, are "texts" in that they incorporate unspecified attitudes and are shaped by a net of largely unacknowledged circumstances. There is—to pick out one difficulty among many—the problem of "self-labeling," as emphasized now by the interactionist approach to the study of deviant behavior. ("Deviance" is, of course, what the visitation protocols were meant to pick out.) The recent literature on this subject shows how easily a "description" of phenomena becomes "ascription" when supposedly factual accounts of behavior are laced with value judgments brought to their observations by investigators harboring a preformed attitude toward what they see.[22] One must, of course. recognize this tendency on the part of six-

[21]See the partial list of printed and archival visitation materials in Ernst Walter Zeeden and Hansgeorg Molitor, eds., *Die Visitation im Dienst der kirchlichen Reform*, 2d ed. (Münster, 1977). For additional references, see my *Luther's House of Learning* (Baltimore, 1978), especially the notes to chaps. 12 and 13.

[22]See, for example, *Theories of Deviance*, ed. S. H. Traub and C. B. Little, 2d ed. (Itasca, Ill., 1980), pp. 241–42; Kai T. Erikson, "Notes on the Sociology of Deviance," in E. Rubington and M. S. Weinberg, eds., *Deviance* (New York, 1973), p. 27.

teenth-century visitors. Still, such circumspection belongs to the historian's basic equipment, and I see no reason why, when used along with other relevant materials, visitation records should not be trusted.

I have been finding additional materials that support my original interpretation. They include the copious records of local and patrimonial courts in Saxony, the so-called *Ehegerichte,* administrative and judicial tribunals on which clergymen had no place.[23] Concerned with problems of law and order in daily life, these bodies produced masses of records in which the picture conveyed of the country's religious condition matches that of the visitations exactly. Another source to be set beside visitation documents is the deliberations of territorial Estates *(Stände)*, notably the unceasing stream of "grievances" *(gravamina, Beschwerden)* addressed by them to their sovereigns.[24] Grievances were very differently generated from visitation protocols. The latter were the products of centralized planning and execution; in the case of the former, masses of local complaints coalesced into regional and corporate protests. In indicating the state of religion and morality in society, however, the two sets of records are in full agreement. From Catholic Bavaria comes still another source to compare with visitation data: the already mentioned reports made to the Munich government by provincial Rentmeister. They contain the very same disappointing descriptions of religious conditions as the records of the duchy's parish visitations.[25]

The evidence from visitation reports seemingly cannot therefore be set aside as inherently untrustworthy. It may be assumed, of course, that exaggerations of failures slipped into the reports. In all likelihood, however, such hyperbole is balanced by some judicious doctoring of evidence in the opposite direction—in order to improve somewhat on the dismal facts of what was observed. Psychologically, the latter distortion makes as much sense as the former. No document is a clear window to reality. Only a much more systematic study of visitations than anything undertaken so far will reveal their real strengths or weaknesses as primary evidence for the consequences of reformation.

There are signs that such studies are now under way.[26] Additional

---

[23]Staatsarchiv Dresden, Locs. 8832 and 9905.

[24]For a lengthy discussion of this grievance literature, see my *Law, Resistance, and the State,* chap. 8.

[25]For a discussion of these reports in one district of Bavaria, see Hans Hornung, *Beiträge zur inneren Geschichte Bayerns vom 16.–18. Jahrhundert aus den Umrittsprotokollen der Rentmeister des Rentamtes Burghausen* (Munich, 1915).

[26]E. W. Zeeden of Tübingen has been overseeing work on visitations for some time. It is one of the projects of the Sonderforschungsbereich Spätmittelalter und Reformation at that university. See the bibliography by Zeeden and Molitor cited in n. 21. In France, the Centre National de la Recherche Scientifique has prepared a useful scheme for content analysis of visitation records.

[208]

visitation material is being unearthed from state, municipal, and church archives where it has been hiding from all but local historians.[27] It is also becoming clear that much more can be accomplished with these documents than has been attempted in the past, perhaps even the kind of serial history of religion envisioned by Pierre Chaunu.[28] But even before the fruits of these fresh labors have been brought in, we may agree with the judgment of Gabriel LeBras that, though visitation records, being human documents, are sure to contain errors, "the critical use of them will give us more truth about the prosperity or the poverty of the faith than is found in our literary fantasies." This, it seems to me, is the salient point: we need to move beyond the stereotypical view of the Reformation so long dominant in our work with the sources. The impulse to this forward step may well come from the lessons to be drawn from the visitations, namely that reform, conceived as religious and moral transformation, was not gaining much ground.[29]

One always returns to the question: why was this so? Why the failure to get through? Why the resistance? I think much more can be said in accounting for this lack of success than was suggested in my 1978 book, though I still think that the explanation offered there is sound. New factors keep emerging. Not until I began to work with the records of regional assemblies, for instance, did I sufficiently appreciate the extent to which the religious policies of state and church governments were impeded by the territorial nobility. As they attempted to implement their religious decrees, governments found themselves stymied by noble landlords anxious to protect their *ius patronatus*. The grievances of most members of the nobility were about the meddling of church consistories and superintendents in their *Gerichtbarkeit* or *Hofmarkrecht* or ius patronatus or Ehegericht—the cherished jurisdictions that defined their aristocratic liberties. Constant reiteration of complaints shows that these liberties were being violated. It also demonstrates, however, that the assault was being

---

See *Répertoire des visites pastorales de la France: Première série: Anciens diocèses (jusqu'en 1790)* I: *Agde-Bourges* (Paris, 1977), *Annexe*. Useful references to archival materials relating to visitations appear in the articles gathered in Georges Livet, ed., *Sensibilité religieuse et discipline ecclésiastique: Les visites pastorales en territoires protestants . . . , XVIe–XVIIIe siècles* (Strasbourg, 1975). See also the notes to pp. 156–59 of Paul Münch, *Zucht und Ordnung: Reformierte Kirchenverfassungen im 16. und 17. Jahrhundert* (Stuttgart, 1978).

[27]For example, Staatsarchiv Weimar, Reg N, *Ergänzungsband*, especially nos. 364–587.

[28]As described by Chaunu in Pierre Chaunu, "Une histoire religieuse sérielle," *Revue d'histoire moderne et contemporaine* 12 (1965), pp. 7–34.

[29]For a strongly dissenting view forcefully argued and well documented, see James M. Kittelson, "Successes and Failures in the German Reformation: The Report from Strasbourg," *Archive for Reformation History* 73 (1982):153–75, and "Visitations and Popular Religious Culture: Further Reports from Strasbourg," in Philip N. Bebb and Kyle C. Sessions, eds., *Pietas et Societas: New Trends in Reformation Social History* (Kirksville, Mo., 1985), pp. 89–101.

resisted. Cities often associated themselves with the nobility in these complaints. Given the utter dependence of princely rulers on their territorial estates for revenues raised from taxes, such parliamentary protests were by no means empty gestures. As for the nobility, its success in resisting intrusions was the measure of its survival as an autonomous estate. This tug-of-war must have been a heavy drag on the efforts of ecclesiastical and political bureaucrats to impose their regulations on the populace. As such it was surely a cause of their inability to make reformation effective.

Their efforts were further enfeebled by the notorious doctrinal dissension that split Lutheranism in the second half of the sixteenth century. Abundant evidence exists for the destructiveness of these divisions, which—touching almost every pastor in the church apparatus—reached down to every parish and congregation. The resulting embitterment of religious tempers may be difficult for us to appreciate. Contemporaries, however, were very much aware of it. Frequent *Änderungen*—doctrinal and administrative alterations—"are making citizens more distrustful, more defiant [*trutzig*], and more insolent every day."[30] Incessant disputes on the fine points of theology were causing "lay people and common folk to doubt the very articles of the faith and to hold the preachers, indeed the entire religion, in contempt."[31] In Saxony, in the 1560s, 1570s, and 1580s, the state frequently intervened to remove ministers from their pulpits following theological readjustments by the territory's chief ideologues. Those allowed to remain had to make open *Damnation und Revocation,* public recantations of their former beliefs and repudiations of those theologians from whom they had been derived—of the "Philippist" Victorinus Strigel, for example, a professor at the University of Jena, a leading advocate of the "synergist" position on divine grace and the human will, and a suspected follower of "Crypto-Calvinism" on the question of the Eucharist.[32] One can imagine the effect on a pastor's flock of such public humiliation. Partisans for one side or the other of this issue must have badly confused their auditors as they held forth from their pulpits with pro-Victorinus and anti-Victorinus fulminations.[33] The vast

---

[30]Christoph Scheurl in a memorandum to the Nuremberg Council, 1530. Germanisches Nationalmuseum Nuremberg, Merkel-Handschrift 129, 20 recto.

[31]From a memorandum by the Saxon jurist Melchior von Osse to Duke August of Saxony, written in 1555. Printed in O. A. Hecker, ed., *Schriften Dr. Melchiors von Osse* (Leipzig and Berlin, 1922), p. 294.

[32]For the effect of the "Crypto-Calvinist" controversy on one small-town Lutheran pastor, see my article "The Mental World of a Saxon Pastor," in Peter N. Brooks, ed., *Reformation Principle and Practice . . .* (London, 1980), pp. 165–67.

[33]Staatsarchiv Weimar Reg N, Nos. 376–88, contains a large number of documents illustrating the situation created on the parish level by this controversy in the 1560s and as late as the early 1570s.

XII

body of writing produced by such a controversy (others concerned "anti-nomianism," "Osiandrism," "adiaphora," "Majorism," and so on) was evidently of absorbing interest to professional theologians.[34] The attitudes that these quarrels created in the minds of the theologically uninvolved are another matter.

The estrangement likely to have been the consequence must have been substantially deepened for the majority of ordinary people by the increasingly class-specific edge given later in the century to the Protestant message. R. W. Scribner has recently shown how the aim of Evangelical propaganda moved from popular to burgher targets and how this shift was made visually explicit in Lucas Cranach's graphic work on behalf of the Lutheran Reformation.[35] Other studies, too, have suggested that the conservative bent of established Lutheranism, particularly its emphasis on patriarchal authority and household property, made its strongest appeal to privileged proprietor groups,[36] a segment of society estimated to amount to no more than 20 percent of the whole.[37] The polarization resulting from this change in the Evangelical message's social direction must have affected the public response. Gabriel LeBras has noted that the practice of religion has never been the same for different classes of Christians.[38] The Reformation did not alter this state of affairs. Whatever Protestantism's original allure as spiritual enlightenment and religious liberation, once it had solidified itself as a politically defined church, it played the part of a provider of theologically and socially safe religious norms. The catechism was the ideal tool for indoctrinating the public in this kind of religion. Once this point had been recognized in the years following the events of 1525, Lutheran pedagogy moved its emphasis decisively from Scripture reading to catechetical instruction.[39] Lamenting the "blasphemous and shameless way in which the children of poor people grow up nowadays," a legal adviser to the government of Nuremberg recommended in 1530 that two German-language schools be set up in that city, "in which simple people's children will be taught some writing and the catechism . . . so

[34]A good impression of the sheer bulk of this kind of writing is given by repertory books in the Staatsarchiv Weimar, Reg. N, "Religionswesen," especially the *Ergänzungsband,* nos. 364–587 and 687–721.

[35]R. W. Scribner, *For the Sake of Simple Folk: Popular Propaganda for the German Reformation* (Cambridge, 1981), p. 247 and illus. 165 and 167.

[36]Berndt Balzer, *Bürgerliche Reformationspropaganda: Die Flugschriften des Hans Sachs in den Jahren 1523–1525* (Stuttgart, 1973). For England, see the suggestive remarks on this subject by J. J. Scarisbrick on pp. 173–74 of the book cited in n. 46 below.

[37]Peter Blickle, *Deutsche Untertanen: Ein Widerspruch* (Munich, 1981), p. 57.

[38]Gabriel LeBras, *Etudes de sociologie religieuse, vol. 1: Sociologie de la pratique religieuse dans les campagnes françaises* (Paris, 1955), p. 363.

[39]For an elaboration of this argument, see Richard Gawthrop and Gerald Strauss, "Protestantism and Literacy in Early Modern Germany," *Past and Present* 104 (1984):31–55.

that these children, who between the ages of five and ten are of no use either as servants or as laborers, will be kept from running wild in the streets.''[40] In this proposal we hear the authentic voice of established Lutheranism. Catechization in the rudiments of religion, with heavy stress on the duties arising from the fourth commandment: such was the approach to be taken now toward the majority of people. A historian looking at a later period has remarked that, ''when the members of a community are divided into classes . . . meeting only in relations of authority and subordination, it is futile to expect that they will meet in the same church.''[41] Lutheran churchmen, however, did harbor such expectations. When their hopes turned to disappointment, they were dismayed and puzzled.

They should not have been. Their own visitation reports showed them that another reason existed for the apathy displayed by so many toward the officially sanctioned faith. Sixteenth-century folk practiced their own brand of religion, which was a rich compound of ancient rituals, time-bound customs, a sort of unreconstructable folk Catholicism, and a large portion of magic to help them in their daily struggle for survival. This underground religion was not necessarily incompatible with the Lutheran creed. Still, when clergymen, intolerant of its primitivism, tried to stamp it out, hostilities developed at every point of contact. We have a somewhat distorted view of this conflict, for our idea of folk magic has been formed largely by the spectacular witch scares of the seventeenth century. The actual practices of folk belief were ordinary, unspectacular, and usually harmless. They had to do mainly with keeping oneself safe and coping with daily life. The facts about them lie buried in local records such as the visitation documents, from which a great deal can be learned about them.

Lutheran clerics abhorred this rival religion, supposing it, quite correctly, to be a popular alternative to the church, its ministers, and its teachings. Until recently, the opinions of modern scholars have reflected this disdain. Their views illustrate the preoccupation with the normative that has traditionally guided Reformation historiography. They also reveal the largely unquestioned assumption that the religious concerns preached so passionately from the pulpit met an equally heartfelt response from the mass of auditors. In such attitudes, Reformation scholarship shows itself to be backward compared with work done in the religious history of other periods. Our knowledge of the Reformation's reception by ordinary people is still largely undifferentiated, and this deficiency explains, I think,

[40]Memorandum by Johannes Müller, 1530, Germanisches Nationalmuseum Nuremberg, Merkel-Handschrift 129, 92 recto–93 recto.

[41]Hugh McLeod, *Class and Religion in Late Victorian London* (Hamden, Conn., 1974), p. 281.

XII

the rather stern rejection by a number of reviewers of my conclusions concerning the "failure" of the Reformation. But the withdrawal, or defection, of groups of people from established churches and official religions is a common phenomenon. Fintan Michael Phayer has described it for nineteenth-century Bavaria, Joseph Moody for the French working class in the Second Empire, and K. S. Inglis, Owen Chadwick, Kitson Clark, Standish Meacham, Hugh McLeod, and James Obelkevich for Victorian England.[42] Obelkevich observes in his excellent study of *Religion and Rural Society* that

> what parishioners understood as Christianity was never preached from a pulpit or taught in Sunday school, and what they took from the clergy they took on their own terms. . . . The Church . . . had become too closely associated with the elite and with elite culture to be attractive to most villagers, [and it] was almost entirely lacking in religious institutions of the middle range—monks, nuns, saints, shrines, processions, pilgrimages, rosaries, candles—which might have reduced the gap between transcendent deity and ordinary villagers. . . . The Church offered no "moral equivalent" to the magic and superstition that proliferated in the villages. Since the clergy were incapable of shaping a more popular version of the faith, villagers were left to do so themselves.[43]

These sentences relate to England in the middle of the nineteenth century, but they could have been written to describe the sixteenth-century German Reformation. "What is popular religion?" asks Obelkevich. He answers:

> First of all, it is religion. To treat it as ignorance, superstition, debasement, or as compensation or mystification is to misconceive it. No less than the religion of the elite, it is a realm of the sacred, with its own pattern of symbol, ritual, and morality. At the same time, popular religion is popular: it grows out of the experience of the many, expressing their wider outlook and values and often their ambivalence toward a hegemonic faith.[44]

[42]Fintan Michael Phayer, *Religion und das gewöhnliche Volk in Bayern in der Zeit von 1750–1850* (*Miscellanea Bavarica Monacensia* 21 [Munich, 1970]); Joseph N. Moody, ed., *Church and Society: Catholic Social and Political Thought and Movements, 1789–1950* (New York, 1953), 138; K. S. Inglis, *Churches and the Working Classes in Victorian England* (London, 1963); Owen Chadwick, *The Victorian Church*, 2 vols. (New York, 1966) 1:325–36, 2:235–36; G. S. R. Kitson Clark, *Churchmen and the Condition of England, 1832–1885* (London, 1973), chaps. 9–10; Standish Meacham, *A Life Apart: The English Working Class, 1890–1914* (London, 1977), pp. 15–16, 200; Hugh McLeod as in n. 41, especially chap. 2: "Who Went to Church?"; James Obelkevich, *Religion and Rural Society: South Lindsey, 1825–1875* (Oxford, 1976).

[43]James Obelkevich, *Religion and Rural Society*, p. 279.

[44]James Obelkevich, ed., *Religion and the People, 800–1700* (Chapel Hill, 1979), p. 7.

If this can be said by a historian of Victorian Britain, why not by a Reformation scholar?[45]

The answer may be that too few of us who work on the German Reformation have grasped the importance of what Keith Thomas has demonstrated for seventeenth-century England and what John Bossy has tried to show for late sixteenth-century France and Italy: that a change occurred in the normative meaning of religion as a result of the Reformation, a shift away from piety and toward doctrine or creed. The result of this shift, which placed unprecedented emphasis on the central necessity of a coherent doctrine, was—Thomas writes—"an across-the-board downgrading of alternative views of religion and knowledge." In this derogation, the word "magic" came to be applied indiscriminately to all forms of popular religion. German visitation records bear out the aptness of this formulation, as they do Thomas's further assertion that, while before the Reformation, the Church was "a limitless source of supernatural aid, applicable to most of the problems likely to arise in daily life," Protestant theologians tried to abolish "this whole apparatus of supernatural assistance," although—plainly—"the problems for which the magical remedies of the past had provided some sort of solution were still there."[46] Because the problems would not go away, and the new religion offered no simple corrective for them, people sought their own remedies.

It seems to me that the reluctance of Reformation historians to accept this view of how ordinary people construct their religion has less to do with a shortage of sources than with the uncritical acceptance by so many of us of what, earlier in this chapter, I called a myth about the Reformation. The proponents of this myth know only the normative faith, the one developed by theologians and delivered from university lecterns and church pulpits. They do not ask how this faith was received by those for

---

[45]The reluctance of Reformation historians to draw the sum even of their own investigations is illustrated by Bernard Vogler, "Die Entstehung der protestantischen Volksfrömmigkeit in der rheinischen Pfalz zwischen 1555 und 1619," *Archiv für Reformationsgeschichte* 72 (1981):158–95. Vogler concludes (p. 195) that Protestantism as a product of a "rational and urban culture" initiated a "secularization of thought" by demanding a piety detached from sacred objects and by banning old fears and anxieties about hell and demons. Vogler's own evidence suggests, however, that things remained the same for most people, thus contradicting his conclusion. Most of the evidence is set out in the three volumes of Vogler's *Vie religieuse en pays rhenan dans la seconde moitié du 16e siècle, 1556–1619* (Service de reproduction des thèses, Université de Lille III, 1974).

[46]Keith Thomas, *Religion and the Decline of Magic* (London, 1971), pp. 76–77; John Bossy, "The Counter-Reformation and the People of Catholic Europe," *Past and Present* 47 (1970):51–70 and *Christianity in the West 1400–1700* (Oxford, 1985). For a vivid picture of the stark contrast between the old faith and the new, see J. J. Scarisbrick, *The Reformation and the English People* (Oxford, 1984), chap. 8: "Rival Evangelisms."

XII

whom it was intended or how it fitted into their world. The reformers themselves were more curious than this about the public reaction to their labors. Holding themselves responsible for people's lives, as well as for their souls, they asked hard questions about the reception of the faith they tried so vigorously to bring to their flocks. Through these questions they discovered that they were failing in their best efforts.

I do not think that we should interpret this failure as a judgment on the worth of their objectives, but it does seem to be a sign of the instinct people have for protecting themselves from uplifting ideas forced upon them from above. Whether we read this sign as a sad comment on human behavior or as an encouraging one depends on how we feel about the idea.

XIII

How to Read a Volksbuch: The Faust Book of 1587

How we see a subject depends first and foremost on how we have framed it. When the subject is a text of little intrinsic depth, frame is everything. It is not to disparage a prominent item in the German literary canon to say that in the *Faust Book* of 1587 we have such a text. This is a fact established by its acknowledged identity as a *Volksbuch* aimed by its makers at a particular class of consumers and intended to serve objectives in part commercial and in part educational (cf. Burke; Muchembled, *Popular Culture*; Bollème). If we are to discover the book's meaning, or point, we must look for it in these objectives. In its peculiar combination of episodic construction, shrewd catering to common tastes, and preachy censoriousness, the anonymous *Historia von D. Johann Fausten* is the very paradigm of a late medieval-early modern *Volksbuch*, a user-friendly article, attractively packaged, designed to grab and hold attention, and capable of leaving some sort of enduring mark on the mind of the targeted reader. Obviously, popular literature should entertain. It has long been understood that it was also intended to uplift, or at least to instruct. But to what purpose? And in whose interest? Reflecting what trends in the cultural and social processes of its time? These questions have not often been put to the products of the early printing press in Germany. I think a review of some current historical thinking on early modern Germany can help us in developing suitable attitudes toward the *Faust Book* itself, and toward the whole literature of sorcery, witchcraft, and devilry of which it is the foremost example.

Frame, to repeat, is everything. As the time frame within which the *Faust Book* must be read, Renaissance and Reformation have exerted a determining influence on our understanding, for they function not merely as chronological labels but also as conceptual tags of great suggestive power. Not so very long ago, »Renaissance« stood for the victory of individuality over collectivism and the triumph of creative innovation over tradition and conformity, while »Reformation« was synonymous with deliverance from spiritual subjugation and a turning away from religious superstition. No longer. We do not nowadays set Middle Ages and Renaissance in such drastic opposition to one another. On the contrary: the weight of scholarship has decisively tipped the scales against the old notion that in the fifteenth century a burst of inventiveness broke the stranglehold of a long period of inertia and stagnation. And as for the Reformation: only the most denominationally committed scholar would now speak of the age of state churches and orthodoxy as a time of religious emancipation. As a result, we have been gaining very different sight lines on the period's personalities, events, and cultural products. Faustus and his book are examples. Faustus as an »echter Renaissancemensch,« as he has been called, becomes, in this revised view, an anachronism. To portray him as a prefiguration of the Enlightenment, a titanic intellectual rebel, is to misread a text distorted by the wrong historical frame. Barbara Könneker argued this twenty years ago in a fine article on what she saw as a coherent central conception at work in the *Faust Book*. But more can be said toward an interpretation adequate to the intention of the book's producers; above all, there is a more appropriate historical setting to be brought into focus.

What preoccupied the sixteenth century, in Europe generally and in Germany in particular, was not the philosophical or aesthetic challenge of Rome and Greece or the promise contained in the rediscovered gospel. It was a much more concrete phenomenon in the lives of people: the all-pervasiveness of political aggrandizement. Saying this is only to repeat the observation of scores of contemporaries, many of them made uneasy by the apparently inexorable drift of events. This drift was speeding the processes of judicial and administrative consolidation in cities and states, vastly strengthening central authorities and the bureaucracies they were putting into place. The Reformation in particular created unprecedented opportunities – in Catholic no less than in Protestant parts – for concentration of powers in the hands of princes and magistrates, for these powers now included oversight of ecclesiastical as well as of secular institutions. In the aftermath of the abortive uprisings of the 1520s, state and church authorities resolved to prevent a repetition of these frightening events by drawing the reins of law and government even tighter. There can be no doubt that life for all but the most inaccessibly situated men and women in urban and rural Germany became more rule-bound, more closely surveyed, and more rigorously directed in the sixteenth century than it had been at any time in the recent or distant medieval past.

All this is quite well understood. What has not been so well established is the linkage between these developments and a contemporaneous effort on the part of Europe's ruling groups to undermine, and ultimately to replace, the expressions of popular culture. Again, it was the religious shakeup of the sixteenth century that created opportunities for what has been called »a systematic attempt by some of the educated ... to change the attitudes and values of the rest of the population« (Burke 207). To give this endeavor some chance of success, Lutheran and Reformed establishments, and the leaders of the Counter Reformation in Catholic regions, felt it incumbent upon them to accustom or – to use a term sometimes given now to this attempt at cultural subversion and substitution – to acculturate the masses to habits of thought and codes of behavior thought fitting and proper by the elites (cf. Muchembled, »Lay Judges«; Wirth).

Fitting and proper in what respects? A small number of mutually reinforcing principles turn up in official pronouncements justifying the inroads being made on popular ways. These principles are, first, order, then reason, next the orderly and reasonable conditions of uniformity and orthodoxy and the authority of the written word, finally, and underlying all of these, an unquestioned faith in the objective existence of truth coupled with the conviction that this truth can be known and can be formulated as laws of belief and conduct. Seen from the eminence of these lofty principles, ordinary life looked chaotic indeed. Its apparently ungovernable profusion of indigenous folkways violated all canons of order and coherence. Most offensive among these motley habits were the religious practices of ordinary folk. They were superstitious, licentious, disorderly, irrational; they blended the sacred with the profane. In every respect they violated the reformers' elitist ethic of »decency, diligence, gravity, modesty, orderliness, prudence, reason, self-control, sobriety, and thrift« – to quote a list of sanctioned virtues offered by Peter Burke (213).

Wherever Lutheran regimes established themselves from the late 1520s onward, they therefore made the achievement of orthodoxy and order a matter of the most urgent priority. But this was an endeavor in which, as they discovered, not much headway was being made. Even half a century after the victory of the Reformation, people seemed stuck in their old habits, paying little heed to the improving doctrines preached to them from above. There is much documentary evidence to allow us to reach this conclusion. It was collected by Reformation authorities themselves in the course of their annual parish visitations. As observers of the contemporary scene, they never failed to deplore the apparent indifference of people to the saving message, and to lament the helplessness of authorities in the face of public apathy. Even after fifty years of evangelical preaching and catechization, says one such observer, Augustin Lercheimer, people still live like heathens, and the pastorate does, or can do, little about it. »Is it any wonder, then,« Lercheimer concludes, »that the Devil has won a place among these people and has taught them superstition and sorcery?« (323) Identical litanies were heard in every part of the country. They sound as plaintive toward the end of the sixteenth century as at its beginning. People are mired in their superstitions. They would rather cast a spell than say a prayer, consult a soothsayer or faith healer than go to church. They are closer to Satan than to God.

Was this rhetoric or description? Did men like Lercheimer really believe that there was a devil-saturated culture of sorcery out there, indifferent to, and heedless of, gospel, doctrine, law, and civility? There can be no doubt that they did. Lercheimer himself was a partisan of a minority position that doubted the reality of magic, attributing its apparent effects instead to deception practiced by the devil. But by far the greater number of commentators maintained the objective existence not only of the devil – no one denied this – but also of acts of sorcery carried out by his human agents. Luther's full acceptance of this view is well known. The depth of his involvement with the devil has been brought out most poignantly in Heiko Oberman's new biography, the subtitle of which is »A Man between God and Devil.« »In no sense is it true,« writes Oberman, »that Luther overcame the medieval belief in the Devil. On the contrary, he deepened it and made it more acute« (109). Most contemporary intellectuals were in the same camp. For every Lercheimer, Plantsch, Weyer, Gödelmann, and Loos who thought that conjuring and necromancing were merely sleight-of-hand or devilish tricks, there were a hundred – and they included the author and publisher of the *Faust Book* – to whom these acts were real phenomena accomplished by real sorcerers with real powers. Both factions, in any case, were in full agreement on the role, the resourcefulness, and the long-term goal of the devil (cf. Hondorff; Russell 35, Midelfort 10–14). In their view, every blameworthy action was a deed done in the service of Satan.

To demonstrate that this was so, German printers issued a host of cautionary books in which – to quote the dedication of the *Faust Book*, which is one of them – »des Teuffels Neid, Betrug und Grausamkeit gegen dem menschlichen Geschlecht« is shown to be the root cause of every ill done or suffered in the world. These so-called *Teufelsbücher*, of which it has been estimated that a quarter of a million copies were circulating in the second half of the sixteenth century (Roos 108–09), are by no means the jolly entertainments they are often made out to be. Deadly serious in their objectives, they set out to brand every deviation as an act of apostasy, ultimately a denial of Christ. It has been pretty well established in the recent literature on these matters that the late-sixteenth- and seventeenth-century fixation on the devil did not originate as a popular notion deep in the grassroots of society. Instead, it was a position developed by the educated and spread by them to the populace, mostly through preaching, literature, and, probably most effectively, litigation. Germany was not the only country to experience this phenomenon. Robert Mandrou has shown how French judges, theologians, and other intellectuals became preoccupied with the devil in the 1580s and 1590s, fully embracing the whole catalogue of satanic atrocities: pacts, marks, sabbats, werewolves, and all the rest (137–52). And Carlo Ginzburg has demonstrated that inquisitors reshaped popular mythic material into accounts of repulsive rituals (39–57).

This sounds like madness to us. But there was method in it. Without doubting that these men believed what they professed, we can see that devilry was of great practical use to them as well. *Die Welt verteufeln* – bedeviling the world – was a way of polarizing in the most radical way the options open to every individual in his or her walk of life. There was no such thing as a trivial decision: you must either choose the devil or choose Christ (*Theatrum diabolorum*, Fii v.). Loaf at work, and you are acting like a follower of the devil. Rebel against your superior, stay away from catechism class, put on the slashed trousers against which your preacher has warned you, and you have declared yourself a loyalist of Satan. It is easy to see the practical value of this linkage. It allowed early modern opinion makers to brand every infraction as, literally, devilish. It facilitated social control and strengthened authorities in their endeavor to bring people into line with the abstract, written, urban, civilized, academic, legal, and theological norms of the great tradition (Delumeau 487). Whatever term we use to characterize this cleansing operation – reform, acculturation, or christianization (and no label has so far gained general acceptance) – it had two essential aims, one ideological, the other political. The former was to root out plebeian folkways and replace them with an approved popular culture congenial to the educated and issuing from their sermons, catechisms, and church hymns, and from an edifying literature of improving instruction. The latter, the political goal, was to eliminate altogether the sprawling network of cunning folk, spell-casters, and fortune-tellers whose activities had, apparently, been competing successfully with the services offered by the ministers of the established church and state. The great problem facing sixteenth-century reformers was to detach people from what was seen as, to all effects and purposes, an alternative religion, and to bond them firmly to the elite-determined obligations of church, court, doctrine, parish, law book, and catechism (Bossy 51–70).

I hope enough has been said to enable us to see the *Faust Book* framed by this comprehensive reforming impulse. It remains to support the argument by considering the text itself. First, its publisher. Johann Spies was anything but a purveyor of best sellers to the masses. Despite his location in Frankfurt, which became in the second half of the sixteenth century a center for the printing of *Volksbücher*, he had other things at heart. In the early 1580s Spies belonged to the orthodox wing of German Lutheranism, which at that time was embroiled in a vehement battle against moderate, that is to say compromise-oriented, followers of Melanchthon. Spies supported the conservative position by publishing, first in Heidelberg, then, after 1585, in Frankfurt, works by its leading theologians and controversialists, also sermons, jurisprudence, and official documents, including the text of the Book of Concordance. (The full list of his titles is given in Zarncke's article on Spies, on which everyone now depends.) The rigorous brand of Lutheranism espoused by his authors, with its polemics against Philippism on the one side and Calvinism on the other, was evidently what Spies regarded as the correct position on matters of religion. He continued to publish heavy theology into the next century, occasionally lightening his program with some books of spiritual advice. But he brought out no reprints and no trendy crowd pleasers, except one: the *History of Dr. Johann Faustus, the World-Famous Sorcerer and Black Magician, How He Contracted Himself to the Devil for a Certain Time, What Strange Adventures He Saw and Pursued during This Time, Until in the End He Received His Just Reward, Compiled and Printed, Mostly from His Own Writings, as a Dreadful Example, Ghastly Case Study, and Faithful Warning to All Ambitious, Curious, and Godless Men.*

Read in the context of the late-sixteenth-century Lutheran world view, these are not the conventional phrases they now seem at first sight. The devil *is* mankind's sworn enemy, as the »Preface to the Christian Reader« assures us (Henning edition 7). Sorcery *is*, to quote the preface again, »without any doubt the greatest and most serious sin against God.« Every approach to magic and the other black arts *was* a willful violation of the admonition from James 4, given on the title page: »Submit yourselves therefore to God. Resist the Devil.« Even Mephistophiles, when asked by Faustus what he would do if he were a human creature, confesses: »I would bow down before the Lord ... that I might not move him to anger against me ... and that I might know that, after death, eternal joy, glory, and bliss await me« (chap. 17). Just how vital and timely a message this was for the still godless masses out there in the lands monitored by Lutheran clerics, only these clerics, deeply imbued as they were with the reforming mentality of late-sixteenth-century Protestantism, could know. The *Faust Book* was no aberration on Spies's list. Far from a mere potboiler to bring in money for printing more low-profit theology and jurisprudence, it was a product of his own rigorous Lutheranism and, more broadly, an instrument in his beleaguered fellow Lutherans' reformist assault on folk occultism as part of their large-scale push for cultural reform.

Everything we learn about the protagonist of the *Faust Book* links him with the deplored scene of common occult dabbling. He craves wealth and the freedom to enjoy it. He wants someone to do his bidding. He likes to have his questions answered. Conjuring can satisfy these wishes, and so – like many others – he conjures, thus initiating the progression leading to the satanic compact. Georg Gödelmann, a contemporary diabologist, comments: »The excessive desire to know future and hidden things (by which our first parents, too, were led astray) is the foremost reason why those who practice the black arts tie themselves to the Devil« (Ci v.-Cii r.). The *Faust Book*, too, reproaches its hero for being a »speculator,« for being »eager to search for all the causes in the heavens and on the earth« (chap. 2). But when read in context, this characterization describes not the protoscientist of the Renaissance, but rather the would-be adept of occult cunning setting out to make a profitable career for himself among the gullible. The point here is that Faustus's world, though described as that of a man of learning, is in all respects the world of ordinary folk as it was observed and denounced by those who were most eager to reconstruct it. Like everyone else, Faustus was brought to his undoing by the damnable trait of *Sicherheit*, that sense of smug self-sufficiency against which every pastor railed from his pulpit. *Sicherheit* was, like magic, a form of superstition. It was placing one's confidence not in God, but in one's own wit and reason, or in idols. *Sicherheit*, magic, and the devil were therefore linked in inexorable sequence, as the preface to the *Faust Book* states explicitly when it asserts that: »Where [the devil] finds a self-assured person [*wo er einen sicheren menschen antrifft*] ... there he enters and makes himself at home.«

There is much in the *Faust Book* that is ideologically Lutheran in a specifically late-sixteenth-century way. The 1570s and 1580s were a tumultuous time in the internal affairs of denominational Lutheranism, a crisis phase in the long conflict among several opposing camps over the correct interpretation of Luther's theology. The issue came to a head in Saxony in 1575 when the elector August, taking the side of the so-called Gnesio – or orthodox – Lutherans, suppressed the rival Philippist, or Crypto-Calvinist, faction by imprisoning its leaders. This group, which was centered at the University of Wittenberg, held positions on free will, on good works, and on adiaphora that were obnoxious to the orthodox. Here, by the way, we have the explanation for the *Faust Book*'s insistent association of its hero with Wittenberg, a connection not found in earlier stories about the magician related by Luther, Johannes Manlius, and Hondorff. To the orthodox, who looked to the universities of Leipzig and Jena for doctrinal authority, Wittenberg was a hotbed of heterodoxy, and Faustus's alleged professorship there must have been intended to bring the place into disrepute.

And there was a particular reason why the orthodox might wish to do this in the late 1580s. In 1586 the situation in Saxony had suddenly changed. August's successor, Christian I, had abandoned his father's crusade against Philippism and moved toward a compromise on the theological points in dispute. This outraged the orthodox, but their battle lines were now redrawn over the adoption of the Book of Concord, which had been printed, after heated debates and long delays, in 1580. Johann Spies published it when he lived and worked in Heidelberg. He did not move from there to Frankfurt until that city accepted the Formula of Concord in 1585. He was very much on the side of the *Concordia*'s anti-Calvinist, anti-synergist slant, and his *Faust Book* is as much an expression of this inclination as are all the other titles on his list. Why did Faustus fall? Faustus himself gives the answer: »Ich habs also haben wollen,« he admits in the last of his three *Weheklagen* (chap. 66). It was the result of »my stubborn, stiff-necked and godless will.« The postlapsarian corruption of the human will was a basic article of faith, as well as a major article of contention among the Lutheran factions, and Faustus is a paradigmatic case of one who comes to grief by placing his trust in his »Vernunft und freyer will« (chap. 63). Lutheran preachers had been trying to drill this lesson into their hearers' minds for more than half a century.

But other things also had to be taught if the book was to do its job as a reforming tract, and, indeed, the *Faust Book* does impart a great deal of conventional wisdom: about the cosmos on the approved Ptolemaic-Neoplatonic model, for example (chaps. 21, 25), and about the influence of the stars on people's lives (chaps. 28, 31, 32). Readers were given the correct line on Catholicism and the papacy, including a picturesquely detailed, very long chapter on the excesses rampant at the Roman court. Marriage and the work ethic, the twin fundaments of civic virtue, are legitimized by the devil's antipathy to them as Faustus learns from him to scorn the domestic state (chap. 10), and as Faustus's life of enjoying rewards without having to work for them is shown to be antithetical to the calling of *ein rechter gottseliger Hausvater*, that central pillar of Lutheran social morality (chap. 9). To those who were obdurate to these and similar counsels, the book offered a vivid description of hell (chap. 16). Stern

Protestantism permitted no escape or reprieve for sinners guilty of collusion with Satan. For Faustus, no alternative exists but despair; understanding has come too late for him. For the book's audience, on the other hand, not yet contracted to the forces of evil, there was still hope. »Always struggle against the Devil,« the sad and sorry Faustus urges near the end of the book, »and never stop trying to defeat him« (chap. 68). This was the chief moral lesson to be learned, a simple one, surely, but to the reformers of the 1580s a most fateful piece of advice.

The point is reinforced by the observation that the *Faust Book*'s didactic thrust is enormously intensified in the several augmentations of the text published at the very end of the sixteenth century. Georg Rudolf Widmann, for instance, comments at great length in his version on the arguments heard in his day against marriage, and shows why these arguments are wrong (112ff.). For every example of an objectionable trait or act given in the *Faust Book*, Widmann and Johann Nikolaus Pfitzer, who wrote a further amplification in the seventeenth century, offer a dozen additional cases suitable for pointing socially valuable lessons. The sequel to the *Faust Book* supposedly written by Faustus's disciple Christoph Wagner takes an insistently modernist stand by contrasting superstition with the procedures of science, reason, and the practical skills. »If you would cure a disease,« argues Wagner, »go and study medical books…. Do you want to prophesy? Turn to mathematics, geometry, astronomy and astrology, navigation, and optics…. « We do not, in other words, need the devil to help us with our problems (»Anderer Teil« 176–85). Wagner's expatiations, and the unbearably prolix commentaries of Widmann and Pfitzer, give us some idea of how the *Faust Book* may have been used by preachers and other advice givers to drive home the points of an approved moral code. No doubt it made for enjoyable reading as well, for author and publisher, practicing a kind of ideological double standard, pandered to tastes of which they sternly disapproved by describing in alluring detail what on nearly every page they admonished their readers to abhor. It is this ambiguous stance of censorious titillation that has obscured for most modern readers the *Faust Book*'s true intention. But in its own time, too, the book probably worked against itself. Emphatic as it is in its declarations of disapproval, these condemnations are embroidered with such rich anecdotal detail that what remains in the memory is an entertaining story, not a grave and salutary caution.

This leaves open the question of who was reading the book, and why. Certainly the *Faust Book* was a favorite with the public. Three additional printings came out in various places during the remaining months of 1587 following the original Frankfurt publication of September of that year. There was also an illicit reprint that same winter, and Spies himself reissued the book in 1588. Twenty-two printings have been counted in all, plus a sequel, adaptations, and translations. Such success was predictable. Books about the devil had been good sellers in Germany for at least half a century, and they must have whetted the public's appetite for more of the same. It seems obvious that the *Faust Book* was aimed at an urban public, whose reading ability, judging by the little impressionistic evidence we can gather about it, increased markedly in the century after 1500 (cf. Burke 251–54; Gawthrop). My own work in the educational history of Reformation Germany has persuaded me that reading skills were on the rise also in the villages and market towns of the countryside, at least among the better-off peasants who made up the leadership of rural society. I do not believe that this growth of literacy had much to do with religion, with any desire, that is, on the part of plain folk to read the gospel unaided by interpreters. Most people had practical reasons for wishing to read, and governments responded by providing basic reading instruction in a host of elementary schools set up in towns and villages. Needless to say, state and church authorities had their own agenda in promoting literacy: they expected it to be of help in their effort to reform public thought and behavior. To nourish the newly stimulated taste for reading, a steady supply of wholesome literary materials was needed, utilizing themes and topics from the chiefly oral popular culture, but subjecting these themes to a process of taste modification in which they were brought into line with the more elevated culture of the elite.

In this way, reading, learning, schooling, and religion worked together as a comprehensive program of acculturation. The *Historia von D. Fausten* is a case in point of this program. By the time the *Faust Book* came off the press in 1587, a large potential readership had been created and rendered receptive to its message, a message which – it was hoped – would strip the crudeness and inconstancy from the lives of common people, and raise them to a condition of willing and obedient Christian subjects.

38

Works Cited

Anderer Teil D. Johannis Fausti Historien, darin beschrieben ist Christophori Wagners Pact mit dem Teufel (1593). In *Doctor Fausti Weheklag*. ed. Helmut Wiemken, pp.137–310. Bremen: Carl Schünemann, 1961.

Bollème, Geneviève. *La bibliothèque bleue*. Paris: Julliard, 1971.

— Les *contes bleus*. Paris: Montalba, 1983.

Bossy, John. »The Counter-Reformation and the People of Catholic Europe.« *Past and Present* 47 (1970): 51–70.

Burke, Peter. *Popular Culture in Early Modern Europe*. New York: New York University Press, 1978.

Delumeau, Jean. »Les réformateurs et la superstition.« In *Actes du colloque L'Amiral de Coligny et son temps*. Paris: Société de l'histoire du Protestantisme français, 1974.

Gawthrop, Richard. »Literacy Drives in Preindustrial Germany, 1500–1800.« In *National Literacy Campaigns in Historical and Comparative Perspective*, ed. Harvey J. Graff and Robert F. Arnove. New York: Plenum Press, 1987.

Ginzburg, Carlo. »The Witches' Sabbat: Popular Cult or Inquisitorial Stereotype?« In *Understanding Popular Culture*, ed. Steven L. Kaplan, pp. 39–51. Berlin: Mouton Publishers, 1984.

Gödelmann, Georg. *Von Zauberern, Hexen und Unholden...*. Frankfurt am Main, 1592.

Historia von D. Johann Fausten. Neudruck des Faust-Buches von 1587, ed. Hans Henning. Halle: Sprache und Literatur, 1963.

Hondorff, Andreas. *Promptuarium exemplorum*. Leipzig, 1568.

Könneker, Barbara. »Faust-Konzeption und Teufelspakt im Volksbuch von 1587.« In *Festschrift Gottfried Weber*, ed. H. O. Burger and K. von See, pp. 159–213. Bad Homburg: Gehlen, 1967.

Lercheimer, Augustin. *Christlich Bedenken und Erinnerung von Zauberey ... , wie diesem Laster zu wehren ...* (1585). In J. Scheible, *Das Kloster*, vol. 5, pp. 263–348. Stuttgart, 1847.

Mandrou, Robert. *Magistrats et sorciers en France au XVIIe siècle*. Paris: Plon, 1968.

Manlius, Johannes. *Locorum communium collectanea*. Basel, 1563.

Midelfort, H. C. Erik. *Witch Hunting in Southwestern Germany, 1562–1684*. Stanford, 1972.

Muchembled, Robert. »Lay Judges and the Acculturation of the Masses.« In *Religion and Society in Early Modern Europe, 1500–1800*, ed. Kaspar von Greyerz, pp. 56–65. London: German Historical Institute, 1984.

— *Popular Culture and Elite Culture in France, 1400–1750*. Baton Rouge: Louisiana State University Press, 1985.

Oberman, Heiko. *Luther. Mensch zwischen Gott und Teufel.* 2nd edition. Berlin: Severin und Siedler, 1983.

Pfitzer, Johann Nikolaus. *Das ärgerliche Leben und schreckliche Ende ...* (see Widmann, Georg Rudolf, below).

Roos, Keith L. *The Devil in Sixteenth-Century German Literature.* Bern: Herbert Lang, 1972.

Russell, Jeffrey Burton. *Mephistopheles: The Devil in the Modern World.* Ithaca: Cornell University Press, 1986.

Theatrum diabolorum. Frankfurt am Main, 1569.

Widmann, Georg Rudolf. *Das ärgerliche Leben und schreckliche Ende dess viel-berüchtigten Ertz-Schwartzkünstlers Johannis Fausti ...,* ed. Adelbert von Keller. In *Bibliothek des litterarischen Vereins in Stuttgart,* vol. 146. Tübingen, 1880.

Wirth, Jean. »Against the Acculturation Thesis.« In *Religion and Society in Early Modern Europe, 1500–1800,* ed. Kaspar von Greyerz, pp. 66–78. London: German Historical Institute, 1984.

Zarncke, Friedrich. »Johann Spies, der Herausgeber des Faustbuches, und sein Verlag.« In *Kleine Schriften,* vol. 1, pp. 289–99. Leipzig: E. Avenarius, 1897.

XIV

The Idea of Order in The German Reformation

When we think of the early modern state—the state that rose to such eminence during the sixteenth and seventeenth centuries in Europe that it could make a credible claim to a monopoly of power—we tend to think first of its highly visible sovereigns: Henry VIII, or Ferdinand of Aragon (Machiavelli's paradigm of a "new prince"), or the Elector August of Saxony, or Duke Maximilian of Bavaria. But these rulers and their well publicized actions were not the essential feature of the Renaissance-Reformation state. What was most characteristic of that state was the proliferation of laws, decrees, ordinances, codes, and injunctions by means of which the state attempted to put its monopoly into practice. These enactments were intended to give firm structure to the body politic, and they did this in a particular way: by placing effective regulative powers into the hands of rulers, more concretely, into the hands of their bureaucratic agents.

Now, laws, directives, regulations always presented themselves as legislative or administrative instruments for bringing or restoring society to, or stabilizing society in, the condition said to be most appropriate to it, a condition usually called "order". This word, order, turns up ubiquitously in the political pronouncements of the time. It designates both ends and means, doing double duty as the name for the grand purpose of legislation, and as the title for prescriptive and proscriptive instruments through which that purpose was to be achieved. It is a rich word, with a multi-layered structure of meanings. Some of these meanings the word is meant, in its official uses, to make explicit; others are concealed by it. In the political documents of the time it acts as defining concept, as programmatic declaration, and as slogan. Its "correct" meaning depends on how one interprets the true intentions of the authorities invoking the word. An analysis of these intentions, and of the real interests that lie behind them, is therefore the only approach that will yield the meaning of "order", and its relation to "law", in a time when these two terms animated much of the political discourse.

I want to give some thought to that highly charged word
"order" as we find it employed in German state and church documents
in the sixteenth and seventeenth centuries. I say "state-and-church"
because in the course of the sixteenth-century reformations—the
Catholic no less than the Protestant ones—these two bodies were
consolidated into a, for all practical purposes, single agency for
promoting the job of reform in the most sweeping sense of that word.
I concentrate on Germany for the simple reason that I am familiar
with the sources there; but also because it is my impression—though
I have not done the comparative work to allow me to quantify that
impression—that "order", *Ordnung*, was invoked more insistently in
that country than in any other. I do not mean to add my bit to the
stereotype of Germany as a land where order reigns and where citizens
react reflexively to peremptory commands coming down to them from
above. If that stereotype was ever true, it is true no longer. But it is
the case that apostrophes to "order" and admonitions about complying
with it are extraordinarily prevalent in the official pronouncements of
state and church apparatuses in early modern Germany. I want to
think about the reasons for this prevalence and draw out, if I can,
their implications for whatever we may wish to learn about the
country, the society, the Reformation, or all of these.

It hardly needs to be noted, by way of getting started, that a
concern with, or—more anxiously—a concern *for* order seems to be
pervasive in all cultures. Certainly it pervades Western culture. It
has been said, though not, I think, very helpfully, that all the sciences,
all organized attempts at learning and understanding, are the products
of the urge to discover, and thereby establish, unity and order in
human experience, and that the fear of disorder, or confusion, is a
basic impetus to reflections upon nature, society, past, future, perhaps
everything else. More useful is the realization, which we are bound to
take from even the most superficial survey of the main currents of
Western speculative thought, that the idea of order has been a
preoccupation of intellectuals from the very beginning. The reason for
this preoccupation would seem to lie in the self-assigned mission of
thinkers not merely to describe things as they are, but to hand down
at the same time a justification of how they must be. Werner Jaeger
points this out in his great book *Paideia*. Cosmos, he notes, is the
term for the proposition that things exist in the world in orderly, that

is to say lawful, which is to say right relation to each other.[1] The force of this proposition, which Jaeger traces back to the pre-Socratics, was powerfully enhanced for the Judaeo-Christian tradition by the Genesis account of a transcendent God imposing law and order upon his creation. "Order", says Saint Augustine in an early treatise on the subject, "is that by which are governed all things that God has constituted".[2] Thus "Order is Heaven's First Law", in Pope's later catch phrase;[3] a facile remark, to be sure, but one behind which lurks an assertion which, when it is believed, or when it is treated as if it were true, gives deep resonance and tremendous weight to every call for law and order sounded in the regions beneath heaven's sway. Order is real; it is not a thinking category only; it exists, transcendently. It is, as the scholastics said, a *fundamentum in re*. We *see* that the course of nature is orderly, but it is not our seeing that establishes order. We sense order, but our experience of it is derivative of the real thing.[4] So far as I know, there was—despite the nominalist challenge—no departure from this realist position in medieval and sixteenth- and seventeenth-century thought.

As the basic formative principle of the universe, order expresses itself as relation. It exists between things, or among things: in other words, when put into effect, it is arrangement. Far from being arbitrary, or adventitious, this arrangement has purpose, just as it had origin. Its end is the good of the whole, which was defined by the scholastics, in keeping with the teleological argument of which this definition is a major component, as cooperation among its parts and

---

[1]Werner Jaeger, *Paideia. Die Formung des griechischen Menschen* (Berlin and Leipzig, 1934) I, 219-221.

[2]"Ordo est, . . . per quem aguntur omnia quae Deus constituit." *De ordine* I:10, trans. as *Divine Providence and the Problem of Evil* by R. P. Russell (*The Fathers of the Church. A New Translation*, vol. 5, New York, 1948), 266.

[3]Alexander Pope, *Essay on Man* Ep.4:47.

[4]Edward A. Pace, "The Concept of Order in the Philosophy of St. Thomas," *The New Scholasticism* 2:1 (1928), 52-54; 68.

4   The Idea of Order

members.[5] This pair of propositions—that the natural order is a ranked and graded arrangement of divinely positioned members (Pope's famous Chain of Being), and secondly, that it is the obligation of each of these members to help accomplish the system's overall purpose by cooperating with all other members—shaped the theory of order and its practical applications during the medieval and early modern periods well into the eighteenth century.

It is the practical uses of the theory that interest me here, and these practical uses I find solidly embedded in even the apparently most abstract philosophical and theological formulations. They give point to Augustine's definition, for example, of order as a place for everything and everything in its place.[6] And they give point also to the many contemporary descriptions of order as fixed hierarchy, in support of which a passage from Cicero was usually cited. Order, Cicero wrote, is "the arrangement of things in their suitable or appropriate places";[7] In other words, in an orderly universe—and who would speak up for a disorderly one?—each thing is settled in its proper place and each place is perfectly suited to the thing that occupies it. This is the formulation that achieves epigrammatic point, and obvious utility, in Pope's famous couplet, already quoted:

> Order is Heav'n's first Law, and this confest,
> Some are, and must be, greater than the rest.

Preachments such as Pope's clearly demand from those to whom they are addressed more than a passive acknowledgment of the world as it is. They require action, right and suitable action: that is to say, they demand conduct consequent upon the acceptance of one's particular place in the universal order. It is easy to see how scholastic definitions could be made to serve mundane thinkers as an ideological launching pad for their own efforts to create order in their respective worlds. We

---

[5]Ibid., 59-60. See also Hermann Krings, *Ordo. Philosophisch—historische Grundlagen einer abendländischen Idee* (2nd ed., Hamburg, 1982), 77-78.

[6]Augustine, *De civitate Dei* 19.13.1.

[7]*De officiis* 1:40. The thought is attributed by Cicero to the Stoics. Edward A. Pace, in the article cited in note 4, points to St. Thomas's use of this passage from Cicero.

will in a moment see these definitions surface in the political documents of the Reformation.

Why calls for order should be so prominent in the programs of the German Reformation from about 1530 on is not difficult to explain. After centuries of perversion by Rome (as Protestants saw it), religion, the church, indeed all of public and private life, had to be restored to their right condition. With the break from the papacy accomplished, a long history of bickering between church and state could now be brought to an end and the two make common cause in pursuit of their common goals. The revolutionary upheaval of the 1520s having been subdued, and the doctrinal disagreements among Protestants having reached a stage where mostly heat and little more light could be expected to be generated, it was time to put together again what had long been falling apart.

In this endeavor, state and church officials were impelled by an ideological conjuncture we should, I think, recognize as a powerfully formative feature of the Reformation period. I mean the acceptance by leading figures in state and church of concentration and conformity as guiding principles and as necessary virtues. It was the objective of both political and religious reformers in early sixteenth-century Germany to put as final an end as possible to what they all considered a deeply offensive state of disarray in secular and spiritual affairs. Reformers detested this chaotic condition because they saw it as a gross violation of fundamental postulates in which they were true believers: that truth is single, that order is paramount, and that both truth and order issue from authentic and binding declarations. Ideologically, the Reformation was first and foremost an exaltation of authorized texts. As a religious event, it was a reduction of the precepts of faith to Holy Scripture as the sole source of truth. As a political event, it was a reduction as well, in this case a reduction of the proliferation of rights and jurisdictions that was so characteristic of the cultural and political pluralism of the Middle Ages to a tight and tidy legal system authenticated, ultimately, by a text of no less exclusive pretensions than the Bible: the Roman law, as codified in the *corpus juris* of Justinian. But the really significant point to be grasped about the role of Bible and *corpus juris* in the Reformation period is not that these texts were raised at that time to a position of unprecedented dominance. It is that both Bible and law came, as a consequence of the Reformation, into the hands of a small number of close-knit coteries who jointly took over the direction of church and

state in Protestant regions (and to an only slightly lesser extent in
Catholic ones). It is *their* views, the views of these men—theologians,
lawyers, academics, professional administrators sitting on joint
executive bodies and closely tied, both organizationally and personally,
to ruling princes and magistrates—that are reflected in the foundation
documents of the new state churches in Germany: in the church
ordinances, catechisms, and school regulations through which
institutional articulation and doctrinal formality were given to the
Lutheran polity. And it is in these documents that the appeal to order
is most clamorously made, most broadly extended, and most directly
applied to civic, social, religious, and working life. Let us look at a few
examples.

A typical point of departure in these basic documents is Paul's
instruction, given in 1 Corinthians 14:40, "Let all things be done
decently and in order" (*Omnia autem honeste et secundum ordine
fiant*). These words often serve as a motto placed at the head of the
preamble to a *Kirchenordnung*, an ecclesiastical ordinance, or
constitution, which was the basic charter establishing, under the
authority of a ruling prince or magistrate, the state church, not only
in principle, but also in punctilious description of everything that
must, and must not, be done in matters concerning religion and related
civic duties in a particular territorial or urban realm. I take as my
example the *Kirchenordnung* for the territorial state of Hessen, issued
in 1566.[8] Paul's charge, "Let all things be done decently and in order,"
binds us to two requirements, its preamble begins. These must be met
if the business of a government, a church, a civic organization is to be
conducted in a godly manner. The two requirements are decorum and
order. Decorum (given in the text as the Latin translation of Paul's
Greek term εὐσχημόνως, German *züchtigkeit* or *erbarkeit*) will prevail
"when due attention and care are given to the persons who do
something, and to the things that they do".[9] That is to say, everything
must be accomplished in a fitting, seemly, honest, and proper way.

---

[8]It is printed in Emil Sehling, ed., *Die evangelischen Kirchenordnungen des 16.
Jahrhunderts* (Leipzig, 1901-13), continued by the Institut für evangelisches
Kirchenrecht der evangelischen Kirche in Deutschland (Tübingen, 1955 ff.), vol. VIII, 179
ff. For some other uses of the passage from 1 Corinthians, see ibid. XI, 624; 731; VI, part
I, 22; 650.

[9]Ibid., VIII, 180.

Fitting and proper to what? The answer provides the point of entry for
the idea of order. In accordance with Paul's Greek term for it—τάξις,
Latin *ordo*—order, *Ordnung*, means arrangement, which demands that
"everything be in its proper place".[10] Why is this contention more
than a platitude? Because it is presented here as an unavoidable
obligation, corresponding to and mandated by the structure of the
universe itself, in which every least particle is situated in a certain
and permanent place, there to do the work for which it was created,
and thereby producing effects beneficial to the whole. Make a change
in this disposition, and everything will go awry or break apart.
Inevitably, the modern reader encountering this image will think of
the great speech given to Ulysses in *Troilus and Cressida*, certainly
the best-known rendering of the vision of an intricately collocated
cosmic order and its inescapability as the law of all being and doing in
the world. Less ringingly than Shakespeare, but forcefully all the
same, the Hessen preamble said much the same thing. "Make even
the slightest alteration in the divine arrangement", the text warns, "or
allow the smallest disturbance to upset it, and the world's very
substance and essence will be corrupted, and its entire force and
operation suffer harm or come to naught".

As in the heavens, so on earth. "Human affairs", the ordinance
explains, "can be conducted . . . with favorable and fruitful results only
by those who understand the operations of Order and conform their
purposes to it".[11] The best instrument for producing this necessary
understanding, and for assuring compliance with it, is—and here we
reach the goal of the entire argument—*eine gewisse Kirchenordnung*,
a definitive, authoritative, written, officially promulgated, authentic
code, a church constitution to be known and obeyed by everyone in the
land, so that "everything will be maintained in good and lasting
order".[12] To frame these codes, and to do all that is needed to
guarantee the replication on earth of the stable configuration that
keeps the heavens on course, there is need of a supreme authority, an
Obrigkeit, a government, defined (I am quoting from another

[10]Ibid., 181.

[11]Ibid., 181.

[12]Ibid., 184.

ordinance, from Saxony, published in 1580) as "a special and particular divine disposition and order, God's own great matter". Like the sun itself, political authority exists to make life on earth possible, although sometimes, again like the sun, it may cause injury or pain. But whether we deem it harmful or beneficial, what we must understand and acknowledge about government is that it is "a divine imposition and *Ordnung* through which justice and peace are maintained, even if it should happen that a particular person uses this *Ordnung* to do wrong."[13] Note the double sense of *Ordnung* in this passage. "Order" refers to the commands, or instructions, given by God for the governance of his people. And it denotes as well the completed arrangement installed by these instructions. This dual meaning of *Ordnung*—as archetypal condition and as instrumentality—by linking law-making and law enforcement to cosmic design, the objective existence and paradigmatic authority of which it was not reasonable to doubt—gave to the political uses of the word their great ideological and executive force. "The Almighty Himself is the enemy of disorder", warns a municipal church ordinance of 1575: "[God] takes special pleasure in good and sound order wherever he finds it in human affairs".[14] Luther's own use of the word touches all these bases: "God's word and ordering",[15] "God's external ordering of worldly things",[16] "the right order of things",[17] "discipline and order",[18] "law and order",[19] and so on. Eventually, order becomes one of the very attributes of God: God is a God of Order, "*ein Gott der Ordnung*, who intends"—I am quoting from a municipal school ordinance—"all the

---

[13]From the preface to the *Kirchenordnung* for Saxony, 1580, Sehling I, 361.

[14]Preface to *Kirchenordnung* for Lüneburg, 1575, Sehling VI, part I, 650.

[15]*D. Martins Luthers Werke. Kritische Gesamtausgabe* (Weimar, 1883 ff.): WA 26, 506.

[16]WA 19, 634.

[17]WA 40, part II, 131.

[18]"Zucht und ordnung": WA 8, 497.

[19]"Regiments und ordnung": WA 32, 393.

estates in the world . . . to stand in their right and good order",[20] where the words "right" and "good" meant ranked arrangement and a posture of strict non-interference with what had been so well designed.

The point is often made that it was only with great reluctance that Martin Luther prompted magistrates to introduce or restore order in human affairs; that it was Calvin, rather, who urged rulers to intervene actively so as "to keep the human community in order", as he wrote in Book Four of the *Institutes*.[21] In fact, however, Lutheran governments did not usually trouble to solicit the reformer's authorization before proceeding with their ordering of things. Nor did they hesitate to associate the business of organizing their realms with God's cosmic arrangements. In most of their declarations, the association between God's universe and a ruler's or magistrate's domain was made quite explicit. "Is there to be no Christian order in the world?" asked an ordinance for the city of Schweinfurt in 1543, inveighing against "willfulness and mutability" among its citizens. "Are we going to set ourselves against nature itself? . . . If God Almighty will not suspend his heavenly order or make any change in it, . . . how much less may we disturb or alter the order and laws governing temporal and worldly life!" This is a lesson, the city fathers go on to say, taught not only by revelation, "but demanded by natural law, which enjoins us to observe order and decorum in all that we do, and which warns us against all meddling in the way things are meant to be".[22]

Such passages make it easy to see the arguments from cosmic design for what they are. They are not statements of natural philosophy. They are political proclamations. They are rhetorical

---

[20]From a memorandum to the school patrons of the city of Wismar in Mecklenburg by the rector of the municipal Latin school, 1644: *Das Unterrichtswesen der Grossherzogtümer Mecklenburg-Schwerin und Strelitz*, ed. H. Schnell, II (*Monumenta Germaniae Paedagogica* 44 (Berlin, 1909), 84.

[21]Calvin, *Institutes* IV, 10, 28. E. W. Zeeden's study of Calvin's correspondence with governments and rulers shows that Calvin persistently urged them to do everything necessary to assure the maintenance of discipline and order: E. W. Zeeden, "Aufgaben der Staatsgewalt im Dienste der Reformation. Untersuchungen über die Briefe Calvins an Fürsten und Obrigkeiten", *Saeculum* 15:1 (1964), 132-52.

[22]*Kirchenordnung* for Schweinfurt, 1543. Sehling XI, 624-25.

turns, too, of course, and very persuasive ones. As Kenneth Burke has pointed out, religious cosmologies are "exceptionally thoroughgoing modes of persuasion".[23] But above all they are political statements. The extent to which their assertions about God's universe are true, or even believed to be true, matters much less than does their utility as legitimizing phrases and enabling clauses for the accomplishment of particular political aims. What do they mean? That is to say, what objectives of governmental policy were they intended to justify? What concrete results were expected? In other words, what, and whose, real interests were at work behind all these assertions about order, coherence, immutability, collocation, and arrangement?

The "whose" part of the question is quickly answered. When observing the making and implementing of policy in the territories and cities of Reformation Germany, we focus our attention on a numerically small and socially homogeneous band of functionaries who had, by the middle of the sixteenth century, come to occupy most of the positions of administrative authority and intellectual influence in the intertwined offices of state, bench, church, and academy. This is the group I referred to earlier in this essay as a "coterie", which I understand in the dictionary definition of a small, usually exclusive group of persons having a binding common purpose and interest. As lawyers, as classical humanists with their mind-set formed by the then fashionable precepts of neo-stoicism, as seminary-trained theologians and preachers, and as organization-minded bureaucrats, these men were imbued with the result-oriented ethos of the reforming activist (which more than compensated for the obligatory anthropological pessimism of their sin-conscious evangelicalism). They did not see eye to eye on every issue. But they were linked by a common over-all objective, which was to drag society, no matter how unwillingly, into the sixteenth century. They were linked in other ways, too: by intermarriage and class consolidation, by the privileges attendant upon social ascent, and by daily working contact with one another in the political, financial, and ecclesiastical bodies whose collective deliberations guided the business of early modern government. They had ready access to their ruling prince or magistrate. They could usually get his ear, and many of them knew how to touch his

---

[23]Kenneth Burke, *The Rhetoric of Religion. Studies in Logology* (Berkeley, CA., 1970), v.

conscience. Some were intellectuals, but their arena was not the study or the lecture hall; it was the political stage. Professors of jurisprudence sat on administrative boards. Theologians staffed investigative commissions. Jointly, lawyers and preachers manned the *Kirchenräte*, the collegiate ecclesiastical councils in which *Kirchenordnungen* were drafted and religious—which in practice often meant internal—affairs were run. They travelled about the land conducting parish visitations. They had a common sense of what the immediate and long-term problems of government were. In addressing these problems, they had a fairly clear pattern of changes in view. "Order" was the code word for this agenda.

To make my point more concretely, let me concentrate on a phrase from a *Kirchenordnung* issued in 1579 for the city of Nördlingen. This document, and the enforcement provisions that went with it, are meant, so the drafters declared, to do away with, and prevent the recurrence of, *alle unordnung, ungleichait und unrichtigkeit*, all disorder (or disorderliness), all lack of uniformity—meaning untidy confusion, bothersome complexity—and all irregularity, that is to say, all departures from established regulations.[24] The suppression of these unsatisfactory conditions is the most urgent object of policy makers. The restoration of their positive opposites—order, uniformity, regularity—is the supreme goal.

Why uniformity (to take up this one member of the programmatic trinity)? Why insist—quoting now from an ordinance for the County of Wolfstein in the Upper Palatinate, published in 1574—on "abolishing and doing away with troublesome multiplicity and diversity . . ., instituting instead, and upholding from now on, a definitive, superior, and correct uniformity (*eine gewisse besserliche richtige gleichförmigkeit*)" in the land?[25] The answer is that "diversity," "variety," "multiplicity" were metaphors for the genuine dismay with which political and ecclesiastical elites regarded the multifarious patterns by which people in all ranks of society lived their collective and individual lives. To the reforming mind, and the interventionist temper usually associated with it, variety in beliefs, diversity in customs, multiplicity as opposed to uniformity in religion,

---

[24]*Kirchenordnung* for Nördlingen, 1579. Sehling XII, 366.

[25]*Kirchenordnung* for Wolfstein, 1574. Sehling XIII, 566.

in judicial procedure, in political and social organization, in local usages and customary ways of doing things were, quite literally, intolerable. Not only was profusion tantamount to confusion, and therefore to chaos, it also represented an obtuse indifference on the part of subjects to the reformers' attempt to remodel, for their own good, people's habits and ways. The principles invoked were order and disorder. But the real matter at issue was power: the power of the stronger to impose versus the power of the weaker to ignore or to resist. Understood as pursuant action rather than as mere phrase-making, "order" meant, and was known at the time to mean, some concrete changes actually taking place in the political, social, and mental status quo. It meant the curtailment of local autonomies and their integration in a spreading system of state offices, most of them newly established or reinforced as part of the process of activating the Reformation or the Counter-Reformation in a particular place. "Order", in practice, meant a single body of civil and criminal law; it meant appellate jurisdiction transferred from local, domainial, village, or town courts to supervening territorial—that is to say, state—benches. It meant the replacement of amateur law finding by professional jurisprudence. It meant that village elders, town councils, seigneurial deputies were being subordinated in their authority to princely bureaucrats. It meant "orderly" administrative channels—which is to say hierarchy, always favoring the upper echelons. It meant that deeply rooted, probably cherished, and possibly even helpful expressions of traditional religiosity were vilified as superstitions. It meant the threat of eradication held over the entire farrago of notions and practices that made up traditional piety, and their replacement by an academically defined and politically sanctioned orthodoxy. It meant common standards for Christian living, improving rules for putting one's house in order, officially declared and enforced canons of civic decency and good citizenship. It meant schools organized to educate, on one level, a culturally homogeneous cadre of lay and clerical office holders and, on the other, an essentially docile mass of subjects. It meant weakening many of the attachments linking people to their native places and bonding them instead to designated administrative units, the parish and the district.

For all these attacks on the untidy status quo, the claim that the assault was mandated by the prerogative of a cosmic call to order served as a philosophical and moral warrant. This is why order was

for so long a favored image in preambles and other programmatic
declarations. But no image was ever less abstract. Behind it stood
groups of individuals with real interests to guard and an ambitious
social program to promote: the clergy to get, at long last, a handle on
popular religion; lawyers to make, again for the first time, the written
law a real presence in people's lives by transforming it from an
intrusive manipulative tool into the chief agent of social cohesion; state
functionaries to consolidate their political, and thereby their social,
position by exalting the virtues of bureaucratic centralism; princes,
dukes, landgraves, patrician town councillors to turn their pretensions
to power into effective instruments for wielding it. Each party in this
contention over the future shape of society had its prodding metaphors:
order, uniformity, consonance, stability, conformity on one side;
tradition, community, freedoms, ancient rights on the other. But no
one proclaiming these epithets, or responding to them, was in any
doubt about what they stood for in the real world, or who would gain
and who would lose in the course of their deployment as ideological
markers in the great sweepstakes of power.

   With all this in mind, we can perhaps begin to feel the force
behind such apparently detached definitions of order as the one lifted
by the Hessen church ordinance from Saint Augustine: "[Order is] a
statute assigning similar and dissimilar things each to the place where
it belongs (*ein satzung, da gleichen und ungleichen dingen einem
jeglichen sein gebürender ort gegeben und zugeeignet wird)*".[26] The
"statute", in this case, is the *gewisse Kirchenordnung*, the duchy's
authoritative ecclesiastical ordinance,[27] which was made basic law in
1566, and backing it up, as in every German territorial and urban
state, a host of additional regulatory provisions that went before, along
with, and after it: rules for the household, *Polizeiordnungen* governing
civic affairs, school ordinances, legal and procedural codes, clothing
restrictions, and so on. For "similar and dissimilar things" in the
definition, read the rights, beliefs, opinions, duties, and daily activities
that made up the lives of people in the land, lives that were being
repatterned by the Hessen ordinance according to their degrees of
agreement with, or deviation from, newly declared rules. All the

---

[26]*Kirchenordnung* for Hessen, 1566. Sehling VIII, 181, quoting *City of God* 19.13.1.

[27]Sehling VIII, 184.

senses of "order" are contained in this formula: fixed arrangement; classification; formal disposition; harmony of parts; status and rank within a hierarchy; mandates; regulations; command; due accord with what is lawful; the right or approved way of being, thinking, inclining and doing.

Made operative in daily religious and secular life—and this is of course what *Ordnungen*, ordinances, were intended to do—order would result in, quoting from an instruction issued by the County of Oldenburg in 1573,"*durchaus gleicheit und einigkeit*: uniformity and unity throughout".[28] Who would resist an appeal to uniformity and unity? Those might, and did, who knew the reality behind the words. Reality was a steamroller geared up to flatten all that lay in its path across the peculiarities and singularities of the medieval landscape. To the reformers, this landscape was a wilderness exhibiting all the flaws and vices associated with "disorder": not only irrationality, or unreasonableness; but also a willful disregard of God's original plan for a harmonious world. To the resisters, on the other hand, it was the familiar scenery of their accustomed ways and time-tested experience. This scene was not especially admirable. It was not sanctioned by reason, nor had it been drawn from design. It was simply there. The threat to its survival was causing chagrin and discomfort; we might call it alienation. Hence the resistance, which took many forms, the least studied of which utilized the proven weapons of the weak: paying no attention, dragging one's feet, looking the other way, playing dumb, and manifesting an exasperating contentment with life lived in a condition of disorderly clutter.

That these are effective weapons is not open to doubt. It is their very effectiveness that explains the reformers' inability, despite the energy and dedication they brought to their efforts, to make, even in the long run, much of a dent in public attitudes and demeanor. Many changes did take place in the sixteenth and seventeenth centuries, and some of these changes did eventually make an impact on the workings of society. But "reform" in the larger sense—reform, that is, as a program of social discipline institutionalized to reconstruct religious and social values and behavior—in other words, making lives conform to "order"—this attempt did not succeed. I imagine that it failed not owing to any deep inherent defects in the principles reform

[28]*Kirchenordnung* for Oldenburg, 1573. Sehling VII, part II, 1, 987.

sought to advance. It failed, I think, because the state and the state church, despite the accretion of power that came to them as a result of Reformation and Counter-Reformation, lacked the socialization mechanisms effectively to direct public conduct, not to mention private inclinations. Thus, while norms and standards were altered to reflect new theological and civic postures, and while fearsome imprecations were hurled down upon those who ignored them, the latitude available to opponents and resisters was not very much narrowed.

One side of this tug of social re-formation has been studied and is quite well understood. We know what ruling bodies tried to do. We know their programs, their declarations, and their instruments: the centralized schools, uniform religious instruction, approved sermons, regulations for the policing of conduct, "reformed" legal codes, and so on. This is the entire panoply of state intervention which some scholars speak of, taking the term from Gerhard Oestreich, as *Sozial-disziplinierung*,[29] and which has been analyzed, for a later period and rather extravagantly, by Michel Foucault.[30] What we do not know much about is the resistance to it. I do not mean the occasional outbreaks of violence and revolts. I mean the latent, mostly passive, ongoing, pervasive, daily obstructionism with which people seem to have braced themselves against the efforts of their betters to upgrade their lives. It seems to me that this sort of resistance to imposed norms of thinking and doing is at least as interesting to know about as are the norms themselves, and the careers of the norm makers. It has been studied in a non-western setting by James C. Scott, whose book, which is titled *Weapons of the Weak*, is enormously suggestive to students of popular culture in the west, partly because he offers such an interesting critique of Gramscian views of ideological hegemony by showing how tenacious, and how ingenious, plain people can often be

---

[29]Gerhard Oestreich, "Strukturprobleme des europäischen Absolutismus", *Vierteljahresschrift für Sozial- und Wirtschaftsgeschichte* 55 (1968), 338. On Oestreich's use of this term, see the article by Winfried Schulze, "Gerhard Oestreichs Begriff 'Sozialdisziplinierung in der frühen Neuzeit'", *Zeitschrift für historische Forschung* 14 (1987), 265-302.

[30]On the whole question of "social discipline," see R. Po-chia Hsia, *Social Discipline in the Reformation: Central Europe 1550-1750* (New York, 1989).

in blocking cultural directives handed down from above.[31] The study of resistance focuses our interpretation of past societies on persistent tensions rather than on the effort to absorb and subdue these tensions, which is to deny them their legitimacy. And tensions *are* revealing: this is a suggestion I have taken from E. P. Thompson. It is not only their "way of life" that tells us what we want to know about people in other cultures. It is their "way of conflict", as Thompson calls it, that opens a society to insightful inspection, because this way exposes the neuralgic points at which power and resistance to power cause discomfort in a social body.[32]

The notion of order is one of the devices we have for concealing this power play. By adopting it, more or less on the terms of sixteenth-century reformers, scholars have let it privilege one side of the struggle. It hides the contest of interests at work. It legitimizes the winner's right to set the rules. It misrepresents the counter-thrust that met every normative directive aimed from above. It therefore underestimates the accomodations always forced upon elite ideas when they encounter popular culture. It overdetermines our judgment: for how can one not be for order and against confusion? In all these ways it mystifies the processes of historical change and disembodies the forces that drive it. It is a ghost that has haunted the historical discourse on the Reformation for a long time.

---

[31]James S. Scott, *Weapons of the Weak: Everyday Forms of Peasant Resistance* (New Haven, 1985).

[32]E. P. Thompson, in a review of Raymond Williams's *The Long Revolution*, in *New Left Review* 9 (1961), 33.

XV

THREE KINDS OF "CHRISTIAN FREEDOM": LAW, LIBERTY, AND LICENSE IN THE GERMAN REFORMATION

Anniversaries of the famous make serious problems for the historian, especially the social historian. We want not only to commemorate, we want to magnify our hero; on the other hand, the professional judgment, reinforced by our experience of life, tells us that individuals—even extraordinary individuals—leave no more than a shallow impression on the course of human affairs. Before a notable life is over or a distinguished career has wound down, the real person has ceased to be and the image, or the myth, has taken over. And it is the myth that determines historical afterlife. Certainly this has been true of Luther. His powerful image dominates the German Reformation, but this may be because we have learned to see the event from the eminence of his personal stature. Once we switch viewpoints, things look very different: not correspondence, but the divergence between the Reformer and the Reformation strikes us as we survey the scene. Such a shift is increasingly being effected now in Reformation scholarship, and this does no dishonor to Luther who never wanted to be, or thought it would be possible to be, the creator of a Reformation. For the historian, this shift in viewpoint means asking the only kinds of questions we now consider adequate to the reality of human existence in the world—questions about the always complex and usually ambiguous interactions between an individual and the human collectivity within which he lives and acts.

I want to focus the remarks that follow on the subject of freedom, because whether proposed as ideal, as criterion, or as program, or sounded as slogan, "freedom" and "free" are words that turn up so regularly in the documents that I'm persuaded we have in them a useful clue to the reception, at all levels of society, of the central issues of the Reformation as these were declared from the lectern and the pulpit, and as they were understood below. The issue of freedom, more specifically of Christian freedom, seems to me to go to the heart of Reformation concerns; in an important sense it is what the Reformation was about. And there is an additional advantage to be gained from a consideration of Christian freedom: it brings us face to face with a problem not only foremost in the age of the Reformation, but of concern also in our own day. The best compliment we can pay Luther as we celebrate him this year is to conclude that what he thought and wrote about is still a live issue in our world. The extent of our agreement with him matters less here than the fact that we are still involved with him.

Let me begin with the best known use of the word "free," in the third of the Twelve Articles of the peasants of southwestern Germany of March 1525. For in the space of three short sentences in this passage, the condition of freedom is invoked in a number of different senses, pointing us to the overlapping meanings of the word in secular and religious discourse. "We find in the Bible," the familiar phrases go, "that we are free and want to be so. Not that we wish to be altogether free, to have no ruling authority over us; God doesn't teach us that. We are taught to live by commandments, not in free fleshly license, but to love God, recognize him as our Lord in our neighbor, and to do all things as we would have them done to us, as God commanded us at the Last Supper."[1]

The careful distinctions drawn here between the state of personal freedom and actions taken in consequence of it, between legitimate and illegitimate uses of freedom, reflect the unsettled position of the word in the political and legal literature of the time, an instability already given in the New Testament reference cited in the margin of the article, 1 Peter 2:16 (on which Luther had preached a cautionary sermon during the troubled months of 1522-23)[2] and very evident in the ambivalent and often contradictory—at least in practice contradictory—uses of the term "freedom" in contemporary political documents. Its most often encountered sense lies in the plural, "freedoms," meaning stated rights and privileges granted to a group or an individual, specifying something that may be done or may not be done. But "free" meant also that something was "free for the taking;" thus, the insurrectionaries in the 1520s argued that birds, fish, and the wild game of the forest should be "free" to all, that hunting and trapping should be free, and so on.[3] Others claimed that they were "free" to do as they pleased with their goods and persons; "the laws of all the nations," they said, "suppose and assume that every person and his belongings are free and untrammelled."[4] This is affirmed as a right. In the face of denials of this right, to be free comes to mean being one's own lord and master,[5] a proposition readily turned into a political slogan, as in the common adage "To be free like the Swiss," or in the insistent reminders of the lost freedom of the German nation given in the writings of Ulrich von

Hutten, who begins his first letter to Martin Luther, in 1520, with the motto *"Vive Libertas".*[6]

If we can fill these and similar catchwords with some political content, they might lead us to an understanding of the common view of what a "Reformation" was expected to accomplish in the early decades of the sixteenth century, for "freedom," or more precisely "Christian freedom," was the issue. Concretely, then, what did "free" and "fair," "just" and "right," "Christian" and "godly" mean in 1525 when these words were used by people in a hurry to see them put into practice? The goal, to put it first in general terms, was "Christian freedom" or, rather, its realization in an equitable, cooperative, brotherly, communitarian society to replace the present state of affairs with its ethic of egoism resulting from the substitution of man's law for God's law, human ambitions for the gospel. Christian freedom, in this view of it, was emancipation from the indignities and insecurities of life lived under the yoke of *Aigennutz,* of self-seeking. It avowed instead the principle and practice of the common good, *Gemeiner Nutz, res publica,* which was expected to follow from the restoration of the New Testament to its proper positon as law giver. It was recognized that attitudes and behavior result from social patterns. The virtues or faults of the latter govern the quality of the former. Hence the need for a thorough-going reconstruction of church and state, "so that the common man will be no longer defrauded of his Christian freedom," to quote from one of the plans.[7] This view of the Kingdom of God as attainable on Earth gave powerful ideological and rhetorical force to demands for a rearrangement of customs and institutions. Nearly all these demands had been made before, in the past. But they had never been drawn together into reform programs on so large a scale or with so wide an appeal as those aired in the years around 1525.

Actualizing Christian freedom in practical terms in society[8] meant above all other things the establishment of equal justice for all, that is to say a new condition of legal equality resulting from the shift from partisan and vested "human laws," now enthroned, to "godly natural laws in accord with Christian freedom." Next, everyone's basic needs were to be met, and each was required to do what he could, and no more. Those who had little to offer, or had suffered misfortune, would be cared for: the sick nursed, the old housed and fed, orphans raised and trained in useful occupations, the needy supported. The minimum mandated by Christian conscience was a fair sharing of the wealth and a redirection of social effort toward supportive caring. the maximum—disappearance of all distinctions between mine and thine—was proposed in schemes like Johann Hergot's

Impending Transformation of Christian Life of 1526, whose language is apocalyptic in the style of much of the social criticism of the time, but whose suggestions for reconstituting Christian society are solidly grounded in contemporary expectations. Hergot's appeal to conscience can stir us even today. "There are three tables in the world," he wrote in the concluding sentences of his *Impending Transformation,* "the first set sumptuously with great abundance of good things to eat; the second modestly, neither too much nor too little; the third meagerly, providing only scraps. And those feasting at the bountiful table came intending to take the bread away from the poorest table. From this arose the struggle [a reference to the events of 1525] and now God will smash the table of surfeit and the table of privation and make broad the table of moderation."[9]

To the Christian reformer intent on bringing about the Kingdom of God on Earth, there was nothing utopian about the grand turnabout announced here in prophetic tones. Thomas Müntzer said much the same thing: "All things should be in common" he insisted in his testimony, "and should be divided up among people according to their needs." His revolt, he maintained, was undertaken "so that all Christians might be made equal."[10] There is some controversy over how faithfully Müntzer's words, which were obtained under torture, reflected his real thoughts. However, what the scribe wrote down as Müntzer's confession in May 1525 could be heard almost everywhere at about the same time. In the spring of 1524, Johann Schilling, lecturer in the Franciscan monastery in Augsburg, began to preach vigorously against church and municipal authorities in that city, particularly against Jacob Fugger, saying, according to one who heard him, "that all things should be held in common, and with this and similar ideas he gathered a great crowd of people together."[11] In Augsburg, a large population of struggling weavers furnished a ready-made audience for this egalitarian message. But elsewhere the appeal was much the same. In Cologne, the slogan was "equal sharing," with reference to both wealth and the special privileges traditionally enjoyed by the rich.[12] In Frankfurt, in April 1525, the leaders of a guild revolution asked for the right of communal consent to taxation and for greater concern for the poor in setting prices of grain and wood.[13] In towns and cities from Ulm to Danzig and Königsberg, the communal idea of Christian freedom was translated into demands for, and of the action toward, a diminution of social and political differences among citizen groups to keep pace with the Reformation's equalization of clergy and laity. R.W. Scribner has recently summed up the underlying principle and its application in these and many similar actions. In the political events taking place in German cities in the early Reformation, he writes, "there is the sense of a considered collective decision, firmly taken and justified by the yardstick of Scripture."[14] "Christian freedom" and Holy Writ demanded no less than this: an equitable sharing among brothers of what life had to offer to all.

Most reform programs, however, were less grandiose in what they hoped to achieve, attending chiefly to matters for immediate improvement.[15] Serfdom was to disappear altogether; excessive and conspicuous wealth was to be channelled to the poor and needy; a host of regulations were to keep merchants honest. At the same time the plans show a conscious drive toward rationalization of economic and administrative procedures: standardization of weights and measures within territories; abolition of road taxes and other impediments to free-moving trade; better control of coinage; streamlining of administrative arrangements; and so on. Governments were asked to reduce cronyism, the tendency of entrenched functionaries to favor their friends and relations in judging, governing, financing. And one notices in these manifestoes, as in so much of the literature of the time, a pronounced suspicion of men of academic learning, and of the enlarged authority lately given them and their book knowledge in the councils of church and state. The strongest animus was against lawyers, deeply rooted by now in political administrations and courts of territorial and municipal governments. A kind of backlash against these unwelcome modernizers (as they were perceived) was one of the forces behind the push to do away, as much as possible, with so-called "worldly laws," and to substitute for them the binding code of the "godly and natural law." A few radical reformers—Gaismair for example—even moved to restrict all academic teaching to the Bible.[16] Man-made statutes not directly drawn from the Bible were reclassified as *Neuerungen,* innovations, a word with strongly pejorative associations in the sixteenth century. *Neuerungen* were held responsible for the corruption of life, and the repair of such perversions was always seen as a return to the past, above all to Scripture. This is the perspective from which we should judge the prominent place given in almost every statement of grievances to the request for freely elected pastors to "preach to us"—that is to every community or congregation—"the holy Gospel purely and clearly, without human additions, human doctrines, or human precepts."[17] "Human additions" were *Neuerungen.* They were deviations from true doctrine and were held responsible for the loss of that Christian freedom whose recovery was the chief ideological objective of the revolutionaries of 1525.

This, then, is what *"Reformation"* meant to a large segment of the German population in the 1520s: a trasformation of secular and religious life to bring it into line with Scripture. A Christian's freedom was his right to live in such a christianized society. It was also his right to help bring it about. To scruples about people's license to alter laws and social arrangements the reformers had a short answer: if their plans were in harmony with Scripture, well and good. The divine law gave them more than adequate authority. Acts 5:29: "We must obey God rather than men." 1 Cor. 7:21: "If a chance of liberty should come, take it." These passages were often cited.[18] But it would be wrong to let them stand for the whole movement. Christian freedom and Christian justice did not insist on insurrection. Only the most rigid apocalyptics advocated violence and destruction as a means to a desirable end. Most leaders had absorbed too much Christian quietism to endorse a code of violence. With the authors of the Twelve Articles they believed that "The Gospel does not cause rebellion and uproars, because it tells of Christ, the promised Messiah, whose words and life teach nothing but love, peace, patience, and unity."[19] On the other hand, though violent overthrows were not usually intended, the reformist movement did develop a true revolutionary momentum, a dynamism given in its belief in God's irresistible purpose, of which human wills were the instruments. "If God deigns to hear the peasants' earnest plea that they may be permitted to live according to His word," the Twelve Articles threatened, "who will dare deny His will? Who indeed will dare question His judgment? Who will dare oppose His majesty?"[20] The insurrection of 1525 thus derived its revolutionary power not so much from a commitment on the part of its leaders to violent overthrow, as from the conviction that their cause was one with the will of God manifesting itself in history and tending to the establishment of the right order in society.

Now, this was a most unLutheran reading of both history and Scripture: an utterly different sense from Luther's of what Reformation meant and what the Reformation was about. On Christian freedom and its responsibilities, Luther and the reformers talked past each other. Scorning all efforts to alter the status quo in the world, Luther condemned every attempt to make of Christian liberty a material kind of freedom. "Christ doesn't want to change worldly states," he said, "nor does he want to do away with serfdom. What does he care how princes and lords govern? It's nothing to him how you plow, sow, make shoes, build houses, pay interest, or take dividends.... Christ speaks of no such external matters. He concerns himself with a freedom that is beyond and above outward things, namely, how you are redeemed from sin, from death, from God's wrath, from devil and hell and eternal damnation.... This Christian freedom comes to a free man and also to a serf, to a man in prison as well as to one who takes a prisoner, to women and to men, to a serving man or maid and to master and mistress. We speak here of a freedom before God, who frees us from sin...."[21] The promise of this spiritual freedom is one of the root doctrines of evangelical Christianity, and Luther described it often and was tireless in distinguishing it from the other, vulgar, carnal freedom after which, he said, the mob hankers, and which it pursues with, he thought, misguided perseverance.[22] After the mid-1520s, and in reaction to the events of those years, his contrasting of the two freedoms against each other grew more polarizing and his excoriation of those who wanted the fleshly sort much more strident. "The freedom of the flesh is the devil's freedom," he said in *Lectures on Galatians* of 1535, "through which Satan rules the world. Those who claim this kind of freedom obey neither God nor the laws; they do as they please. This is the sort of freedom the rabble is after nowadays."[23] It was not for this that Christ had come into the world, he says, adding with some bitterness, "though people would seem to prefer it that way."[24] Luther had few illusions, and he was a close and, by-and-large understanding, observer of the human scene. "Most men interpret the doctrine of faith in a material way," he admitted "and want to make spiritual freedom out to be a freedom of the flesh. You can see this every day," he adds, confessing that he has found himself wishing that "such swine who trample pearls under their feet were still living under the tyranny of the Pope."[25]

Luther, then, had no sympathy with the reformers' struggle for a more just world drawn from the New Testament understood as a gospel of liberation. "Laws don't make you free," he said to the reformists; "Christian freedom has nothing to do with the body or with your ordinary lives. It has to do with the soul."[26] In sentences such as these—and there are many of them—Luther's meaning is unmistakable. On the other hand, his writings do contain passages in which this message is blurred, and these are sure to have led many of his followers along a path Luther came to consider, in the light of later events, fatally wrong. Justus Maurer, who has made a study of over two hundred evangelical preachers active in the years leading up to the revolution of 1525, attributed their success as crowd gatherers and crowd pleasers to the *"Befreiungserlebnis"* their sermons conveyed to their audiences, a sense of exhilaration arising from the newly uplifted status of the pious lay person vis-à-vis the clergy. Maurer concludes that "Freedom was the cue word" for this raising up of the laity with its claim that ordinary people, by their faith, were placed as high as the clerical estate.[27] Now, this is a proposition that, while not original with Luther, owes everything to the force with which he preached it and wrote about it in the early years of the Reformation. In some of his most widely propagated publications, the idea had a distinctly libertarian cast. In *To the Christian Nobility of the German Nation,* for example, "free" and "freedom" are used so often and, for evident propaganda purposes, given such an emotional charge, that some scholars have suspected the pamphlet of misleading its readers into giving Christian freedom a falsely political and social meaning.[28] It is hard to imagine that Luther was not at the time alert to this ambiguity. Everything we know about how people read and listen suggests that they insert words and ideas into their own frames, making sense of them by aligning them with their own familiar social landmarks, and no doubt this is what happened in the 1520s. Luther's contemporaries are not likely to have made tidy distinctions, as he did, between religious and worldly needs and obligations. Nor did they place the former above the latter; nor did they agree that a good Christian is bound to do so. To Luther, reformation was all inward (although he was, of course, all for doing away with any structure that constrained the freedom of the Gospel to form consciences); its central thrust was the acceptance of Christian freedom as emancipation from sin and promise of eternal life. The material reformers had totally misconceived this meaning, with—so Luther thought—disastrous consequences. He did not deny the accuracy of their description of the real world or the justice of their criticism of the inhumanity and rapaciousness of the powerful men who dominated it. But he thought such criticism pointless, and those who made it, misguided. His sense of being implicated in this misunderstanding no doubt explains the forcefulness of his repudiation of all revolutionary aims in 1525 and thereafter, and his decisive denial of the image of reformation as an ideology of political and social freedom.

I have restated some familiar facts and speculations. A more interesting question arises from them. Why are we so willing to accept Luther's strictures of the reformist platform while holding on to our generous view of him as a sympathetic judge of the human scene? The world was, for most people, a cruel place. They had little to expect from their God, from nature, from their fellow men. Was it helpful to tell them that it didn't really matter, that—as he put it in his response to the Twelve Articles—"these things don't concern a Christian, and he cares nothing about them"?[29] Clearly, to most people, rightly or wrongly, worldly cares were precisely what mattered. How could Luther tell them that Christians should be martyrs on Earth, and why does this advice not destroy Luther's image for us?

The answer is, of course, that centuries of Luther scholarship have convinced us of the total honesty of Luther's central outlook: his unshakable acceptance of the absolute priority of otherworldly concerns, the consequences of which he was as ready to apply to himself as to others. The depth of Luther's commitment to taking God's view rather than man's, and the cost to him in human terms of this obligation, has recently been brought out dramatically in Heiko Oberman's warm and compassionate new biography. Professor Oberman's book bears the subtitle: "Mankind between God and Devil." In the tug of war between these two cosmic forces, the only thing that counted for the human individual was the outcome. What were a few years of pain and trouble compared to the promise of bliss everlasting? Life mattered only to the extent that it affected what came thereafter. Luther really believed this, and we believe that he believed it.

But our view of these things is surely swayed also by the knowledge that they relate to history, to the past, in this case the quite distant past. Do we not make automatic discriminations in our value judgments according to whether we appraise events far or near in time and space? Obviously we do; we do it all the time; and our distinctions often trouble us in our conscience, although we don't seem to be able to do much about our tendency to make them. With respect to the past, our frequently cavalier way of presenting it must be due to the fact that it *is* past: done and gone. Elaborate, often strained, demonstrations are needed to link it to the present. We wish only to *understand* the past, no more. When it comes to our own time, on the other hand, we want much more than that: not merely to understand it, but to live in it as well. A very different set of standards is brought into play to serve this much more demanding objective. Understanding in its two-fold sense—not only to grasp or apprehend, but also to gain a sympathetic and tolerant attitude toward something or someone—is routinely awarded in history, from which the passage of time has insulated us. In our dealings with the present it is much more reluctantly given. Were he writing today, in reaction to events in our own time, Luther would be studied with a much colder eye, and judged by much less accommodating standards, than is the historical figure in his safely remote sixteenth century.

Let me make a test of this supposition. Not long ago I picked up a paperback published in 1982 by the Ethics and Public Policy Center in Washington, called *The Pope and Revolution: John Paul II Confronts Liberation Theology.*[30] The book opens with a brief foreword by Richard J. Neuhaus, a Lutheran pastor prominent in conservative circles in the United States. Reading this foreword, a Reformation historian at once finds his attention seized because of the striking way in which its author has repeated the gist of Luther's response to the revolutionaries of his own day. Throughout Christian history, Neuhaus writes, there have been individuals and movements ready to settle for less than the Kingdom of God. Trying to make the world a better place is settling for less because it means confusing the Kingdom with our own programs for making things the way we think they ought to be. Liberation theology is the latest of these confusions. As preached in the Third World, particularly in Latin America, it substitutes short-term gratification for long-term deliverance. "Almost as in a mirror image of earlier illusions," Neuhaus says, "it is often posited that demolishing the social, economic, and political orders . . . is necessary to establish the Kingdom of God." Neuhaus thinks this is understandable, but wrong. We get tired of waiting for the promise, he contends. We long for the fleshpots of Egypt—in this case, for the satisfaction of a cause or a movement to make us feel important and powerful in the world. We want the Gospel to be useful to this cause. "Useful" is settling for less. "When we are no longer sure that the Gospel is true," he writes, "we are eager to prove that it is useful." "What is at stake," he concludes, "is the integrity of the Gospel." The Gospel is truly revolutionary. Compared to its thorough-going radicalism, our little plans for quick and partial changes are conventional, mere accommodations, and Neuhaus dismisses them as such. Instead of dreaming of a few changes we think we can make, we should learn patience and rest content to wait for the promise to be fulfilled. Any other attitude is human presumption; any other action is folly.[37]

I don't know about other readers of this preface,[32] but I find it distasteful in its reasoning and extremely disturbing in its implications. But it is also clear to me that I judge it to be so chiefly because I am much more keenly alert to these implications—specifically to their effect on real men and women in real places—than I would be if they related to events I study in history. The former, the lives of my contemporaries, touch me in a way in which the latter—figures in the past—do not. What Neuhaus says upsets me for this reason, and no amount of scene setting and interpretation can take the callousness out of his remarks. What bothers me about them is their hypocrisy. He tries to have it both ways. He doesn't justify the status quo, he will even admit criticism of it; but he won't have it altered: things must stay as they are while we await the time of the promise. The Bible's absolute truth and utter radicalism preclude any lesser means with which the lot of our fellow men might be eased. Meanwhile people suffer, in concrete ways brought graphically home to all but the most resolutely ivory-towered among us. Witnessing their suffering, I wonder not about the meaning of it, but only about whether it can be lessened, and how this might be done, and how soon. Neuhaus's posture strikes me as both cruel and dishonest. Surely the long wait for the promise to be fulfilled is more tolerable for some of us, favored in the circumstances of our lives, than it is for others, who are not. I do not even want to understand a man who can't or won't see the moral flaw in this position and seems so indifferent to its consequences. Needless to say, this is an emotional reaction on my part. I am free to indulge it in response to what I read in the daily press. But the criteria of our scholarly discipline dictate that it has no place in my study of the past, where it would seriously compromise my understanding of it. And I agree that this is so. What results is a double standard, one which I imagine we all practice, and which has direct and, I think, serious bearing on the character of our work. But I believe it is useful on occasion to exchange the respective attitudes governing our activities. The results can be instructive.

Liberation theology and the opposition to it are interesting to Reformation historians precisely because they let us test the give and take of sixteenth-century arguments in a tangible, present, living situation. Language differs, but arguments are much the same then and now. A few aphoristic fragments must suffice here to show the correspondence.[33] Liberation theology, Gutierrez says, is "critical reflection on Christian praxis in the light of the Word."[34] It admits no distinctions between world and faith.[35] According to Leonardo Boff, it sees the Kingdom of God as expressing "man's utopian longing for liberation from everything that alienates him . . .: anguish, pain, hunger, injustice, death . . .",[36] and accepts as an article of faith the utopian belief in the possibility of constructing a qualitatively different society.[37] It addresses its rhetoric to a society primarily religious, not yet fully secularized[38] and based not on individuals, but on communities.[39] It sees Jesus as a liberator, as one who broke barriers and opposed legalism in all its forms.[40] Above all, it concerns itself with consequences, with the practical results of what is preached and taught. Christianity is considered as action, not merely as doctrine. A serious view of the Christian faith sees it as an instrument not only of individual change, but also of social transformation.[41]

In all essentials, these are the base positions from which the revolutionaries of the 1520s argued their grievances and stated their demands. And the rejection of these positions on the ground of their mere worldliness is also Luther's denial of the Gospel as a charter of secular freedom. We need not, of course, decide for one and against the other of these postulates as we try to make out what happened in 1525. Historians have long maintained—perhaps not always honestly—their right to a posture of impartiality, although others would argue instead the very impossibility of speaking or writing without judging. But when we see Luther's arguments restated in a setting so near, so timely, and so emotionally charged for us, we cannot help but judge them. *How* should we judge them? There is only one fair and sensible way—or so it seems to me: by their consequences in the real world. I have no doubt of the superiority of Gutierrez, Boff, Segundo, et al. over Neuhaus when their respective ideas are tested on this ground. As for the Reformation of the sixteenth century, we might return to it by asking the same question: what were the results of the theologians' denial of the reformist claim that Christian freedom has radical secular applications? Let us remind ourselves that Luther was only the most prominent of the many pastors and preachers who rejected the liberationist position after 1525; among them were men like Johann Eberlin, Jakob Strauss, Christoph Schappeler who had helped direct, lead, or inspire the revolutionary movement in the early 1520s. Now they did their part in showing the way to a passive ethic of acceptance.[42] Luther himself did not indicate his sense of what the consequences might be, beyond suggesting a bad end for unrepentant rebels. But Philip Melanchthon, to whom the events of 1522 to 1525 were even more traumatic and foreboding than they were to Luther, drew a deeply antagonistic lesson from what he had seen. "It would be well," he wrote in his own response to the Twelve Articles, "if so wild and unruly a people as the Germans had even less freedom than they now have." The insurrection had shown, he thought, what happens when you relax the reins. He was all for tightening them now.[43]

And this is exactly what happened. Backing up the preachers' moral authority, Lutheran states made the correct understanding of Christian freedom a matter of legal obligation on all their subjects. From the late 1520s, every German *Kirchenordnung* made the orthodox definition of Christian freedom one of the fundamental laws of state. The object was to discredit the liberationist interpretation of the gospel and to link Christian freedom with the citizen virtues of political loyalty and compliance. Pastors were required to give frequent sermons on Christian freedom, preaching, they were cautioned, not "out of your own heads," but correctly, out of St. Paul and the officially formulated creed. Bible passages were given on which to base homilies on this subject: 1 Peter 2:16 and Galatians 5:13 on the abuse of freedom; Exodus 20 and 22, Matthew 22:21 on the necessity of civil obedience; Romans 13, Titus 3:1, and 1 Peter 2:13-17 on submission to authority.[44] These passages, it was said, "show clearly and sufficiently that Christian freedom does not consist of being free of rents, interest, tithe, tax, service, or any other external burdens and grievances, as subjects call them, but is instead an inner, spiritual thing alone, and that in all external matters and laws, subjects owe their superiors obedience and submission."[45] The established social order is explicitly affirmed. "Christian freedom," the *Kirchenordnung* of Rothenburg states, "is not in conflict with our classes, orders, or Estates . . . ; on the contrary, it upholds them and demands loyalty to the laws that protect them."[46] The authorized view of Christian freedom is presented as the best hope for peace and harmony in society, for instance by Veit Dietrich, in his Agenda book for rural pastors in Nuremberg, in which Dietrich told his colleagues that "if you preach and teach in this way about Christian freedom, you will not only hold down rebellion in the populace . . . but will also encourage people to be dutiful to their worldly authorities and do whatever is best for peace and well being. . . . For Scripture is our witness to this," he continued, "that worldly governments are founded by God, who commands us as their subjects to obey them in all that touches worldly matters."[47] Not all pastors gave the political rationale such a blank check; but many did, and a preliminary and unscientific attempt on my part to plot these on a map of Germany suggests that sternly conservative definitions of Christian freedom tended to appear in governmental pronouncements wherever the revolution of 1525 had been most painfully felt. Indoctrinating their subjects in these definitions became a paramount concern of church and state authorities after 1525. In the process, most of the reform demands that had earlier been deduced from Christian freedom were dropped from the orthodox statement of it. Most notable in its omission from these post-1525 authorized definitions was any and all reference to the right of communities or congregations to choose their own pastors. This change illustrates what was probably the chief lesson taken by church and state authorities from the events of 1525. Everywhere in Germany, governments now devised administrative and educational procedures designed to centralize and control the job of instructing the public. From the point of view of the ruling elites in church and society, this strengthening of their authority, and of the means of exerting it, is what the 16th-century Reformation was all about.

With this dénouement Luther had virtually nothing to do. He was far from approving of, or associating himself with, or sharing the rationale of, the conservative reaction. By his lights, governments policies in the backlash of 1525 were as wrong-headedly carnal, as opposed to Gospel and true Christian freedom, as had been the trouble-making of the rebels. To be sure, Luther accepted and welcomed the need for discipline, and therefore for laws, including restrictive laws, and their enforcement. But the resulting political and judicial order had no claim to being a Christian polity. Its ethos of coercion and involuntary acquiescence, of reciprocal mistrust, revealed it as archetypically worldly. In a true Christian society, association is voluntary, not compulsory. Its bond and drive is love, not force. "A Christian," said Luther, "lives not for himself, but for Christ and his fellow man, for Christ through faith, for his fellow man through love.[48] There was little faith and less love in the crass new society then abuilding. Luther saw this as clearly, and I think as sorrowfully, as the reformers had seen it in the early 1520s. It must have been a consolation to him to know that it would not last much longer.

Notes

1. The German text is printed in Adolf Laube and Hans Werner Seiffert eds., *Flugschriften der Bauernkriegszeit* (Berlin [East], 1975), p. 28. English translation in Peter Blickle, *The Revolution of 1525*, tr. Thomas A. Brady, Jr., and H.C. Erik Midelfort (Baltimore, 1981), p. 197.

2. *WA* 12, 331-333.

3. E.g. Articles of peasants of Allgäu, February 1525, in Günther Franz ed., *Quellen zur Geschichte des Bauernkrieges* (Munich, 1963), No. 35, p. 164.

4. From reply of *Gotteshausleute* of Kempten to complaints of their prince-abbot, September 1525 in *ibid.* No. 27, p. 128.

5. E.g. Articles of peasants of Stühlingen and Lupfen, 1525 in *ibid.*, No. 25, p. 121; articles of Memmingen peasants, February-March 1525 in *ibid.*, No. 40, p. 169; also *ibid.*, No. 34b, p. 153; No. 30, p. 141; No. 29, p. 136.

6. Hutten to Luther, June 4, 1520, *WA Br*, vol. 2, No. 295. On the issue of freedom in early modern German law and politics see Herbert Grundmann, "Freiheit als religiöses, politisches und persönliches Postulat im Mittelalter," *Historische Zeitschrift*, 183 (1957), 23-53; Karl Bosl, "Die alte deutsche Freiheit. Geschichtliche Grundlagen des modernen deutschen Staates" in: *Frühformen der Gesellschaft im mittelalterlichen Europa* (Munich, 1964), pp. 204-219; *id.*, "Freiheit und Unfreiheit. Zur Entwicklung der Unterschichten in Deutschland und Frankreich während des Mittelalters," in: *ibid.*, pp. 180-203; Joseph Schlumbohm, *Freiheitsbegriff und Emanzipationsprozess. Zur Geschichte eines politischen Wortes*, Göttingen, 1973. (especially 14-20).

7. From a reform plan submitted to the Assembly of Franconian peasants, May 1525: Günther Franz, *op. cit.* No. 124, p. 375.

8. For sources of this paragraph, see the following reform plans and manifestos: *An die Versamlung gemayner Pawerschaft* (1525) ed. Siegfried Hoyer, Leipzig, 1975; reform plan by Wendel Hipler and Friedrich Weygandt (1525)—the so-called Heilbronn Program—printed in Laube and Seiffert eds., *Flugschriften*, 75-79 and in Klaus Arnold, "Damit der arm man unnd gemainer nutz iren furgang haben . . . ," *Zeitschrift für historische Forschung*, 9.3 (1982), 288-311; Johann Hergot, *Von der newen Wandlung eynes christlichen lebens* (1526 or 1527) in Laube and Seiffert, eds., *op. cit.*, 547-557; the Meran Articles of Tirol (1525) in Günther Franz, *op. cit.*, No. 91, pp. 272-285; *Michael Gaismairs Landesordnung* (1526) in *ibid.*, No. 92, pp. 139-143; the Franconian plan mentioned in note 7 above.

9. Johan Hergot, *Von der newen Wandlung . . .* in Laube and Seiffert eds., *op. cit.*, p. 557.

10. "Bekenntnis" in Thomas Müntzer, *Schriften und Briefe*, ed. Günther Franz (Gütersloh, 1968), 548. On the problems connected with this "confession," see Walter Elliger, *Thomas Müntzer. Leben und Werk* (Göttingen, 1975), 797-798.

11. Wolfgang Zorn, *Augsburg* (Munich, 1976), pp. 169-173.

12. From the testimony of Tilman Rebein, one of the ringleaders of the Cologne revolution: Hugo Stehkämper, *Revolutionen in Köln* (Cologne, 1973), p. 57.

13. Sigrid Jahns, *Frankfurt, Reformation und Schmalkaldischer Bund* (Frankfurt am Main, 1976), pp. 34-42.

14. R.W. Scribner, "Practice and Principle in the German Towns: Preachers and People" in P.N. Brooks, ed., *Reformation Principle and Practice. Essays in Honour of Arthur Geoffrey Dickens* (London, 1980), p. 98. On political and social instability in German cities, see Rudolf Endres, "Zünfte und Unterschichten als Elemente der Instabilität in den Städten," in: Peter

Blickle, ed., "Revolte und Revolution in Europa," *Historische Zeitschrift, Beiheft 4,* Neue Folge, (1975), 151-170.

15. This paragraph rests on my reading of the printed sources listed in notes 1, 3-5, and 7.

16. Michael Gaismair in Laube and Seiffert, eds., *op. cit.,* pp. 286-287.

17. From the first of the Twelve Articles, English translation in Peter Blickle, *op. cit.,* p. 196.

18. Two examples: "46 Artickel, so die gemeyn einem ersamen rath der...stat Franckenfurt...fürgehalten"(April, 1525) in Laube and Seiffert eds., *op. cit.,* p. 59; "An die Versamlung gemayner Pawerschaft" (1525) ed. Siegfried Hoyer, p. 108.

19. "Twelve Articles" in Blickle, *op. cit.,* p. 195.

20. *Ibid.,* p. 196.

21. From Sermons on John (1530-32); on 8:34-38, *WA* 33, 659-60.

22. Exegesis of First Epistle of Peter (1523), *WA* 12, 331; Second Sermon on Jeremiah 23:5-8 (1526), *WA* 20, 579; Lectures on Galatians (1535), on 5:13, *WA* 40.2, 60.

23. Lectures on Galatians (1535), *WA* 40.2, 2-3.

24. Sermons on John 6-8 (1530-32), *WA* 33, 668.

25. Lectures on Galatians (1535), *WA* 40.2, 60.

26. Second Sermon on Jeremiah 23:5-8 (1526, *WA* 20, 579.

27. Justus Maurer, *Prediger im Bauernkrieg* (Stuttgart, 1979), pp. 34-35.

28. Wilhelm Maurer, *Von der Freiheit eines Christenmenschen. Zwei Untersuchungen zu Luthers Reformationsschriften 1520/21* (Göttingen, 1949), p. 43.

29. "Ermahnung zum Frieden auf die zwölf Artikel der Bauerschaft...," *WA* 18, 328.

30. Quentin L. Quade ed., *The Pope and Revolution. John Paul II Confronts Liberation Theology,* Washington, D.C., 1982.

31. *Ibid.,* vii-x.

32. Neuhaus's preface reiterates the positions framed in the so-called "Hartford Declaration" of 1975 by a conference of scholars, theologians, and pastors of which Neuhaus was one of the conveners. It was answered in 1976 by "the Boston Affirmations" drafted by the Boston Industrial Mission Task Force. Its publication led to a spirited correspondence in the pages of the *Andover Newton Quarterly* (16.4) of March, 1976, pp. 235-270. See especially the "Hartford Declaration's refutation of Theme 12: "The struggle for a better humanity will bring about the Kingdom of God" and the "Boston Affirmations" section "Present Witnesses," as well as correspondents' discussion of these points.

33. Some general works on Liberation Theology are: Francis P. Fiorenza, "Latin American Liberation Theology," *Interpretation, 28* (1974), 441-457, with excellent bibliography; J. Andrew Kirk, *Liberation Theology. An Evangelical View from the Third World,* Atlanta, 1979; Thomas M. McFadden, ed., *Liberation, Revolution, and Freedom. Theological Perspectives. Proceedings of the College Theology Society,* New York, 1975; Dermot Lane, eds., *Liberation Theology. An Irish Dialogue* (Dublin, 1977); Charles R. Strain, "Liberation Theology: North American Perspectives," *Religious Studies Review,* 8.3 (July, 1982), 239-244; *idem,* "Ideology and Alienation: Theses on the Interpretation and Evaluation of Theologies of Liberation," *Journal of the American Academy of Religion* 45 (1977), 473-490.

34. Gustavo Gutierrez, *A Theology of Liberation. History, Politics, and Salvation,* tr. and ed. by Sister Caridad Inda and John Eagleson (Maryknoll, N.Y., 1973), pp. ix, 13.

35. J. Andrew Kirk, *op. cit.,* pp. 31-32.

36. Leonardo Boff, "Salvation in Jesus Christ and the Process of Liberation" in Claude Geffré and Gustavo Gutierrez, eds., *The Mystical and Political Dimension of the Christian Faith. Concilium: Religion in the Seventies* (New York, 1974), pp. 80-81.

37. J. Andrew Kirk, *op. cit.,* pp. 33-34.

38. Francis P. Fiorenza in: *loc. cit.,* p. 443.

39. Mary I. Buckley, "Freedom as Personal and Public Liberation" in Thomas M. McFadden ed., *op. cit.*, p. 40.

40. Leonardo Boff in *loc. cit.*, pp. 83-84.

41. Claude Geffré and Gustavo Gutierrez, eds., *op. cit.*, pp. 10-11.

42. Johann Eberlin, *Ein getrewe warnung an die Christen in der Burgauischen Mark, sich auch füre hin zu hüten vor aufrur...* (1526) in Ludwig Enders, ed., *Johann Eberlin von Günzburg, Sämmtliche Schriften* vol. III (Halle, 1902), pp. 279-280. Cf. Justus Maurer, *op. cit.*, p. 426. Jakob Strauss, *Christliche... Antwort... auf das ungütige Schmähbüchlein D. Johannis Coclei* (1526) quoted in Hermann Barge, *Jakob Strauss* (Leipzig, 1937), pp. 125-132. Christoph Schappeler to Zwingli, May 1525 in *Huldreich Zwinglis Sämmtliche Werke*, vol. VIII (Leipzig, 1914), pp. 324-326. On the about-face executed by many preachers during and after 1525, see Justus Maurer, *op. cit.*, pp. 263-275. For a general account of the reactions of Lutheran pastors and theologians to the revolt, see Robert Kolb, "The Theologians and the Peasants: Conservative Evangelical Reactions to the Peasant Revolt," *Archiv für Reformationsgeschichte*, 69 (1978), 103-130.

43. Philip Melanchthon, *Eyn schrifft... widder die artikel der Bawrschafft* (1525) in Laube and Seiffert, eds., *op. cit.*, p. 234.

44. These citations from *Der Durchleuchtigen Hochgebornen Fürsten... Casimirn and... Georgen..., Marggraven zu Brandenburg... anzeygen, wie die gewesen empörung und aufrurn... auss ungeschickten predigen entstanden sind...* (1525) in: Emil Sehling, continued by the Institut für evangelisches Kirchenrecht der Evangelischen Kirche in Deutschland, eds., *Die evangelischen Kirchenordnungen des XVI. Jahrhunderts*, vol. 11 (Tübingen, 1961), p. 86.

45. *Ibid.*, p. 87.

46. *Ordnung der Kirchen... der Stat Rothenburg ob der Tauber* in *ibid.*, p. 576.

47. Veit Dietrich, *Agendbüchlein für die Pfarrherrn auff dem Land* (1545) in *Ibid.*, p. 552.

48. "Von der Freiheit eines Christenmenschen" (1520), *WA* 7, 38.

THE DILEMMA OF POPULAR HISTORY[*]

It is certainly not the least achievement of current debates on the practice of history to have discredited the old notion that historians can and should separate their work from their personal sympathies. This essay is an attempt to draw out some implications of the readmission of partiality into the historian's performance by considering a problem that has been intruding itself into my own field, the German Reformation. This problem has also attracted a good deal of public attention to the historical discipline itself, while at the same time posing — at least for me, and possibly for others as well — a distinct practical and moral predicament. I refer to the problem of popular history, or, rather, the problem of doing it, of engagement with it, as part of our scholarly programme of exploring and understanding the past.

By "popular history" I am not referring to the writing of history for a broad reading public. I mean scholarship that concerns itself with the affairs of ordinary people: what is usually called "history from below", or sometimes "people's" or "grassroots history". As everyone knows, this "history from below" has enjoyed a great vogue in recent years. Along with the study of popular culture, it has taken some very interesting forms, has attracted highly able practitioners and passionate advocates, and has also drawn vehement critics from all parts of the ideological spectrum. No one doubts that our discipline has been enriched by it, but popular history is not the less questionable for that; indeed it raises a great many questions: conceptual, procedural and methodological. One in particular seems to me to deserve exploration because it has not, to my knowledge, been aired. It is one that I myself have found unsettling, demanding, as the word "dilemma" in my title suggests, that a choice be made between alternatives neither of which is completely satisfactory, thus creating a quandary for those who are active in the field.

* An earlier version of this article was given as a talk at the annual luncheon meeting of the Modern European History Section of the American Historical Association in San Francisco in December 1989.

* This article first appeared in *Past and Present: A Journal of Historical Studies*, no. 132 (August 1991), pp. 130-149 (World Copyright: The Past and Present Society, 175 Banbury Road, Oxford, England).

"History from below" became an issue for me quite unexpectedly a decade and a half ago. I was working on a study of the attempt by the Lutheran establishment in Germany in the second and third quarters of the sixteenth century to meet the uncertainties of the evangelical movement's future by indoctrinating young people with what the leaders of church and state considered to be the essentials of Protestant Christianity and social civility.[1] In using the word "indoctrination" to describe this effort, I had no pejorative innuendo in mind. It seemed an appropriate way to designate an undertaking that involved both theologians and secular bureaucrats (each of these groups having become gravely troubled by the apparent unravelling of order in the early years of the Reformation), that was systematically and vigorously pursued and well supported by state resources, and that, for its overall objective, sought to imbue people — not only children, but unlettered adults as well — with a firm and, it was hoped, permanent mind-set cut to approved norms. Studying this pedagogical undertaking posed no technical problems. Sources were easily identified and readily accessible: government promulgations, church ordinances, consistory records, catechisms, school books, the writings of major and minor reformers, sermons and so on. These told me what was expected and attempted, how it was implemented, and how it all related to the major theological and political concerns of the Reformation.

I knew, of course, that I was seeing things from the perspective of official circles. But this did not at first disturb me. It was while turning the pages of yet another of those innumerable catechisms produced by Lutheran clergy as the safest and most effective instruments for teaching both knowledge and what are now called "values" to their pupils, that I began to wonder how these pupils, a sizeable proportion of whom were adults, had responded to this drilling; how much they had taken in; to what extent they had, as intended, internalized the message; and whether it had made any difference to their lives. I was aware that Lutheran governments had tried to monitor the results of their reforming efforts by means of frequent parish visitations. A sampling of the records of these visitations showed me that most of the (often very detailed) questionnaires from which the visitors worked contained

---

[1] Gerald Strauss, *Luther's House of Learning: Indoctrination of the Young in the German Reformation* (Baltimore, 1978). See also Gerald Strauss, "Success and Failure in the German Reformation", *Past and Present*, no. 67 (May 1975), pp. 30-63.

points of interrogation on the lessons imparted, or which it had been desired to impart, in preaching, in catechism instruction and in schooling. Answers by local pastors, and in many cases by individual villagers, were faithfully taken down; at a later stage they were copied into volumes for the use of various administrative echelons. Masses of these stout tomes, called visitation protocols, repose in archives all over Germany.[2]

Here was a way of balancing the official account of the indoctrination process with the story as observed at ground level. Going through a large quantity of the visitation records, I drew from them what I believed to be a body of trustworthy evidence to help us understand the popular reception of Lutheranism, as well as the social consequences of that reception.[3] This evidence made it apparent that, after three-quarters of a century of Christian instruction, people still remained largely ignorant of, and indifferent to, even the rudiments of the evangelical religion, and quite obtuse as well regarding approved norms of civic conduct. I proposed some explanations of this state of affairs. Most persuasive among these, judged by abundant testimony in the sources, was the persistence of a form of popular religiosity operating independently at the base of society, which constituted, in many respects, an alternative religion that may have rendered the large mass of ordinary people virtually impervious to indoctrination from above. Some reviewers of my book took exception to the approbatory tone in which I described this popular religion. One critic wrote that "it is dismaying to see a historian . . . modishly romanticize the superstitions of folk religion . . . as 'a rich blend of intuitions and observations affording the devotee a satisfying and . . . useful integration of nature and individual life' ".[4] And it *was* true: the account I had given of the reaction of ordinary people in Reformation Germany to the attempts of church and state to improve them was that of a partisan. I was on their side. I was far from disappointed to discover that officially sponsored

---

[2] For a description of visitation procedures and their function in the administration of the early modern state, see Strauss, *Luther's House*, ch. 8. For a useful guide to visitation materials, see Ernst Walter Zeeden and Hansgeorg Molitor, *Die Visitation im Dienst der kirchlichen Reform*, 2nd edn. (Münster, 1977).

[3] For some arguments against and for the use of visitation protocols as indicators of the popular response to Lutheranism in Germany, see Gerald Strauss, "The Reformation and its Public in an Age of Orthodoxy", in R. Po-chia Hsia (ed.), *The German People and the Reformation* (Ithaca, 1988), pp. 194-214.

[4] Steven Ozment, rev. of Strauss, *Luther's House*, *Jl. Mod. Hist.*, li (1979), p. 839.

indoctrination did not, in this instance at least, seem to have worked. I felt heartened, perhaps even a bit gleeful, to see powerfully situated bodies frustrated, and attempts at establishing a far-reaching intellectual and cultural hegemony defeated by grassroots resistance using only what, a few years later — having in the mean time read James C. Scott's book of that title — I learned to call "weapons of the weak".[5]

Caught up in the excitement of shaping a book, especially one whose argument was taking an unanticipated turn, I was not, at the time, aware of the problem I was evading. Even years later, while working on another project, on the losing struggle in sixteenth-century Germany to oppose the political uses of Roman law,[6] I failed to question the contradictions undermining the populist stance when it is adopted with regard to the historical past. More recently, however, I have been having some second thoughts. What seems problematic to me now is this: how can I, in my scholarly work, applaud the ways of ordinary people in former times when, as an inhabitant of my own historical moment and milieu, I feel so little sympathy for, and virtually no sense of kinship with, the popular culture of my contemporaries? This is the dilemma of my title. To put it another way: is it honest for those of us who do "history from below" to extol popular mental habits and behaviour when these are safely distanced from us in the past, while shunning, not to say recoiling from, the expressions of common belief and taste in our own time and place, many of which we find offensive and alienating? A question of professional discrimination is involved here, not only a personal preference, and this obviously affects the disposition in which we approach our work, and thus, ultimately, its results.

There is a background to this dilemma, as I shall show; but it is its consequences in the present that above all call for discussion. I propose to take it as a fact that most "history from below" written in recent years succeeds in valorizing popular culture, an enhancement accomplished by conferring upon it a dignity, a weight and a significance that are intended to change our perception of it from something — here I am using the terms of Natalie Zemon Davis to make my point — conventionally labelled "back-

---

[5] James C. Scott, *Weapons of the Weak: Everyday Forms of Peasant Resistance* (New Haven, 1985).
[6] Gerald Strauss, *Law, Resistance, and the State: The Opposition to Roman Law in Reformation Germany* (Princeton, 1986).

ward", "unchanging", "passive", "naïve", "irrational" and "violent", to something that can fairly be described as "flexible", "innovative", "mindful", "ordering", "artful", "critical" and "vital".[7] Davis's work is a paradigm instance of the valorizing drive behind a great deal of current popular history. Her most recent book, *Fiction in the Archives*, for example, argues that inventiveness and imagination are widely distributed through the social ranks, and that a "common discourse" and "cultural exchange" link the free-wheeling creativity of simple people with the more disciplined literary artefacts of the educated.[8] Elsewhere she has pleaded for an approach to popular culture and its history that dispels its strangeness by analysing its symbolic content, thus discovering recognizable features in it, such as an inherent sense of order and a reflective impulse.[9]

A few other cases in point, all taken from my own area of work, will show that in effect, if not necessarily in intent, popular history tends greatly to elevate its subject. The book that first made "history from below" respectable for many Europeanists was Peter Burke's *Popular Culture in Early Modern Europe*, published in 1978. Burke is a very cautious scholar, bent on avoiding even a trace of sentimentality towards the object of his analysis.[10] When, however, in the last part of his book, he comes to what he calls the "reform" of popular culture by the educated in the later sixteenth and the seventeenth centuries, the neutral tone yields to a partisan voice in which the author speaks, appreciatively, of popular culture's "generosity and spontaneity and a greater tolerance of disorder", in opposition to the "puritanical" and "moralistic" impulses of censorious "godly" reformers, whom he represents as agents of "a petty bourgeois ethic".[11] There is much in the attitude exemplified here that can be traced back to Mikhail Bakhtin's enormously influential *Rabelais and His World*, a book that virtually idolizes the folk as "deep", "rich"

[7] N. Z. Davis, introd. to Jacques Beauroy *et al.*, *The Wolf and the Lamb: Popular Culture in France* (Saratoga, Calif., 1977), p. 14.

[8] N. Z. Davis, *Fiction in the Archives: Pardon Tales and Their Tellers in Sixteenth-Century France* (Stanford, 1987), pp. 111-14.

[9] N. Z. Davis, "Some Tasks and Themes in the Study of Popular Religion", in Charles Trinkaus and Heiko A. Oberman (eds.), *The Pursuit of Holiness* (Leiden, 1974), pp. 307-36.

[10] Cf. his cautionary remarks in Peter Burke, "People's History or Total History", in Raphael Samuel (ed.), *People's History and Socialist Theory* (London, 1981), p. 8.

[11] Peter Burke, *Popular Culture in Early Modern Europe* (New York, 1978), pp. 207-23; quotations from pp. 207, 208, 213.

and "free" in their imaginative power, whose scatology is an affirmative life-force, whose subversive humour puts "a chorus of laughing people" on the world stage to scoff at the drama of history, and whose elemental vigour keeps popular culture forever fresh and unroutinized.[12] More recently, there has been the controversial essay by Carlo Ginzburg, *The Cheese and the Worms*, which is a passionately argued plea for the recognition of common people's traditions as "a culture of their own", autochthonous and independent as an age-old oral heritage, but remarkably similar upon close examination to "the most progressive circles of sixteenth-century [literate] culture", and evidence, therefore, of the grass-roots origins of a great part of European civilization. The book's hero, the obscure Friulian miller Menocchio, whose testimony before the Inquisition allows Ginzburg to hear "as if out of a crevice in the earth" elements of a "deep-rooted cultural stratum", emerges as an admirable representative commoner: tolerant, neighbourly, rational, open-minded, studious and liberal.[13]

Ginzburg's own ideological posture is unconcealed in his book, and it has been noted by nearly every commentator.[14] But political engagement is not a precondition of the valorization process at work here. To take one more recent example: David Sabean's much discussed study of peasant culture in Württemberg, *Power in the Blood*. In this book there is no romanticizing of German peasants and their villages in the early modern centuries; none the less, Sabean bestows substantial worth and dignity on the mental traits and actions of these simple rural men and women, finding rich veins of signification running through their lives by attending very closely to the everyday things they do and say. His conclusion — an important one in light of the sometimes quite strident controversy about popular history — is that, in their own ways, ordinary people were as much involved as their social betters with the great matters of human affairs: justice, responsibility, community, loyalty, vision, faith, exchange and communica-

[12] Mikhail Bakhtin, *Rabelais and His World*, trans. Helene Iswolsky (Cambridge, Mass., 1968), pp. 90, 147-52, 474, *passim*. Bakhtin's book first became available in 1965.
[13] Carlo Ginzburg, *The Cheese and the Worms: The Cosmos of a Sixteenth-Century Miller*, trans. John and Anne Tedeschi (New York, 1982), pp. xiv, 125-6, 58, *passim*. Ginzburg's book was first published in 1976.
[14] For a particularly trenchant, though not hostile, critique, see Valerio Valieri, rev. of Ginzburg, *Cheese and the Worms*, *Jl. Mod. Hist.*, liv (1982), pp. 139-43.

tion. All these themes are present in the lives of the ordinary, though their traces must be teased from the dense fabric of the sources. Throughout, Sabean portrays his people as purposeful in shaping their world. Exploited, but by no means supine, they are actively engaged in waging the lively give-and-take that characterizes all social relationships.[15]

My argument could easily be illustrated from other fields of historical specialization, most pertinently from the work of British Marxist historians. It is evident that the fully conceptualized Marxism of scholars like E. P. Thompson, Christopher Hill and E. J. Hobsbawm keeps them from privileging working people to the exclusion of other classes; it also mutes the celebratory, as opposed to the critical, tone and restrains extravagance in the decoding of symbols. At the same time, their historical writings do immeasurably sharpen our alertness to, and deepen our identification with, the lives of common folk. The influence of Thompson's *The Making of the English Working Class* on "history from below" is too well known to need restating here. But there are highly instructive instances of popular history's ability to channel attention and concentrate sympathy in many of Thompson's other works as well, with their rich description of the festivities and rituals, the songs, dances and legends of eighteenth-century popular culture; with their portrayal of that culture's independence, especially from the church; with their account of its courage, drama and capacity for resolute action;[16] and with their demonstration of the reasonableness and moral purpose exhibited by ordinary people in both their daily routines and their moments of crisis.[17] Thompson's insistence on human agency, on self-making, infuses all his work,[18] and his elaboration of "experience" as a chief category of description and analysis, joined as it is to his great literary skill, virtually assures his

[15] David W. Sabean, *Power in the Blood: Popular Culture and Village Discourse in Early Modern Germany* (Cambridge, 1984).
[16] E. P. Thompson, "Patrician Society, Plebeian Culture", *Jl. Social Hist.*, vii (1973-4), pp. 382-405.
[17] E. P. Thompson, "The Moral Economy of the English Crowd in the Eighteenth Century", *Past and Present*, no. 50 (Feb. 1971), pp. 76-136.
[18] For explicit statements of this position, see E. P. Thompson, "The Poverty of Theory or an Orrery of Errors", in his *The Poverty of Theory and Other Essays* (New York and London, 1978), pp. 106-7, 122. There is a cogent and illuminating discussion of "agency" in Thompson's work in Perry Anderson, *Arguments within English Marxism* (London, 1980), pp. 16-58.

readers' identification with the struggles of ordinary folk.[19] More examples, from the work of Hill, Hobsbawm and others, come readily to mind.[20] But I hope that my point is now clear. The "valorizers", as I shall call them, find much to praise in the history of ordinary lives. Even scholars inclined to cast a much cooler eye[21] end up by raising these lives not only in our sympathy, but also in our esteem. They accomplish this feat simply by doing their subjects the honour of paying them close and caring heed, of taking them seriously; of giving so intense a reading to what people do and say that no incident can any longer be dismissed as trivial, and no detail reduced to a mere splash of local colour.

Now it is obvious that the key question with respect to this honorific turn in writing the history of ordinary people is whether such attention is in fact justified by the — judged by older historiographical standards — rather commonplace nature of the sources. Are all these carnival pranks, village feuds, charivaris and cattle-bewitchings, these more or less identical specimens of

[19] For a highly critical discussion of Thompson's use of "experience", see William H. Sewell, Jr., "How Classes Are Made: Critical Reflections on E. P. Thompson's Theory of Working Class Formation", in Harvey J. Kaye and Keith McClelland (eds.), *E. P. Thompson: Critical Perspectives* (Philadelphia, 1990), pp. 50-77. See also Richard Johnson, "Edward Thompson, Eugene Genovese and Socialist-Humanist History", *History Workshop Jl.*, no. 6 (1978), pp. 79-100. On the whole issue of British Marxist history and "history from below", see Raphael Samuel, "People's History", in Samuel (ed.), *People's History and Socialist Theory*, pp. xxvii-xxxii; Stuart Hall, "Marxism and Culture", *Radical Hist. Rev.*, xviii (1978), pp. 5-14; June Philipp, "Traditional Historical Narrative and Action-Oriented (or Ethnographic) History", *Hist. Studies*, xx (1983), pp. 339-52; Harvey J. Kaye, *The British Marxist Historians: An Introductory Analysis* (Cambridge, 1984), *passim*, esp. pp. 222-32; Harvey J. Kaye, "E. P. Thompson, the British Marxist Historical Tradition and the Contemporary Crisis", in Kaye and McClelland (eds.), *E. P. Thompson: Critical Perspectives*, pp. 252-75, esp. pp. 259-60.

[20] See below, n. 54. There is an immense difference between the fully engaged histories of Thompson, Hill and Hobsbawm and the detached "ethnographical" approach taken by Emmanuel Le Roy Ladurie in *Montaillou*. I do not therefore agree with those who think that the publication of that book in 1975 marks a decisive departure from the *Annales* school's previous preference for a "history without people", whether of material conditions or of mentalities.

[21] In my own field, for example, see R. W. Scribner, *Popular Culture and Popular Movements in Reformation Germany* (London, 1987); Michael D. Bristol, *Carnival and Theater: Plebeian Culture and the Structure of Authority in Renaissance England* (New York, 1985). Bristol presses a vigorous argument against Michel Foucault's contention that the authentic culture of those who have been objectified as "others" by dominant groups is unintelligible to us. He finds popular culture to be rich, evocative and significant, and describes it as such. For a concise statement of Scribner's approach to popular culture, see R. W. Scribner, "Is a History of Popular Culture Possible?", *Hist. European Ideas*, x (1989), pp. 175-91.

adolescent rowdyism, urban rioting, vision mongering and peasant pig-headedness, really worth the heavy hermeneutics lavished on them? The evident importation of this interpretive posture from ethnography and anthropology only sharpens the question. "Thick description" works admirably for bringing the exotic cultures of Clifford Geertz's Bali and Scott's Malaysia within our Western frame of reference, revealing inner connections where, as cultural outsiders, we see only random fragments. But what happens when this procedure is adapted to the study of popular culture in the West? What are we doing when we valorize not extraneous lives, but the common customs of our own plebeian past?

The answer to this question depends to a great extent on the political position from which one observes and judges what is going on in popular history today. Some see it as a threat, not just to the dominance, but to the very survival of our intellectual inheritance. They fear that "history from below" by exalting the commonplace demeans the exceptional, and by legitimizing the counter-cultural endorses — in fact practises — a know-nothing rejection of the entire civilizing process. The most anxious warning of this kind in recent times has come in a sweeping denunciation by Gertrude Himmelfarb, which opens with a cautionary story about a young American historian's refusal to acknowledge that the people of an eighteenth-century New England town, whose lives he was trying to reconstruct, were, in any significant way, affected by great events like the founding of the United States. She concludes with a lament over the loss of coherence and "rational ordering" in human affairs as interpreted by the various approaches she lumps together as "social history", with their insistence on "dwelling on the least dignified aspects of [people's] history".[22] Himmelfarb strikes a crassly anti-populist posture as she reprimands scholars for succumbing to "anthropological history"'s interest in such "non-rational aspects of society as mating customs and eating habits", for enquiring into "intimate feelings that tend to be inaccessible" and for asking "questions of the past which the past did not ask itself". In such ways,

---

[22] Gertrude Himmelfarb, "History with the Politics Left Out", in Gertrude Himmelfarb, *The New History and the Old* (Cambridge, Mass., 1987), pp. 13-32, quotations from pp. 21, 24. This article was first published as "Denigrating the Rule of Reason: The 'New History' Goes Bottom Up", *Harper's Mag.* (Apr. 1984), pp. 84-90.

Himmelfarb suggests, the social historian "denies" or "belittles" reason itself.[23]

While arguments against the practice of popular history have also issued from the other end of the ideological divide, and some of these have been very sharp,[24] most often the attacks have come from the conservative side.[25] Left or right, their political animus is always apparent. But we should not for this reason dismiss them out of hand. Ideas always have consequences, and it is appropriate, in fact it is indispensable, that these be faced and debated. Assuming that the scholarly positions we adopt towards the past reflect judgement and conviction, there is good reason not to be complacent about the effects of these positions in the real world of our own day.

To take another example: in one chapter of his *Power in the Blood*, Sabean tells the story of thirteen-year-old Anna Catharina Weissenbühler, a seventeenth-century Swabian whom reliable witnesses implicated in night-riding and other demonic activities. Although there is nothing especially appealing about the girl, Sabean makes quite a heroine of her for the stubborn resistance she put up to the community's attempt to re-educate her. What he finds especially impressive and, by implication, praiseworthy, is her refusal to allow "them" — the authorities — to force her to accept imposed speech, in the form of a memorized catechism, in place of what he calls the "spontaneous" and "unfettered" utterance of those not yet subjected to "discipline".[26] Certainly

[23] Himmelfarb, "History with the Politics Left Out", pp. 21-2.

[24] See the scornful article by Eugene D. Genovese and Elizabeth Fox-Genovese, "The Political Crisis of Social History: A Marxian Perspective", *Jl. Social Hist.*, x (1976-7), pp. 205-20. The Genoveses direct their ire at the current fad for anthropology in social history, which they see as "a bourgeois swindle" (p. 215) for its evasive and obfuscating agenda of deciphering structural codes and interpreting texts — an activity that, they say, serves to hide the reality of class confrontation under a covering screen of "culture". Social history thus ignores the centre of the historical process. See also Tony Judt, "A Clown in Regal Purple: Social History and the Historians", *History Workshop Jl.*, no. 7 (1979), pp. 66-94. Judt's ill-tempered attack charges current social history with the offence of having followed sociology and cultural anthropology into a non-political stance which ignores the class-based relations of power in society. Social history's "fear of Marxism" has led it to a "loss of faith in history" (p. 87). See also Alan Warde, "E. P. Thompson and 'Poor' Theory", *Brit. Jl. Sociol.*, xxxiii (1982), pp. 224-37, an attack on Thompson for separating historical practice from theory and for conceiving the former "humanistically" in terms of "the 'meanings' and 'experiences' of working people" (p. 234).

[25] For example, Bernard Semmel, "Two Views of Social History: E. P. Thompson and Gertrude Himmelfarb", *Partisan Rev.*, lii (1985), pp. 133-43.

[26] Sabean, *Power in the Blood*, pp. 102-6, 110-12.

it would be foolish, indeed malevolent, to take a lead from Himmelfarb and represent Sabean's choice of sides as an assault on the civilizing impulse, on social decorum, on reason, or on sanity. On the other hand, might one not be apprehensive about a line of interpretation that sees complex metaphors, pregnant symbols, revealing "grammars", and multi-layered "relational idioms" in the most ordinary private acts and social functions? In casual remarks and conventional gestures?[27] For — and this is the point — if we find such a procedure rewarding in our search for a worthy past, we should also, in logic and in fairness, accept it as an appropriate means of decoding the present, of finding comparable significance and dignity in the expressions of popular culture of our own day: in other words, not just Anna Catharina's symbolically loaded way of offering and withholding food, but also eating patterns in the school cafeteria; not only pardon tales dictated to notaries in sixteenth-century France, but letters to the personal advice column; not the village soothsayer's reading of portents only, but resurrection reports from the *National Enquirer*; not only the philosophizing of a Menocchio, but also the splenetic outbursts telephoned to radio talk-shows. Are we, as historians, really prepared to see serious exegesis given to the ever-proliferating symptoms of what many of us regard as trivial and cheap, and sometimes threatening, mass behaviour? Are we willing to accept the consequences of the valorization likely to result from such a procedure?[28] And if not — my sense being that, as a group, historians are still inclined to disparage the work

[27] It is possible that my misgivings are triggered more by the trendy language in which these interpretations are urged on us than by the argument for complex signification. But what troubles me most is the disparity between the claims of significance we make for former times and extraneous cultures, and the claims we allow for interpreting our own time and culture.

[28] An interesting illustration of the discomfort that can be occasioned by such a valorization when it relates to our own time and culture is provided by reactions to an attempt by Henry Louis Gates, Jr., to "decode" the message of 2 Live Crew, a black rap group specializing in explicitly pornographic and violently misogynistic lyrics, against whose recording "As Nasty as They Wanna Be" legal proceedings were initiated in Florida in 1990. Gates's endeavour, using terms familiar to readers of Bakhtin, to represent blatantly expressed phallic aggressiveness and contempt for women as "sexual carnivalesque", "parodic exaggeration", "defiant rejection of euphemism" and "coded ways of communicating" — all part of a "street tradition of 'signifying'" intended to undermine racist stereotypes and, in ethical terms, "so flagrant that it almost cancels itself out" — did not persuade correspondents to whom the objectionable phrases meant what they said. Cf. Henry Louis Gates, Jr., "2 Live Crew, Decoded", *New York Times*, 19 June 1990. For reactions to this article, see letters in *ibid.*, 3 July 1990.

of scholars of contemporary popular culture — is this not tantamount to declaring a decisive qualitative difference between
people's tastes, notions and lives, then and now? And is there
any ground for concluding that such a difference does exist?

An earlier debate answered these questions with a firm "yes".
Throughout the 1940s and 1950s, the phenomenon of popular
culture received intermittent but rapt attention from American
intellectuals on the left, many of them drawing on the theoretical
formulations of the Frankfurt school, especially after the arrival
of most of its members in the United States late in the 1930s. At
first there was some uncertainty about how to label what they
were exposing. Dwight Macdonald's "A Theory of 'Popular Culture'", published in his journal *Politics* in 1944, was recycled a
few years later, almost unchanged, as "A Theory of Mass Culture".[29] "Mass culture" is the more accurate term, Macdonald
suggested, for describing how the commons live because "its
distinctive mark is that it is solely and directly an article for mass
consumption, like chewing gum".[30] This is essentially what
Theodor Adorno and Max Horkheimer say in the chapter on the
"culture industry" in their influential *Dialectic of Enlightenment*,
written in 1944, but not published until 1947. The indictment of
mass culture and, by extension, mass behaviour could hardly be
harsher than it is in this book. *Massenkultur* sells a standardized
uniformity. Absorbing every surviving trace of spontaneity, it
deadens its consumers' senses, serving to reconcile them to existing reality. Fostered by a climate of pluralistic liberalism, it
deceives the gullible by distracting and amusing them; but, to
Adorno and Horkheimer, enjoying yourself means that you have
given your consent ("Vergnügtsein heisst einverstandensein").[31]
Destructive of both folk and élite culture — the former genuinely
popular because community-based but now a thing of the past,

[29] Dwight Macdonald, "A Theory of 'Popular Culture'", *Politics* (Feb. 1944),
pp. 20-3; Dwight Macdonald, "A Theory of Mass Culture", *Diogenes*, no. 3 (summer
1953), pp. 1-17, repr. in Bernard Rosenberg and Donald Manning White (eds.), *Mass
Culture: The Popular Arts in America* (New York, 1957), pp. 59-73. Macdonald further
developed his thoughts on mass culture in "Masscult and Midcult", in Dwight
Macdonald, *Against the American Grain* (New York, 1962), pp. 3-75.

[30] Macdonald, "Theory of Mass Culture", p. 1. For a much more cogent discussion
of the suitability of "popular", "mass" and "folk" as descriptive and analytical terms,
see Morag Shiach, *Discourse on Popular Culture: Class, Gender and History in Cultural
Analysis, 1730 to the Present* (Stanford, 1989), pp. 5, 192-5.

[31] Max Horkheimer and Theodor W. Adorno, *Dialektik der Aufklärung* (Frankfurt,
1981), p. 167.

the latter still precariously preserved by the avant-garde — mass culture offers in their place a cheap product, technologically perfected, homogenized and exalting the average. Instead of the "destructive content" and "subversive force" of high art, we get — in Herbert Marcuse's phrase — "familiar goods and services".[32] There is no prospect of containing what Macdonald calls the "spreading ooze of mass culture".[33] The industrial power behind it is too systemic. It aims at nothing less than a universal cultural *Gleichschaltung*.[34] If this was too apocalyptic a pronouncement for some critics, all were in accord with the general assessment of mass culture as pure trash, "without serious value ... shallow and evasive, and perform[ing] no more important cultural function than tobacco". And, like tobacco, it was habit-forming.[35]

Dissenters from this drastic view pointed to its proponents' credulous acceptance of the myth of an authentic folk culture existing intact at some time in the past, before being corrupted by industrialism and capitalism.[36] They observed that low standards of taste did not begin in the nineteenth century. They rejected the implication that élites had not, in most historical periods, shared and participated in the culture of the masses.[37] They also noted the origin of the radical culture critique in the despairing mood of crisis of the 1930s and early 1940s. They deplored its more or less undisguised élitism.[38] They warned of the distorting effect of an obsessive concern with cultural and political decline.[39] Indeed there seems to be general agreement now that the critique had been — in Jürgen Habermas's words —

[32] Herbert Marcuse, *One-Dimensional Man: Studies in the Ideology of Advanced Industrial Society* (Boston, 1964), p. 61.

[33] Macdonald, "Theory of Mass Culture", p. 17.

[34] Macdonald, "Theory of 'Popular Culture' ", p. 21.

[35] D. W. Brogan, "The Problem of High Culture and Mass Culture", *Diogenes*, no. 5 (winter 1954), pp. 1-13, quotation from p. 5. While agreeing with Macdonald's characterization of mass culture, Brogan attacks the spuriously idealized view of past cultural epochs on which Macdonald's argument rests. He also censures Macdonald's "snobbery" (p. 13).

[36] For a particularly unhistorical invocation of this myth, see Macdonald, "Masscult and Midcult", p. 9.

[37] David Hall, "Introduction", in Steven L. Kaplan (ed.), *Understanding Popular Culture* (Berlin and New York, 1984), pp. 11-12.

[38] Brogan, "Problem of High Culture and Mass Culture", *passim*; Edward Shils, "Daydreams and Nightmares: Reflections on the Criticism of Mass Culture", *Sewanee Rev.*, lxv (1957), pp. 587-608; Karl R. Popper, "The Frankfurt School: An Autobiographical Note", in Judith Marcus and Zoltan Tar (eds.), *Foundations of the Frankfurt School of Social Research* (New Brunswick, 1984), pp. 167-9.

[39] Shiach, *Discourse on Popular Culture*, pp. 10-11.

143   THE DILEMMA OF POPULAR HISTORY

one-sided, incomplete and totalizing.[40] But what has struck me as most disagreeable about it is not its flawed historical sense or its indiscriminate generalizations. It is the derisive, often sneering, tone, and the ungenerous spirit, in which these culture critics took it upon themselves to judge the tastes and habits of millions of their fellow men and women whom they saw only as inert receptacles without features, character or dignity. Nothing nearly so dismissive was written by contemporary conservative writers like Ortega y Gasset, T. S. Eliot or F. R. and Q. D. Leavis.[41] Among the German and North American critics, on the other hand, one looks in vain for a sign of respect for ordinary people, not to mention a hint of empathy or a willingness to enter into their lives and ponder their experiences from within.

This is scarcely explained by Walter Benjamin's rejection of *Einfühlung* for its association with historicism, and with that posture's preference for empathizing with history's winners.[42] Nor could the reason have been lack of information, inadequate exposure or poor data. Concrete examples and vivid illustrations abound in these works, and there is something irresistibly comic in the image of Horkheimer, Adorno, Leo Lowenthal and Marcuse — quintessential Europeans — poring over the funny papers, following the daily radio serial, sitting through B movies, and attending to the tunes of Broadway and Tin Pan Alley. The reason was, as Edward Shils put it in an exceptionally hard-hitting critique, that none of the critics had a first-hand knowledge of working people, their ideas about them being drawn entirely from doctrine.[43] One might add to this their undisguised aversion

[40] Jürgen Habermas, *Der philosophische Diskurs der Moderne*, 3rd edn. (Frankfurt, 1986), pp. 137-8, 153.

[41] José Ortega y Gasset, *The Revolt of the Masses* (New York, 1932; first pubd. 1930); T. S. Eliot, *Notes toward the Definition of Culture* (London, 1948); F. R. Leavis, *Mass Civilisation and Minority Culture* (Cambridge, 1930); Q. D. Leavis, *Fiction and the Reading Public* (London, 1932). There is a very interesting comparison of the Leavisites with British Marxism concerning their respective attitudes towards popular culture in Bill Schwarz, " 'The People' in History: The Communist Party Historians' Group, 1946-56", in Richard Johnson *et al.* (eds.), *Making Histories: Studies in History-Writing and Politics* (London, 1982), p. 64.

[42] Walter Benjamin, *Über den Begriff der Geschichte*, no. 7, in *Gesammelte Schriften*, ed. Rolf Tiedemann and Hermann Schweppenhäuser, 7 vols. (Frankfurt, 1974-87), i, p. 696. For the philosophical background to Benjamin's objection to historicism, see Susan Buck-Morss, *The Origin of Negative Dialectics: Theodor W. Adorno, Walter Benjamin and the Frankfurt Institute* (New York, 1977), pp. 53-4, 168-70.

[43] Shils, "Daydreams and Nightmares", p. 592. Cf. E. P. Thompson's powerful statements about the arrogance of some Marxist intellectuals, including those of the Frankfurt School, *vis-à-vis* ordinary people, in Thompson, "Poverty of Theory",

(cont. on p. 144)

to the United States, for throughout their works mass culture is equated with the American way of life, for which it appears they developed an intense dislike. Adorno claimed after his return to Germany that during his years in New York and California he remained a European "from the first day to the last".[44] Nearly all the nasty examples of one-dimensional culture given in Marcuse's famous book are taken from his experience in the United States. The change of scene must have been a great shock to them. As Shils writes, what had been a vague disdain of popular life in Europe became "an elaborate loathing in America".[45] This was hardly a suitable frame of mind in which to examine a phenomenon made strange by a vast intellectual and social distance.

It has been nicely said that "the popular is perhaps the one field in which intellectuals are least likely to be experts".[46] But my point is a different one. It is that the extreme repudiation of twentieth-century popular culture by the Frankfurt school and its adherents should sensitize us to the contradiction centrally inherent in our penchant for boosting the significance of popular life in the past, while being unable or unwilling to overcome our distaste for common ways in our own day, a contradiction not satisfactorily resolved by insisting on the conventional distinction between societies before and after capitalism/industrialism. As historians we live in two worlds, and our dual citizenship brings conflicting loyalties. These, in turn, induce a compartmentalization of our mental life and set up a double standard for appraising what we see. Two very different outlooks are at work in us, entailing two distinct tests of judgement, with results that are at least questionable. To take my own case again: how sincere, how well founded, is my admiration of the apathy and foot-dragging with which my sixteenth-century commoners shielded themselves from an imposed civilizing process when I deplore the same traits

(n. 43 cont.)

pp. 184-6; E. P. Thompson, "The Peculiarities of the English", in Thompson, *Poverty of Theory*, pp. 295-8.

[44] Theodor W. Adorno, "Wissenschaftliche Erfahrungen in Amerika", in *Gesammelte Schriften*, 20 vols. (Frankfurt, 1973-86), x.2, p. 702.

[45] Shils, "Daydreams and Nightmares", p. 600. Shils developed his own view of mass culture and its relation to intellectual culture in Edward Shils, "Mass Society and its Culture", in Norman Jacobs (ed.), *Culture for the Millions? Mass Media in Modern Society* (Princeton, 1959), pp. 1-27.

[46] Andrew Ross, *No Respect: Intellectuals and Popular Culture* (New York, 1989), p. 232.

as I see them exhibited by my contemporaries, most immediately and painfully by students in my classes? The inconsistency in my respective attitudes is not explained by my personal indifference to one set of enforced values and my partiality to the other. Nor is it answered by asserting, evasively, that one situation presents itself as a historical problem, and the other does not, or not yet. The root of the inconsistency lies elsewhere. It lies in a double perspective, in my choosing (or having been conditioned to choose) to see things from above in the latter, the contemporary, instance, and from below in the former, the historical: in other words, status-induced bias in one case, imaginative escape from it in the other. And it resides, as well, in my fortunate ability to be selective in what I accept from the past, while the present, alas, I must take as it is. Does it make sense to find so much of interest in peasant and artisan life in early modern Europe when I am repelled by what I mostly see as vulgarity in "lifestyles" now? Is it honest to treat with scholarly respect a literary analysis of Shrovetide plays when a close reading of a TV show — "The Incredible Hulk as Modern Grail Quest", from a recent issue of *Studies in Popular Culture* — strikes me as ridiculous?[47] Should I trust my discovery of "order" in the sixteenth-century village when I look with disbelief on a demonstration of aesthetic "system" in the Las Vegas strip?[48] Or, to take a less personal example: how reliable is Robert Mandrou's critique of the *bibliothèque bleue* as a purveyor of "ideological substitutes" intended to depoliticize its formerly autonomous consumers and make them dependent, when he glosses this characterization of the eighteenth-century literature of colportage with a comparison to the television culture of his own time, which he evidently disdains?[49] Ought one to

[47] Elizabeth S. Bell, "The Incredible Hulk as Modern Grail Quest", *Studies in Popular Culture*, v (1982), pp. 56-60. I am not impugning, of course, studies of television as a social phenomenon, such as Raymond Williams, *Television: Technology and Cultural Form* (New York, 1975).
[48] Cf. Robert Venturi *et al.*, *Learning from Las Vegas* (Cambridge, Mass., 1972), esp. pp. 30-2, "System and Order on the Strip".
[49] Robert Mandrou, *De la culture populaire au 17e et 18e siècles: la bibliothèque bleue de Troyes* (Paris, 1985), p. 181. Shiach, *Discourse on Popular Culture*, pp. 9-10, points out that the perception of mass culture as corrupting is a constant feature of the discourse on popular culture. He also suggests (p. 200) that most discussions of mass culture tell us more about the language of cultural analysis than they do about culture. For a finely balanced discussion of a late twentieth-century example of colportage literature, and its effects on its readers, see Janice A. Radway, *Reading the Romance:*

(cont. on p. 146)

place confidence in historical judgements strained by such ambivalence?

Deeply divided responses induce this ambivalence. Living in an age of political democracy and easy access to information, we feel entitled to blame people for falling short of our preferred levels of thinking, doing and responding; but with respect to the past, we know that such an imputation of guilt is utterly inappropriate. Again, the assessments we make of former times impose no burdens: nothing we say about the past obliges us to proceed to actions consistent with our words; with regard to the present, by contrast, our opinions would seem to impose on us the duty to follow through. Unacknowledged considerations of status are also active here. We risk virtually nothing when we bestow attention, respect, even admiration, on the expressions of popular culture in the past. Confronted by comparable expressions in our own day, however, we feel we must guard our cultural and social rank as intellectuals and academics. The contempt shown for a television entertainment is therefore more than a display of one's "taste": implicitly it also affirms status by legitimizing and reproducing distinction. A sentence from Pierre Bourdieu seems apposite here: "Taste is an acquired disposition to 'differentiate' and 'appreciate' . . . in other words to establish and mark difference by a process of distinction".[50] When dealing with sixteenth-century villagers we can, without peril, maintain our scholarly dignity. But there is no ivory tower from which one can safely write about "Dallas".[51]

I am not arguing that in order to be consistent one had better either stay clear of popular history or else adapt oneself to today's

(n. 49 cont.)

Women, Patriarchy, and Popular Literature (Chapel Hill, 1984). Radway acknowledges the reconciling and compensatory function of Harlequin and similar romance novels, but also explores the possibility of their serving as a means of subverting and contesting the dominant culture (pp. 211-22).

[50] Pierre Bourdieu, *Distinction: A Social Critique of the Judgment of Taste*, trans. Richard Nice (Cambridge, Mass., 1984), p. 466. On the exclusion of mass culture by modernism as part of its self-definition as high art, see Andreas Huyssen, *After the Great Divide: Modernism, Mass Culture, Postmodernism* (Bloomington, Ind., 1986), esp. p. viii.

[51] For a strongly dissenting view, see John Carlos Rowe, "Metavideo: Fictionality and Mass Culture in a Postmodern Economy", in Patrick O'Donnell and Robert Con Davis (eds.), *Intertextuality and Contemporary American Fiction* (Baltimore, 1989), pp. 214-35. Arguing that "as television became the primary medium of social exchange, it also began to assume a certain philosophical authority", Rowe makes a good case for interpreting TV shows in "decidedly ponderous ontological terms" (p. 230).

media culture. Nor am I denying that there is value in the study of contemporary cultural forms. I am saying that something is to be gained from sorting out our responses and motives. Two things should be recognized. One of them is the sheer appeal of popular history as a subject. This appeal far transcends the pleasure of having an attractive research task to pursue: a moral impetus is also at work. Largely, perhaps, under the influence of ethnography and folklore (as many practitioners of popular history attest[52]), but in any case owing to the weakening of élitist preconceptions fostered by the great humanistic tradition, popular life and mentality in the past tend no longer to be marginalized as the "other", but to be seen much more sympathetically as a culture that had its own reasons, frames of perception, rules of transformation, processes of reproduction, its own independent dynamics, and above all its own claims to serious attention as an expression of authentic human needs and desires. A mere glance at the (by now very large) body of writings on popular history reveals the reasons for the favour the subject enjoys: the excitement of recovering lost lives; the pleasure of advancing beyond old stereotypes about the folk or the masses; the useful realization that high culture, like everything else, has a social cost; the promise of assuaging a painful longing for community; and in particular the satisfaction of recapturing the history of ordinary people from what Thompson has called "the enormous condescension of posterity".[53] It is hard to do popular history in a serious way without feeling that, in some small measure, you are enlisted in the cause of justice.[54]

All this is true. But what I have just written also demonstrates how easy it is, in the discourse on popular history, to slip into the celebratory mode. This, too, must be recognized. The subject

[52] See, for example, the statements by Burke in the prologue to his *Popular Culture in Early Modern Europe*, pp. xi-xii; Hall, "Introduction" to Kaplan (ed.), *Understanding Popular Culture*, pp. 8-9.

[53] E. P. Thompson, *The Making of the English Working Class* (Harmondsworth, 1968), p. 13.

[54] Some examples of scholarly works conveying this feeling are Christopher Hill, "The Poor and the People in Seventeenth-Century England", in Frederick Krantz (ed.), *History from Below: Studies in Popular Protest and Popular Ideology in Honour of George Rudé* (Montreal, 1985), pp. 75-93; Christopher Hill, "The Norman Yoke", in John Saville (ed.), *Democracy and the Labour Movement: Essays in Honour of Dona Torr* (London, 1954), pp. 11-66; E. P. Thompson, *Whigs and Hunters: The Origins of the Black Act* (London, 1975). A very interesting article by Raphael Samuel, "British Marxist Historians, 1880-1980: Part One", *New Left Rev.*, no. 120 (1980),

(cont. on p. 148)

emits a compelling ethical allure, best expressed by Thompson's memorable and often-quoted phrase, and perhaps by the fervour behind the History Workshop movement in Germany with its "barefoot" historians and grass-roots venues.[55] Such a moral dimension lends a particularly contagious charm to popular history, the pull of which is sometimes hard to control. As we try to come to terms with past realities, we are vulnerable to powerful interventionist incentives. Our work is, for many of us, our chief means of self-definition. Unable to do much to improve the world, but with strong convictions about how this might be accomplished, we make of the past our field of action, seeing it as the site where, belatedly, we rectify wrongs, where retroactive justice is done. Scholars of popular history may well feel the impulse to do this more strongly than most. And I think it is a good impulse. My own brush with it changed the direction of my work. It persuaded me that no understanding of the sixteenth-century Reformation can have much depth until a sense has been gained of its consequences in the lives of the large majority of people. I cannot see how else one can measure the movement's — or any movement's — importance as an event.

But my argument in this essay has been that acknowledging the contemporary implications of this essentially moral stance can

(n. 54 cont.)

pp. 21-96, which traces the intellectual roots and impulses in Marxist historical writing in Britain, derives the moral drive evident in much of this work from the Nonconformist religious strain in British Marxism. Books on everyday life, especially, tend to represent the writing of history as an act of compensatory justice: for example, see Sigrid and Wolfgang Jacobeit, *Illustrierte Alltagsgeschichte des deutschen Volkes*, 2 vols. (Cologne, 1986-7). See also Raphael Samuel's description of the History Workshop activities in the 1960s and 1970s in "History Workshop, 1966-80", in Samuel (ed.), *People's History and Socialist Theory*, pp. 410-17. For an expression of a scholar's longing for community, see Lawrence W. Levine's confession of nostalgia for "a rich shared public culture" which, he argues, once existed in the United States, in *Highbrow/Lowbrow: The Emergence of Cultural Hierarchy in America* (Cambridge, 1988), p. 9. Eric Hobsbawm suggests that bandits may function as the embodiments of our vaguely perceived nostalgia for community and for the "traditional order of things 'as it should be'", in E. J. Hobsbawm, *Bandits*, rev. edn. (New York, 1981), p. 26.

[55] On the *Geschichtswerkstatt* movement, and the "history of everyday life" in general, see Roger Fletcher, "History from Below Comes to Germany: The New History Movement in the Federal Republic of Germany", *Jl. Mod. Hist.*, lx (1988), pp. 557-68, esp. pp. 562-8; Geoff Eley, "Labor History, Social History, Alltagsgeschichte: Experience, Culture, and the Politics of the Everyday — A New Direction for German Social History?", *Jl. Mod. Hist.*, lxi (1989), pp. 297-343, esp. pp. 312-26. For a discussion of some of the ideological problems associated with *Alltagsgeschichte*, see Alf Lüdtke, "Rekonstruktion von Alltagswirklichkeit — Entpolitisierung der Sozialgeschichte?", in Robert M. Berdahl et al. (eds.), *Klassen und Kultur: Sozialanthropologische Perspektiven in der Geschichtsschreibung* (Frankfurt, 1982), pp. 321-53.

help keep us honest as historians. Above all it can guard us against the temptation to exploit the past for our own needs. Our divergent responses towards the past and the present place us in an uneasy tension. To the extent that we are open to the appeal of "history from below" as a good cause, every great historical problem becomes a topic in popular history. To the extent that this inclination calls our own cultural affinities into question, every exercise in popular history turns into a contest between idealism and alienation. I see no way out of this dilemma.

INDEX

Library of
Davidson College